REGIONAL GOVERNMENT INNOVATIONS

REGIONAL GOVERNMENT INNOVATIONS

A Handbook for Citizens and Public Officials

Edited by Roger L. Kemp

McFarland & Company, Inc., Publishers

Jefferson, North Carolina, and London

The present work is a reprint of the library bound edition of Regional Government Innovations: A Handbook for Citizens and Public Officials, *first published in 2003 by McFarland.*

LIBRARY OF CONGRESS CATALOGUING-IN-PUBLICATION DATA

Regional government innovations : a handbook for citizens and public officials / edited by Roger L. Kemp.
p.   cm.
Includes bibliographical references and index.

ISBN-13: 978-0-7864-3155-7
(softcover : 50# alkaline paper) ∞

1. Regionalism — United States.   2. Regional planning — United States.
3. Local government — United States.   I. Kemp, Roger L.
JS408.R44   2007   352.14'3'0973 — dc21   2002008998

British Library cataloguing data are available

Cover images ©2007 Shutterstock

Manufactured in the United States of America

McFarland & Company, Inc., Publishers
Box 611, Jefferson, North Carolina 28640
www.mcfarlandpub.com

ACKNOWLEDGMENTS

Grateful acknowledgment is made to the following organizations and publishers for granting permission to reprint the material contained in this volume.

American Planning Association
Congressional Quarterly, Inc.
Florida League of Cities
Government Finance Officers Association
Intertec Publishing Corporation
National Association of Regional Councils

National Civic League
North Carolina League of Municipalities
State of California
University of Baltimore
Urban Land Institute

CONTENTS

PREFACE

Throughout American history, general and special purpose local governments have provided public services to citizens. General purpose local governments include cities and counties, since each of these levels of government provide general public services to taxpayers. Special purpose local governments, on the other hand, typically provide only one public service to citizens. For example, public services provided by special purpose local governments usually include, but are not limited to, public transportation, street lighting, wastewater treatment, drinking water storage and delivery systems, regional planning, and air quality. In most states, general purpose local governments (i.e., cities and counties) generate most, if not all, of their revenue through real property taxes. Special purpose local governments (i.e., special districts), on the other hand, are either frequently included as a line-item on a municipal property tax bill, or generate their revenues directly through user fees and charges. These traditional lines of authority and financing are beginning to change as our nation enters the 21st century.

There are many types and forms of regional government agencies. These include regional planning commissions, council of governments, regional advisory committees, regional allocation agencies, and special purpose regional agencies. Most of these regional government agencies are created and empowered by their respective state governments. Some regional government agencies, such as the Appalachian Regional Commis-

sion and the Tennessee Valley Authority, are creatures of the federal government, even though these agencies provide services to many states, counties, and communities. In still other cases, such as the Port Authority of New York & New Jersey, an agreement between states permits the agency, but such agreements must be consistent with federal law. Still other regional government agencies come into being as a result of voter mandates. This latter type of regional government, for obvious reasons, is more visible to the electorate. In some cases they even perform a wide variety of public services, such as when a county and city consolidate into a single public agency. They are, however, far fewer in number than government-authorized regional government agencies.

The first section of this volume, *Introduction and Overview*, includes six chapters that provide the reader with a comprehensive introduction and overview to the field of regional government in general, and to recent regional government innovations throughout the nation in particular. The first three chapters provide a brief history of regional planning in America, the evolution of regional governance, and the typical models of regional government as our nation enters the 21st century. The last three chapters of this section include ways to foster regional reform without changing the boundaries of existing public agencies, the status of regional government in America, and highlights of regional government trends facilitated by our nation's fast-moving post-industrial economy. It should be noted that

1

most regional government agencies have policy bodies consisting of elected officials from their member agencies. In only a few cases, where a regional government agency exists as a result of a voter-mandate, will you find governing body of directly elected public officials. This trend is changing, albeit slowly.

The second section of this volume, *Case Studies in Innovation*, examines those outstanding examples of public and non-profit initiatives and programs that promote regional government throughout America.

In total, some two-dozen initiatives are examined in the twenty-five case studies that are contained in this volume. Some of these programs were mandated by higher levels of government — federal, state, and county. Other projects have their origin in the non-profit sector. These public and non-profit initiatives include federal, state, regional, county, and non-profit agencies and organizations in all regions and corners of our nation. The following breakdown is provided to show the reader both the breadth and focus of this volume.

Public and Non-Profit Initiatives

Federal Government Initiatives
- Regional transportation planning.
- Rails-to-trails projects.
- Economic development incentives.
- Public works projects.

State Government Initiatives
- Multi-state transportation planning and programs.
- Corridor planning with counties, cities, and towns.
- Transportation planning as a growth management tool.
- Regional watershed management and water conservation programs.
- State-mandated regional planning.
- Required tax sharing agreements between cities and towns.
- Creating urban partnerships to foster regional cooperation.
- Joint economic development districts for counties, cities, and towns.
- Acquiring conservation easements that promote regional planning.

County-City Government Initiatives
- Regional government between counties and cities.
- A national model for growth management.
- Revenue sharing promotes managed growth.
- Regional financing of scientific and cultural facilities.
- Purchase of public services between counties and cities

Non-Profit Organization Initiatives
- Programs to build regional government leadership.
- Programs to help promote regional government.
- Regional initiatives among fragmented local governments.
- Fostering intergovernmental cooperation.

Case Studies in Innovation

State Organizations
- State of Georgia, Atlanta
- State of Michigan, Lansing
- State of New Jersey, Trenton
- State of Ohio, Columbus
- State of Virginia, Richmond
- State of Washington, Olympia
- State of Wisconsin, Madison

Regional Organizations
- Appalachian Regional Commission, Washington, D.C.
- Atlanta Regional Commission, Atlanta, Georgia
- Denver Regional Council of Governments, Denver, Colorado
- Metropolitan Council, St. Paul, Minnesota
- Metropolitan Service District, Portland, Oregon
- Miami Valley Regional Planning Commission, Dayton, Ohio
- Port Authority of New York & New Jersey, New York, New York
- Puget Sound Regional Council, Seattle, Washington
- San Diego Association of Governments, San Diego, California
- Scientific & Cultural Facilities District, Denver, Colorado
- Triangle J Council of Governments, Durham, North Carolina

Counties
- Allegheny County, Pittsburgh, Pennsylvania
- Contra Costa County, Martinez, California
- Guilford County, Greensboro, North Carolina
- Montgomery County, Dayton, Ohio
- Volusia County, DeLand, Florida

Cities
- City of Akron, Ohio
- City of Dayton, Ohio
- City of DeBary, Florida
- City of Greensboro, North Carolina
- City of High Point, North Carolina
- City of Springfield, Ohio

Non-Profit Organizations
- Center for Greater Philadelphia, Philadelphia, Pennsylvania
- Challenge 95 Leadership Network and Regional Economic Strategies Forum, Dayton-Springfield, Ohio
- The Greater Baltimore Committee, Baltimore, Maryland
- Regional Leadership Institute, Atlanta, Georgia

The final section of this volume, *The Future of Regionalism*, examines current trends in regional governance, the evolving role of regional councils, and the regional challenges posed by increased global competition. The concluding chapters examine regional excellence in the twenty-first century, the future of regionalism based on current trends, and the contemporary regional government renaissance taking place across America. The author of the last chapter concludes, "community leaders and citizens in all regions are already laying the groundwork for a regional governance renaissance" throughout the nation.

A listing of regional and national resource organizations concerning regional government is included at the end of this volume. The *Regional Resource Directory* includes the names and addresses, and other contact information, for each of the state, regional, county, city, and non-profit organizations examined in the case studies referred to above. Readers may wish to contact these organizations for further information about innovations in regional government, or the laws that permitted these innovations to take place. The *National Resource Directory* includes the names and addresses, and related information, for major national professional associations and research organizations serving local and regional governments in the U.S. All of these organizations — government agencies, non-profit organizations, and national professional and research organizations — also have a wealth of material available from their respective internet websites.

Also, a comprehensive *Bibliographic Essay* on regional government is included in this reference volume. Bibliographic information is provided on the historical development of regionalism and metropolitan governance, the forms of metropolitan government and governance, growth management and infrastructure development programs, economic development and regional competitiveness trends and issues, social security and regional asset sharing, as well as practical guidance on regional capacity building. An *Editor's Note* is also provided updating this literature search from 1996, the date this bibliographic essay was first published by the *National Civic Review* (National Civic League, Denver, Colorado).

Innovative approaches to regional government, and cooperation among general-purpose local governments, are a relatively recent phenomenon. Our nation, when it was formed over two centuries ago, was formed as a decentralized republic consisting of numerous municipalities. Regional approaches to governance have evolved in a piecemeal and incremental manner over the years. This is particularly true over the past few decades. While federal and state laws may serve to limit, or even authorize or permit, some of the various types of approaches taken to regionalism, the need exists to codify the available information in this rapidly evolving field. This information must be made available to other elected leaders, our appointed public officials, and, most importantly, to the citizens and taxpayers they serve. For this reason, this volume is important because it is one of the only collections of written resources available focusing exclusively on this important topic — *innovations in regional government*.

I would like to personally thank representatives from the following national professional associations, educational institutions, periodicals covering regional government, state municipal associations, and government organizations for providing the necessary resources for this project, and for granting me permission to reprint the material contained in this volume. Professional associations include the American Planning Association, Government Finance Officers Association, National Association of Regional Councils, National Civic League, and the Urban Land Institute. Educational institutions include the University of Baltimore.

Periodicals include *Governing*, published by Congressional Quarterly, Inc., and *American City and County*, published by the Intertec Publishing Corporation. State municipal associations include the Florida League of Cities and the North Carolina League of Municipalities. Lastly, I am thankful to the Governor's Office of Planning and Research and the Governor's Interagency Council on Growth Management, State of California, for granting me permission to reprint a valuable study published by these organizations.

Roger L. Kemp
Meriden, Connecticut
February, 2003

PART I

Introduction and Overview

CHAPTER 1

THE HISTORY OF REGIONAL PLANNING

American Planning Association

Regional planning is planning for a geographic area that transcends the boundaries of individual governmental units but that shares common social, economic, political, natural resource, and transportation characteristics.[1] A regional planning agency prepares plans that serve as a framework for planning by local governments and special districts.

Throughout the United States, there are regional planning agencies that are either voluntary associations of local government or mandated or authorized by state legislation (e.g., the Metropolitan Council in the Twin Cities or the Metropolitan Services District in Portland, Oregon). These exist for purposes of: undertaking plans that are typically advisory in nature, providing information, technical assistance, and training; coordinating efforts among member governments, especially efforts that involve federal funding; and providing a two-way conduit between member governments and the state and federal agencies. Regional planning agencies may also serve as a forum to discuss complex and sometimes sensitive issues among member local governments and to try to find solutions to problems that affect more than one jurisdiction. Sometimes these organizations have direct regulatory authority in that they not only prepare plans, but also administer land-use controls through subdivision review and zoning recommendations, review proposals for major developments whose impacts may cross jurisdictional borders, and review and certify local plans.

States authorize the establishment of these regional planning agencies in different ways. In some parts of the country, the regional agencies take their structure from general enabling legislation (e.g., for regional planning commissions or councils of government). In other places, they are the product of intergovernmental or joint powers agreements, as in California, or interstate compacts, as with the Delaware Regional Planning Commission in the Philadelphia, Pennsylvania/Camden, New Jersey, area, or the Tahoe Regional Planning Agency in Nevada and California. In some states, regional agencies are created by special state legislation that applies only to one particular agency (e.g., the Northeastern Illinois Planning Commission in the Chicago area, or the Cape Cod Commission in Massachusetts). In still others, they may exist as private, voluntary organizations that seek to

Originally published as Chapter 6 of *Growing Smart Legislative Guidebook: Models Statutes for Planning and the Management of Change*, 1996. Published by the American Planning Association, Chicago, Illinois. Reprinted with permission of the publisher.

FIGURE 1

**Reasons for
Regional Planning**

- Provision of technical assistance to local governments.
- Maintenance of forum for exploring and resolving intergovernmental issues.
- Development of regional plans to guide, direct, and or coordinate local planning.
- Articulation of local interests and perspectives to other levels of government.
- Establishment of two-way conduit between local governments and other agencies.

---

provide a regional perspective through independently prepared plans and studies. Examples of such agencies are the Regional Plan Association in New York City and Bluegrass Tomorrow in the Lexington, Kentucky, area.

The Origins of Regional Planning Agencies

The first regional planning agency with planning powers was the Boston Metropolitan Improvement Commission created by the Massachusetts legislature in 1902. Seven years later, in 1909, the Commercial Club of Chicago, a private organization, financed the preparation of the Plan of Chicago, which was completed by a team headed by Chicago architects Daniel H. Burnham and Edward H. Bennett. The plan placed the city of Chicago in a regional context and contained regional proposals for parks and transportation.[2]

From 1913 to 1915, when the state legislature repealed the statute creating it, Pennsylvania authorized the establishment of a Suburban Metropolitan Planning Commission. Within a 25-mile radius of Philadelphia, the commission could levy assessments and prepare comprehensive plans for highways, parks and parkways, sewerage and sewage disposal, housing, sanitation and health, civic centers, and other functional areas.[3] The commission had the authority to make recommendations to governmental units on a wide variety of issues, including "the distribution and relative location of all public buildings, public grounds, and open spaces devoted to public use, and the planning, subdivision and laying out for urban uses of private grounds brought into the market from time to time."[4]

The major regional planning effort of the 1920s — and for many years afterwards — was the *Regional Plan for New York and Environs*, financed by the Russell Sage Foundation and prepared by an advisory committee. Work began on the plan in 1921 and was completed in 1929. The eight-volume document covered a 5,528-square mile area with 500 incorporated bodies. Even by today's standards, the Regional Plan is an impressive work. It contained regionwide proposals for transportation, land use, and public facilities, as well as specific design proposals for New York City. After its publication, the advisory committee issued periodic reports on its implementation.

In 1922, the first metropolitan area planning commission was established in Los Angeles to advise the County Board of Supervisors on planning for the county and on approving subdivisions. In 1923, the Ohio General Assembly enacted the first enabling legislation for regional planning commissions. That legislation, which was drafted by Cincinnati attorney Alfred Bettman, was to provide the model for the regional planning provisions of the Standard City Planning Enabling Act, on whose advisory committee Bettman would become a member. The same year, the Chicago Regional Planning Association, a quasi-public organization, and the Allegheny County Planning Commission (Pittsburgh) were created.

The SCPEA: Model Legislation for Regional Planning

The Standard City Planning Enabling Act (SCPEA), drafted by an advisory committee to the U.S. Department of Commerce and published in 1928, contained model legislation for regional planning. The SCPEA authorized the planning commission of any municipality or the county commissioners of any county to petition the governor to establish a planning region and create a planning commission for that region. The governor was to hold at least one public hearing before making a determination to grant the application, define the region, and appoint the regional planning commission.[5]

Under the SCPEA model, the regional planning commission was composed of nine members, all of whom would be appointed and removed by the governor. The commission had the authority to prepare, adopt, and amend a "master regional plan for the physical development of the region."[6] After adopting the plan, the regional planning commission was required to certify it to the governor, to the planning commission of each municipality in the region, to the council of each municipality that did not have a planning commission, to the county commissioners of each county located wholly or partially in the region, and to other organized taxing districts or political subdivisions wholly or partially included in the region.

Adoption of the regional plan by the municipal planning commission was optional; however, once the regional planning commission adopted it, the plan would have the same force and effect as a plan made and adopted locally. In addition, the municipal planning commission,"[b]efore adopting any amendment of the municipal plan which would constitute a violation of or departure from the regional plan certified to the municipal planning commission," was required to submit the amendment to the regional commission. The regional commission would then "certify to the municipal commission its approval, disapproval or other opinion concerning the proposed amendment."[7]

Once the regional plan was adopted by the regional planning commission, no street, park, or other public way, ground, or open space; no public building or other public structure; and no public utility, whether publicly or privately owned or operated, could be constructed or authorized in unincorporated territory until the project was submitted to and approved by the regional planning commission. However, the planning commission's disapproval could be overruled by the body or officer having authority to determine the location, character, or extent of the improvement, provided that, in the case of a board, commission, or body, not less than two-thirds of its membership voted to do so and provided a statement of reasons for such overruling in the minutes of records of the body or officer.[8]

One analyst of this period observed that:

> By the end of the 1920s, metropolitan and county planning was a major topic of concern among professional planners. Many city planning commissions found that central city development plans ignored the surrounding local governments and that regional planning and cooperative political solutions were required. Some saw the need for an agency empowered to take an overall view of serious problems besetting the entire metropolitan area.[9]

Regional Planning During the Depression and War Years

The federal government, through the National Planning Board (later the National Resources Committee) in the Department of the Interior, provided the major push for metropolitan, regional, state, and interstate planning. The federal government supported the creation of the Pacific Northwest Regional Planning Commission, a four-state body covering Idaho, Montana, Oregon, and Washington, and the New England Regional Planning Commission, which included Massachusetts, Vermont, Rhode Island, Connecticut, and Maine.[10] It backed a bi-state St. Louis Regional Planning Commission, which it hoped would provide a model for similar efforts elsewhere in the U.S. It also supported the use of interstate compacts, in the words of a report by one federal agency, "as a means of solving regional problems wherever this procedure is found to be feasible."[11]

By the end of the 1930s, according to a report of the U.S. Advisory Commission on Intergovernmental Regulations, federal support had greatly expanded metropolitan and regional planning:

> In 1934, there were only 85 metropolitan and county planning bodies and 23 regional planning agencies in existence. By January 1937, there were 506 metropolitan multicounty and county planning agencies, of which at least 316 were official public bodies. Two years later, metropolitan planning agencies or regional planning boards, commissions, or associations were operating in at least 30 major cities. In addition to these metropolitan developments, by the close of the decade areawide planning had also been extended to a number of small urban areas and several nonmetropolitan regions.[12]

Of note during World War II was the formation of privately financed regional planning councils in San Francisco, St. Louis, Boston, Cincinnati, and Kansas City. In Pittsburgh, the Allegheny Conference on Community Development was established in 1945. Its membership drew from leaders in business, labor, and government, and it emerged as a prime mover in the transformation of Pittsburgh in the postwar era.[13]

Regional Planning in the Postwar Period

In the 1950s, federal aid for comprehensive planning became available with the enactment of Section 701 of the Housing Act of 1954. This statute provided monies for local planning and planning for metropolitan areas by official regional or metropolitan planning agencies.

According to a study by the U.S. Advisory Commission on Intergovernmental Relations, at least 13 states passed regional planning enabling acts in the three years following the enactment of the 1954 Housing Act. This set the stage for a tremendous increase in the number of multijurisdictional planning organizations. During this period, according to the ACIR, the legislatures of at least nine of these states enacted legislation requiring or permitting the establishment of planning agencies for entire urbanized areas. The statutes usually authorized the agencies to apply for and receive federal grants. Some states adopted specific statutes that created planning commissions for certain metropolitan areas. By the beginning of the 1960s, some two-thirds of the nation's metropolitan areas were engaged in some type of areawide planning.[14]

Complementing the "701" program was the Federal-Aid Highway Act of 1962. This statute required a "cooperative, comprehensive, and continuous" planning process as a prerequisite for federal financial assistance for interstate highway development in metropolitan areas. The act required regional transportation plans in urban areas with populations more than 50,000 as a condition to construction funds. In contrast to the "701" grants, which split costs evenly with local governments, the Highway Act provided matching grants of 70 percent of the cost of preparing the necessary studies.

In some parts of the U.S., metropolitan transportation planning was assigned to a special commission or entity. This was the case, and still is, in Boston, San Francisco, and Chicago. In others, the transportation planning function was assumed by a regional planning commission or metropolitan councils of government (COGs), which were voluntary alliances of local governments formed to undertake planning or any type of joint governmental activity that its members could agree upon.

One of the earliest studies of COGs was conducted in 1962 by the American Society of Planning Officials (ASPO), one of APA's predecessor organizations. The study examined eight councils. It observed that the agencies were operating without an overall metropolitan government that would carry out any plans they might propose. As a consequence, the agencies

> must rely on persuasion to convince numerous local governments that joint area-wide action is necessary — a method not notable for its past successes....
>
> Probably the most important advance of the voluntary governmental council is its acceptability to local political leaders. No change in government structure is necessary and there is no transfer of power from local units to a larger agency. The council is easily set up and established by the local governments themselves. Membership is voluntary and the organization is flexible and adaptable to many situations.[15]

During the 1960s and 1970s, the nation was almost completely covered by multistate river basin and economic development commissions and by metropolitan and nonmetropolitan regional councils. The expansion of COGs, prompted by the available of federal funding, was dramatic. In 1961, for example, there were only 36 COGs, including 25 among the 212 metropolitan areas. By 1966, this number included 119 councils, of which 71 were metropolitan. By 1971, there were 247 metropolitan areas, and all of them had official regional planning,

mostly under elected COGs. By 1978, there were 649 councils in the U.S. Of these, 292 were in metropolitan areas.[16]

Four federal laws were responsible for this expansion, and they were all enacted in a watershed year of 1965. The Housing and Community Development Act of 1965 made regional councils eligible for planning funds. The Public Works and Economic Development Act of 1965 provided funding for multicounty economic development districts and authorized the establishment of federal multistate economic development commissions. The Appalachian Regional Development Act established the multistate Appalachian Regional Commission, which accomplished its work through multicounty development districts. Finally, the Water Resources Planning Act of 1965 authorized the establishment of federal multistate river basin commissions.[17] Under Circular A-95, promulgated by the U.S. Office of Management and Budget, regional agencies received authority to review applications for federal assistance for compliance with regional and local plans. In addition, regional agencies began to prepare regional water-quality management plans under Section 208 of the Federal Clean Water Act of 1972.

Bruce McDowell of the U.S. Advisory Commission on Intergovernmental Relations observed:

> This explosion of "areawide" regional councils and the multistate river basin and economic development regions occurred because of very intentional and systematic federal action which drew in the states as well as local governments. In the cases of the areawide councils, the federal actions included establishing 39 grant programs designed to require and fund regional planning, and direct appeal to the governors of all 50 states to establish statewide systems of substate districts to systematize the administration of the federal programs supporting regional councils. And many of the states did so.[18]

New Roles for Regional Agencies

Between 1960 and 1980, there were a number of studies that proposed new roles and authority for regional planning entities. These studies also called for changes in state statutes. Their chief recommendations are summarized below.

1. ASPO Connecticut Report. In 1966, ASPO, assisted by the Chicago law firm of Ross, Hardies, O'Keefe, Babcock, McDugald & Parsons, produced a report entitled *New Directions in Connecticut Planning Legislation*. The report, prepared for the Connecticut Development Commission, recommended major changes in the Connecticut planning statutes. Its major recommendation regarding regional planning agencies was an extension of their jurisdiction to review matters that may have regional significance, such as decisions involving property within specified distances from state highways, and development affecting the region, such as water, sewerage, and utility projects. The regional agency would still not be given veto power over local decisions. If a local or state agency took action contrary to a regional planning agency's recommendation pursuant to a referral, that agency would be required to state in writing the reasons that had led it to a different conclusion. But if the regional agency chose not to comment on a proposal, such an action would be neutral, rather than constitute a project endorsement.

The ASPO report also recommended amending the state statutes to define a regional plan as distinct from a local plan. "The statute should direct the *regional* plan to cover *regional* facilities," noted its authors, "and, especially, to give attention to regional resource and conservation problems."[19]

2. National Commission on Urban Problems (Douglas Commission). In 1968, the National Commission on Urban Problems, also known as the Douglas Commission, after its Chair, Senator Paul Douglas, issued its report, *Building the American City*. The Commission's charge, among other things, was to examine "state and local zoning and land use laws, codes, and regulations to find ways by which States and localities may improve and utilize them in order to obtain further growth and development."[20] To date, the study, with its wide-ranging scope, is one of the most comprehensive and thorough in terms of examining authority of governments to plan and regulate development.

Two Commission proposals to broaden choice in the location of housing called for regional approaches:

> (1) Enactment of state legislation requiring multi-county or regional planning agencies to prepare and maintain housing plans. These plans would ensure that sites are available for development of new housing of all kinds and at all price levels. In the absence of a regional planning body — given the broader-than-local nature of the plan and the importance of political approval of such plans — the state government should assume responsibility for the necessary political endorsement of the plan.

> (2) Amendment of state planning and zoning acts to include, as one of the purposes of the zoning power, the provision of adequate sites for housing persons of all income levels. The amendments would also require that governments exercising the zoning power prepare plans showing how the community proposes to carry out such objectives in accordance with county or regional housing plans. This would ensure that, within the region as a whole, adequate provision is made for sites for all income levels.[21]

3. ACIR Report on Substate Districting. In 1973, the U.S. Advisory Commission on Intergovernmental Relations published *Regional Decision Making: New Strategies for Substate Districts*. This report assessed the effectiveness of regional councils of local elected officials and substate planning and development districts. The report contained a number of recommendations for the federal, state, and local levels of government. The recommendations for state governments are especially relevant to the Growing Smart[SM] legislation. The ACIR recommended that states establish a formal procedure for the delineation and revision of the boundaries of substate districts. It called for a process involving the governor and units of general local government in a substate region, which would result in the governor's designation of a single "umbrella multi-jurisdictional organization" or UMJO in each region, with such designation conferring the legal status of an agency of local governments.[22]

The UMJO's membership should be at least 60 percent local elected officials. The ACIR proposed that such organizations have a voting formula that involved the application of the one-government, one-vote principle in most voting matters, but permitted certain larger local jurisdictions to overrule this procedure on certain issues — such as actions that would affect the finances and operations of constituent local governments — and employ a proportionate, population-weighted rule. The UMJO would be responsible for the adoption and publication of regional policies or plans and of a program for their implementation.[23]

The ACIR called for the UMJO to review and approve, in the context of adopted regional plans and policies, all proposed major capital facility projects of state departments and agencies scheduled for location in the UMJO's region. Similarly, the UMJO would have the authority to review and comment on major capital projects proposed by local governmental units. The ACIR proposed conferring on the UMJO "a policy controlling role" over multijurisdictional special districts operating within the UMJO's region. "The emphasis on a single functional purpose," wrote the ACIR, "often results in decisions which have side effects on other areawide policies, programs, and jurisdictions. *For this reason, a generalist-ori-*

ented and dominated multipurpose regional agency must have authority not only to plan, but also to set basic policy for special districts that transcend city and county boundaries"[24] (emphasis supplied). Means for securing policy control over the special district, according to the ACIR, included: appointment of the special district's policy board by the regional council; review and approval of the district's budgets and basic policies; assignment to the council of the power to halt temporarily or permanently any proposed district project; and empowering the council to serve as the special district's fiscal agent for bonding.[25]

The UMJO could provide member governments with technical assistance and promote interlocal problem solving and contracting. Financing of the regional agency's operations was to come from member governments under a mechanism authorized in enabling legislation and from state funds.[26]

The ACIR recommendations were later translated into model legislation. A portion of this legislation has been adapted for Sections 6-601 to 6-604, which deal with designation of substate districts and substate district agencies.[27]

4. ALI Model Land Development Code. The American Law Institute's (ALI) *A Model Land Development Code* (1976) specifically rejected the establishment or designation of regional planning agencies as having a role in a statewide land development planning and regulation system. Instead, the Code proposed the creation of regional planning divisions of a state land planning agency with regional advisory committees to advise the director of the state agency.

The drafters of the ALI Code were highly skeptical of the potential for regional planning under voluntary associations of elected officials and questioned whether they could provide an independent perspective. "The more that metropolitan agencies have been asked to review functions that bring them into potential conflict with local governments, the more the structural weaknesses of such organizations become apparent," they wrote.[28] The drafters quoted one critic of the system's effectiveness:

> [The COG] receives its legitimacy from its member governments — but those governments do not seem to want the COG to emerge as a force different and distinct from the sum of its governmental parts. Member governments do not generally see the COG as an independent source of regional influence, but rather as a service giver, a co-ordinator, a communications forum, and an insurance device for the continued flow of federal funds to local governments.[29]

Because of these and other political factors, COGs, wrote the Code's drafters, "engage in passive, consensus planning, giving each local government whatever it wants, regardless of the effect on the region," resulting in the "absence of regional planning that really faces tough issues."[30]

As a consequence of this skepticism, the Code required that the basic land planning power "remain at the state level to be delegated by the State Land Planning Agency to the regional divisions or withdrawn therefrom as the state agency sees fit."[31] The ALI Code saw this as "essential to enable the co-ordination of regional land planning with other state activities and to ensure that regional land planning carries the weight and authority of the state government."[32] The Code noted that this would eliminate a "key defect" in most metropolitan planning agencies, which was "the absence of close ties to a governing body and 'a strong chief executive who is able to override the contenders and force resolution of disagreements.'"[33]

Regional Planning in the 1980s and Beyond

In the 1980s, the federal government withdrew almost entirely from its support of regional planning. "Of the 39 programs designed and enacted during the preceding two decades to promote regional organization," wrote Bruce McDowell, "only one — metropolitan transportation planning — remained relatively unscathed by this sudden reversal of federal policy."[34] In the multistate programs, which had created most river basin and economic development regions, the federal government withdrew funding and the organizations died. Only multistate agencies created by federal law or interstate compact survived. The federal economic development programs, through the Economic Development Administration, and the Appalachian programs managed to continue, but in greatly abbreviated form.

A number of states — Connecticut, Florida, Georgia, Kentucky, and Virginia, among them — provided state support for regional planning agencies that replaced the lost federal funds. Florida, in 1972 with the enactment of the Environmental Land and Water Management Act, and Georgia, in 1989 with the Georgia Planning Act, strengthened the authority and responsibility for the agencies in statewide growth management systems. Florida's regional planning councils were required to prepare regional policy plans, review developments of regional impact, and establish mediation and arbitration processes to resolve regional disputes. Under the new Georgia act, the regional planning agencies were recast as "regional development centers" and were given powers similar to the regional councils in Florida. Massachusetts enacted one of the most progressive special purpose regional planning statutes in the nation when it passed, in 1989, special legislation establishing the Cape Cod Commission with broad powers to plan and regulate development in an area of statewide significance.

Regional planning agencies responded to the federal cutback, in some cases, by becoming more entrepreneurial. They undertook joint purchasing programs, forecasting, data collection and dissemination, arranged training, operated programs such as regional ambulance services, or provided consultant planning services to member governments.[35]

Where are regional planning agencies headed? The ACIR's Bruce McDowell suggests that one role of such agencies is the development of "negotiated policies and programs." Regional planning agencies, he observed, are "negotiating bodies" and provide "forums for mediating disputes, finding solutions to tough problems, and working out agreements, and developing cooperative action."[36] A British planning professor, Urlan A. Wannop, predicts that giving regional planning agencies "real duties in planning and implementation" in a statewide growth management system of the type enacted in Florida and elsewhere will make them effec-tive, offering a promise of reinvigorating them.[37] Allan Wallis, an assistant professor of public policy at the University of Colorado at Denver, suggests that, in the current fluid environment, solutions to regional problems will evolve from an identification of "strategic interests over which coalitions already have formed." Thus, there will be no single solution or approach that will work in every region, even if the problems are, in Wallis' words, "fairly generic and common to most other large metropolitan areas." Developing out of the perception of the regional problems and the legitimacy of the coalitions that defined them, the particularized governance structures that result to address those problems "will be highly idiosyncratic, reflecting, as they should, such unique circumstances as local political culture."[38]

ORGANIZATIONAL STRUCTURE

Contemporary Regional Planning Agencies

Regional councils or some type of regional planning organization representing local governments operate in all states except Hawaii, Alaska, and Rhode Island, according to the National Association of Regional Councils (NARC). Regional planning in the U.S. is made institutionally complex by the federal requirement that a metropolitan planning organization (MPO) oversee transportation planning. The MPO may be separate from the established regional planning agencies — the situation in several metropolitan areas including Boston, Chicago, and San Francisco — or governed by a special policy committee inside the agency.

Twenty-five states have "wall-to-wall" regional councils. Regional councils in at least 10 other states serve from 75 to 90 percent of all local governments. For the re-mainder, except for four, reports NARC, councils cover from 60 to 74 percent of all local governments. New Jersey does not have state-designated regional councils. Three councils, two of them MPOs and one a regional planning agency headquartered in Princeton, serve areas of the state. Alaska has divided the state into regions for economic development purposes, but no formal regional agencies exist. In Montana, there are no state-designated regional planning councils, but there are a number of regional planning commissions.[39]

There are at least five possible structures for regional planning agencies:

1. Regional Planning Commission. Regional planning commissions may be single county, multicounty, or composed of multiple jurisdictions. Typically, their governing board is composed of citizens who are appointed by local governments, although elected officials may also serve. They are primarily established to prepare plans, provide technical assistance to member governments, and, in some cases, administer development regulations (such as reviewing and approving subdivision plats). Interstate regional planning commissions cover portions of multistate areas, most typically metropolitan areas. In Ohio, such regional planning commissions are the result of special enabling legislation.[40] In Philadelphia, the Delaware Valley Regional Planning Commission, whose jurisdiction covers portions of New Jersey and Pennsylvania, was created by a special interstate compact approved by Congress.[41]

2. Council of Governments. While they may undertake planning, councils of governments (COGs) are somewhat different than regional planning commissions in that they can carry out virtually any service delivery activity that a member government can undertake, provided the membership agrees that the COG should do so. For example, a council could operate a regional wastewater treatment plan or a regional ambulance service if the members permit. The governing structure of a COG typically involves appointed representatives from member governments but may include others, such as representatives of economic development organizations in the region. A variation includes a COG whose representatives are from local governments and from the state.

In Florida, for example, regional planning councils include representatives of member counties and other local general purpose governments in the geographic area covered by the regional planning council as well as representatives appointed by the governor from the geographic area covered by the council. The governor also appoints, as ex officio nonvoting members, representatives of several state departments.[42] The Metropolitan Washington Council of Governments includes one member of the Maryland General Assembly and one member of

the Virginia General Assembly, representing portions of the Washington, D.C., metropolitan area. Both are selected every two years by separate caucuses of the members of the council from those legislative bodies.[43]

In some states, like Michigan, Ohio, and North Carolina, COGs are creatures of special enabling legislation.[44] In others, like California, they are established through a joint powers agreement.

3. Regional Advisory Committee. The American Law Institute's *Model Land Development Code* rejected the creation of independent regional planning agencies. Instead, it proposed the optional establishment of regional planning divisions for portions of the state. The divisions could be delegated all or a portion of the authority of the state planning agency and would exercise that authority subject to the planning agency's oversight. The governor could also create regional advisory committees and could delegate all or a portion of the powers of the regional planning division to the committees. The committees were also charged with advising the state planning director.[45] The ALI model of regional advisory committees to a state planning agency has not been adopted anywhere in the country.

4. Regional Allocation Agency. Economist Anthony Downs, in his 1994 book, *New Visions for Metropolitan America*, proposed the creation of regional allocation agencies.[46] The regional allocation agency would be responsible for allocating federal funds within various program areas either to local governments or to households, service delivery agencies, or other recipients. At the outset, Downs wrote, the agency would be responsible for allocating federal funding for transportation, environmental control, housing, urban planning, education, welfare, and health care. Within each categorical program, the regional agency would have to develop an allocation plan that addresses the needs and capacities of all potential recipients on an areawide basis and show how it was meeting those needs for persons living in all parts of the metropolitan area.

Examples of such agencies — although they might not reflect all of Downs' criteria — would include the Metropolitan Service District or "Metro" in Portland, Oregon, and the Metropolitan Council in the Twin Cities in Minnesota.[47]

According to Downs, governing members of the agency could be elected by the residents of the entire metropolitan area (as in Portland), appointed by the governor (as in the Twin Cities), or appointed by the local governments in the region. Once chosen, the members of this agency may delegate some of their powers to existing organizations, appoint subagencies to handle funds within each program category, or use any other administrative methods they selected.

With respect to growth management activities, Downs proposed that a single government agency — either at the state level or regional (including county) level — be empowered to review all local land-use plans. The agency would check the plans' consistency with state planning goals — adopted by the state legislature and applicable to all communities in the state — and their consistency with each other, and suggest revisions where inconsistencies of either type are found. Downs contended that the agency must have the power to withhold its approval of local plans and that withholding it should carry significant penalties in the form of ineligibility for various types of state financial assistance.

"In some cases," he wrote, "the agency should have the power to override local government decisions, such as zoning decisions that prevent the creation of low-cost housing. Most often, however, the agency would simply request the local government to revise its plans and repeat the process until final approval is obtained."[48] In order to ensure consistency of state functional plans with local government plans and with each other, the same agency that performed the local plan review would also coordinate activities of state transportation departments, utility regulation departments, environmental protection departments, and other agencies.

5. Special Purpose Regional Agencies. Several states have special purpose regional agencies with the authority to plan and control development in environmentally sensitive areas or areas having statewide resource significance. Examples of such long-standing organizations include the Pinelands Commission in New Jersey, the Cape Cod and Martha's Vineyard Commissions in Massachusetts, the San Francisco Bay Conservation and Development Commission in California, the Adirondack Park Agency in New York, and the bi-state Tahoe Regional Planning Agency in California and Nevada.[49]

The last two alternatives, the regional allocation agency and the special purpose regional agency, require specialized drafting that takes into account regional and local political traditions and the issues that brought about the need for the agency. In the case of the regional allocation agency, the legislation must go beyond regional planning and into the area of restructuring metropolitan governance.

Under model legislation, a regional planning agency can have the planning responsibilities of a regional planning commission and the service provision responsibilities of a council of governments. Various organizational options are also provided including: (a) a voluntary regional agency versus a regional agency mandated by state statute for each substate district; and (b) a structure to be determined by agreement of member governments versus a mandated structure composed of local elected officials, appointees of the governor, and state agency representatives serving in an ex officio, nonvoting capacity.

A related issue is whether membership by local governments will be mandated;

model legislation provides alternative language for this, based on the Florida and Georgia legislation. In Florida, membership by counties in regional councils is mandated by statute, but municipal government membership is not required.[50] By contrast, in Georgia all local governments must be members of a regional development center (RDC), the state's term for a regional planning agency. Georgia, through its department of community affairs, also provides funding support for the RDC.[51] This suggests that where state law mandates local participation in the regional agency (and hence local costs), the state must be prepared to assume a portion of the burden of financing its operation. The model legislation also contains provisions for partial state funding of regional planning agencies.

There is no ideal form for a regional planning agency. The approach taken here, therefore, resists endorsing one, leaving that option up to local officials in the region and the state legislature.[52] For that reason, model legislation does not propose metropolitan or regional "superagencies" or new forms of regional governance, although this may always be an alternative.[53] Economist Anthony Downs has commented that regional growth management policies do not have to be administered "through a single agency acting as a regional policy czar." Instead, he wrote, it might be desirable to have different growth management policies run by different local and regional agencies that are organized in ways best suited to their individual tasks, "as long as they are linked through formal and informal coordination."[54]

As a practical matter, the formal organizational structure of a regional planning agency is less important than the powers and duties that it has, the clarity with which those powers and duties are described, how effectively those powers and duties are actually carried out, and its actual — as opposed to theoretical — relationships with implementing local governments and special dis-

tricts. Conceivably, a regional planning commission whose representatives are lay citizens appointed by their local governments and who are their region's leaders could have just as much informal independence, influence, and authority as the Twin Cities Metropolitan Council, whose board members are appointed by the governor, or the Portland, Oregon, Metropolitan Service District, whose board members are elected. *In adapting these models to local conditions, public officials must look at the desired outcomes of planning and consider modifying the authority of existing agencies before deciding to create new ones.*

Notes

1. See, e.g., Alfred Bettman, "How to Lay Out Regions for Planning," in *Planning Problems of Town, City, and Region: Papers and Discussion* (Baltimore, Md.: Norman, Remington, 1925), 287–301; John Friedmann, "The Concept of a Planning Region — The Evolution of an Idea in the United States," in John Friedmann and William Alonso, eds., *Regional Development and Planning: A Reader* (Cambridge, Mass.: MIT Press, 1964), 497–518.

2. Daniel H. Burnham and Edward H. Bennett, *Plan of Chicago* (reprint of 1909 edition) (New York, N.Y.: DaCapo Press, 1970), esp. Chs. III, IV, and V.

3. This statute appears in Frank B. Williams, *The Law of City Planning and Zoning* (New York, N.Y.: MacMillan, 1922), 594–597.

4. Ibid., 596.

5. Advisory Committee on City Planning and Zoning, *A Standard City Planning Enabling Act* (Washington, D.C.: U.S. GPO, 1928), §26.

6. Ibid., §28.

7. Ibid., §29.

8. Ibid., §30.

9. U.S. Advisory Commission on Intergovernmental Relations (ACIR), *Regional Decision Making: New Strategies for Substate Districts; Substate Regionalism and the Federal System, Vol. 1* (Washington, D.C.: U.S. GPO, October 1973), 54.

10. National Resources Committee, *Regional Factors in National Planning* (Washington, D.C.: U.S. GPO, December 1935), 117–135.

11. Ibid., x.

12. ACIR, *Regional Decision Making*, 55.

13. Judith Getzels, Peter Elliott, and Frank Beal, *Private Planning for the Public Interest: A Study of Approaches to Urban Problem Solving by Nonprofit Organizations* (Chicago, Ill.: American Society of Planning Officials, October 1975), 10–19. See also Jeanne R. Lowe, *Cities in a Race with Time* (New York, N.Y.: Random House, 1967), 110–163.

14. ACIR, *Regional Decision Making*, 57–58.

15. James G. Schrader, *Voluntary Metropolitan Governmental Councils*, Information Report No. 161 (Chicago: American Society of Planning Officials, August 1962), 13.

16. Urlan A. Wannop, *The Regional Imperative: Regional Planning and Governance in Britain, Europe, and the United States* (London, England: Jessica Kingsley Publishers, 1995), 385.

17. Bruce D. McDowell, "The Evolution of American Planning," in *The Practice of State and Regional Planning*, Frank So, Irving Hand, and Bruce D. McDowell, eds. (Washington, D.C.: American Planning Association in cooperation with the International City Management Association, 1986), 56.

18. Bruce D. McDowell, "Regionalism: What It Is, Where We Are, and Where It May Be Headed," a speech given to the 1995 Annual Conference of the Virginia and National Capital Area Chapters of the American Planning Association, Falls Church, Va. (December 4, 1995), 2.

19. American Society of Planning Officials (ASPO), *New Directions in Connecticut Planning Legislation: A Study of Connecticut Planning, Zoning and Related Statutes* (Chicago, Ill.: ASPO, February 1966), 166. The ASPO report recommended that the definition of a regional plan be amended to include the following: (1) conservation and management of water resources, including ground and surface supply, pollution abatement, flood control, and watershed protection; (2) abatement of air pollution; (3) conservation of land resources, including forest, wetlands, wildlife refuges, and seashore; (4) population and general housing types in the several parts of the region; (5) regional facilities, such as major commercial centers, regional parks, transportation, industrial parks, sewerage, and other facilities that would serve the region rather than a single municipality; and (6) a statement of objectives, policies and standards on which recommendations are based. Requiring the factual basis on which policies and standards were derived, wrote ASPO, "will facilitate review of plans by interested public or private group[s] and help them gauge the reasonableness of regional planning proposals. In addition, this requirement will focus attention on development policies underlying specific development proposals such as those for regional land use."

20. National Commission on Urban Problems, *Building the American City: Report of the National Commission on Urban Problems to Congress and to the President* (Washington, D.C.: U.S. GPO, 1968), vii.

21. Ibid., 242.

22. ACIR, *Regional Decision Making*, 354.

23. Ibid.

24. Ibid.

25. Ibid., 360.

26. Ibid.

27. U.S. Advisory Commission on Intergovernmental Relations, "An Act Providing for Designation of Uniform Substate Districts and Coordination Thereof," in *ACIR State Legislative Program: Local Government Modernization* (Washington, D.C.: U.S. GPO, November 1975), 119–132.

28. American Law Institute (ALI), *A Model Land Development Code: Complete Text and Commentary* (Philadelphia, Pa.: ALI, 1976), Note to §8–102, 312.

29. ALI, *A Model Land Development Code*, 311–312, quoting Melvin Mogulof, "Regional Planning, Clearance, and Evaluation: A Look at the A-95 Process," in *Journal of the American Institute of Planners* 37 (1971): 419.

30. ALI, *A Model Land Development Code*, 312.

31. Ibid., 316.

32. Ibid.

33. ALI, *A Model Land Development Code*, 316–317, quoting Melvin Levin, "Planners and Metropolitan Planning," in *Journal of the American Institute of Planners* 33 (1967): 80. See also Richard F. Babcock, "Let's Stop Romancing Regionalism," in *Billboards, Glass Houses and the Law and Other Land Use Fables* (Colorado Springs, Colo.: Shepard's, 1977), 11–23. The late Chicago land-use attorney Richard F. Babcock saw regional planning agencies as "political bastards, the offspring of a loveless dalliance between cynics and dreamers, with no general government willing to acknowledge more than a foster parent relationship." Babcock, who chaired the ALI committee that oversaw the development of the Code and served as the governor's appointee on the Northeastern Illinois Planning Commission, believed that only the state had sufficient independence and power to require the resolution of metropolitan

planning conflicts: "The governor can — if anyone can — compel operating agencies such as the highway department and the state housing authority to recognize in their programs the inescapable interdependence of each with the other. The governor has a broad constituency that permits him to take greater political risks than would be ventured by any mayor or other local representative on a regional commission. If any agency can act as broker between central city and suburb — and perhaps none can — it will be the state. If any negotiation of our bitter metropolitan conflicts is foreseeable, it can occur in our reapportioned and increasingly responsible state legislatures, not in some politically irresponsible regional institution." Babcock's views, of course, colored the approach taken in the ALI Code.

34. McDowell, "Regionalism, What It Is," 3.

35. Wannop, *The Regional Imperative*, 288.

36. Bruce D. McDowell, "Regional Councils Then, Now, and in the Future," a speech to the Board of Directors Retreat, Economic Development Council of Northeastern Pennsylvania (October 7, 1993), in *Regionalism: Shared Decision Making: A Background Reader* (Richmond, Va.: Commission on Population Growth and Development, July 1994), 4.

37. Wannop, *The Regional Imperative*, 292, citing John M. DeGrove, "Regional Agencies as Partners in State Growth Management Systems," *Proceedings of the Joint ACSP and AESOP International Congress*, Oxford, UK (July 1991).

38. Allan D. Wallis, "Investing Regionalism: A Two-Phase Approach," *National Civic Review* 83, no. 4 (Fall-Winter 1994): 447, 450; see also William R. Dodge, "Regional Problem Solving in the 1990s: Experimentation with Local Governance for the 21st Century," *National Civic Review* 79, no. 4 (July-August 1990): 354–366; Patricia S. Atkins and Laura Wilson-Gentry, "An Etiquette for the 1990s Regional Council," *National Civic Review* 81, no. 4 (Fall-Winter 1992): 446–487; Symposium issue on the future of regional governance, Janis Purdy, ed., *National Civic Review* 85, no. 2 (Spring-Summer 1996).

39. National Association of Regional Councils (NARC), *Directory of Regional Councils in the United States* (Washington, D.C.: NARC, April 1995), 3.

40. Oh. Rev. Code §§713.30–713.34 (1994). The Ohio law permits creation by agreement of a board of county commissioners and the legislative authority of a municipality with such boards and authorities of adjoining states. An interstate regional planning commission may also be created by compact which must be reviewed by the attorneys general of the states included in the region and approved and signed by the governors of such states. §713.30.

41. Delaware Valley Urban Area Compact, P.L. 1974, c. 193.

42. Fla. Stat. Ann. §186.504 (West 1987 and Supp. 1995).

43. By-Laws of the Metropolitan Washington Council of Governments, §5.02(e) (December 14, 1988).

44. Mich. Comp. Laws Ann. §124.651 *et seq.* (1991); Oh. Rev. Code, Ch. 167 (1994); N.C.G.S. §160A–470 *et seq.* (1989).

45. American Law Institute, *A Model Land Development Code*, Note to §8-102, 306–319.

46. Anthony Downs, *New Visions for Metropolitan America* (Washington, D.C.: Brookings Institution and Lincoln Institute of Land Policy, 1994), 176–179.

47. Ore. Rev. Stat. Ch. 368 (1993); 1992 Metro Charter; Mn. Stat. Ann., Ch. 186 (1994 and Supp. 1995).

48. Downs, *New Visions for Metropolitan America*, 180.

49. See N.J.S.A. §13.18A-1 *et seq.* (Pinelands Commission); Commonwealth of Massachusetts, Ch. 716 of the Acts of 1989 and Ch. 2 of the Acts of 1990 (Cape Cod Commission Act); Commonwealth of Massachusetts, Ch. 637 of the Acts of 1974 (Martha's Vineyard Commission); Cal. Gov't. Code, §65500 *et seq.* (San Francisco Bay Conservation and Development Commission); N.Y. Executive Law, Art. 27 (Adirondack Park Agency Act, 1990); Nev. Rev. Stat. §278.870 (Nevada Tahoe Regional Planning Agency).

50. Fla. Stat. Ann. §186.504 (4) (West 1987 and Supp. 1995).

51. Ga. Code. Ann. §50-8-33 (1989).

52. For a discussion of the question of support for strong planning roles by regional government, see Mark Baldassare, et al., "Possible Planning Roles for Regional Government: A Survey of City Planning Directors in California," *Journal of the American Planning Association* 62, no. 1 (Winter 1996): 17–28.

53. For an argument favoring metropolitan government or reorganization under a variety of structures, see David Rusk, *Cities Without Suburbs* (Washington, D.C.: Woodrow Wilson Center Press), 91–119.

54. Downs, *New Visions for Metropolitan America*, 182.

CHAPTER 2

THE EVOLUTION OF REGIONAL GOVERNANCE

David B. Walker

Snow White nearly lost her heart. But she overcame the hostility of her stepmother and was kept alive in the forest by a family of dwarfs.

Metro America is Snow White. Migration to suburban areas nearly took the heart out of her. Federal hostility toward taking a role in metro governance has driven metro America into a temporary disappearance from public view. The good news is that she is being kept alive by 17 distinct types of interlocal approaches, on a spectrum from intergovernmental cooperation to full regional governance.

Some view this spectrum as a path out of a dark forest of problems, toward a regional Camelot.

Increasing Need for Metro Approaches

The nation's metro areas are growing, and their problems along with them. Substate regionalism seeks to address problems that spill over the artificial boundaries of central city limits. As metro America expands, the substate regional drama is being played out in more arenas. Note these seven current trends:

1. More Metro areas. More metro areas exist today (1982 data) than ever before, with a more than two-thirds increase since 1962.

2. More People in Metro Areas. Three-quarters of our total population is located there, compared to 63 percent in 1962. More people also live in suburban jurisdictions than previously — some 45 percent of total population compared to 30 percent two decades earlier.

3. Continued Metro Government Fragmentation. Growth in metro areas hasn't meant consolidation. More of the nation's local governments are located in metro areas now: over 36 percent of the 82,000 total as against 27 percent in 1972. The average metro area still encompasses about 100 governmental units, despite the slight increase in the percentage (48 percent of the total) of single county and presumably jurisdictionally simpler metro areas.

4. Increased Metro Diversity. Compared to their situation in the 1960s, metro areas are now more diverse in (a) population and territorial size, (b) the mix of private economic functions and the range of public services offered, (c) the respective position of central cities vis-à-vis outside central city

Originally published as "From Metropolitan Cooperation to Governance," *National Civic Review*, Vol. 76, No. 1, January-February, 1987. Published by the National Civic League, Denver, Colorado. Reprinted with permission of the publisher.

jurisdictions, and (d) the kinds of jurisdictional complexity.

5. Advisory Disharmony. For officials seeking guidance from governmental gurus, theoretically harmony is more elusive than ever. More theories are in vogue as to how metro areas should be run. No wonder actual practice is more eclectic than ever before.

6. Reduced Federal Aid. Direct federal aid to localities, from day care funds to revenue sharing, has been cut back year by year without a concomitant reduction in federal regulations.

7. Reduced State Aid. Because non-educational state aid has been reduced without changes in state mandates and conditions, metro (and, though not the focus of this article, rural) communities' budgets have suffered a double whammy.

These metro area trends point to regionalism as a solution because it can (a) handle certain functions (usually of a capital-intensive or regulatory nature) on a multijurisdictional basis, (b) achieve economies of scale in providing various services by broadening the basis of fiscal support and the demand for certain services, (c) handle "spillover" servicing problems caused by rapid urban population growth and sometimes decline, and (d) confront the necessity for retrenchment by seeking more effective ways of rendering public services.

The 17 Approaches to Regionalism

Regionalism is a gold mine for officials seeking to solve local problems, and 17 different miners may be put to work to extract the gold. These 17 approaches to regional service problems can be arrayed on a spectrum from the easiest to the hardest — from the most politically feasible, least controversial, and sometimes least effective to the politically least feasible, most threatening to

---

FIGURE 1
Regional Approaches to Service Delivery

Easiest

1. Informal Cooperation
2. Interlocal Service Contracts
3. Joint Powers Agreements
4. Extraterritorial Powers
5. Regional Councils/Councils of Governments
6. Federally Encouraged Single-Purpose Regional Bodies
7. State Planning and Development Districts
8. Contracting (Private)

Middling

9. Local Special Districts
10. Transfer of Functions
11. Annexation
12. Regional Special Districts and Authorities
13. Metro Multipurpose District
14. Reformed Urban County

Hardest

15. One-Tier Consolidations
16. Two-Tier Restructuring
17. Three-Tier Reforms

---

local officials, and sometimes most effective, at least in the opinion of many in jurisdictions that have made these fairly radical reforms (see Figure 1).

Easiest Eight

The first eight approaches are the easiest:

1. Informal Cooperation. For many up against the wall, this is the easiest of them all. This approach is clearly the least formal, and the most pragmatic of the 17. It generally involves collaborative and reciprocal actions between two local jurisdictions, does not usually require fiscal actions, and only rarely involves matters of regional or even subregional significance. Although reliable information on the extent of its use is generally absent, anecdotal evidence suggests that informal cooperation is the most widely practiced approach to regionalism.

2. Interlocal Service Contracts. Voluntary but formal agreements between two or more local governments are widely used. Some 45 states now sanction them broadly. Survey data suggest a slight decline (four percent) between 1972 and 1983 in their use, but well over half the cities and counties polled in 1983 had used such contracts to handle at least one of their servicing responsibilities. Metro central cities, suburbs, and counties generally rely on them to a greater extent than non-metro municipal and county jurisdictions.

3. Joint Powers Agreements. These agreements between two or more local governments provide for the joint planning, financing, and delivery of a service for the citizens of all the jurisdictions involved. All states authorize joint service agreements, but 20 still require that each participating unit be empowered to provide the service in question. Surveys indicate that the number of cities and counties relying on joint services agreements for at least one service rose from 33 percent in 1972 to 55 percent in 1983, making them slightly more popular than interlocal contracting, although usage closely parallels interlocal servicing contracts.

4. Extraterritorial Powers. Sanctioned in 35 states, extraterritorial powers permit all or at least some, cities to exercise some of their regulatory authority outside their boundaries in rapidly developing unincorporated areas. Less than half the authorizing states permit extraterritorial planning, zoning, and subdivision regulation, however, which makes effective control of fringe growth difficult. Because a number of states do not authorize extraterritorial powers, and because this approach does not apply to cities surrounded by other incorporated jurisdictions, this approach is less used than other techniques.

5. Regional Councils/Councils of Governments. In the 1960s, no more than 20 or 25 jurisdictions had created wholly voluntaristic regional councils. That figure had soared to over 660 by 1980, thanks largely to federal aid and especially to federal requirements (notably Section 204 of the Model Cities legislation) that required a regional review and comment process in all metro areas for certain local grant applications. Title IV of the Intergovernmental Cooperation Act of 1968 built on the Section 204 base to create a "clearinghouse" structure at the rural and urban regional as well as state levels. Local participation in regional councils still remained primarily voluntary, however, with jurisdictions resisting any efforts at coercion.

Regional councils, also known as Councils of Government (COGs) which rely so heavily on interlocal cooperation, assumed far more than a clearinghouse role in the late 1960s and 1970s. Thirty-nine federal grants programs with a regional thrust sometimes utilized COGs for their own integral parts of a strong state-established substate districting system, as well. Rural COGs tended to take on certain direct assistance and servicing roles for their constituents, while the more heavily urban ones usually served a role as regional agenda-definer and conflict-resolver.

With the advent of Reagan federalism a reduction in the federal role in substate regionalism occurred. Reagan's Executive Order 12372 put the prime responsibility for the A-95 clearinghouse role with the states, while providing a back-up federal role (48 states picked up the challenge). Twelve of the 39 federal regional programs were scrapped, 11 were cut heavily, 9 lost their regional component, and 6 were revised substantially; only 1 was left fully intact.

To survive, COGs had to adapt and the overwhelming majority did so; less than one-fifth (125) of the 660 regional councils shut their doors. Some got greater state support both in funding and in power. Many others sought more local fiscal contributions and became a regional servicing agency for constituent local units. A majority of regional councils now serve as a chief source of technical services and provide certain direct services under contract to their localities. Some state functions have been transferred to [a] regional council and many serve as field administrator of certain state-planned and fund services. All still perform some type of clearinghouse function and some assume specialized regional planning and other related functions under at least 11 federal single-purpose grants and loan programs as of FY 1983.

Most COGs, then, reflect a greater "nativism," "pragmatism," and service activism than their predecessors of a decade ago.

6. **Federally Encouraged Single-Purpose Regional Bodies.** Single-purpose regional bodies came into being when institutional strings were attached to some 20 federal aid programs (as of 1980). According to the 1977 Census of Local Governments, these federally encouraged special-purpose regional units numbered between 1,400 and 1,700 depending on definitions and classifications. A less rigorous, private, and meagerly funded survey identified more than 990 such bodies in 1983. Although the actual number as of 1983 was probably higher, by 1986 the total was probably a lot less, given the number of regional program revisions, budget cuts, and eliminations during the 1983–86 period. Single-purpose regional bodies now exist only in a few federal aid programs (notably economic development, Appalachia, Area Agencies on Aging, Job Training, and metro transportation). Continued federal fundings make them easy to establish and they play a helpful, non-threatening planning role.

7. **State Planning and Development Districts (SPDDs).** These districts were established by the states during the late 1960s and early 1970s to bring order to the chaotic proliferation of federal special purpose regional programs. A state's own substate regional goals were a prominent part of the authorizing legislation (19 states) or gubernatorial executive orders (24 states) that established SPDDs. By 1979 18 states had conferred a "review and comment" role on their SPDDs for certain non-federally aided local and state projects. Sixteen conferred such authority for special district projects and 11 authorized SPDDs to assume a direct servicing role, if it was sanctioned by member governments or the regional electorate.

As a matter of practice, practically all SPDDs adhere to the confederate style of regional councils/COGs. Many regional councils have been folded into the SPDD system, although boundaries have sometimes changed. Approximately the same number of SPDD systems (43) exist today as in the late 1970s, although in the hard-pressed midwest funding problems have rendered some moribund. All of these states took on the devolved responsibilities under Reagan's Executive Order 12372 for the "clearinghouse function," as did five others. Over half fund their SPDDs but only five in a respectable fashion.

Although feasible, SPDDs are somewhat difficult because special authorizing legislation is required, state purposes and goals are involved, and the establishment of a new statewide districting system can at least initially appear threatening, especially to counties.

8. **Contracting (Private).** Contracting with the private sector is the only form of public-private collaboration analyzed here and is the most popular of all such forms. Service contracts with private providers are now authorized in 26 states — far fewer than their intergovernmental counterparts and usually with far more detailed procedural

requirements. Their use has clearly increased from the early 1970s to the present with scores of different local services sometimes provided under contracts with various private sector providers. Joint powers agreements and inter-local service agreements, however, are both more popular than contracting with private firms.

This approach rounds out the cluster of interlocal approaches that we term easiest. Contracting with private organizations has been placed last because authorizing legislation, especially non-restrictive statutes, may be difficult to obtain. Moreover, the fears of public sector unions as well as certain public employees are aroused when local officials seek to contract services privately.

Middling Six

The middle cluster in the spectrum includes four institutional and two tough procedural approaches for new and usually broader territorial service delivery systems. These approaches present somewhat greater hurdles than those in the prior group but each is a more stable way to effectively align governmental and service delivery boundaries.

9. Local Special Districts. These districts are a very popular way to provide a single service or multiple related services on a multi-jurisdictional basis. Three-quarters of all local special districts serve areas whose boundaries are not coterminous with those of a city or county, a situation that has prevailed for at least two decades. Forty-one percent of all special districts were found within metro areas, making special districts the most numerous of the five basic categories of local government in metro America.

10. Transfer of Functions. This procedural way to change permanently the provider of a specific service jumped by 40 percent in a decade, according to a 1983 survey

of counties and cities. The larger urban jurisdictions were much more likely to transfer functions than the smaller ones. Over three-fifths of the central cities reported such transfers compared to 37 percent of the suburban cities and 35 percent of the nonmetro municipalities. Among counties, 47 percent of the metro-type counties transferred functions compared to only 29 percent in the non-metro group. Cities were likely to shift services, first to counties then to COGs and special districts.

Despite its increased popularity, the difficulties involved in transfer of functions should not be overlooked. Only 18 states authorize such shifts (eight more than in 1974) and in half these cases voter approval is mandated. In addition, the language of some of the authorizing statutes does not always clearly distinguish between a transfer and an interlocal servicing contract.

11. Annexation. The dominant 19th century device for bringing local jurisdictional servicing boundaries and expanding settlement patterns into proper alignment remains popular. The 61,356 annexations in the 1970s involved 9,000 square miles and three million people. The 23,828 annexations in the first half of the 1980s affected one million citizens and three million square miles. Although the vast majority of these annexations involved very few square miles, they are an incremental solution to closing the gap between governmental servicing boundaries and the boundaries of the center city.

A look at the larger-scale annexations of the past four decades highlights a dozen municipalities that serve almost as de facto regional governments: Phoenix, Houston, Dallas, San Antonio, Memphis, San Jose, El Paso, Huntsville, Concord (Cal.), Ft. Worth, Omaha, and Shreveport. Most large-scale annexations have occurred in the southwest and west, thanks to the large amount of unincorporated land on municipal peripheries and to pro-city annexation statutes. Students of public finance point out that central cities that were able to annex substantial land are usually in good fiscal shape since they have escaped the "hole in the doughnut" problems of central cities in the older metro areas of the east and midwest.

Annexation is limited by the nature of state authorizing laws (most do not favor the annexing locality); its irrelevance in most northeastern states, given the absence of unincorporated turf in their urban areas; and a reluctance to use the process as a long-range solution to eliminating local jurisdictional, fiscal, and servicing fragmentation. Annexation, then, has limited geographic application and is usually used incrementally; but when it is assigned a key role in a city's development, it can transform a municipality from a local to a regional institution.

12. Regional Special Districts and Authorities. These big areawide institutions comprise the greatest number of regional governments in our 304 metro areas. Unlike their local urban counterparts, these Olympian organizations are established to cope on a fully areawide basis with a major urban surviving challenge such as mass transit, sewage disposal, water supply, hospitals, airports, and pollution control. Census data show there were approximately 132 regional and 983 major subregional special districts and authorities in 304 metro areas in 1982, compared to 230 and 2,232, respectively, in non-metro areas.

Relatively few large, regional units have been established because they (a) require specific state enactment and may involve functional transfers from local units; (b) are independent, expensive, professional, and fully governmental; and (c) are frequently as accountable to bond buyers as to the localities and the citizen consumers.

13. Metro Multipurpose Districts. These districts differ from the other regional models in that they involve establishing a regional authority to perform diverse, not just related regional, functions. At least four states have enacted legislation authorizing such district[s], but they permit a comparatively narrow range of functions.

This option clearly ranks among the most difficult to implement, with metro Seattle the only basic case study. While multipurpose districts have a number of theoretical advantages (greater popular control, better planning and coordination of a limited number of areawide functions, and a more accountable regional government), political and statutory difficulties have barred their widespread use.

14. The Reformed Urban County. Because it transforms a unit of local government, a move frequently opposed by the elected officials of the jurisdiction in question, new urban counties are difficult to form. As a result, though 29 states have enacted permissive county home rule statutes, only 76 charter counties (generally urban) have been created.

In metro areas, however, three-quarters of the 683 metro counties have either an elected chief executive or an appointed chief administrative officer. The servicing role of these jurisdictions has expanded rapidly over the past ten decades or so. Since 1967, outlays for what used to be traditional county functions (corrections, welfare, roads, and health and hospitals) have declined, with expenditures for various municipal-type, regional and new federally encouraged services have risen commensurately. Overall, the range of state-mandated and county-initiated services have risen rapidly in metro counties, during the past two decades, which has necessitated a better approach to fiscal and program management.

In the 146 single-county metro areas this reform county option is excellent. However, since county mergers and modification of county boundaries are almost impossible, in the 159 multi-county metro areas the option is less valuable. It can only provide a subregional solution to certain service delivery problems, not a fully regional approach.

The Tough Trio

The hardest approaches to metro regionalism are the three general governmental options: one-tier or unitary, two-tier or federative, and three-tier or super-federative.

All three involve the creation of a new areawide level of government, a reallocation of local government powers and functions, and, as a result a disruption of the political and institutional status quo. All three options involve very rare and remarkable forms of interlocal cooperation.

15. One-tier Consolidations. This method of expanding municipal boundaries has had a lean, but long history. From 1804 to 1907, four city-county mergers occurred, all by state mandate. Then municipalities proliferated but city-county mergers virtually stopped for 40 years. From Baton Rouge's partial merger in 1947 to the present there have been some 17 city-county consolidations, most endorsed by popular referendum. Among the hurdles to surmount in achieving such reorganizations are state authorization, the frequent opposition of local elected officials, racial anxieties (where large minorities exist), an equitable representational system, concerns about the size of government, and technical issues relating to such matters as debt assumption. Only one out of every five consolidation efforts has succeeded in the past 25 years.

Most consolidations have been partial, not total, with small suburban municipalities, school districts and special districts sometimes left out but the new county government generally exercises some authority over their activities. In addition, the metro settlement pattern in some cases has long since exceeded the county limits, so that the reorganized government may be the prime service provider and key player, but not the only one. This, of course, is another result of rigid county boundaries.

To sum up, one-tier consolidations have generally been most suitable in smaller non-metro urban areas and in smaller and medium (ideally uni-county) metro areas.

16. Two-tier Restructurings. These seek a division between local and regional functions with two levels of government to render such services. These and other features, notably a reorganized county government, are spelled out in a new county charter that is adopted in a countywide referendum. The Committee for Economic Development advanced one of the most persuasive arguments for this approach in the 1970s. Metro Toronto, which created a strongly empowered regional federative government to handle areawide functions and ultimately led to some local reorganization by the merger of some municipalities, is a model for this approach.

The prime American example of this federative approach is Metro Dade County (Miami-Dade). Unlike the incremental reform approach of the modernized or urban county, a drastically redesigned county structure and role emerged from a head-on confrontation over the restructuring issue. Narrowly approved in a countywide referendum in 1957, the new Metro government's cluster of strong charter powers and its authority to perform a range of areawide functions were steadily opposed until the mid–1960s. Since then, its powers have grown and it is widely considered a success. Witness the extraordinary responsibilities Metro Dade assumed during the various waves of immigration since the early 1960s. The level of metro-municipal collaboration is better now than it was a generation ago, but tensions and confrontations are still part of the relationship — as they are in most federative systems. In my opinion, however, its survival is assured.

17. The Three-tier Reforms. This is a rarely used approach, with just two U.S. examples. However, it deals with the special problems of multi-county metro areas.

The first example is the Twin Cities

(Minneapolis-St. Paul) Metropolitan Council. Launched as a metro initiative and enacted by the state legislature in 1967, the Council is the authoritative regional coordinator, planner, and controller of large-scale development for its region which includes seven counties and a dozen localities.

It is empowered by the state to review, approve, or suspend projects and plans of the area's various multi-jurisdictional special districts and authorities; it is the regional designee under all federally sponsored substate regional programs for which the area is eligible, and has the right to review and delay projects having an adverse areawide impact. Direct operational responsibilities do not fall within its purview but it directly molds the region's future development. Like any body that possesses significant power over other public agencies and indirectly over private regional actors, the Council has become somewhat politicized in recent years but its rightful place in the governance of the Twin Cities is not questioned.

The other three-tier experiment is the Greater Portland (Oregon) Metropolitan Service District (MSD), a regional planning and coordinating agency that serves the urbanized portion of three counties. Approved by popular referendum in 1978, the MSD supplanted the previous COG, and assumed the waste disposal and Portland Zoo responsibilities of the previous regional authority. The enabling legislation also authorized the MSD to run the regional transportation agency and to assume responsibility for a range of the functions, subject to voter approval, but these options have not been utilized. A 1986 referendum on a new convention center did pass and this task was assigned to the MSD. Unlike the Twin Cities' Council, the MSD has an elected mayor, an appointed manager, and an elected council of 12 commissioners, which provides a popular accountability that the Met Council has yet to achieve.

Both three-tier examples suggest how other multi-county metro areas might approach areawide service delivery and other metro challenges but they are arduous to achieve and not easy to sustain.

This probe of metro Snow White's current status suggests that she is alive and well, and is being looked after by her 17 regionable dwarfs:

1. Overall Growth in Regionalism. Virtually all of the various approaches have been on the increase. Since the early 1970s, the use of the eight easiest approaches has seen a net increase despite a reduction in the number of regional councils and federally supported substate districts. Meanwhile five of the six middling approaches grew markedly (the exception was the metro multi-purpose authority). Even the three hardest approaches have grown in use.

2. Multiple Approach Use. Very few metro areas rely on only one or two forms of substate regionalism.

3. The easier procedural and unifunctional institutional types of service shifts tend to be found more in larger metro areas while the harder restructurings usually take place successfully within the medium-sized and especially the small metro areas.

4. The expanded use of at least 10 of the 14 easiest and middling approaches is largely a product of local needs and initiatives, as well as of a growing awareness of their increasingly interdependent condition.

5. Jurisdictional fragmentation has not been reduced as a result of restructuring successes, but even incomplete forms of cooperation are useful. Such approaches are used extensively; in a majority of metro areas they are the only feasible forms of regional and subregional collaboration.

6. Like much else in the American system of metro governance, the overwhelming majority of interlocal and regional actions taken to resolve servicing and other problems reflect an ad hoc, generally issue-by-issue, incremental pattern of evolution. However, most of the major reorganizations were

triggered, at least in part, by a visible crisis of some sort.

7. The intergovernmental bases of substate regional activities remain as significant as ever. The states, which always have played a significant part in the evolution of their metro areas, must move into a new primary role if the federal role in this arena continues to erode.

Our Snow White would be ever so happy if her Prince Charming would gallop up soon, wake her from the slumber induced by her stepmother, take her out of the forest and — please — make room in the palace for 17 hardworking dwarfs!

Bibliography

Advisory Commission on Intergovernmental Regulations, *Intergovernmental Service Arrangements for Delivering Local Public Service: Update 1983 (A-103)*. Washington, D.C., October 1985.

_____, *Pragmatic Federalism: The Reassignment of Functional Responsibility (M-105)*. Washington, D.C., July 1976.

_____, *Regional Decision Making: New Strategies for Substate Districts (A-43)*. Washington, D.C., October 1973.

_____, *State and Local Roles in the Federal System (A-88)*. Washington, D.C., April 1982.

Bollens, John C. and Henry J. Schmandt, *The Metropolis*, Fourth Edition, New York, N.Y., 1982.

Florestano, Patricia and Stephen Gordon, "County and Municipal Use of Private Contracting for Public Service Delivery," *Urban Interest*, April 1984.

Hatry, Harry P. and Carl F. Valente, "Alternative Service Delivery Approaches Involving Increased Use of the Private Sector," *The Municipal Year Book*. International City Management Association, Washington, D.C. 1983, pp. 199–207.

Henderson, Lori, "Intergovernmental Service Arrangements and the Transfers of Functions," *Municipal Year Book*. International City Management Association, Washington, D.C. 1985, pp. 194–202.

Jones, Victor, "Regional Councils and Regional Governments in the United States," paper presented at the Annual Meeting of the American Society for Public Administration, Detroit, 1981.

Marlin, John Tepper, ed., *Contracting Municipal Services: A Guide for Purchase from the Private Sector*, Ronald Press, John Wiley & Sons, New York, 1984, pp. 1–13.

McDowell, Bruce D., "Moving Toward Excellence in Regional Councils," based on a paper presented at the New England Regional Council Conference in Portland, Maine on October 26, 1984.

_____, "Regional Councils in an Era of Do-It-Yourself Federalism," a paper presented to the Regional Council Executive Directors of the Southeastern States, March 20, 1986.

_____, "Regions Under Reagan," a paper presented at the National Planning Conference, American Planning Association, Minneapolis-St. Paul, Minnesota, May 8, 1984.

National Association of Regional Councils, *Directory of Regional Councils, 1985-86*, Washington, D.C.

_____, *Matrix of Regional Council Programs, 1985–86*, Washington, D.C.

_____, *Special Report— No. 91*. Washington, D.C., January 1984.

U.S. Bureau of the Census, *Local Governments in Metropolitan Areas* (1982 Census of Governments, Vol. 5-GC82[5]). Washington, D.C.

U.S. Senate, Committee on Governmental Affairs, Subcommittee on Intergovernmental Relations, *Metropolitan Regional Governance*, Hearing, February 6, 1984. Washington, D.C.

Wikstrom, Nelson, "Epitaph for a Monument to Another Successful Protest: Regionalism in Metropolitan Areas," *Virginia Social Science Journal*, Vol. 19, Winter 1984, pp. 1–10.

Wirt, Frederick M., "The Dependent City: External Influences Upon Local Autonomy," paper delivered at the 1983 Annual Meeting of the American Political Science Association, September 1-4, 1983.

CHAPTER 3

MODELS OF
REGIONAL GOVERNANCE

Richard Sybert

This chapter reviews four models and examples of regional government: (1) one-level; (2) two-level; (3) cooperative; and (4) metropolitan council.[1]

Nashville-Davidson County provides an example of the first model, where the city and county governments are consolidated into one. In this case, the new government was able to save its taxpayers an estimated $18 million in the first ten years by providing a more efficient government and cutting duplication of services. The one government could represent both local and regional interests through a combination of district and at-large representation. However, this model has never been successful in metropolitan areas that extend over more than one county or have populations of over one million people, limiting its usefulness in California.

Miami-Dade County's two-level comprehensive government has successfully integrated and coordinated the county's previously disorganized departments and agencies. "Metro" was successful in financing water and sewer treatment, transit, a seaport, traffic, and law enforcement projects in its first two decades. It also established a South Dade Governmental Center to make services such as public works, pollution con-

trol, traffic and transportation, water and sewer, and housing and urban development, more accessible. Metro's main problem is that the growth of the region is extending beyond the Dade County line. With no governing power outside the county, Metro is facing difficulties dealing with the region's problems. This is possibly a problem for California as well, with its urban regions often crossing multiple county lines.

Another two-level model is federation. Through government reorganization, Toronto's Metro, like Miami-Dade County, has been successful in finding solutions considered unachievable in the previous government system. Metro has successfully stabilized the region's governmental finances and resolved specific service crises. Its accomplishments include: water and sewer facilities, a regional highway network, a coordinated public transportation system, a traffic control system, and the establishment of a large parks system. One problem facing Toronto's Metro is factionalism. The Metro Council is often divided by local interests, limiting its ability to deal with regional problems.

The Lakewood-Los Angeles cooperative approach is an efficient and effective

Originally published as *Models of Regional Government*, October, 1991. Published by the Governor's Office of Planning and Research and the Governor's Interagency Council on Growth Management, Office of the Governor, State of California, Sacramento, California. Reprinted with permission of the publisher.

form of government whereby the county provides needed services — generally fire, sanitation, and police services — to the city of Lakewood and others in the Los Angeles County without unnecessarily duplicating government agencies. Opponents say the plan limits a city's powers to land use decisions. Further, Lakewood was a new, small city with no previous service capabilities; the approach may not be applicable to California's existing, large urban regions.

Finally, there is the model of metropolitan councils. Two examples are the Twin Cities Metropolitan Council in Minneapolis-St. Paul and the Portland, Oregon Tri-County Metropolitan Council. Both these plans are examples of regional governments in multi-county areas. Through legislation passed in the Minnesota Legislature, the Twin Cities Metropolitan Council was formed in 1967. Although it possesses rather weak powers, the Council was originally successful in developing regional approaches for sewers, transportation, airports, housing, parks, and open space. However, the Council later encountered difficulties in its effectiveness as a governing body. Portland's Tri-County Council was an evolution of regional agencies. Although it too has weak powers, it has increased its effectiveness through popular support.

One-Level Alternative

Since the beginning of the 20th century, many urban reformers have contended that the entire metropolitan area or "sphere of influence" of the modern city should be brought within its actual legal boundaries. These reformers believe that the creation of single or "one level" governments for an entire urban region would be more efficient, effective, and economical than multi-level governments. However, opponents of this model maintain that it results in the loss of local control, decreased citizen access to public officials, and reduced attention to local services. This is because a one-level urban government in a metropolitan area necessarily is on a larger scale than traditional local government.

The one-level alternative can be accomplished by three basic techniques: (a) annexation (the absorption of nearby unincorporated territory); (2) municipal consolidation (the merger of two or more incorporated units); and/or (3) city-county consolidation (the union of one or more municipalities with the county government).

This chapter focuses on city-county consolidation because it is the most dramatic or strongest of these techniques. To achieve city-county consolidation, two legal battles normally must be won. First, a state constitutional amendment or legislative enabling act must be passed to permit the metropolitan areas to pursue the consolidation. Second, the consolidation must win the approval of the local voters, usually by separate majorities of the city or cities and the unincorporated part of the county.

An example of the one-level alternative through city-county consolidation is Nashville-Davidson County in Tennessee.

Nashville-Davidson County
Background. The metropolitan government of Nashville-Davidson County is located in the north central area of the State of Tennessee. Prior to consolidation, Davidson County had 12 governments within its boundaries: the county, the city of Nashville, six incorporated suburbs, and four special utility districts.

The Nashville region faced problems similar to those of many other medium or small metropolitan areas in the country. There existed a single urban area with overlapping governments — one, the city, with substantial authority but little area; and the other, the county, with substantial territory but little power. This situation created constant attempts between local governments to "pass the buck" and avoid responsibility, with each government trying to keep its own taxes low by taking advantage of the other's services.

The Nashville region also provided an example of a tax dispute often seen between the city government and its "daytime citizens" — i.e., commuters — from the suburbs. Most citizens in the region paid taxes only in their resident communities, despite the fact that their jobs were located in and arguably depended upon the city of Nashville. Suburban commuters also used many city-supported services. While county residents argued that they contributed to the city's wealth, the city believed that its own citizens were effectively subsidizing services to county residents in this manner. The city tried to correct this perceived inequity by over-charging county residents for city-supplied water and electricity. In addition, the city levied a "wheel tax" on all motor vehicles using the streets of Nashville for 30 days or more. However, the strict enforcement of these taxes created considerable resentment on the part of county residents. As an example of conflict, city and county police withheld information from each other. Also, the two school systems fought over how to split state education funds. Additionally, on some roads where the city-county line went down the middle, the speed limit was 35 mph in one direction and 45 mph in the other.

These conflicts made it increasingly evident that the needs of the residents in the Nashville-Davidson County area were not being efficiently and effectively met by the existing multi-level government arrangement. Accordingly, in 1957 the Tennessee State General Assembly enacted enabling legislation permitting city-county consolidation.

A first attempt to approve a county-city consolidation failed in 1958. It was supported by the mayor of Nashville, the Nashville Chamber of Commerce, the Tennessee Taxpayers' Association, labor, and a variety of other groups. Opponents, including sub-urban private fire and police companies, some suburban businessmen, and members of the county legislature (analogous to a California board of supervisors), argued that the consolidation would mean bigger government, higher taxes, and city control over the suburbs. In 1962, a new "Metro" charter election was called for in the Nashville-Davidson County region. This time, with a greater grass roots effort (telephoning, doorbell ringing, and neighborhood coffees), the charter won approval both in the city and the county, by margins of 57–40 percent and 55–44 percent respectively.

The System. The metropolitan government of Nashville-Davidson County merged the functions previously held separately by the city of Nashville and Davidson County. The six suburbs were frozen at their existing boundaries, and given the opportunity to use Metro's services, which most did.

The Metro government has a strong mayor-council system. The chief executive is the "metropolitan mayor," who is elected by the area's voters to a four-year term. His tenure in office is limited to three consecutive terms. The mayor is responsible for the supervision, administration, and control of the executive departments, agencies, boards, and commissions. The mayor is authorized to approve or disapprove council ordinances, subject to an override by two-thirds of the council. The mayor may also veto line-item budget expenditures, again subject to a two-thirds override by the council.

The legislative branch consists of two parts: the metropolitan council and the urban council. The metropolitan county council is comprised of 40 councilmembers and the vice mayor. Thirty-five of these councilmembers are elected from single-member districts of approximately equal population, and five councilmembers are elected at large. The charter provides for a high number of councilmembers to ensure that local concerns [are] represented. The five at large members were included to make sure that regional problems were addressed.

The charter designates two separate service-tax districts with[in] the metropolitan government's geographic limits: the general services district (GSD) and the urban services district (USD). The GSD comprises the total area of Davidson County and provides such services as general administration, police, courts, jails, health, welfare, schools, transit, and parks and recreation. The USD provides additional services, such as urban level fire protection, trash collection, street lights, storm drainage, and additional police protection. Separate taxes are levied in each district to support the level of services within the respective district.

The USD may be expanded whenever areas in the GSD need additional urban services, and when the metropolitan government is capable of providing such additional services within one year after the additional USD tax rate is imposed. While there is no formula to determine when additional services are needed, expansion usually occurs when enough local support is gathered to join the USD and pay the additional taxes. If the USD is not capable of providing the services within the one-year deadline, Metro can delay the application until the services are ready to be provided.

Two-Level Alternative

The two-level alternative of regional reorganization is based on the theory of federalism. With this technique, area-wide functions are delegated to area-wide governments, while purely local functions remain with the local units, creating a two-tier system.

The two-tier system can take three basic forms:

1. Metropolitan district: A governmental unit that usually encompasses all or a substantial part of the entire geographic metropolitan area, but is normally authorized to perform only one function or a few closely related activities of an area-wide nature. California examples would be school districts, water districts, air quality and transit districts and the like. The existing city-county structure is retained.

2. Comprehensive urban county plan: The simultaneous transfer of selected functions from municipalities and other local units to the county governments. The existing city-county structure is retained, with the county performing a number of municipal functions county-wide.

3. Federation: The establishment of a new area-wide government that is assigned new responsibilities and customarily replaces the existing county government. Again, the upper tier performs a number of municipal functions region-wide.

Because metropolitan districts are single-interest entities, with no general jurisdictions to address metropolitan-wide problems, this chapter will focus on the other two systems.

All of these forms are structural variations and may accomplish the same functional result.

COMPREHENSIVE URBAN COUNTY PLAN

Under a comprehensive urban county plan, a county assumes those functions that are determined to be area-wide in nature, while the municipalities continue to administer those functions considered to be of purely local concern. Thus, the county is transformed into a metropolitan government, with the simultaneous reallocation of a variety of functions from all municipalities to the county.

Politically, such a plan can have considerable appeal if the county is viewed by the public as an acceptable unit of local government. Unlike other techniques of reform, the urban county plan does not require the creation of still another unit of government. Instead, it merely strengthens the county to serve as a second tier. The success of this type of regional government in California is questionable because most major metropolitan areas often cross county lines.

An example of a comprehensive urban county plan is Miami-Dade County in Florida.

Miami-Dade County

Background. Dade County, located in the southeast corner of Florida, covers approximately 2,300 square miles. It encompasses all of the Miami area and stretches westward to the Everglades. Population growth in Dade County over the last few decades has been high, increasing six-fold in the 45 years after World War II to over 1.9 million people. Historically, the county had experienced a series of municipal incorporations by the core city, Miami, and its surrounding suburbs.

Metropolitan government, or "Metro," was created in 1957. Prior to this, there was no effective countywide agency responsible for long-range regional planning in such areas as economic development, welfare, recreation, and the environment. Local planning boards did exist, but were ineffective because of relatively poorly trained technical staffs, inadequate financial support, and what some believed to be lack of appreciation by local officials and the general public of the need for adequate planning.

The needs of the unincorporated areas of Dade County, home to one-third of the total county population, constituted a particularly serious problem. These unincorporated areas frequently entered into informal agreements with incorporated municipalities for provision of essential services, such as fire protection and police communication and training, to rapidly growing populations. The major problem with these agreements was that larger cities were burdened with the expenses of providing the services to the smaller areas.

A number of proposals to consolidate Dade County with the city of Miami and a varying number of smaller communities failed in the late 1940s and early 1950s. However, the closeness of a referendum in 1953 led to the formation of the Metropolitan Miami Municipal Board (3M Board) to study the feasibility of governmental reorganization.

In November 1956, the citizens of the State of Florida by a two to one margin, passed a home rule constitutional amendment, thus freeing Dade County and its cities from dependence on the state legislature for the enactment of local laws. The home rule amendment also permitted the county's voters to create a metropolitan government. Following this approval, the 3M board developed a proposal for a metropolitan system.

The principal recommendation of the 3M Board was creation of a two-tiered form of government for the Dade County region. The city level would be responsible for local functions, such as zoning and police and fire protection, the minimum standards for which would be set by the county. The second level would be a reorganized and enlarged county government, responsible for such regional functions as water, sewage, solid waste disposal, all public transportation construction and operation, traffic control, and overall metropolitan planning.

Prior to the referendum election, a Dade County League of Municipalities committee established to study the proposal returned a negative report. In spite of the League's opposition, Dade County voters narrowly approved (51–49 percent with only a 26 percent turnout) a charter based on the 3M recommendations in May 1957.

The System. The powers of the county government under the terms of the charter are separated into four distinct categories: (1) municipal-type functions, (2) responsibilities in unincorporated areas, (3) responsibilities for setting minimum standards, and (4) elastic powers.

The municipal-type functions include transportation systems, traffic control, police and fire protection, county development plans, health and welfare programs, parks and recreation, housing, water supply, waste disposal, and taxing. County government's responsibilities in unincorporated areas include the same municipal-type functions, such as police and fire protection and waste disposal, plus other functions performed by municipalities, such as licensing and regulation of the limousines and taxis, and establishing and enforcing regulations for the sale of alcoholic beverages.

To provide local control of municipal services, the county government is empowered to set minimum performance standards for services provided by all local governmental units. If a municipality does not comply with such standards, the county government is empowered to take over and perform or contract out to other organizations to operate the service. Finally, under the so-called "elastic" provisions of the charter, the county government is authorized "to exercise all powers and privileges granted" to municipalities and counties under the Florida Constitution to "adopt such ordinances and resolutions as may be required in the exercise of its powers" and to "perform any other acts consistent with laws which are required or which are in the common interest of the people of the county."

Although the division of powers under this scheme is strongly weighted on the county government's side, the individual municipalities are given certain protections and prerogatives. The county cannot abolish an incorporated municipality without the express permission of the municipality's voters, nor can the county rearrange municipal boundaries. Municipalities retain the right to change their respective charters, provided the provisions do not conflict with the county charter. Each city can exceed county minimum standards for zoning, and, subject to county standards, regulate taxis and other rental vehicles, determine hours for sale of alcoholic beverages, and provide for fire and police protection.

A board of county commissioners is designated under the terms of the charter to serve as the legislative and governing body of the county and to oversee the entire metropolitan system. The board consists of nine commissioners, with eight elected by the voters of the county at large, subject to the requirement that each commissioner must reside in a different county commission district. The ninth member, who serves as the mayor and chairman of the board, also is elected by a countywide vote. All commissioners serve four-year terms.

FEDERATION

Another variation of the two-level alternative is a federation. This approach involves the creation of an entirely new area-wide government with either multi-county or one-county territorial limits. The newly created unit is usually designated as the metropolitan government and is charged with carrying out numerous area-wide functions. The original municipal units continue to operate and perform local functions that are not performed by the new metropolitan government.

Most of the federation plans proposed in the United States have called for the metropolitan legislative body to be made up of local representatives from the municipalities. Thus, federation, as a metropolitan concept, requires replacing the existing county government with a new metropolitan unit, while the previous urban county plan involves retaining the county unit as the area-wide tier.

Toronto

Background. An example of federation is Toronto, Ontario. Metropolitan Toronto is situated on the northern shore of Lake Ontario in the Canadian province of Ontario. Prior to governmental reorganization in 1953, the 240-square mile metropolitan area contained 13 municipal jurisdictions.

Between 1945 and 1953, there was an exodus of business firms and middle-class citizens from central Toronto to the outlying districts and a steady in-migration of lower-income families. At the same time, new industries were locating in the suburbs rather than the central city. The population shift generated rising concerns over the city's ability to finance and provide water, sewage disposal, housing, and other municipal functions to its residents. To finance these increasing needs, the city was forced to increase its tax rate. However, the smaller, established suburbs, located between the city and the growing industrialized suburbs, benefitted from using Toronto's hospitals, libraries, and parks without taxation, and felt no pressure to expand their facilities or raise their low tax rates. Needless to say, this scenario is strikingly similar to situations faced by the older U.S. central cities in the wake of post-war suburbanization.

The Ontario Municipal Board (OMB), a provincial board, was requested by the province to create an area for joint administration of municipal services in order to redress this situation. In January 1953, the chairman of the board, Lorne Cumming, submitted a report calling for the creation of a metropolitan federation. Although the proposal was controversial, the premier of Ontario's support ensured that the report's recommendations would be adopted by the Ontario provincial legislature.

The System. Under the terms of the 1953 Act for the Toronto Region, a Metropolitan Council was created to serve as both the executive body of metropolitan Toronto ("Metro"), and the legislative body for the 13 represented municipalities. The Metropolitan Council was comprised of 25 members, 12 from the city of Toronto, the mayors from each of the 12 suburbs, with an independent chairman to be elected by the council. Toronto's delegation consisted of its mayor, two controllers, and an alderman from each of the nine city wards.

The chairmanship of the Metro Council was assigned little formal power under the Act, being limited to such functions as presiding over meetings, interpreting the rules of procedure, and casting a vote only in the case of a tie. However, unlike the members of the council, the chairman was a full-time official who could devote his total time and energy to Metro matters, and thereby acquire considerable influence with other council members.

Frederick Gardiner, the council's first chairman, used these limited powers to successfully influence the decision process. Gardiner succeeded in convincing the council that it could work more effectively through a smaller group. A seven-member executive committee was chosen by the entire council and possessed all of the powers of boards of control in municipal governments — preparing budgets, nominating department heads, awarding contracts, etc. Some believe that Gardiner knew that the smaller committee could also be more easily controlled by him.

For the most part, the metropolitan government dealt with the more critical regional problems, particularly finances to build schools, transportation, and water facilities, while such matters as police, fire, public health, and public welfare were left primarily in the preserve of the 13 municipalities. A system of shared responsibilities was set up among the municipalities under Metro in such areas as street construction, road maintenance, traffic control, public assistance, zoning and planning. Only public transportation became a fully Metro function.

While the local communities retained the right to assess taxes, Metro was given the power to cope with regional problems through exclusive borrowing authority for all of the municipalities and independent boards of the region, thereby obtaining very favorable interest rates. It also secured the power to apportion revenue it raised through assessment among the 13 communities, utilizing a formula whereby each municipality's share was based upon a total assessment area.

Cooperative Alternative

The "cooperative" alternative model of regional government, also referred to as "interlocal agreements," calls for greater cooperation between existing governments without the creation of new ones. This approach represents a voluntary technique to address regional problems while maintaining local control.

Supporters of the cooperative alternative view themselves as political realists, because cooperative proposals appear and probably are less radical than other proposed metropolitan structures. Proponents also favor dispersed local government and argue for the right of public choice between competing community locations, services, and tax bases. Proponents argue that the cooperative alternative, although maintaining existing structures, still contributes to greater governmental efficiency and lower costs, since through the possibility of interjurisdictional agreement, it can eliminate the necessity of each local government's hiring its own personnel or constructing new facilities for particular services.

Interjurisdictional cooperation is a broad concept with numerous variations. These range from verbal agreements which may consist merely of the exchange of information, to formal agreements that relate to specific functions or services. Agreements can take the following basic forms:

1. A single government performs a service or provides a facility for one or more other local units.

2. Two or more local governments ad-minister a function or operate a facility on a joint basis.

3. Two or more local governments assist or supply mutual aid to one another in emergency situations.

The cooperative approach has been the subject of considerable criticism. First, critics argue that it is a piecemeal approach since each service agreement normally involves only two governments and one service or facility, resulting in a patchwork of agreements that usually relate to noncontroversial matters. Second, and perhaps the most serious criticism, is financial inadequacy. Cooperative agreements are not devices that equalize public resources among localities within a metropolitan area. Although most interjurisdictional agreements call for provision of services by one local unit in exchange for payment by another, some local governments do not have sufficient financial resources to pay for needed services.

The county of Los Angeles provides an excellent example of the cooperative approach to metropolitan government.

Los Angeles County–Lakewood Plan

Background. Millions of Americans migrated to Southern California to work in aircraft plants and shipyards after World War II. The population of the Los Angeles-Long Beach metropolitan area expanded rapidly during this period.

California state law gives counties control over services vital to all governments, and cities in particular. These include relief for the poor, public hospital care, property tax assessments, registration of voters, the administration of elections and support of the trial court system including jails, prosecution, probation administration, courtroom facilities and staffs. California counties also provide unincorporated areas with many municipal services, including water, sewage, roads, street lighting, and fire [and police] protection.

County provision of such services helped moderate the trend of incorporation of suburban areas within Los Angeles County, which is California's largest county (indeed the nation's) by far in population. Since the county provided services, pressure to incorporate was reduced. However, city-county relations were not always amicable. There had been charges that the county had effectively subsidized unincorporated areas with dollars raised through the county's general fund, which was funded in part by taxes on city residents. In 1950, a study by a League of California Cities committee found that a large part of city residents' county tax dollars were going to provide services to the unincorporated areas of the county. As a result, the county reduced the number of its services available to the unincorporated areas.

The System. Lakewood began as an unincorporated planned housing development within Los Angeles County in 1950. The development was built on land that the city of Long Beach planned to annex to help provide services and increase its tax base. In 1953, Long Beach began a series of annexation proceedings and successfully annexed a part of Lakewood Village with a population of 24,000.

Residents of the remaining unincorporated area of the Lakewood area began a drive to incorporate in order to save it from annexation. An election was set that would have allowed a choice between incorporation and annexation to Long Beach. Pro-incorporation forces argued that incorporation would ensure local control at low costs. On March 9, 1954, the voters approved the incorporation petition.

A new state law, permitting a newly incorporated city in California to contract with its county for all essential services, enabled Lakewood to have a wide variety of services available immediately through Los Angeles County. These services included the county-administered special districts (fire, library, sewer, and lighting), self-governing special districts (sanitation, recreation, and mosquito abatement), and county contracts for general services (animal regulation, assessment and collection of taxes, health services, industrial waste regulation, jails, law enforcement, planning and zoning staff services, street maintenance and construction, and treasury and auditor services).

By contracting with the county for needed services, the new city of Lakewood was able to function with only ten employees and a very reasonable tax rate. While the county lost some tax revenues as a result of incorporation, by contracting with Lakewood it was able to maintain its departments, such as law enforcement and sanitation, at strength.

The Lakewood plan was so successful that it spurred new incorporations within Los Angeles County. Most of the new cities entered into similar agreements with the county for provision of services. However, ultimate control over service levels remained with each city, because each city purchased only specific services that it believed were both needed and affordable. Effectively, this arrangement allowed smaller cities to pool their needs for services and purchase them on a "volume discount" basis from a single, cost-effective provider, the county.

The Lakewood plan eliminated the need for additional municipal service departments and duplication of services. However, it did not attempt to address other pressing regional concerns of planning, water supply, sewage, and education. Further, as the county is the actual producer of the services, the county tends to dominate any bargaining process with the cities over the quality of services and their costs.

Metropolitan Council Alternative

A fourth category of regional or metropolitan government is the metropolitan council. Metropolitan councils are permanent associations of governments that meet on a regular basis to discuss and seek agreement on various issues. While metropolitan councils can be classified as variations of the cooperative approach, there are some key differences. A metropolitan council can be defined as a voluntary association of governments designed to be an area-wide forum for key officials to research and discuss issues and eventually determine how best to address common problems. However, because of its lack of authority, the council mechanism cannot be classified as a true metropolitan government.

Examples of metropolitan councils are Minneapolis-St. Paul in Minnesota and the Tri-County/Portland area in Oregon.

MINNEAPOLIS–ST. PAUL

Background. The Twin Cities Metropolitan Council in the Minneapolis-St. Paul area of Minnesota was created in 1967. It is comprised of 7 counties, 25 cities, 105 villages, 68 townships, 77 school districts, and 20 special service districts.

The problems leading to creation of the Twin cities Metropolitan Council arose from the usual causes: an expanding population, changing population patterns, scattered and uncontrolled growth, and the accompanying need for services such as sewers, waste disposal, housing, and transportation.

There were three main reasons why existing local governments seemed unable to handle all issues. First, some problems, such as pollution, tended to spill over into other jurisdictions. Second, some of the proposed solutions to these problems were potentially very costly and beyond the means of a single local jurisdiction. Finally, no single existing jurisdiction, including any of the involved counties, possessed the authority to make decisions for the entire metropolitan area. Minnesota counties have been traditionally weak, and in this case the metropolitan region crossed county lines.

Unlike many other metropolitan areas, when Twin Cities area leaders recognized that the problems needed to be dealt with from a metropolitan perspective, there was an almost even balance between the central cities and the suburban areas both in population and property value. This prevented either area from dominating the other and made it politically easier to proceed.

The System. Between 1965 and 1967, a consensus was built among metropolitan leaders that an area-wide government body should be created to handle such issues as sewer works, open space, transit, airports, and a zoo. These functions had previously been provided by special purpose districts, not individual municipalities, so that this consensus implied consolidation of various single-purpose agencies or districts.

A group of civic leaders was formed to study regional government in the Twin Cities. By 1967, the group presented its proposal to the Minnesota Legislature. The legislature considered two alternative pieces of legislation, one calling for an elected council with planning and operating control of regional functions, and one creating a council appointed at large by the governor and responsible for planning and coordinating the operation of regional agencies. The latter proposal was passed to establish the Twin Cities Metropolitan Council.

The Council is composed of 16 members appointed by the governor for staggered six-year terms. Each member represents two state senate districts of equal population size. The chairman is selected at large and serves at the governor's pleasure.

The Council's powers are mostly of a coordinating nature. Specifically, the Council is directed to perform three functions. First, it must review all regional plans and projects affecting the Council's metropolitan systems plans for airports, parks, transportation, and sewers, against development guidelines developed by the Council. Within 60 days of submission of such plans, the

Council may indefinitely suspend, in total or part, any project that it finds to be inconsistent with the guidelines. While the Council has the power to delay a project, it uses its powers mainly to leverage changes in projects, not to prevent their development.

Second, the Council reviews and comments on long-term municipal comprehensive plans and any other matters that the Council determines may have a "metropolitan effect," such as a project that would have an effect on the entire Twin Cities region. These local plans must be consistent with metropolitan systems plans developed by the Council for airports, parks, transportation, and sewers, and which together function as the regional comprehensive plan.

Local plans do not have to be updated at any specific time interval, but rather when they affect the regional systems plan, as determined by the Metropolitan Council. The plans are required to include current and future land use; community facilities, such as transportation, airports, sewers, and parks; and implementation — how the plan will be carried out. Local plans are not subject to council veto, although as a practical matter the existence of the Council with its powers generally leads local governments to be consistent with the regional plans. If one local unit objects to the plans of another unit, the Council may hold hearings and mediate any differences.

Finally, the Council performs an advisory evaluation of applications for federal grants emanating from local governments, boards, and agencies.

The Twin Cities Council can be classified as a metropolitan government because it is comprised solely of local representatives, and it is concerned only with regional interests, decisions, services, and needs. Moreover, the Council is empowered to levy an area property tax to finance its operations. It can be viewed in one sense as a state agency, since the governor appoints the representatives who comprise the Council. In addi-

tion, it is the legislature that assigns the Council its powers, controls its finances, determines its structure, and requires it to submit reports.

At the forefront of regional governance in the late 1960s, the Metro council has more recently become less relevant in many regional issues. In its early years, the Council succeeded in creating a regionwide sewer system, founding the Minnesota Zoo, and blocking the construction of an unneeded airport. However, with an ambitious legislature, which did not want to provide the Council with substantial power, and an uninterested governor, the Council's powers dwindled. In recent years, the Council has been left out of the site selection and project definition of the Metrodome, the site selection of a horse racing track in the suburbs, and the consideration of a light-rail system between the two cities. In addition, it was unable to determine a site for a new landfill.

Most of the blame for the Metro Council's recent failures center on its lack of public support: because the Council is appointed by the governor, not elected by the people, citizens and public officials do not believe it has the clout to make necessary changes. In 1985, the Citizens League, a Minneapolis non-partisan research group, concluded that the Council was "in danger of sliding into irrelevance" because it was considered by state and local officials as just another level of bureaucracy. Recognizing the troubles facing the Council, Governor Arne Carlson recently instructed his nine new appointees to revitalize the agency.

PORTLAND

Background. Regional government in the Portland, Oregon, area has evolved over the past six decades. In 1926, in response to rapid and unplanned suburbanization of the area caused by the invention of the automobile, the state established a committee to examine the problems facing the various local governments in the Portland area. The 1944 conference of the League of Oregon Cities passed a resolution that "sporadic, scattered, and unregulated growth of municipalities and urban fringes has caused tremendous waste in money and resources" and requested legislative action at the state level to permit "the creation of metropolitan or regional planning districts and the establishment of metropolitan or regional planning commissions." The state legislature responded by enacting legislation authorizing county planning commissions and county zoning to complement municipal planning programs.

The Metropolitan Planning Commission (MPC) was created in 1957. The Commission had a four-member board representing the city of Portland and the three surrounding counties (Multnomah, Washington, and Clackamas) and was funded by federal grant money. Although it was created to provide planning, the Commission actually provided information and reports on population and industrial sites and assisted local planning departments rather than prepare long-range plans for the region.

In the early 1960s, activists contended that the studies and work produced in the 1950s had done nothing to address the problems of public services in the region. In the 1940s and 50s, the number of special districts in the three counties increased from 28 to 218. In a 1960 study, *A Tale of Three Counties*, the League of Women Voters reported that the local agencies were inefficient and unaccountable, which resulted in poor services. Civic leaders joined together to request that regional options for government services be examined. In response, the state legislature created the Interim Committee on Local Government Problems, whose primary recommendation was the creation of a "metropolitan study commission," later called the Portland Metropolitan Study Commission (PMSC).

The PMSC's *Interim Report* of De-

cember 1966 made ten recommendations for more efficient service, including:

- Special district consolidations where possible.
- Legislation authorizing the creation of metropolitan service districts.
- Formation of a regional council of governments with memberships from counties, cities, and port districts.
- Organization of an area-wide air quality control program.
- Development of intergovernmental cooperative agreements among cities and counties for health, planning, law enforcement and engineering services.

The PMSC's work toward a more regional approach to government services helped produce the Columbia Region Association of Governments (CRAG) in 1966. Structured similar to the MPC, CRAG was a council of governments representing the region's cities and counties. All of the participating city and county governments were represented in CRAG's General Assembly, but its Executive Board was comprised of three county representatives, a Portland representative, and three representatives from other cities in the three counties. CRAG was charged with studying, recommending, rendering technical assistance, and adopting comprehensive metropolitan plans. Although it carried out its duties regarding studies and reports, intergovernmental rivalries slowed its work to develop a comprehensive land use plan. After failing to pass plans in 1970 and 1974, CRAG adopted a general set of goals and objects as a plan.

Another proposal of PMSC was the creation of the multi-purpose Metropolitan Service District (MSD). The MSD governing board was made up of seven elected officials, one from Portland, one from each of the three counties and one representing the other cities in each of the three counties. While the voters approved the District in May of 1970 (54–46 percent), they overwhelmingly rejected a district-wide tax in November of 1970. Thus the new agency was presented with a wide range of problems, with few resources to address them.

In 1975, several regional government supporters applied to the National Academy for Public Administration for an 18-month grant to study the possibilities of multi-level government in metropolitan areas. In November and December of 1975, the "Ad Hoc Two-Tiered Planning Committee," the official recipient of the grant, transformed itself into the Tri-County Local Government Commission. The Tri-County Commission set out to design "an upper tier system of government that will attend to the common needs of the entire Tri-County community." The Commission established a goal of drafting specific legislation for the 1977 Legislative Session.

In 1976, the Commission decided to propose a reorganization of the MSD. Some of the key components to provide a strong and responsive regional government were:

1. Combining the planning functions of CRAG and the regional services of MSD.

2. Direct election of the regional policy makers.

3. A relatively large number of councilors (15) to be elected from relatively small districts.

4. Direct election of the executive director.

The legislature made a number of changes to the proposal, reducing the size of the Council to 12 and deleting a proposed veto for the executive director, before passing it in June 1977. In May 1978, the proposal, Measure 6, passed by 20,000 votes in the three-county area. The new Metropolitan Service District (Metro) was officially established on January 1, 1979.

The System. The enacting legislation did not stipulate any formal relationship between the Council and executive, instead leaving it to them to decide. At the outset, the executive acted more like a city manager, supplying information, setting agendas, and offering recommendations, with the Council being similar to a large city council. However, the relationship gradually changed to one where the Council acts as a miniature legislature, establishing its own policies and programs, with the executive director much like an executive branch, carrying out the Council's policies and programs.

As with most newly established programs, Metro made a number of mistakes in its early years. Its overambitious plan, for example, to address flooding in the Johnson Creek watershed produced one of its first defeats. In 1981, Metro proposed establishing a basin-wide Local Improvement District to fund flood control measures. Although the proposal was technically sound and fiscally creative, it was politically unachievable. Residents on higher lands in the basin were upset that they were, for all intents and purposes, paying assessments to help property owners on the valley floor. Metro's arguments that their paved streets, driveways, and parking lots increased runoff and directly contributed to the flooding in the basin were scientifically correct but politically unacceptable. Metro later withdrew its proposal.

Metro has seen its share of successes as well, both major and minor. In 1979, the Oregon Land Conservation and Development Commission accepted the Portland area's Urban Growth Boundary as designed by Metro. Under Metro's control, the Washington Park Zoo has grown in visitors and national reputation. Metro was able to solve a dispute over the selection of a new landfill site by identifying an alternative site. Metro was also successful in the siting, construction, and operation of the Oregon Convention Center in Portland.

Except for siting regional facilities and accepting or denying the region's Urban Growth Boundary, Metro has not infringed on local jurisdictions' land use powers.

Cities and counties also continue to provide municipal services, except for solid waste disposal which is overseen by Metro.

In response to its success, Metro has gained expanded powers. In 1987, the legislature restored the executive veto power that had originally been part of the Tri-County Commission proposal. The Council has also set up a committee structure, hired a legislative staff, and produced independent policy initiatives. The legislature also passed a measure that now permits Metro to collect an excise tax on its operations to fund its central administration and planning.

Conclusions

This chapter analyzed several different forms of regional structure and consolidated government. All of the models have been valuable in varying degrees in their respective jurisdictions and regions. The variety of options reaffirms the need for flexible state policy in California, allowing maximum local choice to address local needs, priorities, and state goals.

None of the examples in this chapter dealt with regions as large, complex, or diverse as California's. However, there are regions in the state which reflect comparable situations to each of the noted examples. City/county consolidation has been considered and rejected in Sacramento, and is being discussed in Stanislaus County. Models proposed by cities and the county under the auspices of San Diego Area Association of Governments (SANDAG) resemble the structure in Miami/Dade County. Coordinated planning between multiple counties, similar to the Twin Cities approach, can be anticipated as one option in the nine Bay Area counties, as per the recommendations of Bay Vision 2020.

However, the similarities and differences between these examples also raise a number of considerations in dealing with regional problems. First, a common element in all models is recognition that there are regional problems that need to be addressed. Regional entities were created to deal with specific problems that existing local governments could not or did not appropriately address.

Second, each model was implemented with assistance from the state (or provincial) legislature. There were different levels of involvement, ranging from legislation forming or authorizing the government (Twin Cities), to requesting that a board review regional problems and governments (Miami-Dade County and Toronto), to removing possible roadblocks (Nashville-Davidson County and Lakewood).

Beyond recognition of a problem and the need for some form of regional solution, the models go in separate directions. One key difference is in the varying selection methods for representatives selected to the regional body. While Nashville-Davidson County had districts and at-large representatives to ensure local and regional responsiveness, the Twin Cities had gubernatorial-appointed representatives to ensure regional responsiveness. Toronto had city representatives, while Portland's Tri-County Council members were elected directly by the people, in both cases to ensure local responsiveness. It appears that directly elected officials, such as in the Portland area, have proven to be more successful than appointed officials, such as the Twin Cities.

Another notable difference between the models is the scope and powers of the regional body. These were often dependent on the pre-existing government structures and the size of the region. Nashville-Davidson County was able to consolidate all the powers and responsibilities into one government; Toronto and Miami-Dade County had strong powers to deal with regional problems, leaving other "local" matters to the cities; Lakewood decided to temporarily contract out some of its powers to Los

Angeles County; the Twin Cities Council had only advisory powers on limited regional issues; and the Tri-County Council assumed the planning and service responsibilities of existing agencies.

Finally, each body's finances were determined by the problems that each specific region faced and the form of the government it decided to pursue. While most of the governments received tax funds directly from the taxpayers, regional governments can also be financed by the state or by participating cities or cities and counties.

As one model was not appropriate for all the cited examples, so too one model may not be right for all or any of California's regions. While many of the state's urban areas face similar problems, such as traffic, air pollution, and housing, their differences including population and geographic size, could lead to solutions using different or variable models.

Although it is possible for the state to determine whether a regional government is needed, and the appropriate structure, choosing whether or which approach is best for a given region may also be left to the individual areas. California has a long history of home rule, and the state can continue to respect this concept by giving local jurisdictions the opportunity to solve regional problems on their own. Under this approach, only after giving local governments in a region a reasonable opportunity to deal with problems should the state intervene and impose some form of regional approach on specific issues.

This need not mean the state necessarily must take a hands-off approach. General goals can be set for the entire state. Each region would then be responsible for establishing its own more specific goals consistent with the state's, and a specific plan, including means of meeting stated goals and the structure of regional governance if any; goals might also be met through local coopera-

tion. The state would be responsible for certifying that each region's goals were consistent with the general state goals, and that the regional plan [was] feasible. Alternatively, a regional plan could be self-certified against state goals. If not consistent or not achievable, the plan would be returned by the state for adjustment. Plans would also be reviewed and updated periodically.

The strengths of this proposal are that it provides regions with local control to deal with regional problems, while the state oversees the process. It emphasizes that the state has a role in determining the regional problems that need to be addressed, but provides local jurisdictions the opportunity to develop their own solutions. This is, of course, a general notion. Other details, such as financing, state oversight agency, region composition, and default regional governments, would still have to be addressed.

Ultimately, the effectiveness of any regional structure will be up to the credibility and effectiveness of the leadership in each region. The "local heroes" who can convene a political constituency for change, and bring together the interests which must cooperate for solutions, will provide the leadership and direct the structure of the region. Even now, within the cities and counties of California, there are many local differences in program administration and structure. Nothing in the state's growth management policy should restrict the ability of strong local leaders to work within their own agencies and organizations to form whatever planning or service delivery system meets the needs of the local area best, so long as state goals are reasonably met.

Note

1. These models were developed in *Experiments in Metropolitan Government*, James F. Horan and G. Thomas Taylor, Jr., Westport, Conn.: Praeger Publications, 1977.

CHAPTER 4

REGIONAL REFORM WITHOUT BOUNDARY CHANGES

David Miller

Metropolitan regions across the United States are faced with the need to design governance systems that preserve and protect their constituent communities while maintaining or developing a more competitive economic climate. In the face of a globalizing world economy, most regions are seeking to rationalize their local government structure, but effectively adapting to the changing nature of the global economy has proven elusive.

Regionalist Neil Peirce, who popularized the term "citistates," has identified two overarching issues. The first is physical sprawl, defined by Peirce as "the alarming environmental and social consequences of America's inability or unwillingness to contain urban growth within reasonably compact geographic areas." Indeed, the social and environmental impact of sprawl has resurfaced as an important regional and national issue. Traffic congestion and crowded schools are leading to a renewed call for more rational strategies that do not lead to growth occurring in areas unable or unprepared to deal with its consequences. The second issue, Peirce argues, is "America's hesitation, one might say their paralysis, in

creating effective systems of coordinated governance for citistates." America has one of the most diffuse, or decentralized, systems of government in the world. This chapter will focus on this second issue of decentralization.

American Governance

Governance in metropolitan areas is, fundamentally, built around local governments. Although many reformers would argue such an assumption is invalid and leads to inappropriate outcomes, the monopoly position of local governments in two key policy areas makes the assumption a practical reality. The first is local governments' exclusive ability to locally raise public funds through taxation. Although regulated by state governments, this power helps organize how public funds are allocated. The second factor is local governments' exclusive ability to make land-use decisions through the exercise of, primarily, zoning powers. As with taxation power, this monopoly position is tempered by state regulatory responsibility.

Originally published as "Fiscal Regionalism: Metropolitan Reform without Boundary Changes," *Government Finance Review*, Vol. 16, No. 6, December, 2000. Reprinted with permission of the Government Finance Officers Association, publisher of *Government Finance Review*, 180 N. Michigan Ave., Suite 800, Chicago, IL USA 60601 (312/977-9700; fax: 312/977-4806; e-mail: GFR@gfoa.org). Annual subscriptions: $30.

Efforts to improve governance in metropolitan regions, therefore, must deal with one or both of these issues and recognize that local government participation in designing improvements is essential for any change.

The Missing Link

More than 40 years ago, Arthur Maas defined the structure of local governance in the United States as an "areal" division of power. By that, he meant that the territorial-bounded local governments were, by culture and practice, an integral part of a system of organization that divided power between the federal, state, and local governments. The "missing link" in this division of power, Maas argued, was a general process to address governmental issues at the metropolitan level. Such a missing link required the development of four separate processes. They were:

- a last-resort way to settle inter-jurisdictional disputes and questions of jurisdiction;
- a process of inter-jurisdictional cooperation;
- a process by which the governments in a region can act separately and independently; and
- a process of change that cannot be dictated or stopped by a minority of the jurisdictions.

The need to work together in a cooperative fashion in this "areal" environment has never been greater. The Metropolitan Initiative, a partnership between national foundations and the Center for Neighborhood Technology, conducted a series of workshops with key leaders in 12 regions across the United States. The purpose of the workshops was to identify public policy problems associated with growth and regional competitiveness. These 1997 sessions identified eight common themes which every region shared with every other region; namely:

- regions and the communities within them cannot deal with transportation, housing, environment, and economic issues in isolation;
- the large number of governmental jurisdictions in a region makes it very hard to work together. Indeed, participants, regardless of the region they were from, argued that governmental fragmentation and fiscal disparities in their region was the worst;
- individual jurisdictions do not want to lose their identity;
- metropolitan approaches to governmental reorganization require support of state governments and legislators and that is often seriously lacking;
- this is a pivotal time for regional cooperation in each region, but most regions have experimented with regional cooperation in the past with only marginal results;
- sprawl and its dysfunctional effects exist in every region and pose a serious threat to quality of life;
- any success a region is experiencing in metropolitan cooperation is in its early stages; and
- crisis seems to be the strongest motivator for regional cooperation.

Strategies for Regional Reform

Few regions have been idly standing by as the need for reform has emerged. Indeed, a number of cooperative strategies have historically been used, representing a range of options from relatively modest to extensive, highly controversial changes. Perhaps the most controversial of regional strategies involve consolidation/merger and annexation. In annexation, one government takes over part or all of the territory of another government. Today, it is a strategy used primarily in metropolitan areas in the south and west. For instance, through annexation, Charlotte, North Carolina, has grown from 30 square miles to 200 square miles since the end of World War II.

Consolidation/merger is a process by which a government actually goes out of business. One government merges into another existing government, or two or more governments consolidate to form a new government. It was a heavily used process in the 19th century. Many of the great cities of today—like Boston, New York, and Pittsburgh—were formed through the absorption of contiguous municipalities. Because of the implications associated with a government actually ceasing to exist, it is now considered a historical artifact and an infrequent event. Since World War II, voters have adopted only 20 out of 120 consolidation/merger efforts.

Councils of governments (COGs) are a more modest effort at regional cooperation. They are voluntary associations of local governments that work on issues of common interest to their members. Because they are voluntary, most COGs require unanimity before they can enter a policy area. As a result, they have most commonly focused on non-controversial and non-threatening issues. Joint purchasing and sharing of capital-intensive equipment and services represent primary areas of COG activity. Although every region should, and most do, have a COG, its presence may have limited value in addressing the broader public problems facing the region.

A stronger form of intergovernmental organization is the metropolitan council. A council may or may not be a council of governments. Although deeply dependent on the support of the local governments in the region, some councils have moved into a broader role in their respective regions. In the Portland, Oregon, region, the council is directly elected and delivers services in areas

such as growth management and transportation development. The Twin Cities Council (Minneapolis and St. Paul, Minnesota) has assumed responsibilities in the areas of wastewater and regional transit.

Although the development of metropolitan councils or other organizations that have some ability to compel local governments to act consistent with a regional plan has broad implications on local governments, a more promising category of regional cooperation is "fiscal regionalism."

Fiscal Regionalism

Fiscal regionalism is a set of cooperative strategies that recognize the governmental structure of the existing configuration of local governments but create regional funding mechanisms for a wide variety of public purposes. As such, they are relatively recent innovations in metropolitan cooperation. There are three broad forms of fiscal regionalism that will be discussed in this article: cultural asset districts, tax and revenue sharing programs, and peaceful coexistence plans.

Taken as a broad set of strategies, fiscal regionalism addresses a number of important metropolitan policy issues. Initially, strategies that create a metropolitan government with taxing authority appear or are perceived to lessen or eliminate local decision-making authority. Fiscal regionalism approaches create the fiscal equivalent of a regional government without the government. Second, fiscal regionalism mechanisms or institutions create the capacity or the authority to distribute benefits from economic growth or to develop growth policies that reflect the distribution of benefits across the metropolitan region. Third, fiscal regionalism mitigates the worst effects of fiscal mercantilism. Local government reliance on property tax revenues requires those governments to engage in competitive fiscal mercantilism — encouraging only the location of net revenue-producing developments within their boundaries. Such practices have the effect of exacerbating the difficulties associated with the location of undesirable or marginally desirable land uses within a region. Fourth, costs for economic development are not always borne by the government within whose boundary the growth has occurred. Although every government would like to derive economic benefit without cost, the opportunity itself is dysfunctional because a government is rewarded for "free-riding."

Fiscal regionalism approaches allow for a more equitable distribution of both costs and benefits. Few means exist whereby governments in an urban environment can share in the region's growth, as the only determinant of benefits is location within a particular jurisdiction. Fiscal regionalism approaches create means by which such sharing can occur. In addition, annexation laws create a "win-lose" outcome for governments — the government getting the new territory wins, but at a significant loss to the government losing the territory. Fiscal regionalism allows for the development of "win-win" outcomes. Finally, wealthier jurisdictions are able to provide services with lower tax rates than less affluent jurisdictions. This disparity results in a vicious circle of greater disparity as wealth gravitates to wealth, and the poorer jurisdictions become even less competitive. Over time, the gap between rich and poor communities in a region grows wide. Fiscal regionalism aids in "leveling the playing field."

Cultural Asset Districts. One form of fiscal regionalism is the cultural asset district. This institutional arrangement has emerged in the last several years as a direct result of the dispersion of population. Even after World War II, the majority of Americans lived and worked in the center city of our metropolitan areas. Cultural and civic activities were usually, and appropriately,

financed by the center city. For instance, in 1948, 73 percent of business activity in Allegheny County, Pennsylvania, took place within the City of Pittsburgh. For the City of Pittsburgh to be financing the zoo, as an example, was consistent with its economic base and its fiscal capacity. However, by the late 1980s, only 38 percent of business activity conducted within Allegheny County occurred within the City of Pittsburgh. As people and business disbursed to the suburbs, however, they continued to utilize the civic facilities financed by the center city. But the city no longer had the fiscal base to support those services, and non-city residents were becoming the primary users of those facilities. Cultural asset districts are a way to finance civic institutions by the regional public.

Denver and Kansas City are representative of regions that have adopted cultural asset districts. In 1988, the Denver region approved the "Scientific and Cultural Facilities District." It is an example of the first wave of this regional approach to public services. Approved with a 65 percent positive vote at a referendum, the district is financed by .1 percent increase in the sales tax. The district supports institutions like the zoo, museums, performing arts, and a wide variety of local and regional arts organizations.

The Kansas City region enacted (again by referendum) a "Bi-State Cultural District" in 1997 to finance the capital and operating costs associated with historic Union Station. Unlike Denver, this district goes out of business in six years. In this respect, it represents the next generation of districts in that it is organized for a specific purpose and, when that purpose is served, the district ends.

Tax and Revenue-sharing Programs. The second form of fiscal regionalism is tax or revenue-base sharing. Tax-base sharing is a simple idea — take a regional resource of revenue, such as the property tax or sales tax, and distribute the proceeds to constituent local governments on some other basis that reflects the needs of the region, taken as a whole. Its asserted benefits are its more effective and equitable impact on economic development and growth. To the degree that the fragmentation of government services and decision making in an urban area prevent any rational approach to the distribution of the gains and benefits from development and growth policies, tax-base sharing can help mitigate the adverse effects of that fragmentation.

The largest, and perhaps most well-known tax-base sharing plan is in the Twin Cities of Minnesota (Minneapolis and St. Paul). The Minnesota model of tax-base sharing has been in place for about 25 years. Today, the program covers 2.5 million people, 7 counties, and 200 local jurisdictions, and involves $200 million in tax proceeds. The Metropolitan Council administers the program.

In its simplest form, 40 percent of a municipality's growth in commercial and industrial real estate valuation is diverted from the municipality's direct control to a "pool" shared by all municipalities in the region. A uniform millage is applied to this "pooled" value, and the proceeds are distributed back to the municipalities on a need-based formula. The amount a government contributes to the pool has no relation to what it will receive in distributions — a participating government may receive much less than it contributes to the pool, and conversely, it may receive substantially more than it contributes. In this fashion, tax-base sharing serves a redistributive function. Since its inception, the plan has reduced fiscal disparities between jurisdictions. For the period 1987 to 1995, measured inequality in total tax base per capita between jurisdictions was reduced by 20 percent. By some estimates, it has significantly reduced disparities from a ratio of 50:1 to a ratio of 12:1.

Most of the arguments used to develop

the fiscal regionalism program in Minnesota were included in the enabling legislation. Although reduction in fiscal disparities has become one of the major benefits of tax-base sharing as implemented in Minnesota, it was not mentioned in the legislation. The explanation for this omission centers on the difficulty associated with the "selling" of redistributive programs at the local level. The arguments that were used to develop the tax-base sharing program in Minnesota are identified below.

First, the plan was a means to allow local governments to share in the growth of the area without taking away any resources that local governments currently enjoy. By taking a percentage of future or new revenues, governments were not giving up resources that they were currently receiving. Second, the plan would create more rational urban development by minimizing the fiscal impact of locational decisions. Third, the plan would create an incentive system that would encourage all parts of the regions to work for the growth of the whole. Fourth, and perhaps most important, the plan would develop regional strategies that employed the existing structure of local governments and local decision making. Fifth, the plan would assist those communities either in the early stages of development or those facing disinvestments by allocating additional resources to them. In summary, the proponents of this form of fiscal regionalism were supporting the existing structure of local government in the area while recognizing a need to minimize some of the dysfunctions associated with that structure.

Although the fiscal success of the Minnesota plan is documentable, as a form of fiscal regionalism, it continues to come under attack locally and has yet to be totally replicated in other areas. Based on the Minnesota Plan, jurisdictions in Montgomery County, Ohio, have agreed to pool a portion of future growth in exchange for revenues from an economic-development fund. Unlike Minnesota, where some jurisdictions lose more than they contribute, the Ohio plan guarantees, through an economic-development fund, that every jurisdiction will be a net beneficiary. If contributions to the tax-base sharing pool exceed distributions from the pool, the jurisdiction will receive more from the economic-development fund to compensate.

The Meadowlands Area in New Jersey represents a planned commercial and economic development area that spans 14 separate jurisdictions. In 1972, the State of New Jersey established a commission to develop a master plan for the site. Recognizing that not all jurisdictions would benefit equally from the developments, particularly if open and public spaces were to be incorporated, a property tax sharing program was developed for the affected jurisdictions.

A program that captures both of the first two forms of fiscal regionalism has been developed and adopted in Allegheny County, Pennsylvania. Mirroring Denver, an asset district has been created to help finance many of the region's cultural and civic institutions; mirroring Minnesota, a redistributive tax base-sharing plan has been adopted that assists in reducing fiscal disparity between rich and poor local governments.

There were a number of issues confronting Allegheny County and the City of Pittsburgh in the early 1990s. Initially, there was a need to correct inequities caused by the City of Pittsburgh bearing a significant financial burden for regional assets. For instance, less than 15 percent of attendees at Pittsburgh Pirate games were city residents, even though the city was the sole public underwriter of the stadium. A second problem was the growing fiscal disparity between the county's richer and poorer communities. Research had demonstrated that the gap had been accelerating. Third, many public- and private-sector leaders believed that, to be economically competitive, the region needed

to address the issue of over-reliance on certain taxes such as those on amusement events, real property, and personal property. Fourth, given the deteriorating fiscal condition of the city, there was a need to stabilize and perhaps increase funding for maintenance of existing assets. In addition, the region had no real mechanism for the funding or development of new assets. Lastly, given the highly fragmented governance structure of the region, it was necessary to establish precedent for future cooperative approaches to the resolution of public problems.

The Allegheny County Regional Asset District was created and funded through an additional 0.5 percent on the sales tax. This funding stream generates more than $60 million annually to provide funding to the region's shared assets. Facilities like the zoo, aviary, libraries, parks, and stadiums are now the fiscal responsibility of the region.

Two important regional funding issues have been addressed through this program. First, approximately $40 million is provided to the region's assets directly from the sales tax proceeds, replacing funding that previously had been provided to the assets by individual local governments. This transfer of funding responsibility, primarily away from the City of Pittsburgh and Allegheny County, has helped to make those governments more fiscally sound and competitive than they would be otherwise.

Second, the asset district provides a more stable and elastic funding base for the region's assets. Initially, approximately $13 million was available annually to increase funding to new or existing assets. This discretionary portion of the program has grown to more than $20 million in several years.

The "other half" of the legislation created in the first form of fiscal regionalism also brought into existence the second form. This less visible reform has created a tax-base sharing program second in size only to the Minnesota plan. Through an additional

0.5 percent on the sales tax, more than $60 million is available annually to assist Allegheny County governments in shifting a portion of their funding requirements away from the property tax and other taxes.

The distribution is as follows: 50 percent goes to the Allegheny County government, and 50 percent is shared among the participating municipalities in the county. Although all municipalities in the county have a right to participate, the formula used for this distribution targets the less affluent. Per capita distribution under this program ranges from $9.81 in the county's wealthier communities to $18.86 in the most fiscally distressed of the county's communities.

Peaceful Coexistence Plans. The third form of fiscal regionalism involves peaceful coexistence strategies. Particularly in states where territory is divided between incorporated areas (usually run by cities) and unincorporated areas (generally run by counties or townships), fiscal equity arrangements have emerged to address the problems surrounding the economic loss of one governmental jurisdiction when territory transfers from one government to another.

The City of Louisville and Jefferson County, Kentucky, entered into a 12-year agreement in 1986 (which was subsequently renewed in 1998) that has become known as the Louisville Compact.

As a center city, Louisville was faced with severe fiscal problems and repeated attempts to consolidate the city and county had been rejected by voters. Although it was a difficult legal process, the city was posed to engage in a significant annexation campaign that would have serious financial implications for the county. Rather than conduct an adversarial battle with each other, both parties agreed to negotiate a plan for the delivery of services and the funding of those services. Predicated on the assumption that there would be a moratorium on annexation, the parties divided service delivery between them. Services like air pollution control, public health, and planning were assigned to the county. Services such as the zoo, museums, and emergency services were assigned to the city. The glue that held the compact together was an agreement to share tax revenues. The resulting agreement has been beneficial to both the city and the county and has led to an institutionalizing of cooperation.

Laws in Virginia represent another example of governments working together to avoid adversarial battles over territory. Agreements entered into by the City of Franklin with Southampton and Isle of Wright counties are representative. In areas of the counties that are experiencing significant commercial and industrial growth, the city has agreed to no annexation in perpetuity, but has agreed to deliver essential utility services in exchange for a percentage of all local tax revenues collected in the designated areas.

In Michigan, several peaceful coexistence strategies have been developed that create "win-win" outcomes for the states' cities and townships. One in particular is Michigan's Land Transfer Act. Rather than annexation, the township conditionally transfers the land that would have otherwise been the subject of annexation to the city in exchange for a share of the tax revenues and state aid. Typically, the agreements are for a 50-year period at which point the land is scheduled to revert back to the township.

Conclusion

A review of the fiscal regionalism approaches taken by local governments demonstrates how they are addressing a number of important regional issues. As such, they represent pragmatic responses to the need for cooperation within a metropolitan area. Given the difficulties associated with altering the governmental boundaries within a region, the strategies identified in this article are creating the equivalent of what a regional government would do fiscally were it to be created. Fiscal regionalism mechanisms or institutions are distributing benefits from economic growth across the metropolitan region. They are mitigating fiscal mercantilism while creating a more equitable distribution of both costs and benefits to participating jurisdictions. They share an ability to level the playing field and create win-win solutions that improve the overall fairness and competitiveness of the regions in which they occur.

CHAPTER 5

THE STATE OF REGIONAL GOVERNMENT

Bruce D. McDowell

What Is Regionalism?

The United States is a nation of regions. Some are big, like the major river basins, the cornbelt, the sunbelt, the frostbelt, and the northeastern megalopolis. Some are small, like the 300 or so metropolitan areas and the numerous rural commutersheds defined by the federal government. Some cross state lines, while others are in one state. Even among the "small" areas, there are about three dozen interstate metropolitan areas that cross state lines, greatly increasing their governmental complexity.

Each region has problems and opportunities that its citizens and governments strive to address. Yet most are not governed as single units; they span the jurisdictions of many governments.

The most common means of coping with these regions' issues has been to establish regional planning commissions or councils to study pressing problems and advise local, state, and federal agencies about potential remedies. In the American experience, these planning bodies almost always have been advisory only — without the power to govern by themselves. If they cannot convince the regularly constituted local, state, and federal authorities to act on their recommendations, those recommendations simply sit on a shelf somewhere — until there is another study, another set of recommendations, and another opportunity to persuade the regular governments to act — often against their own individual self-interests.

Exceptions to this general pattern are so rare that they draw immediate, excited, and hopeful attention. Some of the most prominent examples of authoritative regional bodies are

- Tennessee Valley Authority;
- Susquehanna and Delaware River Basin Commissions;
- Metropolitan Service District in Portland, Oregon;
- Twin Cities Metropolitan Council in Minnesota; and
- Metropolitan Transportation Commission in San Francisco/Oakland, California.

But then they usually are dismissed as special cases, not appropriate for replication anywhere else. They were the product of a unique set of circumstances that required

Originally published as "Regionalisms: What It Is, Where We Are, and Where We May Be Headed," *The Regionalist*, Vol. 1, No. 4, Spring, 1996. Published by the National Association of Regional Councils, Washington, D.C. Reprinted with permission of the publisher.

emergency action that is not justified in a normal situation.

In contrast, the advisory regions abound. It is just too local and politically attractive to have an organization that can geographically "get its arms around the problem." Since many regional problems deserve this degree the recognition, many regional organizations have been created, and many of them lie on top of each other.

Where We Are and How We Got There

In the early part of this century, there was great excitement about regional solutions to governmental problems. Much of it was pushed along by planners, political scientists, public administrators, economists, water resources professionals, and the "good government" movement that brought so many other reforms to government during that period. And, from about 1920 until about 1960, there was a great deal of experimentation with regional planning commissions, statewide planning, and river basin commissions. By 1960, these organizations spotted the continent at wide intervals and whetted the public's appetite for more.

THE 1960S AND 1970S

The 1960s and 1970s saw the nation almost completely covered both by multistate river basin and economic development commissions that had state and federal participation and by metropolitan and nonmetropolitan regional councils dominated by local government officials. Most of the metropolitan and nonmetropolitan regional councils were carefully designed to be "areawide" according to some criteria—such as commutersheds or areas of interdependent economic influences. By the end of the 1970s, 99 percent of all the nation's counties (or county areas in New England) were participating in regional councils.

This explosion of areawide regional councils and multistate river basin and economic development regions occurred because of very intentional systematic federal action that drew in states as well as local governments. In the cases of the areawide councils, the federal action established thirty-nine grant programs designed to require and fund regional planning, and it appealed directly to the governors of all fifty states to establish statewide systems of "substate districts" to systematize the administration of the federal programs that support regional councils. And many of the states did so.

By 1977, the areawide regions spurred by federal programs were so pervasive and so firmly established that the Census of Governments taken that year included a special report on them. The census found 675 general purpose (or multipurpose) regional councils and 1,257 special purpose regional organizations serving federal program purposes. On average across the nation, the general purpose regional councils were designated to carry out 3.73 federal programs, while the special purpose ones generally carried out a single federal program.

In the Southwest and Appalachia, the general purpose regions were designated to handle more than five of the federal government's regional programs together. The federal government strongly supported multiple designations, but the states had a lot to do with making some of these designations and they took differing approaches. Some states reinforced the federal policy of multiple designations, while others did not.

During the golden age of regional organizations in America, the federal government was committed to the idea that regional planning could help solve many of the nation's urban, rural, economic development, environmental, and water resources problems. Federal funds for regional planning flowed freely throughout the country, and the regional bodies prepared many planning studies, yielding comprehensive regional plans with an array of specific functional elements and multi-year action programs.

The federal funds supplied the big bucks in the budgets of most regional planning organizations — often up to 75 percent. And the accompanying federal planning requirements defined the type of planning that was done.

THE 1980S

The 1980s tell a very different story. The federal government abandoned most of its commitment to regionalism. Of the thirty-nine programs designed and enacted during the preceding two decades to promote regional organizations, only one — metropolitan transportation planning — remained relatively unscathed by this sudden reversal of federal policy. By 1984, the rest had been terminated, substantially defunded, or relieved of their region-promoting features. Most of this decline had occurred by 1982.

For the multistate programs, which had created most river basin and economic development regions by agreements between the governors and the president, President Reagan withdrew his approval, left them unfunded, and watched them die. The only ones that survived were those that had been created directly by federal law or interstate compact.

The metropolitan and nonmetropolitan areawide councils rapidly lost federal designations and funding. By 1984, their budgets and staffs had been reduced by about half. Their functions were beginning to migrate away from the federal government's areawide planning agenda to activities more in tune with services for which local governments, who were starting to pick up the funding responsibilities dropped by the feds, were willing to pay.

By the end of the 1980s, 80 percent of the areawide regional councils still existed, but they had changed dramatically. They were beginning to rebuild as data sharing, joint services, and regional service bodies. Even the councils still designated for metropolitan transportation and planning saw a decline — the land-use elements formerly funded by the Department of Housing and Urban Development and the environmental planning for wastewater treatment and air quality formerly funded by the Environmental Protection Agency had to be absorbed by DOT funds, which were at the same time being stretched thinner by the addition of a large number of new urban area designations following the 1980 census.

The federal economic development and Appalachian programs, though suffering significant cutbacks, managed to survive, maintaining some planning and other support to many of the nonmetropolitan regional councils. Thus, the federal abandonment of regions, though drastic, was not complete.

Through the 1980s, as the areawide councils struggled to adjust to the decline in federal support and raised their local government dues, state support remained almost as it had been. The state support, of course, differed greatly from one state to another at the beginning of the 1980s, and that remains true today. In those few states that provide direct financial support to the regional councils and rely on them for delivering federal and state programs, the councils have been somewhat insulated from the federal abandonment, but the number of states taking this position did not change much in response to the federal action. Independently, those few states that enacted new growth management programs during the 1980s tended to give additional important roles to their regional councils.

THE 1990S

In 1995, we cannot write the whole story of the 1990s. But we can begin.

The most significant occurrence so far

has been the enactment of the Intermodal Surface Transportation Efficiency Act of 1991 (ISTEA). For those metropolitan planning organizations (MPOs) designated to satisfy ISTEA planning requirements (about 47 percent of which are areawide metropolitan regional councils), the federal funding and expectations have increased significantly. But, the clear consensus is that the increase in expectations has been greater than the increase in funding.

Before discussing this development further, it is significant to note that about 75 percent of the MPOs had been areawide regional councils in the mid–1970s when the federal government was intentionally supporting those organizations.

A recent U.S. Advisory Commission on Intergovernmental Relations (ACIR) study of the capacity of MPOs to meet the expectations of ISTEA turned up mixed results.

A broad range of participants in eighteen MPOs across the country agreed that ISTEA had brought about many desirable changes, including the following:

- increased public participation,
- more air quality planning,
- better intergovernmental coordination,
- better relationships between the state department of transportation and the MPO,
- new or increased attention to intermodal issues, and
- new or increased attention to long-range planning.

But, these same interview respondents identified many difficulties they were encountering:

- increased regulatory and workload burdens,
- unachievable expectations,
- uncoordinated deadlines among the various federal requirements and between the federal requirements and related state and local requirements,

- disrupted relationships within the MPO, and
- new strains in the MPO relationship with the state DOT.

Of course, great differences exist from one state to another, and these findings are generalizations from cases that spanned the country.

Nevertheless, the bottom line of ACIR's *MPO Capacity* study, released in May 1995, was that MPOs need a lot of help to keep up with the great expectations of ISTEA. The challenges they face are institutional, technical, and political — and the political ones were seen by all as the most difficult. ACIR recommended a comprehensive capacity-building program for MPOs, but the political part deserves special note.

The MPOs are intergovernmental **processes**, not governments. But ISTEA assumes that they are governments with strong independent decision-making powers capable of speaking with a single voice for all local governments in the region and competing on an equal footing with the power of the governor, the state DOT, and a variety of federal and state agencies. In reality, even the best of the MPOs are lucky to be able to bring all these parties together to reach a modicum of consensus on a few of the key issues.

The MPOs, of course, must help themselves. No one can perform their roles for them. Striving for excellence in everything they do should be their first priority.

Nevertheless, they cannot do it alone. And, on the key political power issue, state support is crucial. ISTEA sets the MPOs in a mutual veto situation with the governor, the state DOT, and the air quality agency — and the MPO's veto is the weakest one by far. If the MPO process gets to the veto stage, it is probably a failure. Therefore, it is essential for all parties to use the MPO process as a good-faith bargaining forum in which everyone tries as hard as they can to reach consensus and to adhere to the agreements reached there.

Where We May Be Headed

Not much indicates that the multistate regions are on their way back. The only hint I have seen of that is the proposal in Congress to replace the Economic Development Administration (EDA) in the Department of Commerce with a series of eight regional commissions — modeled after the Appalachian Regional Commission (ARC). These multistate regions, with a federal co-chair, would make grants to the metropolitan and nonmetropolitan areawide regions in economically depressed parts of the country, as EDA does now. But this proposal is not expected to pass. Meanwhile, there are continuing proposals to do away with ARC itself— proposals that must be continuously defended against, year after year.

At the areawide level, there may be two different tracks — one for MPOs and one for the majority of regional councils that are not MPOs. The MPOs now have a strengthened federal planning role, and they may be able to make something of it *if* the state DOTs let them. The other areawide regional councils appear headed for a much more limited local services role — a non-planning role. But both of these tracks are quite uncertain.

On the MPO track, the state DOTs already have signaled that they will challenge the enhanced roles for MPOs in ISTEA when that law comes up for renewal next year. The recently adopted policies of the American Association of State Highway and Transportation Officials (AASHTO) — spurred by the thirty-one Republican governors — call for cutting back on the planning funds for many of the MPOs and giving special weight to the planning of only the MPOs with populations of one million or more. If the state does not see that its own success is tightly linked to the success of all of its MPOs, then the MPOs probably will not be able to do what ISTEA expects. And there is little likelihood that the federal government will step in to save the MPOs in the current political environment, which is leaning heavily toward giving the states greater leeway in determining their own policies.

For the other regional councils, the local services function is one that increasingly will not attract federal or state funding. So it will have to be justified primarily on the basis of saving money for the local governments. Activities of that type — joint purchasing; shared personnel, equipment, data, and technical services — are important, but they leave the most significant regional issues untouched: issues such as infrastructure, the environment, and the social and economic disparities between inner cities and suburbs. The local consensus approach cannot deal with controversy unless there is also some outside-the-region mechanism for forcing the tougher issues to be confronted.

So, where should we look for hope of a better region? I have three suggestions for you to ponder:
- the business community,
- reality, and
- benchmarking.

THE BUSINESS COMMUNITY

In the Washington area, the Board of Trade has taken a hand in pushing for (1) a solution to the Woodrow Wilson Bridge replacement — a three-state facility on the area's only beltway, which is too narrow, has a draw-span that opens too much, and is in danger of collapse from overuse; (2) thinking more generally about the region's gridlocked transportation problems; and (3) marketing the whole region as a good place to do business. It also has taken the lead in convening joint meetings of public and private leaders to explore key public policy issues together. There is nothing earth-shaking here, except that it does show a recognition that businesses operate throughout the whole region and have more on their minds than the concerns of the individual localities.

REALITY

Sooner or later, reality will catch up with us, and something will have to be done. The Woodrow Wilson Bridge may actually fall down. The beltway may actually grind to a halt. Regional problems are not imaginary. They do make a difference in the lives of people, and they demand response — however ad hoc that response may be.

BENCHMARKING

The way to make the federal, state, and local governments accountable to the people and regain the people's trust and confidence is to set quantified goals, devise methods of measuring progress toward them, and report their status back to the people to show that they are actually getting something for the taxes they pay. This "benchmarking" system sets up a new kind of public dialogue about the effect governmental activities have in the lives of real people. Is the environment getting cleaner? Is congestion easing? Are our lives getting safer?

San Diego's growth management process is designed around such a "quality of life" performance measurement system. We should watch to see whether it makes a difference in restoring people's confidence in their governments. If it does, we may have another path open to us for helping to solve regional problems.

Conclusion

I wish the future were more clear for those of you following the regional path. The only real advice I can give you is to keep at it. We need regional approaches to regional problems, because regional problems are real. Sooner or later, our approaches to these problems will get real, and you will be there to lead the way.

CHAPTER 6

REGIONAL GOVERNANCE AND THE POST-INDUSTRIAL ECONOMY

Allan D. Wallis

In 1991 Denver lost out to Indianapolis in a competition to win construction of a $250 million United Airlines maintenance facility. After a speech in Denver a year later, former Indianapolis mayor Bill Hudnut was asked why Indianapolis had been successful even though Denver's incentive package was more generous. His answer was that in his city when negotiations took place with a major corporation, only three people had to be in the room: the corporate executive, the mayor, and someone from the governor's office. Because of Unigov — the consolidated city-county government — the mayor could speak for the region.[1]

A story with similar implications is told by Clarke County (Georgia) commissioner Tal DuVall. Several times the county and its core city of Athens attempted to win voter approval of a consolidation plan. The primary rationale presented to the voters had always been economical service delivery and infrastructure development. Although analysis demonstrated that consolidation would achieve significant savings, the voters weren't buying.

But in 1992, a consolidation referendum passed. Success resulted from a change in strategy. Rather than using an argument based on service and infrastructure cost savings, commissioners justified consolidation this time as a way of improving economic competitiveness. DuVall said,

> When you have a corporation that wants to locate, they want to know that you can provide the necessary permits and deliver the services they need. If you can't give them an answer quickly, then they start to look elsewhere. It's easier to provide a timely response when you're speaking as one government.[2]

Across the country communities are beginning to realize that economic competitiveness requires a regional approach. The real competition is not among communities of the same region, but among regions here and abroad. Even regions long divided by bitter rivalries among local governments are finding common cause in the threats of job and population loss. This shift in attitude is evident in places like the Mon Valley that previously comprised the heart of Pennsylvania's steel-producing region. The mills are now closed, and the 37 local governments in the valley are having to learn to cooperate

From *The Regionalist*, Vol. 1, No. 3, Fall, 1995. Published by the National Association of Regional Councils, Washington, D.C. Reprinted with permission of the publisher.

regionally in efforts to restore their economy (Ehrenhalt 1995).

The desire to achieve economic competitiveness has always been one of the basic reasons for strengthening regional government (Wallis 1994a). In the nineteenth century city, size was equated with economic strength. The rapid expansion of central cities to encompass their populated suburbs was justified as making the city more competitive. Size assured an adequate labor supply, as well as the capacity to deliver the services and infrastructure necessary to support industrial growth.

In today's economy, size does not necessarily result in strength. Instead, competitiveness comes from the ability to mobilize regional resources in response to rapidly changing demands. Most regions in the United States have not figured this out yet. Communities within the same region continue to compete with one another for economic base, and in cases where metropolitan communities do unite, it is often against the central city, which is seen as a common enemy. This internal competitiveness assumes that the United States maintains economic hegemony among nations. By contrast, regions in other advanced industrialized nations are reorganizing to become effective competitors in a global economy. They realize that in such an economy national policy may be less important than effective regional governance.

Characteristics of the Global Economy

In a mass-production economy, wealth is made by transforming raw materials into consumer products — for example, coke and iron into steel, and steel into automobiles. The process is labor- and resource-intensive. In a post-industrial economy, wealth is generated by the exchange of information and the transformation of ideas (Reich 1991).

Microsoft has become one of the wealthiest corporations in the world by manufacturing information-organizing products for a market that did not exist 20 years ago. U.S. communities may compete for a Japanese automobile assembly plant, but the real wealth of the parent corporation is generated by its design, engineering, and marketing side, which it is not likely to ship overseas.

A post-industrial *global* economy is characterized by three interrelated trends (Accordino 1992):

- **Globalization of Production.** In a mass-production economy, manufacturing is concentrated in metropolitan regions, especially in central cities. But in a post-industrial economy, routine production activities are transferred to rural areas and or less developed countries. Such relocation is motivated by the search for lower labor and land costs in a politically stable environment. It is made possible by such technological changes as wide-body cargo jets, which reduce transportation costs, especially for valuable electronic goods, and by electronic communications, which allow a high level of production control from remote headquarters.

- **Globalization of Consumption.** In a mass-production economy, efficiency requires a market that demands large quantities of a standard product. If the market can be controlled by a few major manufacturers, they can regulate the product obsolescence cycle to assure profits. In a post-industrial economy, the product obsolescence cycle is accelerated as consumers in advanced industrial nations seek newer products from an ever broadening range of suppliers. Shorter product obsolescence cycles place pressure on manufacturing to become more flexible and market responsive, while remaining cost competitive. Lowering or eliminating tariff barriers also served to promote a global flow of products.

- **Globalization of Investment.** In today's economy, capital is increasingly free to move around the world, seeking the highest return. This mobility has significantly increased with the free-floating exchange rate system that was initiated in the early 1970s. Moreover, participation in global capital markets is no longer restricted to large-scale investors. Today, anyone with an interest can become involved.

Globalization of the economy has been occurring for several decades, but the end of the Cold War, combined with a lowering of international trade barriers, has accelerated the pace. A recent study sponsored by the German Marshall Fund of the United States (1992, 6) concludes, "As national trade barriers are lowered ... 'city-regions' in the European Community and the North American Free Trade Area are [becoming] the real arenas of global economic competition... ." Similarly, urbanologists Richard Knight and Gary Gappert (1989, 11–12), writing about city-regions, observe,

> With the advent of the global economy, nation building is becoming more and more synonymous with city building. Cities serve as the nexus of the global society. As the global society expands, a nation's welfare will be determined increasingly by the roles its cities play in the global society.

Effects on the Structure of Regions

The global shifts just described have produced a significant restructuring of what economic geographers refer to as the "system of cities" that consists of the patterns of production and labor dependencies among metropolitan centers (Bourne and Simmons 1978). A mass-production economy results in a system characterized by dominant central cities and, in later phases, polycentric regions. By contrast, because a post-industrial economy depends more on the flow of information than on the movement of material goods, the system of cities it produces is less dependent on spatial proximity (Castells 1984). Consequently, the vitality of suburban and "edge-city" employment centers has become less dependent on the health of the central city, or cities, in their region. Instead, they may depend on the vitality of corporations located in wholly different regions.

One manifestation of changing employment locations is that incomes for central-city residents, which historically have been higher than those of suburban households, today are significantly lower and declining (Rusk 1993; Barnes and Ledebur 1994). Another manifestation is that an increase in vehicle miles traveled in urban areas is now primarily generated by intra-suburban trips rather than in commutes between central cities and suburbs (Federal Highway Administration 1990).

The transformation of the system of cities is also evident in the restructuring of labor markets within regions. In the mass-production era, metropolitan regions with an economic base of heavy industry supported a high proportion of blue-collar employment. Workers in this segment — often benefiting from organized-labor negotiated wage agreements — could expect to achieve relatively high salaries that outpace inflation. By contrast, the service-based economy of a post-industrial era consists of significantly fewer blue-collar workers on one end and a growing number of highly skilled service professionals and semi-professionals at the other. This labor market reflects a dual economy in which employees in the low-skilled segment have little opportunity to earn wages comparable to those in the skilled segment (Noyelle and Stanback 1981).

The loss of middle-income jobs in both manufacturing and services has produced a widening gulf between classes, with fewer bridges of opportunity. It has also produced a socially isolated "underclass" with extremely poor access to new job markets (Kasarda 1989). Again, in socio-spatial terms, this earnings gap manifests itself in the form of suburban alienation from the central city.

These changes often are used to question the central city's significance in the region's economy. But that debate draws attention away from a more fundamental point — the importance of the interdependency of all of a region's communities for its economic competitiveness. The implication of the foregoing analysis is not that a post-industrial economy allows all communities to function as free agents, independent and indifferent to their neighbors. Rather, it suggests that the communities of a region are now bound up in a far more complex set of interdependencies, and the relationship between central cities and their suburbs is only one aspect (Savitch 1992).

Pathways through the Post-Industrial Economy

Over the last 20 years, regions across the country have been struggling to keep pace with the trends associated with globalization of the economy. Some regions, faced with factory closings, offer extremely attractive incentives to keep existing manufacturing plants and lure new ones. Others have abandoned efforts to maintain their old industrial base and seek either to attract or incubate firms capable of competing in the new high-tech service sector (Miller and Cotes 1987). Some approaches clearly are predicated on a desire to restore the old economic order, while others attempt to comprehend emerging trends and apply them in their plans. Major corporations similarly are

engaged in prognostications on how best to restructure.

How a region chooses to respond to the changing economic realities reshaping it depends very much on how current trends are interpreted and future directions are perceived. At this point in its evolution, the post-industrial economy appears to have at least two distinct pathways through it. Each has very different implications for the competitive mobilization of regions and, in turn, for their governance.

THE NEO-FORDIST PATH

Many of the largest corporations in the United States continue to adhere to mass-production, or "Fordist," principles. These corporations are attempting to extrapolate those principles on a global scale by promoting an international division of labor on one hand and an international organization of markets on the other. This is especially evident among automobile manufacturers (Barnet and Cavanagh 1994). Such corporations continue to be structured hierarchically, with a strong division between upper-management decision makers and line production workers. Neither trust nor power flows downward through their organizational structure.

Variants of the neo–Fordist approach, however, accept a degree of decentralization. In some cases, individual factories or firms are encouraged to diversify. More power is given to the worker on the line, especially where total quality management principles have been adopted.

Large firms also create smaller subsidiaries focusing on specialized production and innovation. For example, major steel manufacturers have created or acquired subsidiaries that produce relatively small batches of special alloy steels. These mills often are built in new locations, rather than replacing older mills that have been closed due to technological obsolescence and changing demands. Likewise, chemical companies have subsidiaries specializing in products ranging from new fibers to insecticides (Sabel 1982; Bianchi 1992).

Some analysts suggest that the neo–Fordist approach contains inherent contradictions. Its attempts to achieve greater flexibility to respond to rapidly changing consumer demands require a redistribution of power and responsibilities that is antithetical to the corporate hierarchies that continue to concentrate control (Sabel 1982; Lorenz 1992).

THE REGIONAL INDUSTRIAL-DISTRICTS PATH

In the early phases of the industrial revolution, efficient production occurred in districts where skilled artisans learned to employ machines to increase their output of traditional goods. Some shops produced only components of a finished good — fabric but not cloth, cloth but not clothing — but the district as a whole created market-competitive products. Such districts maintained a high level of craft, but they also provided an environment conducive to continuous, if relatively modest, innovation. In addition to a shared ethic for quality craftsmanship, such districts cultivated strong social solidarity. Indeed, analysts of such districts emphasize the importance of trust and reciprocity in structuring social relations (Sabel 1982; Lorenz 1992).

The manufacturing districts of early industrialization were largely displaced by mass-production techniques that sought to reduce reliance on craftsmanship by dividing production tasks into small steps that could be reproduced, without variation, by machines. But the idea of industrial districts never wholly disappeared. The production of highly specialized goods, especially those sufficiently high priced to cover rising labor costs (e.g., musical instruments), continues in a district form of organization. In some cases, districts have developed a symbiotic relationship with mass producers. The fash-

ion industry, for example, still relies on highly specialized districts to create new designs that subsequently provide the basis for mass-produced imitations.

In addition to traditional industrial districts such as those associated with the garment industry, new high-tech districts have grown in prominence since the end of World War II. The Draper Labs of MIT helped provide the knowledge base for many of the firms that now dot Route 208 west of Boston. Similarly, Stanford University helped give rise to Silicon Valley. These high-tech districts have several characteristics of their traditional counterparts. They, too, rely on shared craft knowledge that can best, and perhaps only, be gained by being immersed in the environment of production — an environment that typically includes proximity to major research universities (Miller and Cotes 1987).

The vitality of both traditional and high-tech districts relies on orderly competition among local firms, but this internal competition limits itself to maintaining and enhancing competitive advantage over similar districts located elsewhere. Both types of districts develop strong reciprocal relationships among firms — relationships built on trust and mutual advantage.

Implications for the Governance of Regions

Each path through the post-industrial economy has significant implications for the definition and conduct of governance, especially at the regional and even at the neighborhood level.

GOVERNANCE SUPPORTING THE NEO-FORDIST PATH

Under a neo–Fordist regime, large firms become even larger through mergers and acquisitions and more global in their expanse. In effect, they operate in a "borderless world" (Ohmae 1990). As such, it might be expected that they would want an end to all government regulation of trade. In fact, they lobby for streamlining and or eliminating certain forms of regulation that are costly to large corporations, such as those pertaining to environmental protection, workplace safety, and minimum wage and benefit levels. Nevertheless, such firms continue to support national policies offering specific market protections, production subsidies, funding for research and development, and advantageous tax policies.

Since neo–Fordist firms benefit from the flexibility to relocate where labor-market conditions are most favorable, they presumably support federal policies that are non-place specific — for example, policies that favor accelerated obsolescence of capital investment in factories. Conversely, they oppose funding that is directed toward the problems of declining cities or regions.

At the state, regional, and local levels, governments respond to conditions of neo–Fordist competition by offering generous incentives to attract new industry. Regional cooperation often is required to put together an adequate package of incentives, and the communities of a region often must lobby collectively to secure sufficient state support. The resulting bidding wars among regions is advantageous to locating corporations but not always advantageous to the regions.

In many cases, winning a bid for a new industry can result in downstream losses. The public sector may be left with debts from up-front incentives if companies move out within the payback period (Faux 1987). States have tried to protect themselves by implementing "clawback" provisions, requiring corporations to pay back incentives if they relocate before a specified period (Ledebur and Woodward 1990). But if such policies have real talons, they can act as disincentives to locating in those states. Alternatively, some neighboring regions and states have agreements not to compete to avoid bidding wars, but these agreements have proven to be conspicuously nonbinding when a large relocation prospect is highly prized. In short, although competition for jobs can result in increased intergovernmental cooperation, especially at the regional level, it is just as likely to result in predatory competition.

Even when public-sector cooperation is achieved, the private sector may maintain a tenant-at-will mentality, failing to commit itself to the region's long-range future. If firms are not committed to being regional citizens, neither are their executives. Local nonprofit institutions have long been dependent on the involvement of such executives to raise funds and lend expertise. But executives in neo–Fordist corporations are more likely to identify with their firm's worldwide network, rather than the local social networks of the communities in which they are located. When the Rockefellers left Cleveland they still felt a strong civic obligation to the community, leaving it with a significant endowment. Will British Petroleum feel a similar obligation?

All this is not to suggest that corporations are totally footloose. Many have significant plant investments, as well as concentrations of skilled employees, at specific locations. Consequently, they continue to have a strong vested interest in the ability of local and regional governments to deliver essential public services and infrastructure in an efficient and timely manner. One potential implication for governance growing out of this demand is increased use of single-purpose regional authorities, for example, port and or airport authorities, water districts, sewage districts, and the like. Such authorities overcome local fragmentation, and corporations can work with them easily.

However, many corporate requirements are not amenable to such an approach. For example, providing an adequate supply of affordable housing so that skilled employees can be attracted to and retained in an area often involves working with local governments on reform of their land-use policies. In this case, corporate interests may promote regional governance designed to override local controls that limit the supply of needed goods and services (Association of Bay Area Governments et al. 1990; Danielson and Doig 1982).

Similarly, corporations may find it necessary to become involved in issues of public education to assure an adequately trained workforce. Again, promoting regional governance to address the problem may be more attractive to corporate interests since it provides an organized forum through which to influence performance. By contrast, social equity issues, such as concentrated poverty and fiscal disparities among communities of a region, are not likely to be issues of central concern to neo–Fordist corporations (Mollenkopf and Castells 1991). The collective implication for regions is a somewhat strengthened form of governance, but in areas of narrow and strategic corporate interest.

GOVERNANCE SUPPORTING THE INDUSTRIAL-DISTRICTS PATH

In contrast to the neo-Fordist path, which focuses attention on federal policies that can promote mobility, the industrial-districts path is much more concerned with developing effective regional and local policies. Likewise, whereas the neo–Fordist path prefers policies that are not place-specific, the industrial-districts path is firmly rooted to place and emphasizes building local capacity.

Nevertheless, advocates of an industrial-districts path see a strong role for federal policy if it is structured to support and enhance local and regional efforts at strengthening the industrial-districts approach (Accordino 1992). Developing a national industrial policy could have this effect, depending on how it is crafted. Like-

wise, a federal enterprise zone program could be structured to support industrial districts. Unfortunately, the current empowerment zone/enterprise community program, although emphasizing the importance of community capacity building, does not embrace an industrial-districts philosophy.

Since the industrial-districts approach emphasizes development of local production networks, advocates of this position see benefit in creating a regional government capable of providing a wide variety of public goods ranging from training and education to support for research and development, medical care, and housing (Lorenz 1992; Clavel 1986).

Economists Piore and Sabel (1984, 301) conclude,

> Successful industrial reorganization in the United States will require reinvigoration of local and regional government — not necessarily its supersession in favor of an expansion of corporate autonomy. Industrial policy will have to be regional policy; to be effective, the coordination of training programs, industrial research, transportation networks, credit, marketing information, environmental protection, and other elements of infrastructure will have to be done at the regional level.

In addition to suggesting a strong role for regional governments, the industrial-district paradigm also suggests a restructuring of *governance*, defined as participation in the processes of public decision making. In this conception, governance involves considerable interaction between the public, private, and nonprofit sectors. This restructuring goes beyond the creation of partnerships, focusing more broadly on achieving genuine collaborations in which all sectors — public, private, and nonprofit — provide distinct services and capacities in pursuit of a common regional vision (Wallis 1994b).

The type of governance advocated to support industrial districts also emphasizes neighborhood/community participation in decision-making processes (Peirce et al. 1993). Interest in neighborhood-level governance is indicative of the place-based orientation of an industrial-district approach, as distinct from the "borderless world" of the neo–Fordist alternative.

Emphasis on cross-sectorial governance also recognizes the importance of strengthening local civic infrastructure as an integral aspect of economic development. Robert Putnam (1993a, 106), drawing from his research on regions in Italy, observes,

> Of two equally poor Italian regions a century ago, both very backward, but one with more civic engagement, and the other with a hierarchical structure, the one with more choral societies and soccer clubs has grown steadily wealthier. The more civic region has prospered because trust and reciprocity were woven into its social fabric ages ago.

Part of the effort to strengthen civic infrastructure involves reengaging the poor living in isolated neighborhoods, as well as tapping into the talents available from new immigrants. The justification for placing resources in these populations of a region is that they represent human capital, which if abandoned creates inertia to competitive development.

Comparing the Paths

The two paths through a post-industrial economy, which are briefly described here, are ideal types. Most U.S. regions are of a scale and complexity that elements of both types are evident, but neither exists in a pure form. Nevertheless, distinguishing between these two paths may help regions in thinking about their current economic structure, how it is changing, and where it might be heading.

Each path through the post-industrial economy has very different implications for regional government and governance. The neo–Fordist alternative, based on the grow-

ing dominance of large multinational corporations, requires regions with the capacity to deliver necessary infrastructure and services. This demand could be met by developing and or strengthening special regional authorities or by enhancing the capacity of existing organizations, such as metropolitan planning organizations and councils of government.

In many regions, a neo–Fordist alternative also would benefit from strengthening regional capacity to siting various supportive land uses, ranging from power plants to landfills to affordable housing. None of these requirements necessitate a radical reinvention of regional government or governance, but all involve a degree of state and interlocal commitment that to date has been very difficult to achieve.

By contrast, the industrial-districts scenario implies a substantial restructuring of regional government and governance. Few if any U.S. regions have developed an effective means to analyze adequately the linkages of industries comprising their current or nascent industrial districts, and few have the ability to connect such analysis to the formulation of a complementary, strategic policy agenda.

If the emerging global economy favors industrial districts, then U.S. economic competitiveness will be substantially disadvantaged by its lack of governance capacity to support such development. European and non-western regions appear to be ahead of the game in this respect, not simply due to recent efforts at "harmonization," a term for reducing local government fragmentation (van den Berg et al. 1993), but because of well established political cultures in many regions that already support the types of governance conducive to industrial districts (Lorenz 1992; Putnam 1993b; Sabel 1982; Piore and Sabel 1984).

Which Path?

Global restructuring of the economy is no longer an esoteric phenomenon confined to specialized conferences and journals. It has become material for the evening news. Increased awareness of change can motivate desire for shared dialogue and eventually for collective action.

Asking the question "Which path?" assumes a deliberative process by which interest groups in a region get together and think about what is happening to their economic structure and what they need to do to change it. In some cases this does occur, but only rarely. There are many efforts at visioning, but few engage in the kind of rigorous economic analysis necessary to generate informed conclusions. Several regions have developed coalitions of corporate interests dedicated to developing strategies to enhance regional economic competitiveness.[3] Some of these coalitions even include public agency members, but more often community dialogue occurs in an environment of crisis defined by the threat of a factory or military base closing.

If the question "Which path?" is to be asked, several things have to happen:

- **Identity.** If interests from different sectors within a region are to enter into dialogue, they must first identify themselves as active participants in the life of their region.
- **Citizenship.** People not only need to see themselves as part of a region, they need to develop a sense of citizenship for its well being (Cisneros 1995).
- **Dialogue.** Once identity is established, opportunities must be provided for genuine dialogue. Coming together in dialogue helps reinforce identity with the region.
- **Vision.** Beyond dialogue, visioning involves a structured attempt to think about the future. It works best when it is strategic (about specific, pressing issues) rather than general (Dodge 1992).
- **Mobilization.** If visioning is effective, it should lead to mobilization to implement elements of the vision.

Realistically, regions do not have the capacity to control global economic forces, but they can actively decide how they want to respond to them. In formulating their responses, alternative forms of regional governance should be a central consideration.

Notes

1. William Hudnut, keynote speech at Town Meeting West (Denver, Colorado), April 3, 1992.

2. Personal interview with Commissioner DuVall, April 21, 1993.

3. Examples of such coalitions include Cleveland Tomorrow, Greater Philadelphia First, and the Greater Seattle Trade and Development Alliance.

References

Accordino, John. 1992. *The United States in the Global Economy.* Chicago: American Library Association.

Association of Bay Area Governments et al. 1990. *Bay Area Housing.* The Local Housing Element Assistance Project.

Barnes, William, and Larry Ledebur. 1990. *Toward a New Political Economy of Metropolitan Regions.* Washington, DC: National League of Cities.

_____. 1994. *Local Economies: The U.S. Common Market of Local Economic Regions.* Washington, DC: National League of Cities.

Barnet, Richard, and John Cavanagh. 1994. *Global Dreams: Imperial Corporations and the New World Order.* New York: Simon and Schuster.

Bianchi, Patrizio. 1992. "Levels of Policy and the Nature of Post-Fordist Competition." In *Pathways to Industrial and Regional Development,* edited by Michael Stroper and Allen J. Scott. New York: Routledge.

Bourne, Larry S., and James W. Simmons, eds.

1978. *System of Cities*. New York: Oxford University Press.

Castels, Manuel. 1984. "Space and Society." In *Cities in Transformation: Class, Capital and the State*, edited by Michael Smith, Vol. 28, Urban Affairs Annual Reviews.

Cisneros, Henry. 1995. *Regionalism: The New Geography of Opportunity*. Washington, DC: U.S. Department of Housing and Urban Development.

Clavel, Pierre. 1986. *The Progressive City*. New Brunswick, NJ: Rutgers University Press.

Danielson, Michael N., and Jameson W. Doig. 1982. *New York: The Politics of Urban Regional Development*. Berkeley: University of California Press.

Dodge, William R. 1992. "Strategic Intercommunity Governance Networks." *National Civic Review* (Fall-Winter).

Ehrenhalt, Alan. 1995. "Cooperate or Die." *Governing* (September): 28–32.

Faux, Jeff. 1987. Industrial Policy and Democratic Institutions. In *The State and Local Industrial Policy Question*, edited by Harvey Goldstein. Chicago: American Planning Association.

Federal Highway Administration. 1990. *Personal Travel in the United States*. Washington, DC: U.S. Department of Transportation.

German Marshall Fund of the United States. 1992. "Divided Cities in the Global Economy" (November).

Hanson, Royce, ed. 198. *Rethinking Urban Policy: Urban Development in an Advanced Economy*. Washington, DC: National Academy Press.

Kanter, Rosabeth Moss. 1994. "Collaborative Advantage." *Harvard Business Review* (July-August): 96–108.

Kasarda, John. 1989. Urban Industrial Transition and the Underclass, in *The Annals of the American Academy of Political and Social Sciences*, v. 501.

Knight, Richard V., and Gary Gappert. 1989. *Cities in the Global Society*. Newbury Park, CA: Sage.

Ledebur, Larry, and Douglas Woodward. 1990. "Adding a Stick to the Carrot: Location Incentives with Clawbacks, Rescissions and Calibrations." *Economic Development Quarterly* 4(3): 221–237.

Lorenz, Edward H. 1992. "Trust, Community and Cooperation: Toward a Theory of Industrial Districts." In *Pathways to Industrial*

and Regional Development, edited by Michael Stroper and Allen J. Scott. New York: Routledge.

Miller, Roger, and Marcel Cotes. 1987. *Growing the Next Silicon Valley: A Guide for Successful Regional Planning*. Lexington, MA: Heath and Company.

Mollenkopf, John, and Manuel Castells. 1991. *Dual City: Restructuring New York*. New York: Russell Sage.

Noyelle, Thierry J. 1983. "The Implications of Industry Restructuring for Spatial Organization in the United States." In *Regional Analysis and the New International Division of Labor*, edited by Frank Moulaert and Patricia W. Salinas. Boston: Kluwer/Nijkoff Publishing.

_____ and Thomas Stanback, Jr. 1981. *The Economic Transformation of American Cities*. New York: Conservation of Human Resources, Columbia University.

Ohmae, Kenichi. 1990. *Borderless World: Power and Strategy in the Interlinked Economy*. New York: Harper Collins.

Peirce, Neal, Curtis Johnson, and John Stuart Hall. 1993. *Citistates: How Urban America Can Prosper in a Competitive World*. Washington, DC: Seven Locks Press.

Piore, Michael J., and Charles F. Sabel. 1984. *The Second Industrial Divide*. New York: Basic Books.

Putnam, Robert D. 1993a. "What Makes Democracy Work." *National Civic Review* (Spring): 101–107.

_____. 1993b. *Making Democracy Work: Civic Traditions in Modern Italy*. Princeton, NJ: Princeton University Press.

Reich, Robert. 1991. *The Work of Nations*. New York: Random House.

Rusk, David. 1993. *Cities Without Suburbs*. Baltimore: Johns Hopkins.

Sabel, Charles. 1982. *Work and Politics: The Division of Labor in Industry*. New York: Cambridge University Press.

Savitch, Hank. 1992. "Ties That Bind." *National Civic Review* (Summer-Fall).

van den Berg, Leo, H. Van Klink, and J. Van Der Meer. 1993. *Governing Metropolitan Regions*. Brookfield, VT: Avebury.

Wallis, Allan. 1994a. "Regionalism: The First Two Waves." *National Civic Review* (Spring).

_____. 1994b. "Inventing Regionalism: A Two-Phase Approach." *National Civic Review* (Fall-Winter).

PART II

Case Studies in Innovation

CHAPTER 7

REGIONAL TRANSPORTATION PLANNING THROUGH FEDERAL LEGISLATION

Bruce D. McDowell

Governmental regions often are difficult to build and maintain. Resistance to them frequently comes from state and local governments and state agencies that feel threatened by the prospect of having to share power with regional organizations. However, federal initiatives can stimulate and nurture effective regional organizations that are deemed helpful to the proper administration of federal programs which spill across the boundaries of state and local governments that divide natural service areas.

One of the most effective federal initiatives supporting regional organizations in recent years has come from the Intermodal Surface Transportation Efficiency Act of 1991 (ISTEA). This act's innovations have strengthened many regional organizations and led both practitioners and scholars to suggest the ISTEA approach as a model for other functions of government that have regional dimensions. Congress has continued ISTEA's innovations with only modest refinements for another six years by enacting the Transportation Equity Act for the 21st Century (TEA-21). The ISTEA/TEA-21 approach brings well-funded planning together with strong links to the implementation [of the] decision-making processes.

This chapter briefly:

- reviews historic federal roles in supporting regional organizations;
- describes how ISTEA has refined the federal government's role in region building;
- draws some key principles from the ISTEA experience that might be applied to other federal-aid programs; and
- suggests six other federal program areas in which the ISTEA model of regional problem solving could be applied beneficially.

Originally published as "The ISTEA Model of Region Building," *The Regionalist*, Vol. 3, No. 1/2, Fall, 1998. Published by the National Association of Regional Councils, Washington, D.C. Reprinted with permission of the publisher.

The Federal Role in Supporting Regions

Regions are natural for almost everything but governance. For example, nature has its watersheds, river basins, mountain ranges, ecological regions, wildlife habitats, wetlands areas, estuaries, and outstanding natural features worthy of preserving as parks, wilderness areas, and marine sanctuaries. Economies have their market areas, commuter sheds, labor markets, newspaper circulation and broadcast areas of influence, and international trading regions.

But, when it comes to governments, we have the nation, the states, and local governments, all with relatively fixed boundaries and presumed monopolies over the authority to govern within their borders.

For certain special purposes — single functions with demonstrably essential needs not being met by general-purpose governments — limited-purpose units of government have been established. Examples are special districts, school districts, the occasional river basin commission, the Tennessee Valley Authority, and the Appalachian Regional Commission. The latter two organizations are historical anomalies, originally intended to be models for establishing regional organizations to boost economic development in other underdeveloped areas, but they were not replicated after the concepts they represented lost political favor.

In general, however, the boundaries of nature and the boundaries of markets do not match the boundaries of governments. Yet, governments must respond effectively and efficiently to nature and to markets. The concept of governmental regions attempts to bridge this gap between natural, economic, and political realities.

The idea that regional analysis is the only way to "get your arms around" certain types of governance issues makes common sense, and is tolerated by state and local governments as long as the organizations responsible for preparing regional analyses have no governing authority. Therefore, most regional organizations in the U.S. are largely limited to planning responsibilities. Although a few also have some service delivery responsibilities, and one is an elected government, most use only persuasion and the serendipitous confluence of favorable political conditions to lead state and local governments to think regionally and act accordingly.

Relying only on advisory powers, many regional planning bodies have had rather limited success, leaving many people wondering whether they are worth the money, time, and effort it takes to keep them going. Too often, it is difficult for them to point to tangible benefits they have produced.

The federal government generously supported regional planning organizations with some three-dozen programs in the 1960s and 1970s, and assisted the states in blanketing the nation with metropolitan and nonmetropolitan planning regions by the end of the 1970s. Then the federal government lost faith in regions for many of its programs (ACIR, 1982; McDowell, 1986).

In the early 1980s, federal support for regional planning declined precipitously. The Environmental Protection Agency, the Office of Management and Budget, and the Departments of Housing and Urban Development, Health and Human Services, Labor, Agriculture, and Justice dropped their regional planning programs. Today, federal aid for regions survives primarily in two programs; one (administered by the Department of Transportation) supports transportation planning for 340 metropolitan areas, and the other (administered by the Department of Commerce, Economic Development Administration) supports economic development planning for 320 small metropolitan and nonmetropolitan regions.

Although three-fourths of the regional planning organizations once supported by the larger array of federal programs have survived, many of them have abandoned most of their planning and regional problem-solving roles. Instead, they now emphasize technical and convener services to local governments. The 1998 directory of regional councils, prepared by the National Association of Regional Councils, lists 501 currently active general-purpose regional councils.

Two lessons emerge from the recent history of regional organizations. First, the federal and state governments can cause the creation of regional organizations and give them areawide problem-solving roles. Second, when the forces supporting regional roles from outside the regions are withdrawn, local support tends to lead them toward technical service roles, and away from contentious interjurisdictional problem-solving and policy-making roles.

In sum, a federal role makes a real difference in how regional organizations are structured, what they do, and how well they do it. The federally-supported metropolitan planning organizations (MPOs) required by ISTEA provide very clear current examples of the effects the federal role can have.

The ISTEA Model of Region Building

The most important thing that ISTEA has done for metropolitan regional organizations has been to give them effective leverage over funding decisions in a group of high-stakes federal-aid programs for surface transportation worth $20–$30 billion per year. Before ISTEA, the states ran the majority of these programs with a pretty free hand. Now, the designated MPO in each metropolitan area over 200,000 population shares in many of those decisions. They do the detailed planning for the metropolitan transportation system, take the lead in setting the priorities for spending the federal funds allocated for use within their areas (consistent with recognized funding constraints), and negotiate with the state department of transportation (SDOT) for the use of statewide funds within the metropolitan area.

MUTUAL LEVERAGE

The MPO's negotiating leverage for state funding rests on the mutual vetoes that the MPO and SDOT hold over the use of each other's federal funds in the region. In short, ISTEA made the larger MPOs into real decisionmakers that allocate funds in an essential public works program, and put them into a close partnership with the state.

The MPOs are better suited to these detailed planning roles because of their greater ability to involve the citizens, local governments, and other affected parties in the heavily populated portions of the state. Giving these responsibilities to the MPOs frees the state DOTs to concentrate their efforts on statewide issues.

Although some of these state-metropolitan partnerships have been rocky, ISTEA brought the destinies of the nearly 140 larger MPOs and their SDOTs closer together. It is more difficult, now, for one to succeed without the other.

It should be noted, however, that even though the approximately 200 smaller MPOs are required to meet the same planning requirements as the larger ones, they have neither the assured level of planning funds, the regionally allocated program implementation funds, nor the federally enforced decisionmaking partnership with the SDOT that the larger MPOs have. Thus, the full ISTEA model applies to less than half of the MPOs. Nevertheless, it sets a precedent that the smaller MPOs and many other federal-aid recipients envy.

ISTEA also broadened the scope of transportation decisionmaking. Planning and funding decisions now are supposed to be made on the basis of intermodal analyses that show how people and goods can be moved most effectively and efficiently by the combination of means that will produce the greatest benefits for customers, while minimizing adverse impacts on the environment, energy resources, and social equity. That is far different than the single-minded highway construction goals of the past.

To support this new style of planning, implementation funds from the federal highway and transit programs now can be used flexibly, not just for construction and equipment purchases, but also for operations, maintenance, and demand management, and for such related programs as bicycle and pedestrian facilities, goods movement, and intermodal connections (including port access). And the larger MPOs have a strong voice in determining the use of these funds.

Fortunately, MPOs are funded generously by the federal government to do their required planning using set-asides from the surface transportation programs to a large extent. (The ISTEA/TEA-21 construction, operations, and maintenance funds still go to the state DOTs or the transit authorities, rather than to the MPOs.) These federal planning funds make the MPOs the best funded and most stable regional planning bodies in the country today. For those MPOs that are regional councils, their federal transportation funding helps to strengthen their broader regional planning programs.

However, in return for these new responsibilities, the MPOs are required by the act to pursue a more thorough and more comprehensive planning process, and to more thoroughly involve a much wider range of interested and affected parties than ever before. Although federal law has required transportation planning organizations to exist ever since 1962, they played less important roles in earlier years and received less attention. ISTEA added the following very ambitious new requirements:

- provide a level playing field for involving all the affected parties as they make broad-ranging transportation decisions;
- produce flexible "performance-based plans" that integrate all the transportation modes to move both people and goods more effectively and efficiently;
- use better analytical techniques to study broad sets of alternatives and produce higher quality plans;
- develop "financially constrained" implementation programs that establish priorities among alternative proposals to achieve the greatest performance improvements consistent with available funds; and
- broaden and intensify public involvement in the planning process from beginning to end.

Each of these five far-reaching MPO requirements is described below, based on two recent studies by the U.S. Advisory Commission on Intergovernmental Relations (ACIR, 1995; ACIR 1997). They offer potential for emulation in other federal-aid programs that use regional organizations.

THE LEVEL PLAYING FIELD

ISTEA requires the MPOs to provide a decisionmaking process that includes all the affected local government officials in the region, as well as state transportation officials, transportation providers, and state and regional air-quality officials when transportation plans and implementation programs are being developed and approved.

Although ISTEA does not specify exactly how this requirement must be met, the ACIR research has shown that many MPOs have increased the numbers and types of members on their governing bodies and established new intergovernmental agreements to broaden participation in the decisionmaking process. In addition, technical committees and special committees for new topics such as freight planning have been established or expanded to provide a wider range of inputs to transportation decisions. The idea is to get all the key stakeholders involved in the MPO decisionmaking so that the results will be sustained by strong and consistent local, state, and federal support.

ISTEA's ideal of broad and deep involvement frequently is difficult to achieve, however. For example, federal field personnel (especially those from FTA) may not attend MPO meetings regularly because of time and travel constraints. In addition, both federal and state representatives may hold different views than local officials, but not resolve these differences within the MPO process. Such factors may lead to MPO decisions being overturned at a later time by either state or federal action, or both.

It takes great skill and patience by the MPO to draw the federal and state officials into the decisionmaking process deeply enough to ensure that the MPO decisions can be relied on to be implemented with state and federal support in all but the most unusual circumstances.

PERFORMANCE PLANS

The transportation performance plan is expected to bring all the related programs together to allow the flexible funding mixes needed to get desired results, skirting the arbitrary program barriers that often have stood in the way. ISTEA provides a substantial amount of funding flexibility among separate transportation programs if the planning process supports it.

ISTEA's substitution of flexible performance goals for the mode-specific goals of individual programs may be reinforced by the Government Performance and Results Act of 1993 (GPRA). U.S. DOT has taken the outcome-oriented performance goals supported by both acts to help it move beyond the individual programs in ISTEA and other DOT legislation toward the "One DOT" concept. This means that U.S. DOT now expects all 10 of its major organizational units to work together to achieve the following five performance goals:

- mobility of people to jobs and services (including a new welfare-to-work objective) and access of goods to production sites and markets;
- economic vitality of the nation enhanced by efficient transportation and trade;
- safety and security of transportation in America (to save lives and protect property);
- environmental protection and community livability features of transportation systems in America; and
- national defense capabilities of America's transportation system.

Thus, DOT is taking steps intended to take the integration of Federal Highway Administration and Federal Transit Administration programs established by ISTEA even further under GPRA to include railroads, ports, airports, pipelines, and shipping. ISTEA (and now TEA-21) requires each MPO to take into account all the modes relevant to its region, and GPRA provides an extra push to get the additional modes to join the integrated effort.

Obviously, these goals also have a lot in common with goals of other federal departments and agencies, including HHS, Labor, EDA, EPA, and Defense. This suggests that there may be advantages if the MPOs also have relationships with those organizations, and if these federal departments and agencies have relationships with each other regarding these closely-related programs. Many MPOs, indeed, do have such relationships, often continued from the 1960s and 1970s when they were promoted heavily by the federal government. (ACIR, 1973, pp. 226–227.)

CPRA requires all federal departments and agencies to promote interagency coordination where it can help to improve the performance of federal programs. DOT has already built such coordination into its programs for such matters as air quality, water quality, wetlands, and welfare-to-work.

Common performance goals and measures, and coordinated reporting of performance, are becoming essential parts of the federal-aid process (McDowell, 1998). They are the means by which the federal, state, regional, and local partners can support each other's success in meeting broad performance goals. In the past, it often was so difficult for federal agencies (sometimes even in the same department) to coordinate with each other that regional planning organizations were expected to coordinate the federal programs. Although that is an attractive idea, it often is difficult to accomplish because of the separations and incompatibilities built into the individual federal programs. ISTEA bridged some of those difficulties with its flexible funding provisions, and GPRA encourages DOT as well as the other federal departments and agencies to go even further toward program integration.

ENHANCED ANALYTICAL TECHNIQUES

The kinds of outcome-oriented performance goals that are beginning to drive transportation and other federal programs require more powerful analyses that can look into the future and estimate the potential impacts on society of new facilities, better maintenance, more efficient operations, no action, and other program options.

Transportation programs have depended on simulation models for many years, but ISTEA has created the need for even better models requiring still more and better data. DOT has geared up by spending significant money to:

- upgrade transportation simulation models;
- develop better data to support the new models;
- make transportation data more readily available to support new models

and powerful geographic information systems (GIS);
- develop realistic performance measures;
- create and support interactive decision-support systems; and
- train MPO and other planners how to use the new data and analytical techniques effectively.

REALISTIC IMPLEMENTATION PROGRAMS

Before ISTEA, transportation implementation programs were largely limited to capital improvements listed in the Transportation Improvement Program (TIP). Now, implementation plans include much more than capital improvements. The new elements are: innovative finance plans; regulatory plans aimed at reducing travel demand or improving air quality; and system management, routine maintenance, and operating plans aimed at squeezing greater service out of the same facilities and equipment.

Noncapital and low-capital alternatives for meeting performance goals stretch public transportation dollars, but they require a different type of planning and analysis than traditional transportation planning programs. ISTEA's "financial constraint" requirement — limiting proposed spending to the revenues demonstrated to be available during the implementation period — put a premium on low-cost alternatives and criteria for systematically assigning priorities to the projects and programs that will produce the greatest amount of performance per dollar.

ENHANCED PUBLIC INVOLVEMENT

"Inclusive," "early," and "often" are the watch words of ISTEA's public involvement requirement. MPOs are required to reach out to all the affected parties, and seek to involve them in the MPO process from beginning to end. This is true particularly for the hard-to-reach sectors of the population such as: persons with disabilities (who may need special means of communicating and special accommodations at meetings); ethnic groups (that may have language and other cultural barriers to overcome); and the poor and disadvantaged (who may be transit-dependent but unable to participate in public forums to make their needs known).

This enhanced involvement is intended to make the transportation programs customer-oriented, to take advantage of the unique insights that come from viewing the programs "from the other end of the telescope," and to help create a body of support for the programs that will best meet the needs of the customers. Successful public involvement programs typically use a wide variety of techniques appropriate to reach the diverse groups found in most communities and to match the different stages of the planning process.

DOT funded a new inventory of these techniques (Howard/Stein-Hudson) and made case studies available to illustrate the benefits that can come from such activities. The time and resources required to pursue sincere and creative public involvement programs may be substantial, but the effort can pay off in plans and projects that have the breadth of support necessary to be implemented.

MPO Capacity Building

FHWA-sponsored studies (ACIR, 1995; ACIR, 1997) found that the MPOs have adapted very significantly to the ISTEA innovations, but they still need to make further improvements, and they are looking for help. One reason they are looking for help is that the larger ones (over 200,000 population) must be certified by the federal government every three years. The certification process assesses the extent to which these MPOs are meeting the federal planning requirements outlined above, and makes recommendations for improvement. A number

of conditional approvals have been issued, allowing brief periods to rectify deficiencies (ACIR, 1997). Although MPO funding and implementation funds in the MPO's region could be cut off, that has not yet happened. Nevertheless, the certification requirement provides a strong incentive for MPOs to meet the federal requirements.

To help all MPOs meet federal requirements, FHWA is funding development of a learning network through the Association of Metropolitan Planning Organizations (AMPO). The primary goal is to share good practices quickly and effectively among the MPOs to help them become high-performance organizations. It is expected that a permanent website will be operating as part of this network in 1999 to help MPOs get up to speed and maintain their high performance well into the future as techniques continue to improve.

The main point to emphasize here is that DOT is making very substantial investments in building MPO capacities to help ensure that they will be the strong partners needed to help implement the national transportation policies spelled out in ISTEA.

Principles for Federal Support of Regional Institutions

The ISTEA experience suggests that the federal government could substantially enhance its support for regional organizations in ways that could significantly improve the performance of other national goals. This could be accomplished by distilling the lessons of ISTEA into a multipurpose model of region-building and applying it to additional federal-aid programs. Five principles that should be included in such a model follow.

Define Regional Interest

The federal government should carefully delineate the program areas in which it has a regional problem-solving interest. This delineation should include the scope of the federal interest, the existing programs that relate to it, and the federal performance goals established for the program area.

Each program area should incorporate a significant amount of federal funding over which a designated regional organization would have authority to assign spending priorities consistent with an adopted performance plan and realistic financial constraints. Within the program scope, flexibility should be created for transferring funds among related programs to help meet performance goals more effectively and efficiently.

The following areas are suggested for consideration, along with some of the major departments and agencies that might be involved.

Economic Development. Major related programs exist in the Economic Development Administration, the Appalachian Regional Commission, the Small Business Administration, and the Departments of Housing and Urban Development, Defense, Transportation, Agriculture, Education, Interior, and Labor.

Community Development and Housing. Major related programs exist in the Departments of Housing and Urban Development and Agriculture.

Social Opportunity, Health, and Public Safety. Major related programs exist in the Departments of Health and Human Services, Labor, Education, and Justice.

Pollution Control. Major related programs exist in the Environmental Protection Agency, the Departments of Energy and Defense, the Nuclear Regulatory Commission, and the Federal Emergency Management Agency.

Natural Resource Use and Preservation (including water resources). Major related programs exist in the Environmental Protection Agency and the Departments of Interior, Agriculture, Commerce, and Defense.

Disaster Mitigation. Major related programs exist in the Federal Emergency Management Agency and 27 other federal departments and agencies.

ASSIGN REGIONAL INSTITUTIONS

The federal government should assign a federally-assisted regional planning and coordinating role to appropriate regional institutions for each of the "regional interest" program areas defined above. In general, the choice of institutions should be the general-purpose regional councils already established for other federal and state programs. Multiple programs should be assigned to the same regional organization whenever possible to facilitate coordination and encourage program synergies.

Where regional councils are not the best choice (perhaps because they lack capability and authority, or appropriate geographic scope), some flexibility should be provided to allow conformity with other applicable state laws, interstate compacts, watershed or river basin organizations, or other regional structures that may already exist for other purposes. Combinations of regional councils may be appropriate in some cases. If regional councils are not designated for a particular program area, coordination with those that exist in the geographic area should be required. The federal government should play a special role in helping to support or create interstate regional councils where needed to address areawide concerns that cross state lines.

Opportunities for coordinating related federal programs and agencies should be seized. Regional planning requirements should be as consistent as possible from one program area to another to allow efficiencies in meeting federal planning requirements. Duplicate planning should be avoided by incorporating the relevant elements of related regional, state, and local plans into the designated regional organization's planning reports and policies.

To the extent possible, planning assumptions (such as population growth rates and future development patterns) should be consistent from one program to another. This practice was heavily promoted by the federal government in the 1970s, but was de-emphasized until ISTEA renewed the emphasis on coordinating land use, environmental protection, and transportation. TEA-21 increases that emphasis.

The planning funds to support designated regional organizations should be provided as a percentage set-aside from the related implementation programs. This arrangement has worked well in the transportation field, while the use of separately appropriated planning funds has not worked well in other fields.

REQUIRE REGIONAL DIALOGUE

The federal government should establish performance requirements for (a) inclusiveness in the policymaking bodies of the designated regional institutions, (b) a collaborative decisionmaking relationship between the regional institution and the related state agencies, and (c) ISTEA-style public involvement. The designated regional organization should be a partnership mechanism, responsible for bringing the affected and responsible parties together to help broaden consensus. This is not always easy to accomplish, so the federal government may have to assist some regional organizations in getting some of the parties (such as a state agency) to the bargaining table and keeping them there in a constructive relationship. DOT has found this role necessary in a few cases.

EMPOWER REGIONAL PARTNERSHIP

Federal officials in the field should be active partners in the regional planning and problem-solving process. They should attend regional planning meetings faithfully, participate fully, and abide by the regional decisions made in the collaborative process, except in clear cases when the regional decisions violate federal law.

This role will be a significant culture change for many federal officials who have been accustomed to monitoring compliance with detailed federal-aid regulations. In addition, it will require a greater federal field presence than is available presently in many of these programs. However, this approach would require less time for regional office and headquarters reviews, and would diminish the need for unilateral federal decisions made from afar. Special training for federal field representatives should be provided to facilitate the transition from "compliance officer" to "full partner." A recent report by the National Academy of Public Administration (NAPA) is available to support such training.

BUILD REGIONAL CAPACITY

Federal agencies should help to build the capacity of regional councils and other designated regional organizations, and facilitate their operations. Federal research, program evaluations, and training programs are important sources of information for regional organizations about what works.

In addition, the federal government is in a position to sponsor "learning networks" for regional organizations to help them share experiences about good practices. Federal agencies, including DOT and HUD, also are beginning to package data conveniently to assist their grantees in performing required planning analyses and preparing helpful maps and graphic displays for decision-support purposes — a technique that should be applied more fully to regional programs. Finally, federal agencies are beginning to establish nationally comparable regional indicators and automate many aspects of the grant management process — from applications for funds to disbursements and project closeouts.

Precedents for these helpful practices have been cited above, but most are not widespread outside the ISTEA/TEA-21 orbit. Fuller use by federal agencies in a wider range of regional programs could significantly aid the effectiveness and efficiency of regional organizations and enhance the performance of many federal programs.

Conclusion

After nearly two decades of neglect by most federal programs, it is time for renewed initiatives by the federal government to take advantage of the benefits that regions can provide. The partnership model embodied in ISTEA, and continued by TEA-21, is effective and worthy of broader application.

Now is a particularly good time to pursue this regional initiative because of the outcome-oriented performance management requirements of GPRA. Many federal-aid programs have regional dimensions, and it is in the regions that their benefits will be produced. These programs will be delivered by federal-aid recipients, not by the federal government itself. So the partnership idea takes on new meaning; federal program performance will need to be measured largely by the success of the partners. The federal interest in strengthening regional councils, therefore, is the same as its interest in seeing its own programs succeed.

References

Howard/Stein-Hudson Associates, Inc., and Parsons, Brinkerhoff, Quade & Douglas. 1996. *Public Involvement Techniques for Transportation Decision-Making*, prepared for the Federal Highway Administration and the Federal Transit Administration. Washington, D.C.: U.S. Department of Transportation.

McDowell, Bruce D. 1986. "Regional Planning Today," Chapter 6 in Frank S. So, Irving Hand, and Bruce D. McDowell, editors, *The Practice of State and Regional Planning*. Chicago: American Planning Association.

McDowell, Bruce D. 1998. "The Results Act: Implications for Managing Federal Grants," *Assistance Management Journal*, Volume 8, No. 4, pp. 1–10.

National Academy of Public Administration. 1997. *Principles for Federal Managers of Community-Based Programs*. Washington, D.C.: The Academy.

U.S. Advisory Commission on Intergovernmental Relations. 1973. *Regional Decisionmaking: New Strategies for Substate Districts*. Washington, D.C.: U.S. Government Printing Office.

U.S. Advisory Commission on Intergovernmental Relations. 1982. *State and Local Roles in the Federal System*, Chapter 5, "Areawide Organizations: Metropolitan and Nonmetropolitan." Washington, D.C.: U.S. Government Printing Office.

U.S. Advisory Commission on Intergovernmental Relations. 1995. *MPO Capacity: Improving the Capacity of Metropolitan Planning Organizations to Help Implement National Transportation Policies*. Washington, D.C.: ACIR.

U.S. Advisory Commission on Intergovernmental Relations. 1997. *Planning Progress: Addressing ISTEA Requirements in Metropolitan Planning Areas*, A Staff Report. Washington, D.C.: ACIR.

CHAPTER 8

RAILS-TO-TRAILS PROJECTS IN REGIONS OF GEORGIA, MARYLAND, AND MISSISSIPPI

Terra Hargett

When transportation funds are mentioned, most community leaders think of building highways and interstates, but a growing number of cities and counties across the United States are setting a different trend. Residents are telling their legislators and city representatives that they want alternatives to concrete and congestion. Those communities are using abandoned rail corridors, which normally sit unused or are sold off in sections, to create trails. Rail-trails can be used for bicycling, walking, in-line skating, cross-country skiing or horseback riding. Some rail-trails preserve historic landmarks, and others help preserve wildlife.

Rail-trails are not new, but since the 1980s the number of trails has increased because of federal and state legislation allowing for alternative transportation spending. According to Karen Stewart, director of communications at Washington, D.C.–based Rails to Trails Conservancy (RTC), more than 1,200 rail-trails, totaling about 11,000 miles of converted track, have been completed since the 1960s. The trails have been built in rural and urban areas alike, using a variety of funding and construction methods.

ISTEA Refreshes Growth

Because transportation funds have traditionally been used to build highways and transportation systems, trail supporters have had a difficult time convincing some government officials to allocate funds for alternative transportation methods. The Intermodal Surface Transportation Efficiency Act (ISTEA), signed into law in 1991, has made it easier by giving state and local governments latitude in spending the money. Additionally, the legislation includes language mandating that recipients spend 10 percent of their surface transportation dollars on transportation enhancement activities. City transportation enhancement funds can be used to build trails as long as 20 percent of the project budget is raised locally.

Originally published as "Rail-Trails Gather Steam," *American City & County*, Vol. 116, No. 1, January, 2001. Published by the Intertec Publishing Corporation, Atlanta, Georgia. Reprinted with permission of the publisher.

Longleaf Trace Trail, a converted rail corridor that stretches 39 miles from Hattiesburg, Miss., to Prentiss, Miss., benefited from that provision. In 1994, two retired attorneys, Stone Barefield of Hattiesburg and Bobby Garraway of Bassville, wanted to use federal funds to convert an abandoned Illinois Central rail line into a trail. The lawyers worked to pass a bill in the state legislature that would allow counties and cities in Mississippi to form recreational districts, which would qualify for ISTEA funding.

Supporters of the bill hoped that recreational districts would be able to raise the 20 percent of funds that were necessary to use ISTEA money for trail construction. After the bill was passed in 1994, several residents worked to encourage the formation of a recreational district between the four cities and three counties that ran along Longleaf Trace Trail.

James Moore, trail advocate and owner of a bike shop, became the lead spokesperson for forming a recreational district and building the trail. "The trail was a much needed addition to the area," Moore says. "We are not a very bike-friendly area. There are no bike lanes or trails. We have a state park, but, as far as getting into nature quickly, this met the need."

Moore traveled through the counties, giving speeches to civic and business organizations. From those organizations and other private entities, the group raised $160,000 before it approached cities and counties to ask them to form the recreation district.

The four cities and three counties along the rail line agreed to join the coalition and invest public funds in the venture. Each county agreed to contribute a total of a quarter of a mil for the trail. With the $160,000 already in hand, the counties' contributions brought the total amount to $520,000, giving the $2.5 million project the 20 percent in local funding it needed to use ISTEA funds.

The Mississippi Department of Transportation purchased the rail line from Illinois Central and leased the land to the recreation district. The trail, which opened on Labor Day 2000, took nearly two years to complete. Its opening brought a surge of tourism to the area.

"All of a sudden, towns with 300 and 1,200 people have new businesses," Moore says. "It was difficult, but in the end it was so worthwhile. When I go out there, I see kids and mothers with their children. It is a place where they feel safe. We have had nothing but positive feedback, and it has been very much worth the hard work."

Banking on the Right-of-Way

In many cases, railroads are supportive of rail-trails because they allow the rail corridor to remain intact should the railroad ever need it in the future. Railbanking, a process that grants a trail group temporary control of an abandoned corridor, has become a common practice since it was established through 1983 amendments to the National Trails System Act.

A railroad company may sell, donate or lease an inactive corridor to a trail agency that will assume taxes, legal liabilities and maintenance of the corridor. According to the act, the railbanked lines will remain intact because they are treated as if they had not been abandoned. The Surface Transportation Board retains control of the railroad right-of-way.

Congress passed the act to protect the corridors for future rail lines, which would take precedence over the interim trails built on the corridors. Because of increased freight traffic, a few railroad companies have repossessed rail corridors that have been railbanked.

Georgia took advantage of railbanking when the state Department of Transportation paid $7 million for a 57-mile railbanked trail that runs through Cobb, Paulding and Polk counties. The counties partnered with the Georgia Department of Natural Resources, which leased the land on which the counties created a state trail.

"In the past, a railroad would abandon a corridor, and farmers would buy it piece by piece," says Ed McBrayer, executive director of Atlanta-based PATH, a non-profit organization that promotes greenways. "Suddenly, it is strips of land instead of a continuous corridor."

The counties created the Silver Comet Trail to preserve the corridor and to provide recreation resources for their residents. (The trail is named for the Seaboard Coast Line passenger train that operated in the corridor.) Construction began in 1993, and 37½ miles have been completed. Ultimately, the trail will reach Anniston, Ala.

Trail Controversy

Despite their popularity with preservationists and railroad companies, rail-trails have been known to spark conflict. Because valuable land is in question, with many groups and individuals claiming rights to the outcome of the land, controversy is inevitable.

When the B&O Railroad abandoned an 11½ mile corridor in 1985, many groups, including an historical society that wanted to preserve the rail line and another group that wanted to install a light-rail line, had plans for the unused corridor. The Coalition for Capital Crescent Trail in Silver Spring, Md., lobbied for a trail. The process was not easy.

Residents who lived near the rail line had expressed concern about traffic and crime if a trail were built. "Neighborhood communities tend to be nervous with anything they are not familiar with," says Wayne Phyillaier, president of the coalition. "The key is to get them on board, show

them a vision and give them an opportunity to express their views and participate in the process."

The coalition took steps to garner support for the trail. Members visited local communities and civic associations to present their vision of the trail and showed 40 to 50 slides of other trails and pictures of the right-of-way in its current condition.

With the help of RTC and the Washington Area Bicyclist Association, the trail coalition lobbied the National Park Service and the Montgomery County government to build the trail. Convinced that the idea was worthwhile, Montgomery County purchased the railbanked corridor from Silver Spring to the D.C. line in 1988 for $10.5 million. The following year, a local businessman acquired the remaining land and leased it to the National Park Service, which purchased it in 1990.

Local utility Potomac Electric Power and Project Open Space, a non-profit organization in Montgomery County, joined other groups to provide 20 percent of the project budget; the county also received $867,000 in ISTEA funds. The Washington, D.C., section of the trail was constructed and is managed by the National Park Service.

Seven miles of the Capital Crescent Trail have been paved and completed. The trail connects two national park trails — the C & O Canal and the Rock Creek Park Trail. Because the trail also connects Washington, D.C., with its suburbs, commuters use it. "The trail is a good alternative to being stuck in the busy streets," Phyillaier says.

What happens to the remaining three miles is a hotly contested issue between those who want to extend the pedestrian/bike trail and those who want to install a light rail line. While officials are determining its fate, the stretch is serving as an interim trail.

Despite the conflict and hard work involved, communities that attempt rail-trail projects are rewarded for their hard work, Phyillaier says. "When we first built the trail, people were worried," he says. "Now, people have found that it is a great recreational asset."

Communities that want to preserve rail lines and provide additional recreation opportunities for their residents are continuing to build rail-trails; about 1,200 projects are currently under way. Although the trails require hard work and innovation, communities attest that the end result is well worth the effort.

RAILS-TO-TRAILS RESOURCES

Rails to Trails Conservancy, Washington, D.C., offers information for communities interested in building rail-trails. Visit the organization's Web site (www.railtrails.org) to get information on existing trails; to obtain technical information and resources for building trails; or to obtain information about federal funds available for rail-trail development.

Additional articles about rail-trails can be found in *American City & County's* online archives at www.americancityandcounty.com.

CHAPTER 9

ECONOMIC DEVELOPMENT IN THE APPALACHIAN REGION

Howard J. Grossman

Regionalism has entered the "thirty-something" age group. Its form and function have evolved, its ability to perform its original mission of planning has expanded, its funding base has been broadened, and its astonishing capacity for mind stretching has only begun.

While these characteristics represent the hidden strength of sub-state regionalism, very few new regional agencies have been established in recent years. Some regional agencies have significantly expanded their roles while others have not kept pace with the 1990s. In fact, some have folded their tents due to lack of financial resources.

The most intriguing, and perhaps most difficult role for regional agencies is the prospect for changing the nature and structure of regionalism from a purely governmental activity to one that is truly cross-sectoral, as may have been envisioned by the two cataclysmic events of 1965 that prompted establishment of the Appalachian Regional Commission and the Public Works and Economic Development Program. As a result of these initiatives, new regional development agencies were founded in various parts of the nation, and public-private partnerships for rural development encouraged.

Equally difficult may be the introduction of substate regionalism as a true national strategy, stretching across the entire country and involving every county in a participatory planning process for the 21st century. Regionalism, as a definitive national strategy, has not taken a path that guarantees its place in the intergovernmental/cross-sectoral partnership of the coming century. However, it is precisely through a national regional policy and process that a comprehensive and viable vision for U.S. competitiveness, social equity and environmental sustainability could be most easily created.

Clearly, if the president and Congress agreed, such a strategy could be promoted and implemented.

Reinventing Regionalism

Can we reinvent regionalism in the 1990s as David Osborne and Ted Gaebler

---

Originally published as "The Future Is Now: The Case for a National Sub-State Regional Policy," *National Civic Review*, Vol. 83, No. 1, Winter/Spring, 1994. Published by the National Civic League, Denver, Colorado. Reprinted with permission of the publisher.

have stimulated the reinvention of government? The powerful surge of regionalism that occurred in the 1960s may be shifting in the 1990s and more likely in the 21st century toward public-private-nonprofit partnerships whereby the private sector becomes more embedded and deeply involved in regional issues.

How this can be accomplished and the exact structure and form it may take remain to be determined. Sub-state regionalism 1) needs the strength of the private sector; 2) requires delicate relations among all levels of government; 3) is more influential when congressional and state legislative representation is enabled; and 4) is much more powerful in partnership with the private and voluntary sectors.

To gain acceptability, regionalism must constitute a unique institutional framework to supplement — rather than supplant — existing governing institutions, as well as a potent source of positive production, not a bureaucratic impediment.

Achieving this dream will require a strategic vision of where the nation wants to go and how it wants to get there. It requires new thinking beyond the pale of conventional wisdom, which holds that what went on before is what should happen tomorrow.

Local governments are straining under the burden of mounting financial demands. They will not withstand the pressures of service delivery in many regions without securing a new institutional framework. This does not mean local governments must be eliminated or lose identity. It does not mean state government must preempt local government responsibilities. It does not imply a loss of power, either political or financial. It *does* mean those services that can no longer be delivered affordably at the municipal or county levels be provided by renewed and strengthened sub-state regional organizations. It means that certain programs that may traditionally have been provided at the local level be managed and administered at the regional level.

The threat of take over, the threat of job loss and tarnished prestige, the threat of "big brother," and the threat of lost identity all are phantom images that do not do justice to the grand opportunities of regionalism. These opportunities include the proven efficiency and effectiveness gains of regional service delivery and program coordination.

Networking the Nation

The structure of regionalism already varies from state to state and in some cases within states. Uniform legislation exists in a number of states enabling establishment of regional councils in a variety of ways, including executive order of the governor, interstate compact, intergovernmental cooperation, nonprofit incorporation, and a range of other ways. No single format fits the entire nation. By whatever means, sub-state regionalism can flourish only if an appropriate analysis of the entire U.S. intergovernmental structure is conducted and acted upon.

Just as statistics can not tell the whole story of the economy or the quality of life of a given jurisdiction, they can not tell the whole story about regionalism. The professional competence, decision-making capacity, and ability to deal with controversial issues crossing boundary lines are some of the positive characteristics reflecting the best that regionalism can offer. Already, a regional council network exists in most states. The nation, however, is not carpeted with regional councils, and a fractured system can not mobilize the positive forces that a fully unified and standardized system might unleash if it were enabled across the length and breadth of the United States. Orchestrating a uniform, national regional process would make an outstanding contribution to the long-term economic performance and quality of life of the nation. Delivering federal and state services, creating a natural base for data management and a clearinghouse of information, developing regional plans coordinated with state planning and economic growth policies, and, most importantly, establishing a national focus, are only a few advantages of such a networked system.

Regionalization implies a network, and such a network exists in a substantial portion of the nation. Some states have a complete structure of regionalism in which many types of programs are delivered through a sub-state system. Other states have a less comprehensive system, in which only part of the state is served by regional councils.

Federal acts mandated the establishment of what are called, in federal language, local development districts under the Appalachian Act, and economic development districts under the Public Works Act. These measures suggested that economic development could best be stimulated through a multi-jurisdictional system in which decision making would be shared by a variety of local governments within a given region, and in some cases the private sector. In fact, private sector involvement in the administration of development districts was mandated.

Designation of national boundaries can be controversial. When the Appalachian Regional Development Act was framed, some states designated regions as the basis for regional organizations and the delivery of services available through the Appalachian Regional Development Program. Over time, these regional boundaries largely have remained intact. More of a controvers[y] is the issue of whether or not regional councils are another form of government and an obstacle rather than an opportunity. Regional agencies in many places, however, are mature enough that the traditional objection raised to regionalism — that it constitutes another layer of ineffective "big government" — does not hold up vis-a-vis their success in delivering a range of services.

Global Regionalism

A new dimension has been added to the justification for regionalism. This is the global connection. The rhetoric of global interdependence has spread like prairie fire, and now inhabits the language of diplomats, economists and politicians. But it is a language of true meaning. As the nation, thus far unsuccessfully, bids for renewed leadership in a variety of arenas, new strategies must be identified. In economic performance, the United States is no longer at the top of its game, and has fallen behind in a number of other categories, such as health and educational attainment. Sub-state regionalism is not designed to resolve these problems. The severity of problem, however, calls for significant and enlightened leadership for economies of scale and more efficient means of production, as has already taken place in the private sector.

Clarifying the Role of Regional Councils

Down-sizing of government and service delivery mechanisms is possible only through appropriate substitution, such as that offered by sub-state regionalism. Too often, regional councils have been looked upon as paper shufflers and gatekeepers for federal grant programs. While there is a noticeable change in this regard, much more remains to be accomplished. One difficulty, while an asset at the same time, is that regional councils differ in philosophy and responsibility from state to state. Some regional councils focus on economic development, others on transportation and land use. Even the diversity of nomenclature adds complexity to the subject. Known as regional councils, regional planning commissions, economic development districts, councils of government, metropolitan planning organizations, and perhaps three or four other names, these entities will not soon acquire the status of a national treasure unless we can state simply and succinctly what they do. Some attempt is being made to rationalize and clarify this patchwork, but no clear answer is ready to hand. Federal action could introduce some standardization once and for all, identifying sub-state regional councils as instruments of national policy and clearly delineating who they are, what their roles are to be, and how they would interact with the public and private sectors.

As the 21st century approaches, the challenges and opportunities for a true national regional strategy grow more apparent. If anything, the national recession which began sometime around 1990 and continues to plague a great swath of the nation should awaken more public officials and citizens to the benefits and attributes of regionalism. Some of the fiery and controversial words normally associated with regionalism must be appropriately explained. Planning, accepted by many governments today, still is not necessarily an acceptable word in all circles. Since planning is included as a mainstay of regionalism, the meaning of the word and how it translates into appropriate production of goods and services from an economic development and quality-of-life standpoint demands further attention. Since many sub-state regional councils engage in environmental sensitivity, human services, training and education, and planning work, these roles require careful definition.

Obstacles to Success

During the years of the Reagan Administration, regional councils faced serious obstacles to survival. Not only were multistate commissions abolished with the exception of the Appalachian Regional Commission, but regional councils that relied on federal financial support for much of their staffing were thrust into a defensive posi-

tion. Some were eliminated while others had to curtail services. Still, the structure of regionalism was kept alive by the innovation and creativity that have become the hallmark of many regional organizations. Some have displayed the entrepreneurial impulse to deliver new services and become more market-oriented in dealing not only with governments but also the private sector. In fact, the private sector may emerge as the principal advocate of a national policy for regionalism in the United States.

Public-Private Partnerships

Public-private partnerships were the hallmark of economic revitalization throughout much of the 1980s, whereby the private sector actively participated in promoting economic revitalization while utilizing public funds as incentives. In fact, lessons can be learned from the massive changes occurring in Eastern Europe, the privatization growth process occurring in several Latin American nations, and the increasing interest shown by other nations in the public-private partnership model. To a large extent, the success of the Appalachian Regional Development Program, a true partnership among the federal government and 69 local development districts representing 13 states or portions thereof (Alabama, Georgia, Kentucky, Maryland, Mississippi, New York, North Carolina, Ohio, Pennsylvania, South Carolina, Tennessee, Virginia and West Virginia), should rivet attention on the potential of this problem-solving model.

The Appalachian model of regionalism should be stretched and stroked throughout the nation as a unique and structured process that can softly but effectively open new horizons for interjurisdictional governance. The ability to work with governments while working outside the public sector arena to marry private sector programs with government incentives is a beautifully timed, sensitive and sensible arrangement offering the benefits of top-quality services across large geographic expanses. This model also offers the expertise and involvement of the private sector which makes the investment decisions that directly impact the people and institutions of the American landscape.

The post powerful and potent argument for some type of structural change and the development of a national policy for regionalism is the very essence of American ingenuity and growth. The American federal-state-local system has served the nation well, but clearly is not equal to the issues faced by regions today. A national strategy for regionalism means a more disciplined approach to the normally helter-skelter, irrational rivalry among urban, suburban and rural interests, as well as a more rational and responsible decision-making process for those issues that clearly cross boundary lines and resist reconciliation at the local level. Perhaps the most meaningful advantage of regionalism is its ability to bring to the table the major power brokers of the public and private sectors in a given region. While regionalism in its early days brought to the table only government leaders, its more advanced form invites involvement of private sector leaders, although to a large extent regional councils are still predominantly governmental agencies and viewed in that context. If it is assumed that the private sector produces the goods and services that support the economy, the logic of a public-private form of regionalism becomes even more seductive.

Regionalism as a public-private partnership is a different institution from that established 30 years ago. While it is difficult to convince local officials the two sectors should have equal voting rights and status, with appropriate discussion, sensible solutions surely can be found.

The important principle is to recognize reality, utilize all public and private resources, and create, nurture, expand, and enhance the already successful relationships that have been built on the "thirty-something" foundation called sub-state regionalism.

Regionalism and Empowerment

Regionalism is neither an art nor a science. It is, to the extent that federal support is maintained, a tenuous system and strategy. For the most part, regionalism is neither a full-fledged agent of government nor a fully developed private sector force. Regionalism currently is a professional discipline that needs recognition as such. It can be a quasi-public-private-non-profit partnership, although many regional councils, as has been noted, only represent the governmental side. When fully developed, a national regional strategy would enable seemingly unlike areas and diverse opinions to work toward common solutions to a range of issues and problems. While it is very difficult to translate regionalism into appropriate actions that truly can address an issue involving many diverse viewpoints of the public and private sectors, its neutrality, objectivity and professionalism make it a focal point for defining the public good. This assumes appropriate staffing, policy board process and empowerment that help separate regionalism from other disciplines.

Collaboration

The words "partnership" and "collaborative" represent a philosophy and process by which regional councils are legitimate contenders to lead in economic and quality of life improvements. This is true whether or not the region in question is undergoing population growth and economic development or experiencing distress. The strength of regionalism is the very diversity in which appropriate actions can be measured against a particular problem or issue. This does not negate the central roles that other types of organizations play. It is to say that a partnership and collaborative program are key elements within which regional organizations can be partners with others. That most regional organizations are concerned with all factors and aspects of a variety of issues, rather than a single target or function, is a fact that should not go unnoticed as it has in some parts of the nation. A single-issue focus impedes regional councils from pursuing broader courses of action, such as "planning" or "research." Some argue that those words lack specific meaning and that a well structured and carefully contoured educational process is essential.

Conclusion

Thinking local governments are the most logical agents of service delivery because they are "closer to the people" is not a logical response to the societal issues U.S. communities must confront. Thinking that the future will take care of itself without a legitimate process, an action plan or a strategic vision is no solution to the great dilemma facing this nation today and tomorrow.

With the passage of time, regionalism has proved its worth. Its ability to be at the cutting edge of institution building represents a rare opportunity for the nation to turn a new page in planning and development history. A national strategy for regionalism not only represents an opportunity whose time has come, but also a strategic means of regaining international competitiveness and stature.

Editor's Note: Although this regional "flagship" planning agency was created by the federal government nearly four decades ago, the actual implementation of the programs authorized under this federal law (public works and economic development) have been solely implemented by numerous state, county, and municipal governments. For this reason, this chapter is shown in this portion of this volume.

CHAPTER 10

COOPERATIVE TRANSPORTATION PLANNING IN NEW YORK AND NEW JERSEY

Emanuel Tobier

It is not easy to characterize the recent economic performance of the New York metropolitan region, much less speculate about its future. After all, it has changed course rather dramatically several times over the past three decades or so. The expansion of the global economy since the 1970s certainly has provided the region with new opportunities but also has exposed it to a good deal more instability than it faced in the past.

The region is huge, complex, and affluent. As defined by the Regional Plan Association, it has a population of 20 million and sprawls across parts of three states. With a per-capita income one-third above that of the United States as a whole — and accounting for 10 percent of the nation's gross domestic product — it is not a market to be ignored.

The region's complex economy is a product of nature, policy, and history. From its origin in the 17th century as a trading post at the tip of Manhattan Island, the region always has been influenced by the shift-

ing fortunes of the global economy — inevitable, perhaps, when for three centuries its economic life pivoted on its deepwater harbor.

Well into this century, the region's massive, sprawling waterfronts contained busy piers, warehouses, bulk storage and processing facilities, and railroads that received and shipped manufactured goods and commodities to and from all parts of the world. Many products that passed through the port were produced outside the region, but by the late 19th century the region had a considerable manufacturing sector that owed a great deal to the skills, stamina, and entrepreneurial energy of the vast numbers of immigrants who arrived during the 19th and early 20th centuries. The region's manufacturing sector, which was dominated by production of nondurable goods such as apparel, underwent vast expansion between the 1870s and the period just after World War II, when it reached its apogee.

Originally based on the production and distribution of manufactured goods and

Originally published as "New York Revs Its Economic Engines," *Urban Land*, Vol. 56, No. 10, October, 1997. Published by the Urban Land Institute, Washington, D.C. Reprinted with permission of the publisher.

commodities, the region's economy slowly shifted to management and finance — in other words, to the provision of services, which was on the whole [is] a more lucrative line of business. The region's physical infrastructure thus shifted from what were by then extensively developed waterfront and factory districts to central business districts. Of the latter, the most spectacular were skyscraper-dominated midtown and lower Manhattan. By the 1930s, these two districts contained the world's leading concentrations of office space, and they still do today.

Recent Trends

The region's vital signs are encouragingly good. Although its population fell by three percent in the 1970s, it regained that much and a bit more in the 1980s. It has added several hundred thousand more residents during the current decade, putting it over the 20 million mark.

This overall stability, however, gives little hint of the significant changes that have taken place in the composition of the population, among them the replacement of a significant portion of the native-born population by persons born outside the United States. The region (and New York City in particular) continues to be a magnet for newcomers to America. With just 7.5 percent of the nation's population, the region has steadily drawn 20 to 25 percent of all legally admitted immigrants over the past 15 years. In 1970, foreign-born persons accounted for 13 percent of the region's population; by 1996, the figure was 22 percent and rising. (For the nation as a whole, proportions of foreign-born persons were five percent in 1970 and nine percent in 1996.) Accommodating so many newcomers can be difficult, especially for the region's hard-pressed public sector, but the overwhelming consensus is that the latest round of young, energetic immigrants has made a significant contribution to the region's service sector and rejuvenated many fading inner-city neighborhoods.

While the region's population remained virtually unchanged between 1970 and 1995, its labor force — those working or looking for work — grew a great deal more, by 20 percent. The job deficit was greatest in the 1970s, when employment grew by a modest four percent. In the 1980s, by contrast, employment growth of 17 percent outpaced the 14 percent growth in the labor force. Thus far in the 1990s, employment has contracted at twice the rate of the labor force. The result is that the region's unemployment rate, currently about six percent, has been running steadily at between 1.0 to 1.5 percent above that of the United States as a whole.

Employment in the region fell by seven percent between 1989 and 1992, amounting to three-quarters of a million lost jobs. Through 1996, the region appears to have recaptured about 400,000 of those jobs. A decline of this magnitude is a first for the region in the post–World War II period. The feebleness of its economic recovery, particularly in the context of a national economy that currently is in the midst of a seven-year-long expansion, is disconcerting.

However, the region's performance in the 1990s does have some strong points. Between 1989 and 1994 (the latest year for which data are available), inflation-adjusted average earnings advanced by six percent. (Nationally, the figure was under one percent.) In the 1980s, the difference in gains in average earnings was even more striking: up nine percent in the region, down four percent for the nation. These longstanding discrepancies imply that the region has been replacing low-wage with high-wage jobs. This process seems to have taken place across industry lines, but it has proceeded furthest in the financial services industry, in which the region's wage premium rose from

43 percent to 88 percent over a 25-year period. With an economic mix dominated by high-value-added activities, the region's firms can afford to pay above-average wages and still earn above-average profits.

The Challenge of the Global Economy

Will the region's economy lift off in the reasonably near future and climb again as rapidly as it did in the 1980s, when it added 1.6 million jobs? A repetition of those heady days is too much to hope for and certainly unwise to count on. But if caution is in order, pessimism is unwarranted; the signs pointing to further expansion and prosperity are impossible to miss. Tourism, entertainment and leisure activities, financial and information services, upscale retailing, telecommunications, and the media (new, old, and multi-) are big growth industries in the global economy and have a natural affinity for places like New York City.

While the ability of its entrepreneurs to navigate the global economy successfully always has been crucial to the region's economic success, the stakes have been raised considerably during the last few decades. For one thing, there has been an enormous expansion in the scale and relative importance of the global economy. In addition, the global industries that are growing most rapidly and offer the greatest rewards are those that involve the production and exchange of ideas, knowledge, information, and images. The region's movers and shakers need to maintain a significant edge over the competition in that area if the economy is to flourish.

And they had better be keen competitors. This is no longer a largely uncontested market to be divided up among a handful of global economy old boys like New York, London, and Tokyo. Dramatic changes in information and communications technol-ogy have made it possible for a host of new competitors to vie for a piece of the global economic pie. Top prizes will go to those city-regions that offer key participants the kinds of microenvironments they need.

What those might be will depend on the part of the global economy in which they happen to be operating: in other words, different microenvironments for different folks. Purveyors of newly created financial instruments are likely to need a different mix of supporting services and facilities than such global economy denizens as cutting-edge fashion designers or the diverse cast of characters populating the fast-merging worlds of media, culture (high and low), and entertainment.

While each part of the global economy has distinctive requirements, they share the need for many kinds of support facilities and services — libraries, museums, universities, and hospitals are leading examples. But they also need hotels, restaurants, and entertainment options that appeal to a wide range of tastes, interests, and pocketbooks. The winning global city-region will provide them all.

The Importance of the Manhattan CBD

Manhattan's only significant — but still distant — U.S. competitors for global city-region status are Chicago, Boston, San Francisco, and Washington, D.C. In competing for global industries, the region has one outstanding asset: the Manhattan central business district (CBD), defined as the area south of 72nd Street to the Battery. The part of the regional economy that matters most — the export sector — is located there. While many of the region's export firms always have operated outside the CBD and while there has been a steady dispersal of the city's export base to other parts of the region, the Manhattan CBD still represents its chief drawing card.

As of the mid 1990s, Manhattan had about 2.5 million jobs, of which the lion's share was located in the CBD. Close to one of four of the region's jobs are in Manhattan. The importance of Manhattan to the region's economy shows up even more vividly with respect to its contributions to overall earnings. In 1994, Manhattan-based earnings represented one-third of the region's total, slightly higher than its 1979 level and just a bit below its 1969 showing. The average earnings figure for Manhattan was 43 percent above the regional figure as of 1994; a quarter of a century earlier, the Manhattan earnings premium was only 17 percent.

The big question for Manhattan's future and, by implication, for that of the region, is how much agglomeration is economically productive. Does it really make sense to have more than two million people beavering away in a nine-square-mile area? Or will digitized global television and computer networks soon overthrow the ancient tyrannies of time and space, thus making such artifacts as the Manhattan CBD redundant? No one really knows. In the global economy, more and more business will be conducted by electronic means. But the need for face-to-face dealings will continue to grow, and it will make economic and social sense for them to continue to occur in a handful of world-class central business districts.

The Public Sector Role

In a market economy, the identification and provision of inputs needed by global firms to produce and distribute whatever it is they are engaged in can, generally speaking, best be left to those firms. But in the New York metropolitan region, the public sector's role in providing transportation services — subways, buses, suburban transit, air travel, long-distance rail — represents a special case. Given the scale and density of Manhattan, the destination of so many of the region's trips, its economic viability depends on keeping its immensely complicated transportation system in reasonably good working order.

The responsibility for this task is divided among three states, numerous localities, and the federal government. This division of responsibility, implemented through myriad subsidies and regulations, is a sure recipe for conflict and missed opportunities; it is a wonder that it works as well as it does. The negative implications for important sectors of the global economy such as tourism and business travel can best be glimpsed in the still unresolved, long-running dispute over how to link Manhattan directly to the region's major airports through high-quality transit services.

Implications for Development

Predictably, the region's construction activity swooned along with its economy in the early 1990s. While construction has rebounded somewhat, it is still far below its late 1980s' peak. The modest economic gains of the last few years plus the expectation of, at best, comparably modest gains going forward have dampened the spirits of developers, not to mention those of their bankers. But in a region of this size and complexity, opportunities for new construction always will present themselves, and there always will be substantial activity in the capital maintenance and upgrading of the existing building stock.

The area's office sector took the hardest hit as far as new construction is concerned. The contraction in white-collar employment in the early 1990s followed what proved to be an unsustainable surge in new building during the 1980s. By the end of the 1980s, office vacancy rates had reached high double-digit levels in Manhattan as well as in the surrounding suburbs; more recently, they have fallen to the low double-digit levels. But combined with inflation-adjusted asking rents that are half their level a decade earlier, this is unlikely to lead to much new building. Indeed, when white-collar employment heats up in the future, its impact on demand for office space is likely to be less than in the past, as office managers are under constant pressure to use space more efficiently.

Where the region's building stock portfolio is most overweight is in the industrial sector. Manufacturing employment has fallen continuously since the 1950s, and over the last quarter of a century the region's manufacturing jobs have been reduced by half. Many redundant buildings have been put to, or are awaiting, the wrecking ball, but a surprising number, along with office buildings that have seen better days, are finding new uses as residential lofts or hotels.

Last, vast expansion in the leisure and entertainment industries, as reflected in the enormous growth in tourism, has stimulated hotel building in all price ranges. This phenomenon has benefited Manhattan most of all, but it also has spread to nearby areas.

Back to the Future

The region's origins and its economic livelihood for much of its history revolved around the comings and goings at the Port of New York. The considerable decline of the port for shipping, passenger travel, and industrial use throughout the 20th century has, by default, created a major opportunity for the century to come.

In the years ahead, the region has a chance to reorient itself to its waterfronts and waterways by introducing new uses, including those that can be incorporated in old buildings and landscapes. This process is, in fact, already under way. Announcements of major projects in the port are made on an almost monthly basis. While the port of yesteryear was a place of industry and the physical movement of goods, the port of the future will focus on amenities, leisure, and recreation — and on how to attract residents of the surrounding region. Making this happen is a major challenge for a city-region that remains a top contender in the global economy.

CHAPTER 11

CORRIDOR PLANNING IN CALIFORNIA, ILLINOIS, MASSACHUSETTS, MISSISSIPPI, AND OREGON

Pamela Freese

Corridor planning is a familiar tool for transportation infrastructure planning. The concept has also successfully been redefined as a comprehensive tool for a range of planning applications, including economic development, environment, and historic or heritage-related efforts. As the applications continue to diversify and the land-use implications increase, it is important for planners and zoning professionals to be familiar with corridor planning as an effective planning tool.

Corridor Planning Basics

All corridor planning processes share four general characteristics: clearly delineated spatial boundaries, stakeholder participation, a need for authorizing legislation and intergovernmental agreements, and a comprehensive planning process. These characteristics interact differently based on the scope and objectives of each individual corridor planning application.

Spatial Boundaries. Corridor planning efforts have a linear designation, either connecting two points or preserving a large area to maintain unrestrained movement or development within specified boundaries. For example, the Heritage Corridor Planning Council was established in Illinois to consider a highway corridor connecting Interstates 55 and 80. Alternatively, river corridors often prioritize preservation of the aesthetic and ecological elements of waterways, in addition to maintaining healthy waterway linkages.

Stakeholder Participation. Regardless of whether a corridor crosses jurisdictional boundaries, a wide array of stakeholders is often involved, including planners, mayors, developers, environmentalists, property owners, and forest preserve districts. Section 1 of the Indiana Code mandates the creation of a corridor planning board to ensure broad-based representation of the parties. The board must consist of a commissioner, director, representatives from the agricultural and railroad industries, local govern-

Originally published as "The Evolution of Corridor Planning," *Zoning News*, December, 1998. Published by the American Planning Association, Chicago, Illinois. Reprinted with permission of the publisher.

ment representatives, and two other individuals, one of whom must own corridor property. All parties are appointed by the governor, and not more than five members of the board may belong to the same political party. Public participation requirements also attract developers, taxpayers, environmentalists, and other interested stakeholders.

Authorizing Legislation. State legislation can authorize zoning controls helpful in corridor preservation, such as overlay zones, planned unit developments, site plan review, and interim uses employed primarily for transportation corridors. Other planning and zoning tools include discretionary review power, land-use intensity review, comprehensive plan review, density transfers, and development agreements.

Authorizing legislation can also establish a corridor, such as the Mississippi River National Heritage Corridor, created in recognition of the unique and nationally significant resources associated with the Mississippi River. The corridor's planning commission calls for the boundaries to coincide with existing political and administrative boundaries, and that they include the regions of concern or interest to the organizations and individuals involved in the Mississippi River. The recommendation welcomes stakeholder involvement and strives to limit intergovernmental disputes.

Planning Process. Corridor planning traditionally includes identifying the proposed corridor, securing necessary authorizing legislation and intergovernmental agreements, seeking public input, refining corridor goals, identifying funding, and implementation.

The planning process is perhaps most clearly defined in the Transportation Equity Act for the 21st Century (TEA-21) as it applies to transportation planning. TEA-21 calls for all transportation planning efforts requiring federal funding to undergo a Major Investment Study (MIS). The MIS requires that the project area be well-defined,

that the planning process consider all feasible alternatives, and ample opportunities for input be allowed for by all interested parties, including the public. Only when the process has met the designated planning requirements for scope, participation, and evaluation, will funding be approved for the "preferred alternative."

The Northeastern Illinois Planning Commission (NIPC) has defined a corridor planning process encompassing projects that may not require federal funding, but can benefit from the cooperative analysis process. The NIPC approach creates a local corridor planning council representing a diverse range of environmental, municipal, local, and pro- and anti-development perspectives to ensure the best solution.

In Oregon, transportation corridors are defined as broad geographic areas served by various transportation systems that provide important connections between regions of the state for passengers, goods, and services. In Phase 1 of Oregon's corridor planning program, strategies are established to address the goals and policies of the state transportation plan and statewide mode plans. Phase 2 focuses on developing corridor improvement and management elements, and city and county transportation planning. Phase 3 calls for the refinement of all particular land-use, access management, or related issues that demand more in-depth analyses than typically required to prepare a corridor improvement and management plan.

Technology. Advancements in geographic information systems (GIS) allow for faster evaluation, analysis, and presentation of planning elements. Sophisticated technology makes it possible to consider the implications of a proposed project on a wider scale through modeling and illustrative techniques. In Duxbury, Massachusetts, the Metropolitan Area Planning Council implemented GIS technology to better serve its 101 member communities. One of the first applications of the new technology involved defining a one-eighth mile corridor or "buffer" around major transportation networks to guide business location and help in rezoning decisions. The technology improved the speed and quality of analyses while reducing long-term costs.

Corridor Planning Adaptations

Corridor initiatives have evolved into the areas of economic development, tourism, industrial retention, environmental conservation, and historic and heritage preservation. Transportation-related corridor planning projects remain the most common adaptations.

Corridors for Tomorrow, a grassroots environmental organization in Illinois, advocates using highway rights-of-way to provide much needed habitat for native plants, birds, mammals, and insects. Proposed revegetation buffers potentially soak up pollution, capture and store carbon dioxide, filter and dilute dust and exhaust pollution, retard erosion and loss of top soil, prevent siltation of streams, rivers, and lakes, and reduce maintenance practices, including mowing and herbicide application.

Multi purpose public paths created from abandoned railroad corridors, called RailTrails, also build upon obsolete transportation facilities. To date, more than 900 RailTrails (totaling almost 10,000 miles) have been created across the country. RailTrails also serve as historic and wildlife conservation corridors, linking isolated parks and creating greenways through developed areas. According to the Rails-to-Trails Conservancy, many corridors also stimulate local economies by increasing tourism and promoting local business.

Economic Development Corridors

Corridor planning is sometimes used to foster or increase economic development. Integral to each effort is a common thread — often a linear path — that holds the corridor together. The Central North American Trade Corridor Association has as its mission statement "promoting and developing tourism, trade, and commerce throughout the North-South corridor from Alaska and the Port of Churchill through Canada, the United States, and Mexico, with a focus on rural revitalization."

Washington State's 10-mile Technology Corridor caters to master-planned business campuses and advanced technology employers. Developed originally as a marketing tool, the corridor's business parks have attracted more than 200 companies in the last five years, encouraging software, electronics, biotechnology, communications, and computer equipment companies to locate in Snohomish County. The Technology Corridor includes 1,600 acres zoned for research and development, light manufacturing, and technology facilities. Landscaped lots and boulevards, jogging trails, and open space grace the corridor. Employers include well-known firms such as Microsoft and Motorola. Exploiting the region's transportation links, businesses located in the corridor can access shipping ports in Seattle and Everett in less than 30 minutes. Two interstate freeways and five state highways network the corridor to the rest of the state.

Central to the development of the Technology Corridor was cooperation between public planning entities, private developers, and the Snohomish County Economic Development Council, which now markets and promotes the corridor. According to George Sherwin, former Snohomish County planning director, planning and zoning officials worked closely with private sector developers to create a business park ordinance. The ordinance allows for business/industrial uses capable of being constructed, maintained, and operated in a manner uniquely designed to be compatible with adjoining residential, retail, commercial, and other less intensive land uses. The business park ordinance was adopted into the zoning code for Snohomish County. Nearby Bothell, Washington, and Snohomish County amended their comprehensive plans to reflect the new business park classification. Developer involvement pushed the plan forward quickly, making the Technology Corridor an excellent marketing tool and allowing the area to target high-tech companies worldwide.

Seven industrial parks currently share the corridor. Aesthetic standards help to create cohesiveness while retaining individual park identity. The parks have comparable

ingress and egress design, access points, a three-story height limit, building material restrictions, and centralized parking and park-and-ride features. According to Michael Cade of the Economic Development Council, open communication between the public and private entities, especially zoning and planning officials, has been the biggest asset in ensuring the corridor's success.

Chicago's 22 industrial corridors are part of a comprehensive economic development initiative to link predefined industrial areas. Retaining Chicago's ability to meet the needs of industrial interests while allowing for neighborhood growth and development was considered essential in the corridor development plans.

Industrial corridors are a zoning overlay that allows for greater flexibility to meet industry's changing needs. To assure stable

---

FIGURE 1

What Planning and Zoning Professionals Need to Know

Planning and zoning professionals can use corridor planning as tool to inform decision-making on a range of land-use, environmental, and economic development issues. Planners interviewed for this issue of *Zoning News* offer the following six suggestions on what other planners should know about corridors and whom they should be in touch with on this issue:

- Find out if authorizing legislation for establishing corridors exists and what attributes it has. If none exists, explore the option of creating one, using examples from other states.
- Become familiar with the details of other zoning controls, including: zoning overlays, interim uses, density transfers, and development agreements. These tools are beneficial for other planning purposes as well.
- Be familiar with projects underway in your planning department and related departments. Is there potential for using corridor planning techniques to meet a broader range of stakeholder needs and land-use planning objectives?

- Be involved with organizations for developers, planners, and land-use groups to become familiar with relevant stakeholders and their positions and objectives.
- Become familiar with intergovernmental agreements and how they can position the planning organization. Determining each stakeholder's role at the outset of a project can help streamline the planning process and expedite planning and implementation of effective strategies.
- Become familiar with corridor planning terminology and concepts from various applications, such as "functional connectivity."

land use within the corridors, proposals for nonindustrial development in the corridors are required to undergo full review through the planned development process. City planners are given full consideration of the operational needs of existing industries when reviewing proposals to rezone property near industrial corridors and when updating the existing zoning standards for manufacturing districts.

According to Donna Ducharme, former deputy commissioner for the city's Department of Planning and Development, each industrial corridor plan has five objectives: to ensure safety, accessibility and function, competitiveness and marketability, manageability, and attractiveness. Designated improvements to the Ravenswood Model Corridor project improvements include viaduct enhancements, park-and-ride facilities, decorative lighting, an external building improvements program, landscaping, security initiatives, and traffic and public transit studies. A preliminary budget of $1.25 million was proposed for the project.

Species, Environment, and River Conservation Corridors

Conservation-related corridors are defined by the Ninth U.S. Circuit Court of Appeals (1990) as "avenues along which wide-ranging animals can travel, plants can propagate, genetic interchange can occur, populations can move in response to environmental changes and natural disasters, and threatened species can be replenished from other areas."

Protecting core reserves and landscape connectivity for species conservation is the goal of the Sky Island/Greater Gila environmental corridor, spanning from Arizona and New Mexico south to Mexico. An acknowledgement of mating needs and migration patterns of area species prompted a coalition of environmental organizations to support a corridor preservation plan. Plan proponent Andy Holdsworth, Sky Island Alliance's Arizona field coordinator, recognizes the importance of working cooperatively with other stakeholders, including county planning departments in both states and Mexico.

Holdsworth says a critical element in biological corridor development is the need to maintain or restore functional connectivity, or provide flexible corridor boundaries to accommodate species' changing needs. If adopted into actual corridor planning efforts, the concept will require zoning solutions such as overlays and interim uses.

Historic and Heritage Corridors

Also evolving out of corridor planning are historic or heritage linkages. The Royal Missionary Road of the Californias corridor stretches from the Los Cabos region in Mexico north to Sonoma, California. The historical significance of the corridor dates back to the establishment of the Mission Nuestra Senorade Loreto in 1697. Mission and archaeological sites, ancient structures, and important ecological zones add to the corridor's unique heritage. Preservation efforts are being led by a diverse team of stakeholders in Mexico together with a group that represents wide-ranging American interests, including California's parks and recreation department.

In the East, corridor planning was presented in numerous bills to link historic locations such as revolutionary war sites so tourists can more easily follow the history of the region. American heritage corridors would be a "museum without walls," says Connecticut State Representative Sherwood Boehlert (R–New Hartford). The legislation recommended a partnership between the federal and local governments to coordinate corridor improvements such as road signs and better preservation of historic sites.

Corridor Planning Challenges

Achieving broad participation and stakeholder cooperation is a major challenge of corridor planning. In 1992, the Oregon Department of Transportation (ODOT) adopted the Oregon Transportation Plan to address corridor planning. A case study tracked the experience of ODOT in its efforts to develop a corridor plan, parts of which would have to be adopted and/or implemented by 34 local jurisdictions and 4 other state and federal agencies. A key element of the process was the creation of several groups to maximize stakeholder participation. The groups included an intergovernmental policy and coordination committee comprised of an elected official and a key staff member from each of the participating 27 cities and 7 counties, a management-level staff person from each of the four other key states, and federal agencies. Over the next two years, each participating jurisdiction's commitment to the planning process and outcome deepened. ODOT came to recognize the benefits of broad public involvement in decision-making and land-use planning.

Unanticipated outcomes are another common challenge with corridor planning efforts. Recent developments in transportation planning suggest that capturing the true implications of corridor development requires a broader geographic analysis. A 1998 *ITE Journal* report by Decorla-Souza notes "the only way to ensure that all benefits are accounted for is to perform the analysis at the region-wide level." Others argue in defense of corridor planning, noting that regional planning misses many important local considerations, such as neighborhood density and character.

In a June 1998 *Urban Land* article, William Hudnut III, former mayor of Indianapolis and senior fellow at the Urban Land Institute, says "building relationships across boundary lines that traditionally have divided and diminished a community is more important than constructing new systems of government. The emphasis now is on collaboration, networking, engaging, participating and sharing, not on empire building." As an intermediary between regional planning and local planning efforts, corridor planning provides an important perspective to an increasing range of land-use issues.

Organizations and Contacts

Central North American Trade Corridor Association (CNATCA). P.O. Box 1356, Minot, North Dakota 58701.

Corridors for Tomorrow. 607 East Peabody Drive, Champaign, Illinois 61820.

Lower Saluda Scenic River Advisory Council; c/o South Carolina Department of Natural Resources, Land, Water, and Conservation District. 2221 Devine Street, Suite 222, Columbia, South Carolina 29205.

Rails-to-Trails Conservancy. 1100 17th Street, NW, 10th Floor, Washington, DC 20036.

Sky Island Alliance. 1639 East 1st Street, Tucson, Arizona 85719.

Snohomish County Economic Development Council. 728 134th Street SW, Suite 219, Everett, Washington 98204.

Snohomish County Planning and Development Services, 4th Floor, Administration Building, Mail Stop 604, 3000 Rockefeller Avenue, Everett, Washington 98201.

CHAPTER 12

TRANSPORTATION PLANNING FOR GROWTH MANAGEMENT IN CALIFORNIA, NEW JERSEY, AND WASHINGTON

Lawrence D. Frank and Robert T. Dunphy

Because traffic congestion is one of the public's major objections to growth and because extending transportation facilities is necessary to support growth, transportation is an integral component of any smart growth strategy. Growth management most often is politically acceptable when a region is perceived as experiencing extreme traffic congestion, which is usually attributable to unplanned growth. Planners need to propose programs that address these conditions. Once adopted, the programs must be able to weather economic downturns as well as changes in the political composition of the legislature. Growth management programs in the states of Washington and New Jersey and in California's Contra Costa County all have had to withstand political pressures resulting, in part, from periods of economic hardship.

Washington State: Sprawl and Environmental Degradation. The state of Washington has witnessed significant population growth in the latter half of this century, with most growth occurring in the Central Puget Sound region — from 1.5 million in 1960 to 2.8 million in 1990, an 87 percent increase. Employment grew at the even faster rate of 147 percent. More than two-thirds of the growth during the period occurred in the unincorporated areas of the region, while the central cities of Tacoma, Seattle, Renton, and Everett began to show signs of decline. During the 1980s, traffic grew at six percent annually, two to three times the rate of population increase; agricultural land and open space was lost; air, water, and land pollution problems began to appear; and pristine habitats throughout the state began to be degraded, threatening many plant and animal species.

By the late 1980s, the impact of unplanned growth led to elected officials' recognition that growth management had become a popular and in some cases required component of a successful political platform. In 1990, the Washington legislature adopted the Growth Management Act. The unexpected decision was attributable to a political deal: Democrats would support a

---

Originally published as "Smart Growth and Transportation," *Urban Land*, Vol. 57, No. 5, May, 1998. Published by the Urban Land Institute, Washington, D.C. Reprinted with permission of the publisher.

gas tax increase to fund transportation improvements if Republicans supported a growth management bill, including a transportation concurrency provision implemented at the local level.

Contra Costa County: Growth Management as an Afterthought. One of the San Francisco Bay area's fastest-growing localities, Contra Costa County, provides its residents access to jobs in both San Francisco and Silicon Valley in Santa Clara County. A growth management program (GMP) was established in the late 1980s as part of a comprehensive effort to deal with growth and traffic. Bay area jobs surged and growth boomed in the 1980s, just as the tax-cutting fervor of Proposition 13 and other limits on government spending kicked in. California's resulting cuts in highway investment during this period of economic prosperity, coupled with low-density development patterns, made traffic congestion the region's number-one concern. In response, Contra Costa attempted to replicate nearby Santa Clara County's successful sales-tax initiative to raise money for transportation. A 1986 vote for a one-half percent sales tax increase to pay for $1 billion in transportation improvements in Contra Costa failed, however, causing advocates to reexamine their approach.

Proponents learned that a significant portion of the opposition did not object to the tax or the projects but wanted to ensure that new development did not swallow up the increased capacity resulting from transportation improvements. Industry, environmental, and citizen groups were brought together to devise a two-part plan for a one-half percent sales tax increase coupled with a growth management program that would encourage localities to develop plans that might lead to more coherent regional growth. The revised plan, known as Measure C, passed by a 58 percent vote in 1988, promising an estimated $1 billion over 20 years, of which about 40 percent was ear-

marked for highways and arterial roads and 30 percent each for transit and transportation management programs.

New Jersey: Combating Urban Decline and Traffic Congestion. In contrast to the state of Washington and Contra Costa County, there has been limited growth to manage in New Jersey and few governmental programs to manage it. New Jersey had a home-rule tradition of highly local control of planning, and the key actors were municipalities and townships, which covered the entire state. New Jersey has no unincorporated areas.

New Jersey is the most urban state in America. When the state's economic resurgence began in the 1980s, especially along the Route 1 corridor in central New Jersey around Princeton, traffic congestion became an issue. The state needed to do something, given its other pressing problems — the increasing concentration of poverty and minorities in urban areas, crumbling urban infrastructure, spiraling housing costs, loss of farms and open space, and inadequate consideration of spillover effects in local land use decisions.

A state development and redevelopment plan was initiated during Governor Thomas Kean's administration in 1986 and adopted in 1992, under Governor Jim Florio. The current governor, Christine Todd Whitman, who took office in 1994, strongly endorsed the plan, which emphasizes concentrating growth into urban centers — known as "communities of place" — along main transportation corridors, in contrast to the prevailing spread of development to rural areas. The terminology was carefully chosen to avoid more common planning terms such as "urban villages," which were felt to have a negative connotation. The plan is supposed to allow the state to maintain and improve transportation facilities in established urban areas and to avoid expensive and/or underused highways and transit in undeveloped regions.

Organizing to Manage Growth

Washington State. Local control is a cornerstone of Washington's growth management program. The state department of community, trade, and economic development is responsible for implementing growth management. Washington has what is often characterized as a bottom-up growth management program, leaving the balance of power at the local level. Unlike in New Jersey, Oregon, and Florida, there is no state-level plan. The Growth Management Act does, however, provide the state with some review and legal authority. Washington requires *internal* consistency among the elements of the comprehensive plan.

The state's growth management legislation stipulates that a developer must mitigate the effect of a proposed project on transportation along all arterials and transit routes so that within six years they meet a preestablished level of service (LOS). This transportation concurrency requirement is an adaptation of Florida's growth management policies. Each jurisdiction must adopt a concurrency ordinance that establishes an LOS standard on all arterials in its jurisdiction and monitor their performance; transit routes have yet to be addressed. Developers whose projects would bring the LOS below the adopted standard are required to mitigate its impact or improve traffic conditions to comply with the standard. Each jurisdiction also is required to limit transportation plans assumed over a six-year period to projects that are affordable based on current funding levels adjusted for inflation. The intent is to ensure that transportation investments support the land use policies adopted in the jurisdiction's concurrency ordinance and conversely that land use policies support earmarked transportation investments. A Growth Management Hearings Board was established to settle conflicts relating to the implementation of the Growth Management Act.

Contra Costa County. The newly formed Contra Costa Transportation Authority (CCTA) found itself with fresh revenues from Measure C and a mandate to improve transportation and manage growth. The transportation mission was pretty clear, since voters had approved a concise expenditure plan along with funding. The growth management component was less precise. It

---

FIGURE 1
Washington's Growth Management Goals

Because the state of Washington has strong private property rights, local control, and limited capabilities for public sector intervention in the private development process, goals identified in the growth management program represent a balance of public and private sector concerns. Public sector goals include the following:
• Creation of an efficient multimodal transportation network;
• Promotion of sustainable development patterns;
• Preservation of pristine lands;
• Promotion of economic development; and
• Provision of affordable housing to all segments of the population.
Private sector goals stipulate that:
• Private property shall not be taken for public use without just compensation and private property rights shall be protected from arbitrary and discriminatory actions; and
• Applications for both state and local government permits shall be processed in a timely and fair manner to ensure predictability.

consisted of a two-page description — which had been on the ballot — that took two years to develop into a five-volume set of codes to make the program operational. The carrot for local governments was the opportunity to share in 18 percent of the revenues from the sales tax, which were reserved for transportation-related projects — from potholes to bike lanes. That incentive became increasingly attractive as the Bay area boom of the 1980s turned into a bust and tax revenues became increasingly scarce. To comply, local governments needed to adopt LOS standards for streets and a five-year capital program for transportation projects and to participate in a multijurisdictional planning process. Measure C projects would be used to pay for the "past sins" of neglect and to improve congestion for current residents.

Paying for new growth —"future sins"— became the responsibility of new residents through development fees. In the sprawling eastern part of the county, 50,000 new homes are expected to be built. At fees of $5,000 per house, this area is expected to contribute $250 million for the expansion of a state highway from four to eight lanes, including high-occupancy vehicle (HOV) lanes, and for a future Bay Area Rapid Transit (BART) line. According to Martin Engelmann, who manages the GMP, "the impact fee program established in the eastern part of the county represents a major commitment on the part of new development to fund a significant regional facility that will serve as the transportation lifeline to that development. The agency never has to tell project proponents that we don't like their project or that they won't get their project — simply, that if they want it, they will have to pay for it themselves."

New Jersey. A major challenge for New Jersey was gaining localities' support for a state development plan. The state office of planning was established as a division of the state treasury department to oversee the ongoing development and implementation of the state plan; the office is chartered to review and report the progress made toward achieving specific plan goals. Rather than a top-down process such as Florida's, which was recognized as politically unacceptable, or Washington's bottom-up approach, New Jersey chose an informal process called cross-acceptance. Cross-acceptance involves reaching agreements among state, county, and local governments regarding the appropriate level of development for specific land areas. This process is designed to generate a written statement of areas of agreement and disagreement. An update of the state plan, currently underway, is scheduled for adoption next spring.

Influencing Transportation Investment

While the Contra Costa program is focused on raising and spending money on transportation projects, the Washington and New Jersey programs can change state transportation spending priorities to support local growth management plans.

Washington State. Since the implementation of the Growth Management Act in 1994, the Central Puget Sound region has seen rapid growth. A review of the impact of growth management and transportation concurrency ordinances on land use and transportation investment suggests that central cities have been affected less than their suburban counterparts. The city of Redmond, home of Microsoft, is located 15 miles northeast of Seattle. This suburban community, bounded on the east by the adopted urban growth boundary, has nearly met 90 percent of its employment target and 25 percent of its residential growth projected for 2012. Redmond has 42,000 employees, but only approximately one in four resides in Redmond. As a result, a reverse commute has emerged between Seattle and Redmond. Redmond is one of several suburban communities in the area that have experienced significant job growth resulting in complex commute patterns for the region.

As a result of the rapid rate of growth in suburban communities such as Redmond, meeting the concurrency requirement has been a challenge. In many instances, developers in Redmond have to pay the normal impact fees and bankroll projects adopted in the long-range transportation plan for which public funding is not yet available to bring them into compliance with LOS standards. In some instances projects have been delayed and in a few cases even denied, not because their developers were unwilling to pay for additional transportation improvements, but because the city felt that the projects were not in keeping with its comprehensive plan. This is a fundamental growth management issue. The types of improvements that the current vehicle-based level of service method would suggest — for instance, double or even triple left-turn lanes — are not compatible with the type of community that Redmond is trying to cultivate.

Contra Costa. In 1991, the CCTA was designated the county's congestion management agency under a new state-mandated program with goals similar to CCTA's. This gave the transportation authority a say in how federal and state dollars would be spent and enhanced the connection between the growth management program and transportation investments. In addition, the agency has managed to expand the multijurisdictional, cooperative planning process to include adjacent counties, allowing them to openly discuss multicounty transportation issues with counties that are not part of the Bay area. Surprisingly, despite California's reputation as a regulatory hell, there are no state or regionwide growth management programs with any real clout.

The Measure C revenues have had enormous leverage. For example, sales tax revenues paid for the $100 million local match for the BART extension, which cost $500 million. Even the "future sins" money being raised from developer fees is being leveraged. For the three urban portions of the county currently imposing impact fees on new development, it is estimated that a total of $189 million in impact fees will be matched by $214 million in federal and other public funds.

New Jersey. In addition to the state development plan, two major transportation initiatives were adopted to further focus development priorities and state investment. An access management code for developments that need driveways along state highways gives the state even greater say over adjacent development than the state plan, requiring consistency with the department of transportation's (DOT's) functional plan. If a development project requires an extra lane on a state highway or intersection improvements nearby, the developer is responsible for paying a fair share. This code also provides incentives for developers by relaxing LOS standards to encourage development in established centers.

Transportation development districts

FIGURE 2
Robbinsville, New Jersey

Robbinsville, New Jersey, is a small rural village crossroads on a main highway. The town center plan calls for developing the entire area as New Jersey's first pedestrian-oriented, mixed-use community based on neotraditional design principles. It is located in Washington Township, which was an early advocate of the state plan and has developed policies to direct development into compact, mixed-use nodes; preserve open space and farmland; and discourage suburban sprawl. The state DOT has supported plans, which call for on-street parking downtown and reduced traffic speeds on a state highway.

identify areas designated by the county and the DOT commissioner for planned growth and document the transportation infrastructure needed to serve them. A fee schedule is then developed so that development fees will supplement the funding needed to provide adequate multimodal transportation for the area, allowing development to proceed. A new initiative, the Public/Private Partnership Act, signed into law last year, allows the transportation commissioner to negotiate with the private sector to design and/or build transportation projects.

The DOT has been the only state agency to dedicate funding to designated centers. In addition, its programs are reinforced by the federal transportation enhancements program, which took effect as part of the 1991 Intermodal Surface Transportation Efficiency Act (ISTEA), just before the state plan was adopted.

With local agreement on key aspects of the state development plan, Governor Whitman directed state agencies to coordinate their efforts, giving the state plan more clout with the DOT. In establishing the state's transportation program, consistency with the state plan now counts for 25 percent of the weight in DOT's rating system, up from a mere 10 percent when the state plan was first adopted. Other factors, including system preservation, safety, congestion mitigation, and political realities, still count, but the state plan is beginning to affect how transportation dollars are spent. Further reinforcement comes from the three metropolitan planning organizations — the North Jersey Transportation Planning Agency, the South Jersey Transportation Planning Organization, and the Delaware Valley Regional Planning Organization — that also select projects that are consistent with the state plan.

Access management plans are beginning to have an influence as well. A planned connection to the Garden State Parkway is finally under design, and it also will facili-

tate access to expanding retail development in the area. The state was able to develop a comprehensive approach to access permits, rather than reviewing them one at a time as it did in the past. While there has not yet been a thorough cost accounting, John Jennings, supervisory planner for the DOT, feels there has been "more attention to transit and pedestrian projects and greater investments in the older cities, including Camden and Trenton." Despite the state development plan's official support for the older cities, it was not until 1998 that Governor Whitman announced a $400 million program to promote infill development, a strategy that until then only the DOT was backing with its pocketbook.

Results and Lessons

Washington State. While growth management has increased coordination between state and local agencies, it also has met with significant resistance. If the growth management program provides for a timely and predictable permitting process, developers may be strong supporters. Another form of resistance has come from local governments concerned with the impact of development on state-owned highways. They have proven to be very reluctant to include limited-access, state-owned highways in their concurrency ordinances because of the high costs of mitigating that impact and the inability to predict state investment in the roads.

Coordination among adjacent jurisdictions has been hampered by the fact that each local government has adopted a unique system to monitor the level of service on its roadways. The ability to receive credit for diverting some of the traffic generated by new development to transit has been limited because the measures do not give credit for transit access. Broadening the transportation measures beyond traditional LOS measures could give planners a wider range of choices to serve the needs of new development, including public transit and pedestrian and bicycle routes rather than road improvements only. This is essential to ensure that the highway system maintains or exceeds a desired capacity. The city of Renton developed a level of service system based on travel time to address system performance from a multimodal perspective. This first, admittedly limited, approach provides the theoretical basis required to compare the benefits of various investments across a variety of transportation modes.

Contra Costa. While Contra Costa's transportation tax is now ten years old, it was not until 1995 that county and local plans were fully operational. Different parts of the county have developed different levels of tolerance for congestion before requiring mitigation. In the more urban western part of the county, it is accepted that there will be extended periods of congestion during both morning and evening rush hours, continued growth in developed areas, higher congestion as the norm in such areas, and transportation investments that emphasize carpooling incentives and transit. The program also has been successful in reducing distrust between upstream jurisdictions undergoing development and established downstream jurisdictions through which the new traffic passes, by creating forums in which all parties have a say. The program has kept a number of confrontations out of the courts and has brought relative harmony to neighboring jurisdictions that historically were in conflict.

Efforts to push the bounds of development densities have been less successful. Urban village concepts repeatedly have encountered significant backlash from residents who live near transit stations. Ironically, at the Pleasant Hill BART station in Walnut Creek, plans for a major transit-supported retail center have been stalled by residents who, only a few years earlier, had

first bought into the village concept. They argue that higher densities will bring only more traffic, noise, and crime.

Now that the economy is back on track, local programs are doing little to stem the tide of new growth, nor were they designed for that purpose. What the growth management programs have accomplished is to ensure that new development will be approved only if the developers can demonstrate that standards for traffic, police, fire, and other services will be met. Martin Engelmann of the Contra Costa Transportation Authority has said that "this has been somewhat of a disappointment to those people who thought our new programs would put a stop to sprawl on the county's suburban fringes."

New Jersey. The implementation of New Jersey's plan dates only from 1992. The plan was conceived under a Republican administration and a Democratic legislature in good times and had to survive shifting party control and a recession. Funding waned during that time. For the time being, there appears to be good support, with Governor Whitman making the state development plan the centerpiece of her second term and the subject of her inaugural address earlier this year. Building consensus among state and local officials proved difficult, however, even in a state that is so highly urbanized.

Adapting to the new business environment is a significant challenge. The vast majority of New Jersey's growth in such key growth industries as telecommunications, pharmaceuticals, and chemicals has come in corporate campuses outside designated centers, and it creates special transportation challenges. Stephen Dragos, president of the Somerset Alliance for the Future, which serves as the transportation management association for Somerset County, points out that in a state that developed along rail corridors, "the trains run the wrong way today, serving the outbound commuters from New Jersey communities to New York and

Philadelphia, rather than bringing them in to emerging job centers." Even then, getting commuters from the train station to the office requires a route carefully tailored to the needs of office workers, who may not tolerate long waits and slow speeds.

The Bottom Line

Growth management needs to carefully balance the interests of both the public and private sector to survive. To make a difference in transportation, it needs to alter local development policies to significantly reduce the impact of growth on state roads, which would allow current transportation dollars to go further. State governments can use their control of transportation funds to encourage land use actions that are consistent with adopted growth management policies and, in the process, become consistent with these policies themselves.

On the other hand, political expediency could make smart growth policies an excuse to avoid undertaking important transportation improvements. Contra Costa's billion dollars was considered a shot in the arm compared with the $4 billion needed. In New Jersey, a 1991 study by the Foundation of the New Jersey Alliance for Action, Inc.

(just as the state plan was being adopted), estimated infrastructure needs of $10 billion annually, half of which was for transportation, and called for doubling current spending levels. The state of Washington similarly estimated needs for $27 billion over the next 20 years, which represented a $16 billion shortfall from current revenues, or a $9 billion gap assuming historical trends that would imply a gas tax increase.

The Contra Costa County experience, where growth management was an afterthought, illustrates a clear policy on increasing revenues to finance new transportation facilities. Perhaps its lesson, that citizens are willing to pay for new transportation initiatives as long as the increased capacity is not "wasted" on new development, is relevant elsewhere. New Jersey raised additional revenues by a constitutional change dedicating the gas tax to transportation. According to the DOT's John Jennings, "it is easier to make a case for increasing spending to the citizens and the legislature if you can show that it will be spent to support smart growth." Smart transportation will increasingly require that transportation agencies convince the public that new facilities are part of an agreed-upon strategy for managing growth.

CHAPTER 13

WATERSHED MANAGEMENT AND CONSERVATION IN GEORGIA

Kim O'Connell

For decades, the United States has been fighting with Canada and Mexico over rights to rivers along national borders. In the arid West, rapidly growing cities are competing for water rights along state borders in Arizona, California, Colorado and elsewhere.

Even in regions where water has traditionally been plentiful, bitter battles are erupting. Georgia, Alabama and Florida, for example, are wrestling over two river systems that cross state boundaries.

Nationwide, water battles are intensifying, as booming populations, migration to urban areas and chronic drought conditions strain metropolitan water supplies. However, the same phenomenon that has produced conflict also has given rise to cooperation.

Many local governments have begun planning and managing their watersheds regionally. Working with other local jurisdictions, they are addressing stormwater, wastewater, land use and development to ensure that the quantity and quality of water supplies in their regions remain ample.

Common Goals

Two years ago, acting on a statewide directive issued by the Georgia Department of Natural Resources, three Georgia localities embarked on a watershed assessment study to determine how to best protect the region's beleaguered water sources. Gainesville, Forsyth County and Hall County are — like the rest of metropolitan Atlanta — facing a severe water shortage and a water quality crisis. They assessed three different watersheds, with the primary focus on popular Lake Lanier and the Chattahoochee River watershed.

"Watersheds don't know political boundaries, so from a scientific standpoint, it made the most sense [to work together]," says David Dockery, environmental services administrator with the Gainesville Utilities Department. "We also realized that some restrictions on development and watershed protection measures would come out of this study. We wanted to approach it in a regional fashion to not drive development from one side [of the watershed] to the other."

Originally published as "Regionalizing Watershed Management," *American City & County*, Vol. 116, No. 8, June, 2001. Published by the Intertec Publishing Corporation, Atlanta, Georgia. Reprinted with permission of the publisher.

The local governments tested the water chemistry in more than 30 streams. They found that, in urban areas, the streams were affected by altered hydrology, erosion, degraded habitat and sedimentation. Then, using the collected data as a baseline, the governments developed computer models that simulated how future development or other changes would affect the watersheds.

The governments also outlined several options that each could use to protect the watershed. For example, they recommended establishing buffer zones around rivers and streams, building regional detention ponds, improving erosion controls, and using trenches and semi-pervious surfaces to aid in stormwater filtration and groundwater absorption.

The results of the watershed assessment can be applied by each locality individually. For example, in a proposed ordinance, Gainesville is calling for a 100-foot buffer zone, while rural Hall County — where residents are concerned about infringement on private property — is proposing a 50-foot buffer.

"All three entities aren't doing exactly the same thing as far as implementing watershed protection, but we're all basically on the same page," Dockery says. "We're [proposing] ordinances that are seeking the same ends, but the means vary a little from entity to entity."

That flexibility helps stave off resentment, which can result when one or more regional partners dictates what the others should do. Public resentment also is possible, which is why public meetings about regionalization are important. During the assessment, Gainesville and Hall County held 26 public meetings — two for each of the 13 community watersheds identified in the region.

"Politically, no one wants to give up their turf, to a certain extent," Dockery says. "There are also cultural issues — when we're dealing with the way rural folks look at water as opposed to how urban folks look at water. There's a private property rights issue to deal with, and we're sensitive to that."

Dockery notes that the three governments still handle their water supplies separately and that the regional assessment is not part of a source water protection plan. (A separate regional development commission is working on guidelines for source water.) However, he says that protecting the region's watersheds will have peripheral benefits, such as a cleaner water supply.

Inclusion and Education

Cleaning up the water supply was the motivation for forming the Medford Waste Commission early in the 20th century. At the time, the residents of Medford, Ore., were plagued with foul-tasting and odorous water that had tadpoles and other aquatic life floating in it.

Medford is situated within the Bear Creek watershed, which joins the Big Butte Creek and Rogue River watersheds (owned primarily by the U.S. Forest Service and Bureau of Land Management) in making up the Rogue River Valley. Within decades of MWC's formation, the commission had secured rights to groundwater within the Big Butte Creek watershed and rights to surface water within the Rogue River watershed. By default, it became the regional water manager.

The jurisdictional mosaic gets even more complicated, however. The Big Butte Creek and Rogue River watersheds cross three counties, private timberlands and cattle grazing areas.

Building consensus among those entities has been an important part of managing the region's water, says Medford geologist Bob Jones. "It's a long, steady process, and you have to keep working at it," he says. "One of the things that will help you achieve success in working together is having all the main entities, people with jurisdictional authority, at the table at the same time." Talking to stakeholders separately opens the door to miscommunication and suspicion, he notes.

The commission is involved with two local watershed councils, which include a cross-section of stakeholders — environmentalists, loggers, landowners and others. The groups meet monthly to discuss project status and proposals.

Sometimes, projects are put to a simple majority vote, Jones says. When parties are unable to negotiate an agreement, opponents are sometimes willing to step out of the proceedings to let the project continue.

The commission also has undertaken efforts to educate the public about watershed management. For example, it has published brochures with other entities in the region, and it has made door-to-door visits to discuss programs with residents.

"So often people say we need an ordinance to stop something from happening, and I'm not saying that's not sometimes true, but what happens so often is they don't get enforced," Jones says. "So we've taken the tack that it would be better to do an education campaign."

Rather than correcting harmful behavior with short-term punitive responses, the MWC assists stakeholders in identifying ways to eliminate or modify the behavior to produce long-term improvements. For example, when a private entity recently sprayed herbicides that affected a spring in the Big Butte watershed, the Waste Commission convinced the owner to stop spraying over water and to allow monitoring by the commission. In another instance, the commission helped to work out a master plan for cattle grazing that protected particularly sensitive areas of the watershed.

A Matter of Necessity

Long-term, cooperative relationships are key to successful regionalized management, says Chip Norton, watershed manager for Cambridge, Mass. Massachusetts is divided into numerous watershed regions, with much of the populated area around Boston served by the Massachusetts Water Resources Authority. However, since the mid–19th century Cambridge has had its own water supply, drawn from the city and four nearby communities.

Although Cambridge does not supply water to the region, it relies on regional partners to help protect its watershed. "One of our problems is we own five percent of the watershed, so it makes things difficult," Norton says. "A lot of water suppliers own most of their watershed. I think regionalization is a trend that comes out of necessity."

Cambridge has learned to communicate with and rely on the cooperation of other entities and stakeholders in the watershed. As part of the Cambridge Watershed Advisory Committee, the city works with conservation commissions, fire departments, planning boards, sewer departments, health boards and other groups to protect its water supply.

It builds relationships and resolves issues via meetings on a case-by-case basis, and it keeps residents informed through a quarterly newsletter. According to Norton, the city has dealt with a variety of issues, including those related to highway runoff, urbanization and development.

"We're really looking at the next 100 years," he notes. "This water supply has to be here forever."

The Wave of the Future

With chronic water shortages and water quality problems throughout the country, regionalization is likely to become more commonplace, according to Dockery. Instead of staging never-ending turf wars, local governments are now more apt to look for ways to work together.

The process can have several benefits. For example, taking a holistic view of watersheds makes good environmental sense, and, by pooling resources, local governments can implement changes more efficiently and less expensively than they could individually.

Regionalization is not always easy. However, by bringing all stakeholders to the table, local governments can reduce conflicts, build consensus and, in some cases, avoid the time-consuming and politically charged process of developing ordinances.

CHAPTER 14

A STATE AND ITS REGIONS PLAN TOGETHER IN GEORGIA

Susan R. Crow and Gail M. Cowie

Planning for growth management in Georgia is structured by the Georgia Planning Act of 1989. Nationally recognized as a model for growth management and coordinated planning, the act defines an integrated, bottom-up process for comprehensive planning. The process begins at the local level, with subsequent activity at the regional and then state levels. Local comprehensive plans were developed during 1990–1995. Regional plans, drawing on the results of local planning, are currently under development by regional councils (regional development centers [RDCs]) in the state. Regional plans, then, will provide the basis for a state-level planning effort.

In contrast to this emphasis on bottom-up comprehensive planning, the planning act incorporates a different process for natural or historic resources that have regional significance and span multiple local jurisdictions (known as regionally important resources [RIRs]). The act authorizes the Georgia Department of Community Affairs (DCA), working with regional councils, to identify and designate RIRs. Designation requires development of a management strategy specific to that resource. Once the strategy is adopted and final designation is granted by DCA, local governments' proposed actions affecting the RIR are subject to regional review for consistency with the management strategy.

Although partially congruent with the principle of bottom-up planning, this structure places state government and regional councils at the front end of the planning process along with local governments. The lead roles of the state (primarily) and regional councils (secondarily), embedded in a context that emphasizes local primacy, pose substantial challenges in implementation of this portion of Georgia's growth management program. This article describes planning for one resource of regional importance in Georgia, the Pine Mountain Ridge.

In June 1993, the Pine Mountain Ridge was one of four resources selected from more than 150 statewide nominations to receive preliminary RIR designation. Development of a resource management strategy for the

Originally published as "Georgia's Pine Mountain Ridge: Lessons for Regional Planning," *The Regionalist*, Vol. 1, No. 4, Spring, 1996. Published by the National Association of Regional Councils, Washington, D.C. Reprinted with permission of the publisher.

Ridge began in March 1994 and was completed in September 1995. In December 1995, however, planning participants were notified by the DCA board of its decision to suspend RIR designation for the Pine Mountain Ridge for an indefinite period of time. This outcome was particularly unexpected because, throughout the process, the value and vulnerability of the Pine Mountain Ridge was acknowledged by everyone involved. Yet, resistance to the RIR was so significant that final designation was suspended. This experience with the first RIR initiative in Georgia provides some clear lessons for future attempts at regional planning.

Preliminary Designation of the Pine Mountain Ridge RIR

The Pine Mountain Ridge, spanning four counties in west-central Georgia, is approximately 100 miles south of Atlanta in the southernmost mountainous area in Georgia. Rising dramatically from adjacent Piedmont lowlands, the Pine Mountain Ridge is visible for miles, and its slopes offer commanding views of the neighboring countryside. The mountainous character of the ridge makes it host to plant and animal life contrasting with that of surrounding areas.

Much of the ridge is in a natural state that provides area visitors a wilderness-like experience. In addition, the substantial influence of Franklin D. Roosevelt in the Pine Mountain area is apparent in the historically important sites of Pine Mountain Valley and the Little White House. The unique natural features, important cultural resources, and considerable development pressure from Columbus, to the south, and Atlanta, to the north, led to the nomination of Pine Mountain Ridge as one of the state's first RIRs.

The cities and counties with jurisdiction over portions of the Pine Mountain Ridge are members of three regional councils. In 1992, one of these, the Lower Chattahoochee RDC, prepared the initial RIR nomination for a segment of the Pine Mountain Ridge. The boundary specified in the nomination encompassed portions of three counties — Harris, Talbot, and Meriwether. Although the nomination alluded to the historic resources in Warm Springs associated with Franklin Roosevelt, the clear focus of the nomination was the vulnerability of the ridge's natural resource base. In fact, the primary threat to the ridge was said to be its susceptibility to piecemeal loss of character (e.g., from commercial buildings and second home developments).

The nomination was actively supported by the Pine Mountain Trail Association, a non-profit organization based in Columbus, Georgia. The association has a significant presence in the area and supported the nomination as a way to ensure that the natural character of the ridge be maintained and enhanced by excluding commercial development, unnecessary signs, and roadside landscape treatments that interrupt the hardwood canopy along the ridge highway.

Following preliminary designation of the RIR by DCA, the adjacent regional councils, Macintosh Trail and Chattahoochee-Flint RDCs, reviewed the original nomination. Staff from the three RDCs decided that the extent of the RIR should not be limited by the boundary of a single regional council; rather, natural features and historic characteristics should be the determining factors. Their recommendation that the scope of the RIR be expanded beyond the Ridge's natural resource base and that the boundary be changed to include important historic resources associated with the Ridge was subsequently accepted by the Board as part of the preliminary designation. This change in boundary substantially increased the RIR area in the three counties and added a portion of a fourth, Upson County.

Resource Management Planning Process

Following preliminary designation, DCA staff was charged with developing the Resource Management Strategy (RMS) required prior to final designation as an RIR. DCA contracted with the Institute of Community and Area Development (ICAD), a public service unit of The University of Georgia, for assistance. DCA and ICAD worked as partners in developing and implementing a planning process conforming to the RIR program at the state level, yet tailored to the Pine Mountain region.

The planning process for the Pine Mountain Ridge RIR corresponds to the transactive approach to planning conceptualized by John Friedmann (1973). In this stakeholder-centered approach, significant responsibility for development of the plan is placed with those who will be involved in subsequent action steps and those who will be affected by the plan. Planners and other staff support and assist this process but are not the primary decision makers. Transactive planning emphasizes exchange between participants and planners, dialogue, and mutual learning. Ownership of the plan, laying the groundwork for successful implementation, is the goal.

RESOURCE MANAGEMENT STRATEGY COMMITTEE

A transactive approach to developing the resource management strategy is consistent with the intent that the RMS be locally driven. (The locally-driven process also is evident in local resource nomination vs. state resource assessment and nomination.) A Resource Management Strategy committee was formed to accomplish this. RMS committee members were identified by the RDCs through interviews with the initial members and at two regional public meetings. The meetings were held to announce preliminary RIR designation and introduce the resource management planning process. RMS committee members included local elected officials from the four counties; staff from the three RDCs, business and industry (including forestry and agriculture), relevant state and federal agencies, and environmental organizations; planning commissioners and staff; educators; private landowners; local leaders; and interested citizens. Although the majority of members were from the Pine Mountain region or adjacent areas, the group had a diversity of expertise, interests and opinions from federal, state, regional, and local perspectives. The original committee had 40 members; a core group of 19 participated throughout the planning process.

The RMS Committee was formally charged with developing the content of the resource management strategy. Members also were asked to serve as a conduit for information exchange with the general public and their local governments. That is, members were expected to provide information about the RIR and resource management planning, as well as communicate the concerns or ideas of others to the committee for its consideration. It also was expected that a group of local advocates for the RIR would emerge from the committee.

ANTICIPATED PLANNING PROCESS

The anticipated RIR planning process had two specific tasks. The first was to develop the substance of the Resource Management Strategy. Consistent with a transactive planning approach, the committee was asked to generate the content of the management strategy, with DCA and ICAD providing technical and decision-making support. In a series of monthly meetings, the committee addressed the following substantive elements of the RMS:

• Identification of important natural and cultural resources.,

- Development of resource goals and objectives.
- Delineation of the final RIR boundary based on the resources.
- Generation and selection of preferred management strategies for the region.

These elements are intricately linked with one another; therefore, it was expected that individual elements would be re-examined at key points throughout the process in the context of the committee's ongoing work. For example, the initial RIR working boundary might be adjusted in response to identification of specific resources or management strategies.

Modifying the planning sequence became necessary early in the process. Some group members were very uncomfortable dealing with the more abstract concepts of resource goals and objectives. They preferred to delineate a definite boundary for the RIR before considering goals, objectives and strategies. As described below, this decision became a focus of strategic maneuvering as external events began to affect the planning process.

The second aspect of the planning process concerned public involvement. To assist with distribution of information, staff sent out monthly meeting summaries to "interested parties" and to the elected officials in the affected counties. Staff also distributed press releases summarizing monthly meetings to local newspapers. Interested citizens were invited to attend the monthly committee meetings. Early meetings attracted a few observers; some meetings near the end of the planning process attracted more than 30 citizens who actively participated in discussions.

On several occasions, the RMS Committee discussed the need to have greater public input. There was, however, considerable tension within the group about additional public involvement. Committee members expressed a strong desire for greater awareness of the RIR among local elected officials and residents, and they wanted more local citizens involved in the planning process. At the same time, they were reluctant to hold public meetings until they had a product to present. Consequently, they decided to postpone formal public involvement efforts until late in the planning process.

After the committee completed a full draft of the RMS, four public meetings were held (one in each affected county). The meetings were established as informal drop-in sessions designed to provide information to interested citizens, as well as to gather public input regarding the RIR and the RMS. Committee members and DCA staff were present at each of the meetings to explain and discuss RIR planning and the RMS. Copies of the RMS and descriptions of the RIR planning process and the proposed Pine Mountain Ridge RIR were available as handouts.

A questionnaire soliciting public response was distributed and a recorder made available to take citizens' comments. All comments received at each meeting were posted in a central location readily accessible to everyone attending that session. Public meeting participants, RMS committee members, DCA board members, and "interested parties" were subsequently provided verbatim comments from the four meetings. The most significant result of the public meetings was that responses primarily addressed the concept or existence of the RIR rather than the substance of the Pine Mountain Ridge Resource Management Strategy.

External Developments

While the RMS Committee was considering the substantive elements of the management strategy, external developments began to affect their work. Ultimately, these developments had a profound impact on the development of the RMS for Pine Mountain

Ridge. In November 1994, local elections resulted in significant changes in the county commission representatives in the four counties, which affected the RIR in two major ways.

First, the newly-elected officials were uninformed regarding the RIR. As liaisons to local governments, staff from the participating regional councils attempted to inform the new officials about the RIR. DCA staff provided copies of meeting notes and press releases to all elected officials in the four counties. ICAD staff contacted many newly-elected officials, attempting to recruit participants for the RMS Committee. These efforts had limited success in obtaining the active participation of local elected officials in the RIR process.

Second, official elected representatives on the RMS Committee changed. At this time, the committee had met for 10 months, delineated a working RIR boundary, and generated resource management goals and objectives. The group was beginning to identify management strategies, and the change in committee composition was difficult. Some members felt that they were starting over because issues that had been addressed earlier were resurfacing and disrupting the work flow.

Furthermore, one of the new committee members who represented Meriwether County was fundamentally opposed to the RIR. This change was particularly influential in creating a platform for local opposition to the RIR. During initial public meetings and early committee meetings, some local opposition to the RIR was apparent. This opposition, however, was low level and loosely organized. As the planning process progressed, local opponents began to organize. With an ally formally designated as a member of the RMS Committee, local opponents gained a platform and became more vocal.

Corresponding to the national mood, local opposition was expressed as a desire for decreased state involvement in local affairs or decreased governmental intrusion on property rights. Local opposition characterized the RIR as "state control," "other counties telling us what to do," and "the biggest land grab in the history of this state government." These efforts culminated in a petition to withdraw from the RIR, submitted by the Meriwether County Commission to the board of the Department of Community Affairs. Meriwether County commission members also actively lobbied other jurisdictions to withdraw as well.

Strategic Maneuvering and Boundary Changes

As indicated above, the RMS Committee began its work with a proposed RIR boundary delineated by the staffs of the three regional councils. Early in their work, the committee decided to delineate a boundary that encompassed significant natural and cultural resources and was readily discernible to local residents. During the boundary deliberations, a committee member who opposed the RIR saw an opportunity to make the affected region so large that completion of the management plan would be difficult and, more importantly, opposition would be heightened.

Committee members who supported the RIR, however, felt there were strong resource justifications for increasing the boundary. Working with surface features that would be clearly identifiable on the ground (e.g., roads and streams), they agreed to expand the boundary substantially to include an upstream portion of the Flint River, western portions of the Pine Mountain Ridge to Lake Harding on the Alabama border, and the viewshed from Pine Mountain to Oak Mountain. Rationales for inclusion of these areas were river corridor and water quality protection, viewshed protection, recreation benefits, and tourism.

During consideration of management strategies, the committee identified some areas within this expanded boundary as critical to maintaining significant resources and other areas as important or influential. The two designations were important in that more stringent management approaches were indicated for the critical area, while voluntary and educational approaches were seen as sufficient for the surrounding area deemed important to the resource base. This change seemed to make development and implementation of an RMS for the larger area more feasible.

Meriwether County's petition to withdraw from the RIR subsequently led to reconsideration of the boundary as a whole. After difficult discussion, the committee decided to continue to work with the expanded RIR boundary because it reflected the original intent of the RIR program in general and the Pine Mountain Ridge RIR in particular — that is, to develop management strategies for significant regional resources beyond limitations imposed by individual jurisdictional interests. Recognizing the political reality, however, the committee highlighted the portion of the RIR in Meriwether County as an area where implementation of the management plan was likely to be difficult.

The final action regarding the boundary came from the DCA board. Responding to the view that it would be politically impossible to deal with the expanded RIR area, the board issued its first and only interim guidance to the RMS Committee. Despite repeated assurances that the boundary changes were within the committee's purview, the board strongly urged that the committee go back to the original boundary. With great reluctance, resistance to political manipulation, and some sense of anger at the wasted work, the committee acquiesced.

Status of the Pine Mountain Ridge RIR

The activities of the Meriwether County Commission led to several responses by the DCA board. Board members met with the commissioners to hear their concerns, and initiated and participated in a public meeting in the City of Manchester specifically to address Meriwether County residents' concerns. Also, DCA staff met with elected officials in other jurisdictions within the proposed RIR boundary. The board indicated that it would respond officially to the Meriwether County request after the RMS Committee completed its work and submitted the draft Resource Management Strategy for review.

In November 1994, after reviewing the draft RMS and public comments, the DCA board voted

> to suspend regionally important resource (RIR) designation for the Pine Mountain Ridge for an indefinite period of time.... Critical to the board's decision to defer RIR designation for Pine Mountain were assurances given by the six local governments sharing the ridge that they would cooperate in management of Pine Mountain without state involvement. The board decided to honor this commitment to voluntary cooperation by the area local governments by suspending the RIR designation.

However, in the board's resolution, it called upon the area local governments to use the Resource Management Strategy as a guide for planning and decision making on matters affecting the Pine Mountain Ridge.

Lessons Learned

Major criticisms during the development of the Pine Mountain Ridge RIR focused on the very concept of coordinated regional planning. Critics characterized the Pine Mountain Ridge RIR as an invasion of private property rights and another layer of governmental regulation, which was redundant with existing rules and regulations and therefore unneeded. Opponents asserted that local jurisdictions do not want to be told, or to tell other jurisdictions what to do. In addition, some felt that the public was not adequately informed about the RIR and suggested that all landowners within the proposed RIR should have been contacted personally.

These criticisms, along with strategic maneuvering by opponents of regional planning in the Pine Mountain area, ultimately served to block implementation of the RIR as it was originally envisioned. This occurred despite general acknowledgment of the region's unique natural and historic characteristics, substantial concern about the effects of uncoordinated development activities, and significant investment of time and effort by representatives of a number of constituencies. Six lessons for regional planning in contexts like that in Georgia are highlighted below.

Provide incentives for participation in regional planning and clearly communicate anticipated benefits.

Some of the criticisms cited above are powerful and difficult to counter. Most importantly, they suggest the need to communicate clear and tangible benefits or advantages for participation in regional planning. Four benefits are associated with the RIR program in Georgia. Most tangibly, state funding may be available for regional or local actions to implement elements of the resource management strategy. Less tangible benefits include building the capacity for regional coordination and planning, promoting public values associated with resource protection, and enhancing economic growth through appropriate resource management and development guidelines.

Such benefits should be clearly com-

municated from the beginning of the process. In addition, it is important to tailor benefits and messages to the various participant groups — benefits are viewed differently by particular interest groups. For example, elected officials may not view benefits in the same way as the general public.

Obtain endorsements from local jurisdictions and maintain their commitment.

A representative committee of stakeholders is unlikely to provide sufficient local government involvement; therefore, a parallel effort is needed to inform and involve local elected officials. Local government endorsements were obtained prior to beginning work on the Pine Mountain Ridge RIR. However, in spite of significant efforts by staff to inform and involve local officials in the RIR process, their participation in development of the resource management strategy was extremely limited. Also, as demonstrated by the successful lobbying efforts of Meriwether County, local governments may, late in the process, resolve to withdraw from the RIR altogether, undermining considerable effort and expense and fatally affecting the RIR designation.

Since the successful implementation of regional plans often lies in large part with local government, the participation of elected officials and planning agents is critical. Based on the low level of participation on the RMS Committee and the apparent consequences, additional means for involving elected officials in regional planning and ensuring their support throughout the process seem critical.

Define participant roles as clearly as possible at the beginning of the process.

The Pine Mountain Ridge RIR planning process included the RMS Committee, staff from three RDCs, the DCA board and staff, ICAD staff, interested parties, and local elected officials. The following examples illustrate some of the problems with uncertainty in role definition and limited development of some roles.

One aspect of the RMS Committee's role that could have been developed further was in the area of public information exchange. Throughout the process there was tension within the committee regarding public information and input. This problem might have been relieved by developing informal drop-in sessions for local residents to stop by and speak with committee members and staff about the RIR. An informal meeting format might have alleviated some of the tension between the committee's desire for public information and input and its need to have a "product" to present for public comment.

A second example relates to the important and difficult role assumed by the staffs of the regional councils. In the Pine Mountain case, RDC staff was expected to serve multiple functions, some of which conflicted. On the RMS Committee, RDC staff was expected to provide technical expertise. As liaison with local governments, the staff was expected to keep local officials informed and to measure their understanding and support for the RIR/RMS. Serious professional conflicts can result when RDC staff is in the position of advocating a regional planning process and serving elected officials who do not support the effort. In addition to these concerns, the role of the RDC, with regard to dissemination of public information and technical support for the RIR, may require clarification.

Finally, the role of the DCA board in this process was somewhat unclear. This was particularly apparent when the RMS Committee's difficult decision regarding the RIR boundary was essentially voided by the DCA board. To some extent this board decision undermined significant committee work and fueled the fire of RIR opponents. This situation could have been managed more easily if the committee had explicitly understood that the board would provide interim review and guidance throughout RMS development.

Recognize the importance of local advocates.

The process by which RIRs were nominated was designed to demonstrate local support for regional planning. However, since the genesis of such planning efforts can vary, the extent of local support should be assessed carefully. In this case, the Pine Mountain Trail Association, an apparent source of advocates for the project, is actually centered in Muscogee County ... outside the four-county RIR area. The association did not seek to gather support in the RIR counties and, consequently, did not serve as a core advocacy group.

In the absence of an organized advocacy group, it may be desirable to expand support for a regional planning effort by cultivating local advocates beyond local governments. The absence of organized local advocates may make opposition seem greater than it really is. Apparent opposition may serve to intimidate planning committee members and undermine political support for regional planning. Local advocates could serve the very important function of countering or balancing small but vocal opposition to the regional effort.

One of the advantages of a transactive planning process such as this is the potential emergence of strong local advocates for important area resources, as well as for regional coordination and management. There is no guarantee, however, that this will occur in a timely fashion. The benefits of local advocacy for regional planning are clear, and the question of who can or will groom local advocates should be considered early in the planning process, certainly before opposition becomes entrenched.

Recognize regional communication as a significant outcome.

An essential element of Georgia's RIR program is the communication required among local jurisdictions. In the Pine Mountain area, more resistance was demonstrated to the concepts of regional communication and regional review than to any specific elements of the Pine Mountain Ridge RMS. This was true of elected officials as well as private citizens. Some elected officials asserted that they were beholden to their constituents and not people in other counties. They wanted to be responsive to their constituents (avoid needless development delays, red tape, etc.). They did not want to be accountable to residents of other counties for their actions.

Similarly, private landowners were concerned about the loss of private property rights. Some landowners objected to the RIR as an imposition of additional governmental restrictions without compensation. They also asserted that they did not want to have their development plans reviewed, with possible delays and objections from multiple jurisdictions.

Implementation of a regional plan may require profound changes in the way local governments and private citizens do business. Thus, in a program like the RIR initiative, the substance of a Resource Management Strategy may, in the long run, be secondary to establishing a mechanism for communication among local jurisdictions. Such a mechanism is necessary for progress toward regional coordination and planning. Therefore, maintaining a regional communication as a clear and significant goal in developing an RIR, is important. Given the compromise in substantive rigor that is possible in this type of planning effort, this goal may be especially important for committee members and advocates who may become discouraged as the management plan seems significantly compromised.

Balance competing needs to promote local ownership of the regional plan.

The RIR process is, by definition, state-imposed. Current national and local sentiments do not favor big government or additional regulation. Furthermore, the political context in Georgia demands that regional plans or resource management strategies be, to the extent possible, locally developed. The significance of local participation is highlighted by the fact that implementation of many of the RIR's elements is at the discretion of local jurisdictions.

Thus, for regional plans to be meaningful and implementable, adequate time and resources must be invested up front and throughout the process to ensure appropriate local participation and to foster regional communication. Bringing together diverse interests from multiple jurisdictions, however, has inherent difficulties. The process can be facilitated if the planning committee has clear standing and authority for developing the plan or Resource Management Strategy. It is particularly important that the planning committee knows from the beginning what is expected of it, and within what time frame, and has adequate staff support to accomplish its goals.

Although it is critical to invest time and resources to ensure local participation and facilitate regional communication, these efforts must be balanced with the need to complete the planning process in a timely fashion. The Pine Mountain Ridge RIR planning process attempted to ensure local ownership by providing the RMS Committee maximum flexibility in decision making. In retrospect, RIR designation might have been better served by limiting decision choices and expediting the process. In addition, the process depended too heavily on the RMS Committee to meet all planning requirements. In future regional planning initiatives, other means of public outreach, advocacy building, and local government participation will be necessary to expedite the planning process without compromising the critical elements of local ownership and regional communication.

Reference

Friedmann, John. 1973. *Retracking America: A Theory of Transactive Planning.* Garden City, NY: Anchor Press.

CHAPTER 15

ANNEXATIONS AND TAX SHARING AGREEMENTS IN MICHIGAN

William Beach

Annexation battles have created an atmosphere of mistrust between local units of government in Michigan. A state supreme court ruling stating that "no governmental authority, individual, or person has any legally protected interest in the boundaries of a city, village or township"[1] had led Michigan municipalities to the brink of boundary wars. If developers even use the "A" word, townships muster petitions for detachment, not only of the area the developer sought to be annexed, but in some cases, half of the territory of the city itself.

For example, Frenchtown Charter Township adopted a petition to detach about a third of the City of Monroe without a developer in sight. Their rationale was the formation of an aggressive defense against any and all loss of territory due to annexation. Likewise, Williamston Township filed a petition to detach all of the City of Williamston north of the Cedar River, which included the city's wastewater treatment plant and its electric utility. The two units of government were forced into court to stop the detachment election after they had resolved their differences.

To address these and other annexation battles and rekindle peaceful coexistence between cities and townships, the state legislature has proposed several innovative solutions. The legislature's main policy tool has been tax and revenue sharing programs. The State Boundary Commission, which controls boundaries between home rule cities and townships, now is required to attempt to persuade local governmental units to enter into tax-revenue-sharing agreements. Some of those attempts have succeeded, and now, tax-revenue-sharing agreements have emerged as the main tool of boundary mediators in Michigan.

Background

Originally, governmental boundaries were changed in Michigan through a process of petition and referendum. Petitions were filed for annexation with the county clerk. If the signatures were verified, the county commission ordered an election to be held. If the electors in the city, the area to be

Originally published as "Tax Revenue Sharing Agreements in Michigan," *Government Finance Review*, Vol. 16, No. 6, December, 2000. Reprinted with permission of the Government Finance Officers Association, published of *Government Finance Review*, 180 N. Michigan Ave., Suite 800, Chicago IL USA 60601 (312/977-9700, fax: 312/977-4806, e-mail: GFR@gfoa.org) Annual subscription: $30.

transferred, and the township, voted to approve the annexation, the annexation passed. If any one of the affected areas voted it down, the annexation went down with it.

If a petition for detachment of territory from the city was filed, the signatures verified and the election ordered, it only took a majority of all votes cast to make the detachment occur. The resulting inequities only added to the border war fires and caused emotions to boil. The initial solution of the state legislature was to turn over the jurisdiction of home rule cities boundary changes to a State Boundary Commission. It held public hearings, conducted fact finding and attempted to make an equitable decision on each petition filed. The only time a referendum was held was when the number of residents in the transferred area was more than 100 residents. If they numbered more than 100, those residents could call for a referendum, despite the ruling of the State Boundary Commission on the annexation petition. The Boundary Commission's decision could be overturned in that election.

The results of this move did little to slow down the boundary wars. Instead, it breathed new life into the art of gerrymandering. City boundaries began to look like snowflake patterns as boundaries were structured to avoid the 100-resident rule. As more and more of the annexed areas became used for industrial parks and commercial strip malls, the townships felt victimized by having to provide more services with less of a tax base. They continued to lobby the legislature to look for other remedies.

In 1979, the officials at the General Motors (GM) plant in Flint wanted to expand their assembly plant. The only vacant land lay across the border in Genesee Township. GM brought the two local governments together and worked out a contractual arrangement whereby the township would transfer the land to the City of Flint in exchange for a share of the ad valorem property tax revenues collected by the city. With the boundaries so expanded, the city water and sewer could be extended to serve the expanded plant.

Despite the fact that this was a win-win situation for both local governments and General Motors, many questioned the authority of using a contract to skirt the authority of the State Boundary Commission over annexations. There was no recognized statutory authority for contractual annexation between two local units of government at the time. The dissenters were never able to test the strength of their objections, however. The economy took a downturn and the plant was not expanded into the township. The agreement never took effect.

Act 425

The interest in using a contract to affect annexation gave birth to Act 425 of the Public Acts of 1984, creating a procedure whereby two or more local units of government could, by contract, authorize the conditional transfer of property for the purpose and undertaking of an economic development project in the governmental unit to which the property was to be transferred. The act was drafted to define an economic development project as industrial, commercial, or residential development.

The decision to enter into Act 425 agreement has to be made by a majority of the members elected in both local legislatures, after conducting a public hearing on the question before each legislative body. The act does not become effective until 30 days after the public hearing, during which time 20 percent of the registered voters in the transferred area, or 50 percent of the property owners can petition for a referendum on the question. If no petition is filed, or a petition is filed and the election fails to override the votes of both legislatures, Act 425 becomes effective.

Act 425 mandates the inclusion of a number of clauses, including a term not to exceed 50 years (which may be extended an additional 50 years), the method of enforcement, and the manner of termination. The heart and soul of Act 425, however, recognizes that the major basis of annexation fights is the gain or loss of tax revenues. To respond to this issue, Act 425 requires the two governments to establish the amount of tax revenues to be shared by the two units of government. It also requires the agreement to identify the governmental services to be provided by each unit to the transferred area. Ultimately, the act requires the two local governments to decide which unit of government will permanently retain jurisdiction over the property upon the termination of the agreement.

Act 425 agreements immediately became popular. One hundred thirty agreements were entered into between 1985 and 1997. The average length of the 425 agreement was 37.9 years. Townships initially request the maximum time. However, because the current practice is to attempt to establish an urban limit line out in the township under a global agreement, shorter terms are becoming more popular. A majority of the agreements permitted the city to retain permanent jurisdiction over the transferred area upon termination. The average tax revenues shared or given to the township was 1.3 mils. The agreements range from no revenue sharing up to a maximum of 5 mils. One 425 agreement shares 50 percent of all tax revenues from the transferred property between the two local governments. The most often used formula was to give the township the millage they otherwise would have earned on the transferred property as developed with a five-mil add-on as an additional incentive.

Most local officials report that 425 agreements do improve intergovernmental cooperation, minimize the threats of annexation/detachment, and create an environment favorable to economic development. One exception was when all the townships surrounding a city entered into 425 agreements amongst themselves, claiming that the statutory prohibition of annexation of any of the transferred property under the 425 agreement kept the city and the boundary commission from entertaining any further notions of annexation. The courts did not agree with the townships' position. The State Boundary Commission now asks if the petitioner has attempted to secure a 425 agreement with the local governments before filing the annexation petition and it often adjourns the review of the petition pending that step being attempted first.

Act 425 precludes a city from annexing property within the 425 agreement area. Michigan common law requires contiguity of boundaries between the property to be annexed and the city boundary. These provisions in the act prohibit cities from continuing their outward growth if 425 agreements are entered into on all of the city's boundaries. Developers are very cautious about starting a project in the city only to have their development revert late to township jurisdiction. Cities do not want to expend enormous amounts of capital on water and sewer services for property, only to have that property potentially revert to the township.

Act 287

These concerns and other city concerns influenced the state to search for additional means of using tax revenue sharing to solve boundary disputes. That led to the state amending its Urban Cooperation Act in 1987 with Act 287.

The aim of the 1987 amendment to the Urban Cooperation Act was to encourage neighboring communities to work together on economic development projects by reducing the concerns over who would "win" and "lose" in efforts to attract business and industry. It was meant to serve as an alternate, useful tool for dealing with boundary disputes, particularly annexation. The amended act permitted the sharing of property taxes and specific taxes levied in lieu of property taxes on any real and personal property within the annexed area.

Similar to Act 425, an interlocal agreement to share property taxes must specify the duration of the agreement, the method of termination, the formula for sharing the revenue, and a schedule for distribution of tax revenue. It, too, requires passage by a majority of elected legislators, after a public hearing and a referendum period of 45 days in which a referendum could be petitioned by at least eight percent of the registered voters in the local unit. An interlocal agreement would become effective if no referendum was filed within the 45-day period or if it survived the referendum called for within that period of time.

Two things distinguished the use of the interlocal agreement from an Act 425 agreement. First, the Urban Cooperation Act in and of itself is simply a mechanism by which two or more local governments can share tax revenues for activities either one could do on its own. The language of the act does not address boundary changes. To implement an economic development project in conjunction with a transfer of governmental jurisdiction, the two local governments have to covenant in the interlocal agreement to adopt mutual resolutions permitting the transfer of jurisdiction under Section 9(8) of the Home Rule Cities Act. The transfer of jurisdiction takes place only after the approval of the interlocal agreement and the adoption of a separate resolution to allow the annexation of the property. Upon completion of those two steps and the required filings, the property immediately falls within the jurisdiction of the city. The city does not have to wait until the completion of the term of the interlocal agreement before permanent change of jurisdiction takes place as it does under Act 425. Because it permits immediate annexation, Act 287 became the preferred revenue-sharing act requested by developers and by cities.

Second, an interlocal agreement under the Urban Cooperation Act is much more flexible than Act 425. It provides a process to settle inter-jurisdictional disputes by being an inter-jurisdictional act of cooperation. It is also subject to the independent and separate act of each local government. The act requires a majority of votes cast in a referendum of both the township and the city to stop it from occurring. The Urban Cooperation Act applies equally to townships, villages, cities, counties, school districts, state governments, the federal government, and even foreign governments bordering the State of Michigan

Combined Strategy

Some cities have combined the use of both Act 425 and Act 287 in a single agreement. In Richmond, the future outer limit of the city boundary was drawn and a joint planning commission established to create a micro master plan for what they called the Urban Limits Area. As property developed within the Urban Limits Area, it would be annexed to the city so long as it was contiguous to the city boundary. If it was not contiguous, a 425 agreement could be developed in order to provide city utilities to the property until such time as the property became contiguous to the city boundary. The 425 agreement would then terminate and the property would be annexed into the city. The township would receive, as consideration for entering into the agreement, the current operating millage the township would otherwise be entitled to had the property not been included in the Urban Limits Area.

The City of Williamston and Williamston Township entered into several agreements in 2000, which treated an agreed upon, common, transferred area similarly to the way it would be treated under urban cooperation agreements and Act 425 agreements. Residents within certain areas were given the option to permanently become part of the city or township. The monetary consideration for providing water and sewer for economic development projects differed with each agreement from a fixed-dollar amount, to the prevailing township millage rate plus two mils, plus the townships state revenue sharing money, plus the right of special assessment of everything but water and sewer. The services each government provided in each different area changed with each agreement. This solution occurred after an unsuccessful annexation fight and a counter filing of a detachment petition by the township.

Conclusion

Tax revenue sharing has given intergovernmental cooperation in Michigan a new avenue for local governmental cooperation. As long as local communities are willing to discuss economic development between themselves and are willing to discuss the parameters for that development, both Act 425 and the Urban Cooperation Act in Michigan give those local governments the means to accomplish economic development projects and resolve future boundary changes for years to come. Both acts provide the ability to share the economic benefits of economic development through tax and revenue sharing, and Act 425 and Act 287 provide a nationwide model to help local governments resolve the paralysis of urban sprawl.

Notes

1. *Midland Twp v. State Boundary Commission*, 401 Mich 641, 259 NW2d 236 (1977) citing *Hunter v. Pittsburgh*, 207 US 161 (1907).

CHAPTER 16

URBAN PARTNERSHIPS AND REGIONAL COMPETITIVENESS IN VIRGINIA

Roger Richman and James B. Oliver, Jr.

During the past few years a new literature has linked public-private sector collaboration with issues of regional governance.[1] This is an account of some nontraditional policy responses by a traditional state that found itself falling behind economically. It describes the temporary organization that was created and its program aiming at reshaping Virginia public policy toward regional cooperation.[2] It describes the statute that resulted, creating state-supported incentives for regional public-private partnerships within substate regions, and putting into law regional performance benchmarks. Finally, it describes the evolution of a successful strategy that generated support for new policy directions by empirically demonstrating the economic interconnectivities among neighboring localities (cities and suburbs, and among rural communities) and by adopting creative approaches that appealed to the imagination and commitment of the business sector.

A specific objective was adopted from the beginning of this ongoing Virginia program — to introduce and pass in the 1996 state legislative session laws that would improve the state's economic competitiveness by introducing incentives for regional cooperation and by changing old images of adversarial relations among units of local government and between business and government. After two years work the group that was formed, the Urban Partnership, accomplished its primary objective with passage of the Regional Competitiveness Act of 1996.

The law sets out new and untested directions in state support for regional cooperation among local governments, in relations between the state agency implementing the statute and the new regional partnerships, and in the rules guiding public-private partnerships for public purposes in a conservative state. These new directions emphasize state support for the formation of regional partnerships among local governments and

Originally published as "The Urban Partnership and the Development of Virginia's New Regional Competitiveness Act," *The Regionalist*, Vol. 2, No. 1, Spring, 1997. Published by the National Association of Regional Councils, Washington, D.C. Reprinted with permission of the publisher.

business and citizen representatives. The new regional partnerships are provided incentives to begin regional strategic planning programs keyed to local government regional action, and to collaborative intersectoral decision making. To be eligible for continued state funding, partnerships must develop benchmarks of economic competitiveness on a standard set of indicators (specified in the enabling legislation), and must issue "report cards" on their progress toward their objectives. The legislation has a single leading goal — to encourage and support as state policy the formation of regional partnerships building trust and a constituency for positive regional action among neighboring local governments and nongovernmental participants.

What's in the Regional Competitiveness Act?

Virginia's new statute[3] enables and provides state funding for the creation of partnerships of local governments and private sector actors to promote and conduct regional activities. The statute brings together traditional concerns with economic development and job creation with public policy rewarding functional regionalism of local public services. The act provides financial incentives which may be used to guide or support voluntary regional approaches to economic development, education, transportation, human services, land use controls, housing, and other services, and to interjurisdictional revenue sharing.

The new statute goes beyond conventional state and local government support for economic development. It is based on the idea that economic competitiveness is a regional phenomenon; that an individual local government's competitiveness is a function of the overall economic and social well-being of the region of which it is part, and that the economic performance of even

large suburban localities, when compared to peer communities in other metropolitan regions, is linked to the economic health of its own region including its central city. The statute is based on the idea that regions, not localities, compete and that it is in the self interest of each locality in a metropolitan region to take steps to improve the economic and social conditions in all localities in the region. Voluntary movement toward regional provision of public services is proposed in the act as an important step toward reducing interjurisdictional competition and increasing regional competitiveness. Regional economic performance is the measure. The statute is also policy acknowledgment that the state is ultimately affected if regions in Virginia grow more slowly than regions in other states, especially southeastern states. Adoption of the act added the state as an interested party to this unique policy partnership concept that included localities, private business leadership, and now the state.

The new statute enables parties their own regional boundaries, their own community of interest. Existing planning district boundaries (Virginia's equivalent of Council Of Government [COG] or state planning district boundaries) are initially accepted as defining regions; but additional local governments may by agreement be added to the region, and may, with the approval of the state agency charged with implementing the legislation, establish a different regional configuration[4] not employed as predetermined regional boundaries. Thus regions can define their own boundaries, an important element of regional governance.

The act requires qualifying regional partnerships to benchmark their competitiveness using indicators of the long-term economic health of regions, not of short-term measures. Under the statute, regional partnerships must regularly compare their region with competitor regions in other states using three explicit criteria: median family income; job creation; and differences in median family income levels among the localities in the region.[5] Progress toward increasing relative performance on the first two measures, and in decreasing differences in median family income among localities in the same region, are statutory criteria to be evaluated for continued state funding. To be eligible for funding, the state's Department of Housing and Community Development (DHCD) must certify that applicant regional partnerships include, beyond local government officials, representatives of the region's business, educational, and civic leadership in their membership,[6] and that their strategic planning process addresses important regional issues in a regional context.

The statute offers financial incentives to qualifying regions adopting strategic plans promoting functional regionalism. The premise is that increased cooperation among municipalities in urban regions and between public and private sector actors is a prerequisite for making the state more economically competitive. The act sets up a point system for major joint interjurisdictional activities and requires that applicant regions reach 20 points to be eligible for state funding.[7] The point system allows regions to balance past achievements and future efforts, and also assigns points according to difficulty of achievement. It creates a merit system for awarding state incentive funds to regions. Three regional joint activities have a designated value of 10 points (job creation/economic development, regional revenue sharing/growth sharing agreements, and education). A region undertaking two of these activities and receiving full point values for each, would reach the 20-point total necessary for eligibility for state funding. Existing interjurisdictional programs would receive partial but not full point credits. The emphasis is on creating new regional efforts.

Three other regional activities have an assigned value of eight points each (human services, local land use, and housing); and other regional approaches to areawide issues have lower point values (five points — transportation, law enforcement); (four points — solid waste, water and sewer services); (three points — corrections, fire services and emergency medical services); (two points — libraries, parks and recreation). The state agency administering the state funding has considerable discretion in assigning values to these activities. The statute indicates that the agency may determine the significance of each joint activity as measured by fiscal resources committed to it; the number of regional localities participating; the complexity of the activity; the general impact on relations between affected jurisdictions; and other factors including up to five points for joint activities that increase governmental efficiency or lower local property taxes throughout the region.[8]

In its first year, the statute was modestly funded with $3m for the regional partnership incentive fund, with an additional $5m available for approved activities. This funding level is essentially a startup program. With an ultimate goal of $200m dollars per year as regions across the state become certified, the Urban Partnership's objective in the 1997 legislative session is dramatically to increase funding from the current level to $50m for the 1997-98 period.

Inventing a New Direction

How did this innovative statute, which opens many possibilities in regional and city-suburban cooperation, in public-private joint action, and not the least in changing traditional approaches to state-local relations, emerge from a coalition of interests and agendas? The following sections review the odyssey of the Urban Partnership in developing the policy options that led to the legislation. We will see how, through an unfolding process of research, dialogue, political pragmatism, public conference advocacy, negotiations among key actors, and lobbying, the partnership invented itself and its programs.

New Ideas and Virginia's Local Government Structure

In August of 1993, three central city mayors: David Bowers of Roanoke, Walter Kinney of Richmond, and Mason Andrews of Norfolk, met in response to an invitation by Bowers. The Roanoke mayor had read David Rusk's *Cities Without Suburbs*[9] and thought the book's message especially important for Virginia's central cities.

Virginia's structure of local government offers an unusually clear separation of cities and suburbs, with important consequences for the state's central cities. In Virginia, cities and counties are geographically separate. Counties begin where city boundaries end and there is no functional overlap of jurisdictions; even school district boundaries follow local government boundaries. In this structure the central cities are denied even the limited benefits of suburban growth outside their boundaries that accrue to cities in states where county services are provided to city residents. In those settings some cost shifting occurs as service districts include central cities and suburban communities. In Virginia, even more so than in other states, the old central cities have been left behind, participating only in indirect spillover benefits of surrounding suburban growth.

Virginia cities traditionally grew through annexation, transferring land and its tax base and population from counties. Annexation battles in the 1950s through the 1970s were extremely contentious, often embittering interlocal relations for years. Indeed, in southeastern Virginia rural counties became cities

in order to forestall annexations, because state law prohibited one city annexing another. By the late 1970s as suburban communities located in surrounding counties became the state's most populous areas, the legislature made annexation by cities more difficult, and, in certain circumstances, impossible. Finally, in 1987 the legislature established a moratorium on city-initiated annexation, and since has extended it three times. The current moratorium expires in 2000. In essence, Virginia's General Assembly has ended city annexation, but it has not addressed the issues about city-suburban disparities raised by this policy. Fiscal stress in the central cities, with increasing numbers of dependent populations with disproportionate numbers of poor elderly and young children, is compounded by lagging household incomes, and by the location of most new taxable plant and equipment in suburbs. Blocked by the legislature from expanding their boundaries, the future economic and social well-being of the older cities is at risk.

Searching for some means of addressing their cities' needs, the three mayors wondered if David Rusk's analysis could help them. In particular, they focused on his idea of "elastic" cities, cities able to expand their boundaries. The mayors decided to bring their policy experts, city managers, and city attorneys to a second meeting where the issues of the state's control of local government structure and its consequences for the economic and political welfare of the cities were reviewed. The participants felt that Rusk's ideas offered one important way of talking about these issues. Another meeting was scheduled, this time including seven CEOs of large corporations or banks headquartered in the three cities.

The meeting took place in December 1993. The corporate leaders listened to the mayors and from their own perspective added a new dimension to the urban problem. They expressed strong feelings that Virginia and its urban areas were not competing effectively in the nation and internationally. Individually they recounted cases where in other states where they did business local governments cooperated in service provision or else actually merged services, including the public schools, providing more positive business environments than did Virginia's urban areas. The corporate leaders indicated a certain impatience with the level of interjurisdictional conflict they found in Virginia and indicated their interest in improving the state's economic competitiveness by improving its cities. They noted that the Virginia Chamber of Commerce had stated the need to revitalize the state's central cities. In a follow-up meeting in January 1994, the president of the Virginia Chamber of Commerce and his immediate predecessor, the secretary of commerce-designate in the new state administration, indicated support for the group's central themes.

Directed by their mayors, more meetings were initiated by the city managers. Among the city and urban county representatives a consensus emerged that a long-term view, built around making the state more competitive, could provide the basis for a new regional initiative; that all issues should be examined and that a "compelling case" by put together. A commitment was made to set up a process to study the issues rigorously. In subsequent meetings the expanding group, having added officials from three additional central cities — Hampton, Charlottesville, and Alexandria — and new representatives from the private sector, began to put together a consensus view linking the Chamber of Commerce's vision document, David Rusk's assertions, the initial research results from faculty at the University of Virginia on city-county indicators in the Richmond area, and the work of a 1993 report of the Governor's Advisory Commission on the Revitalization of Virginia's Urban Areas. In effect, the working group focused on some

theories and associated data as parameters to outline their discussions. Two city managers were asked to develop a process and scope of work plan to bring back to the full group in March.

At its next meeting the working group adopted an initial mission statement and a work plan to create "...a long-term mechanism to fund the research and development of urban economic policy initiatives and to secure legislative and executive action to achieve implementation of these initiatives..."[10] The work plan recommended establishing a continuing forum to discuss these issues and adoption of an urban policy agenda and strategy, and identified fund raising, research development, and planning functions and recommended that sub-committees be established. The agenda and strategy adopted at the meeting included: recommendations for formally approaching the state Chamber of Commerce's executive board for an endorsement and support; soliciting more municipal members; approaching participating municipalities' governing boards for contributions of $10,000 each; approaching leading corporations for support; establishing the research program; hiring an executive director for the new organization; and establishing a communications program including the announcement of the formation of the Urban Partnership in a news conference in early summer.

The working group endorsed this plan and strategy. In early May, the Business Council, an informal group of chief executive officers of the largest employers in the state, endorsed the new Urban Partnership and agreed to financially match the contributions of local governments. Meanwhile, the group of city managers met to prepare materials describing the organization, its mission, structure, calendar, and other details.

ORGANIZING THE PARTNERSHIP

On July 19, 1994, a news conference in Richmond announced a "partnership for urban Virginia." In attendance were representatives of the state Chamber of Commerce, Virginia Business Council, 11 central cities, and one urban county. The press release described the partnership's image and goals. It was to be joint project with a limited life — "an 18-month collaborative effort" — with goals to "promote a better understanding of how the problems that plague Virginia's urban areas are eroding the economic vitality and competitiveness of the state as a whole, and to develop and gain passage of a highly-specific legislative strategy that will address these problems in a manner that benefits all."[11]

> From its opening public statement the partnership reflected the very interesting idea that it needed to research and define the problems it was seeking to address within 18 months in highly-specific legislation. It had set itself a real challenge.

The new organization began with a large board of directors (44 members), half public sector and half private sector. The board continued to expand as new cities and counties joined the partnership. One year after its founding, 18 of the state's largest municipalities had joined.

An executive committee was appointed, also with equal private and public sector membership. The committee hired Neal Barber, immediate past director of the Virginia Department of Housing and Community Affairs, as its executive director. The committee set an initial target budget of $350,000 for the partnership's activities, which was pledged by board members. Receipts for the first 18 months totaled over $400,000, but ambitious research and communications efforts required additional fundraising efforts.

The Research and Issues Committee

During the partnership's first year the largest workload fell on the research and issues committee, the committee responsible for developing the partnership's policy recommendations. Over the course of a year: it commissioned a series of economic and policy research studies; it sponsored two large well-attended conferences (urban summits); it held regional working group meetings of public and private sector leaders to develop policy options and to synthesize all the material generated; and it convened groups of experts to develop the details of the partnership's policy recommendations.

Led by one of the authors (Oliver), the committee began its work in fall 1994 by soliciting its members' opinions about the urban condition and the future of Virginia's cities. Initial meetings included brainstorming sessions about the real "causes" of the cities' problems including the intractable social conditions associated with the concentration of poverty in central cities. These broad discussions proved frustrating for those public and private sector executives on the committee interested in clearly defined problems to which focused policy prescriptions might be addressed. Yet the more general discussions on race, crime, public education, and joblessness broadened the committee's view of the partnership's agenda. Indeed, realization that traditional governmental policy options would have only limited impact on the dismal conditions of concentrated urban poverty gave impetus to the idea that the statewide partnership needed to advocate state-level support for nontraditional policies. The early discussions about the pathologies of the poorest core city neighborhoods and their impact on perceptions of the urban area as a whole, for example, focused the committee's attention on the issue of neighborhood development. This direction became an im-

portant recommendation in the partnership's legislative package.

BENCHMARKING

In one of its first meetings the partnership's executive committee defined "competitiveness" as an aid to communicating the
organization's objectives. With the chair as
facilitator, corporate and public sector leaders put forward their individual views on
competitiveness. Perhaps unexpectedly, their
views complemented one another and a consensus statement by the chair was adopted.
In the context of Virginia's urban areas, after
reviewing various elements of what "competitiveness" meant to the business persons
in the partnership and what it meant to the
public sector participants, the following
definition was put forward:

(Competitiveness is) ... the ability of a metropolitan area to achieve higher rates of income and job growth, and lower economic
disparity between its central and suburban
sectors than its major competitors by providing an attractive business climate and
quality of life.[12]

Adopting a definition that could be
measured became a persuasive plank in the
ultimate model. Virginia has rarely developed performance measures in its public
policy and this effort may well offer more
general application to other critical Virginia
policy discussions and solutions as well.

The criteria reflect the business and
public sectors' common interests in measures
of individual and community well-being—
calculating personal income growth and job
growth over time. The third measure, the
reduction in disparity in average personal

TABLE 1
Benchmarks for Improving the Competitiveness
of Virginia's Urban Regions

Measurable Impact Criteria (Adopted)
• Growth in personal income
• Employment growth
• Reduction in disparity in personal income, core city relative to suburban communi-
  ties

Additional Impact Criteria Considered (Not Adopted)
• Increased tax base
• Improvement in the business climate
• Improvement in the quality of life
  — fosters regional action
  — improves the efficiency of government
  — reduces social discord or strife
• Deconcentration of the poor

Other Criteria for Evaluating Policy Options
• Operational feasibility and timing
• Political feasibility
• Benefits v. costs
• Win-win or win-lose context
• Short-term v. long-term result

Source: The Urban Partnership. Staff memoranda: Working papers, 1995.

incomes between core cities and their suburbs, was suggested by the results of analyses of census data indicating widening disparities between Virginia's central and
suburban communities, and by Rusk's contention that avoidance of extremes of economic well-being among jurisdictions in a
given metropolitan area will be a positive
factor in regional competitiveness. Published
research had indicated that regions with
higher levels of income disparity between
core cities and suburbs do less well economically than regions with lower disparities within the region.[13] Research commissioned by the partnership supported these
conclusions within Virginia.[14]

Within a few weeks other "impact criteria" for evaluating emerging policy alternatives were suggested by Executive Director Barber, and reviewed by the research
committee. These criteria are identified in
Table 1 as Additional Impact Criteria (Not
Adopted). In essence the committee decided
to focus on three clearly measurable criteria,
indicated at the top of the table.

In addition to the impact criteria, Director Barber offered additional feasibility
and timing, political feasibility, cost and
benefits, win–win or win–lose, short-term
or long-term results. These criteria implic-
itly had great significance as the research
program turned into deliberations on policy
choices. While explicit weighing of policy
options by the committee did not occur
through a formal process, consideration of
these criteria guided the committee's deliberations and their decisions. Moreover, the
partnership's final policy recommendations,
draft legislation, and ultimately the new
statute, adopted the research committee's
three primary criteria as the standard for
evaluating the work of the regional partnerships.

COMMISSIONING RESEARCH

Another principle that the leadership
of the Urban Partnership established was
that all conclusion about findings of competitiveness and its apparent causes need to
be compelling and backed by rigorous empirical analysis. This principle was thought
necessary both to hold the interest of the
business leadership and to weather the vi-
cissitudes of the state legislative process.

As one of its first projects, the research
committee commissioned studies comparing economic growth in Virginia with other
southeastern states and comparing growth
in Virginia's metropolitan regions with growth
patterns in a selected set of similar regions
around the country. The Center for Urban
Development at Virginia Commonwealth
University supported the research effort which
was led by Dr. William Lucy of the University of Virginia. Lucy's reports indicated that
Virginia's economic growth was about average when compared to all states, but that its
growth rate had lagged its peer group of
southern states over the past two decades, and
significantly lagged bordering North Carolina's rapid economic growth. Overall, the
data supported the contention that Virginia's
metropolitan areas have a competitiveness
problem. Comparing, for example, the three
most populous metropolitan regions wholly
within Virginia and North Carolina from
1970–1990 (excluding from the analysis the
Virginia suburbs of Washington, D.C.).
Virginia's regions lagged North Carolina's
regions in growth in personal income per
capita, in growth in earnings per private sector employee, and in employment growth.[15]
No Virginia metropolitan region was found
in the top 10 Southern regions ranked based
on percentage increases in earnings per private sector employee.[16] And only two of six
Virginia regions had earnings per private
sector job growth above the Southeast average in 1988.[17] These and other data presented in reports to the research committee
supported the basic case that Virginia's metropolitan regions were indeed lagging its
neighbors and offered a factual basis for the
partnership's ongoing work.

City-Suburban Comparisons. The research committee asked the university faculty to investigate claims by David Rusk and others that suburban communities have a real stake in the economic success of their core cities. National data had suggested that suburban income levels are in fact linked to the success of the central cities; that regional economic performance is a major factor in suburban success; and that large income disparities between central cities and suburbs are linked to lower average suburban incomes. Dr. Michael Pratt of Virginia Commonwealth University and Dr. William Lucy of the University of Virginia were asked to present their research on this issue using data about Virginia cities and their suburbs. Their work became a mainstay of the partnership's research effort and public communications programs. Dr. Lucy's analyses and graphic presentations documenting the spread of poverty and social problems from the central cities to the inner suburbs made a convincing case that Virginia's central cities and their suburbs' economic and social futures are linked and that municipal boundaries would not confine city problems within city limits. To the extent that competitiveness is affected by the expansion of poverty and of social problems in urban regions, Dr. Lucy's findings suggested that Virginia's urban areas were becoming less competitive than those in neighboring states. Here, clearly, were research results that confirmed the partnership's assumptions.

Citizen Attitude Survey. Another project involved survey research. Soon after its organization, the executive committee suggested that a study of citizen attitudes towards the cities might be of great value in communicating the partnership's message to the state legislature. The research committee contracted with the Survey Research Laboratory at Virginia Commonwealth University for a fair-sized study including telephone interviews with 800 adults plus six

focus groups. The study was performed in November 1994, and results, which generally supported the significance of the cities to all Virginians, were presented at the first Urban Summit Conference in December.

Policy Scans. In October 1994, the research committee approved a set of nine projects relevant to the partnership's concerns. Each of these policy scans, as they were called, was to review both the national "best practices" in the particular subject under review, and Virginia's experience. A set of suggested alternative approaches was requested. Projects in the following subjects were commissioned and performed by academics and/or nationally prominent practitioners with experience in Virginia. These studies, several hundred pages long, proved an ambitious undertaking. They indicate the scope of the partnership's concerns in its formative stage, in effect addressing the

---

TABLE 2
Reports and Studies Commissioned by the Research Committee (Public Policy Scans)

1. Local Government Structural Alternatives for Virginia
2. Revitalizing Virginia's Urban Government Finance
3. Interjurisdictional Revenue and Tax Base Sharing
4. Economic Development
5. Violent Crime in Virginia: Policy Implications for Urban Areas
6. Urban Revitalization for Economic Competitiveness
7. Urban Poverty
8. Community-Based Economic Development
9. A Guide to Regional Governance for Local Study Groups

Source: The Urban Partnership, 1995.

range of urban ills facing the nation. While a few studies proved valuable to the committee's further work, most of the scans had limited direct impact on the partnership's policy development. They were suitable for a continuing urban policy research program, but in the context of the partnership's need for deliberate policy choices suitable for evaluation by the benchmarks it had established, the policy scans were too narrowly focused. Accordingly, the Weldon Cooper Center for Public Service at the University of Virginia was commissioned to produce a "synthesis document" pulling together the recommendations from the individual scans in a common framework. In the end the policy scans and synthesis document raised more questions than they answered and with limited exceptions did not form the base for extended deliberations about policy options. The scans were, however, valuable in a different venue. They were well used in the organization of the first urban summit conference, and other public education materials.

Case Studies. Yet another approach collecting information was made in the form of specially commissioned case studies of local government and private sector interactions in several southeastern cities. Faculty at Norfolk State University performed the case studies, the scope of which were limited by time and funding considerations. Within these practical limitations researchers were able to collect and present background social and economic data and from interviews some anecdotal data about the reasons for the competitive success of those urban regions. While the restricted scope of the cases limited the studies, some suggestive information was developed via interviews with local leaders in urban regions in North Carolina about the necessary preconditions for successful regional collaborative action.

Making Policy Choices: Regional Meetings

By February 1995, six months after its beginning, the research committee had commissioned and received hundreds of pages of studies documenting Virginia's competitiveness problem and reviewing best practices in major traditional public policy arenas. A clear direction for the partnership's policy initiatives had not emerged from these background studies and the research committee, facing deadlines, decided to move in a new direction.

The committee decided to rely on its own members' expertise in Virginia local government. The public sector committee members, city and county managers, took the lead by setting up four regional meetings to select policy directions for the partnership. These individuals invited participants drawing from government, the private sector, or academia in their region. The policy scans were made available as background for the new regional working groups, and the impact criteria and feasibility criteria, the benchmarks developed earlier, were introduced as practical means for considering policy options. The program was to bring together some of the most knowledgeable people in local government affairs in each of the state's four major urban regions for a few hours or a day to come up with their best set of policy options. The results were varied and full of content. They formed the basis for the development of the partnership's emerging legislative program.

The four work groups met separately in March 1995. Each group was charged to develop an "agenda to increase the competitiveness of Virginia's urban areas." One group represented North Virginia, the most populous area of the state, led by the Washington, D.C. suburbs of Fairfax County, Arlington County, and Alexandria city. Another group represented the cities in the Western portion of the state and included representatives from the Roanoke and Charlottesville areas. A third group represented the state capital region, with members from the Richmond and Petersburg areas. The last group represented southeastern Virginia, an urban region including 15 municipalities and 1.4 million residents. Each group developed a distinctive set of recommendations reflecting the views of the leaders addressing unique conditions in their own urban regions. Forming a statewide urban agenda to increase competitiveness clearly would have to integrate the perspectives of different urban environments.

SYNTHESIZING A PARTNERSHIP POSITION

In early April 1995, barely two weeks after completion of the four regional working group meetings, a two-day retreat was held to brief the board of directors and to settle on the partnership's main policy directions. Attending the retreat were the partnership's board and invited mayors and managers, and the presidents and CEOs from some of the largest businesses in Virginia, as well as representatives from small business and the Chamber of Commerce.

On the first day the participants reviewed the results of the regional groups, and, with some difficulty, attempted to define the most important objectives for the coming legislative season. More work refining the options and prioritizing them was needed.

That evening research committee members developed a set of strategic objectives for the partnership, which they presented to the group as a whole the next morning. These objectives were designed to order consideration of the partnership's selection of particular policy directions. They filled a need for consensus about the partnership's direction, though the 50 board members were not yet ready to select particular policy options.

These strategic objectives were refined and presented at a second Urban Summit Conference in June 1995, in Norfolk, Va. Approximately 300 local government, business, and professional groups, and civic association members attended the day-long sessions. Feedback from breakout sessions was positive, supporting the directions set out in the strategic objectives. The most common comment, apart from general support for the effort, was that the objectives needed to be filled out with specific policy proposals, and that the partnership needed to offer specific recommendations to the legislature.

These objectives were then translated into initial policy proposals or a "framework for competitiveness." Four proposals were identified in midsummer:

TABLE 3
Urban Partnership, Strategic Objectives, June 1995

- Increase the economic performance of each region and every locality within the region.
- Decrease the economic disparity among localities and neighborhoods within each region.
- Promote regional and neighborhood endeavors by revising state and local governance structures.
- Develop new systems of governance that utilize partnerships among government, business, educational and community leaders.
- Seek solutions that benefit, wherever possible, all regions and localities of the commonwealth.
- Provide significant incentives to increase regional collaboration, remove barriers to cooperation, and increase regional options.

Source: The Urban Partnership. Urban Summit Brochure, *June 1995.*

- Regional economic development incentives to encourage localities to function as integrated political entities;
- Increased options for restructuring local government;
- Restructuring service responsibility and taxing authority between the state and its local governments
- Continual reinvestment in urban neighborhoods and communities, allowing each to participate in regional growth.

After the board of directors endorsed the strategic objectives, the research committee began developing specific policy options to be translated into legislative strategies and proposals for new and modified statutes. An informal subcommittee led by one of the city managers, Robert O'Neill, of the City of Hampton, began a new process generating policy options. At this point the rather reflective and research-oriented perspective that had dominated the committee's work was replaced with a strategic task orientation. In great measure the April meetings convinced the committee that it was time to move forward with an agenda addressing the state's role in providing competitive urban regions.

From its beginning the partnership had adopted the goal of putting legislation before the state General Assembly for the 1996 legislative session. At a board of directors meeting in February 1995, the communications committee noted that it couldn't develop its lobbying plan until the research and issues committee finished its work on developing the appropriate legislative package. By early summer the gap between the policy development process and development of a legislative package, which lobbyists believed could be adopted was, wide enough for all to be concerned. Under severe time pressure a new pragmatic discipline now shaped the development of the partnership's agenda; past legislative packages

which addressed many of the issues which concerned the partnership, and which had previously considered by the legislature were closely reviewed.

PRIOR LEGISLATIVE INITIATIVES

The 1995 session of Virginia's General Assembly saw several initiatives addressing the regional context for urban issues. The most important, from the viewpoint of the Urban Partnership, enabled local regional planning agencies to create Regional Cooperation Incentive Funds. The fund's purpose is to encourage "...inter-local strategic and functional area planning and other regional cooperative activities..." The act does not specify the form of the Incentive Fund, but directs appropriate executive branch personnel to develop regulations guiding its implementation. In this innovation the research committee saw seeds for the creation of a new program offering strong incentives for interjurisdictional cooperation within the state's urban areas.

The Legislative Agenda

In midsummer 1995, the research committee set up subcommittees addressing three broad policy areas: creation of a regional development incentive fund, and realignment of state/local service and taxing authority; structural options for local government; and neighborhood and community-based solutions. These subcommittees met in July and August and developed recommendations for changes in state law and policy to achieve the partnership's strategic objectives. Some recommendations were controversial, particularly a proposal for financing the regional incentive fund by providing for an optional increase in the state sales tax within metropolitan regions. Another controversial proposal called for changing the state's boundary laws. Subcommittees decided to limit their agendas to the most important issues. In a lively meeting the whole research committee slightly modified the subcommittee recommendations, prioritizing them and de-emphasizing certain controversial recommendations. The research committee then reviewed the recommendations with the partnership's executive board, and after further modifications to eliminate proposals known to be unacceptable to key legislators or the governor (proposals which, if included, would have killed the legislative package), the committee presented its recommendations to the full board of directors at a day-long meeting at the end of September. This meeting was a milestone for the partnership. With a few changes, deleting the tax increase option and certain of the boundary change policy recommendations, the partnership's directors adopted the research committee's report as the partnership's recommended legislative program.

THE REGIONAL DEVELOPMENT INCENTIVE PROPOSAL[18]

This proposal went to the core of the partnership's idea of promoting effective regional cooperation among local governments and the private sector. The original proposal was for significant state-provided financial incentives ($200 million per year) advancing regional perspectives in local government and private sector decisionmaking. Its aim was to encourage but not mandate the formation of functioning regional and metropolitan partnerships across the state engaging in regional strategic planning and regional decisionmaking.

Under the proposal the state was urged to create a regional development incentive fund increasing in four years to $200 million annually to be dispersed by formula to local governments within qualifying urban regions. Eligibility for participation in the incentive fund would be conditioned on two basic criteria for the state's urban regions: creation of a functioning regional partnership, and completion of a strategic regional plan and planning process.

Regional Partnerships. Under the partnership's policy proposals regional partnerships could take various forms from enhanced regional planning districts to traditional nonprofit organizations, to a corporate style regional "holding company." The essential idea required participation from diverse regional stakeholders, e.g., local elected officials, and government administrative officers, civic leaders, business community representatives, and representatives from major local institutions, e.g., higher education and local school systems. The intent of these proposals was to create forums for regional governance able to join public and private policies and able to influence public sector decisionmaking as it affects regional well-being and regional economic performance. The proposed legislation did not prescribe particular partnership structures and it was assumed that such structures will vary significantly among the different urban regions. The regional partnerships were intended to bring public, private, and nonprofit sector leaders together to address important regional issues affecting each metropolitan area.

The second proposed requirement for eligibility for the regional development incentive fund was a regional strategic planning process. The regional partnership, that is, would develop a regional strategic plan to guide and reflect regional policy development and regional cooperative efforts. Each region would delineate its own program for achieving its self-determined regional objectives. Each planning process would include periodic assessments of progress on critical issues in the form of a regional "report card," and each would track the region's progress on the adopted benchmarks: income growth, job creation, and reduction in disparity among localities in median family income.

TABLE 4
Proposed Eligibility Points for Regional Incentive Funds

Regional Revenue/Growth
    Sharing Arrangements .... (10)
Education .... (10)
Human Services .... (8)
Local Land Use .... (8)
Housing .... (8)
Special Education .... (6)
Transportation .... (5)
Law Enforcement .... (5)
Economic Development .... (4)
Solid Waste .... (4)
Water and Sewer Services .... (4)
Corrections .... (3)
Fire Services and Emergency
    Services .... (3)
Libraries .... (2)
Parks and Recreation .... (2)

Source: The Urban Partnership, Draft Legislation, October 1995.

Eligibility for Funding. In Virginia, as in most states, political support for regional governance is weak and state mandates requiring regional approaches to local problems are unpopular. Accordingly, there were no mandates in the partnership's proposals; they were incentive based, relying exclusively on voluntary participation by local governments within metropolitan regions. By creating strong financial incentives for local government participation and by allowing locally-determined strategies to become eligible for participation, the partnership's design was to attract local government support for the regional partnership program.

Under the partnership's initiative, a regional partnership's strategic plan would be submitted to a state agency or commission for approval. The determination of eligibility for the regional incentive funds by this agency would follow legislative standards. This agency or commission would employ the following criteria and weights in evaluating a region's strategic assessment and plans.

Each region would be required to reach 20 points to be eligible for funding, with no more than 50 percent of the total points from activities in place prior to 1996. In its regional strategic plan, each regional partnership would identify regional services it currently provided and future activities it intended to undertake. The state agency determining eligibility for incentive funds would consider the extent to which proposed activities promote the effective provision of services and regional approaches to more fundamental issues requiring regional responses.

Sorting Out Service Delivery and Taxing Authority. The research committee's report also addressed the perception by the business community and local government officials that the existing pattern of government service delivery responsibilities and taxing authority is less effective than it might be. The existing patchwork of service responsibilities evolved in rather an ad hoc fashion. Current imbalances between services that localities are required to provide and the revenues available to provide them impede regional effectiveness. Similarly, partnership members strongly expressed the view that the legislature should "rationalize the array of local taxes and review any adverse impacts on business growth and job creation, and make them uniformly available to all localities."

In its legislative recommendations, the partnership asked the legislature to extend and support its Commission on State and Local Service Responsibility, and to adopt changes that rationalize service responsibilities and tax authorities.

THE NEIGHBORHOOD DEVELOPMENT PROPOSAL

The second of the partnership's legislative proposals deals with neighborhood stabilization and development. As the partnership focused on regional approaches to urban problems, relationships between regions and neighborhoods became more apparent. Where past urban policies focused on declining neighborhoods as targets for remedial projects, the partnership's vision was that urban and suburban neighborhoods are vital elements in the regional economy that can help or hinder the region's well-being.

Strategies to assist declining urban and suburban neighborhoods most fully develop the partnership's theme of a collaborative model that draws upon and combines the resources of government, the private sector, the nonprofit sector, and individual citizens. The key recommendations of the committee in this area are listed below.

State and Local Development Corporations. The partnership proposed to expand the Virginia Community Development Corporation's mission to include support for neighborhood and community revitalization. The legislative proposal called for increased authority for the agency to provide financial, technical, and organizational support to local nonprofit corporations supported by local governments, the private sector, and neighborhood organizations. Recommendations were offered for expanding the mission state, regional, and local development corporations to address critical neighborhood needs for housing, risk capital for small business development, labor force training, etc., including issues that cut across local political boundaries.

STRUCTURAL OPTIONS FOR LOCAL GOVERNMENT

Virginia's structure of local government is unique, with independent cities surrounded by counties. While this historic system has the advantage of simplicity of structure (there is no overlap either of local general governments or of school districts), the system does not allow for the orderly expansion of cities. Increasingly, Virginia's mid-sized cities suffer fiscal stress and an inability to provide adequate services. Because boundary adjustments under this system involve counties actually losing land areas, residents, and tax base to annexing cities, annexation is exceedingly controversial. For over a decade the legislature has set a continuing moratorium on city annexations. This structure of local government creates adversarial city-county relations with much suspicion about future relations. The structure of local government apart from the major urban centers in the state (those areas are not directly affected by this proposal) thus works against the Urban Partnership's theme of regional integration to achieve a better quality of life and competitiveness.

The subject of restructuring local government proved to be a controversial one for the partnership. Modest proposals dealing with specific elements of Virginia's local government law were adopted, including recommendations removing existing barriers to joint revenue sharing and growth sharing programs, and recommendations as an extension of its regional incentives proposal, that the state provide financial incentives to localities that consolidate, merge, or create a regional governance structure. Recommendations for major changes in state law affecting city and county relations were not included in the partnership's legislative package.

Conclusions

Using competitiveness as a metaphor for healthy communities, a powerful coalition of large corporations, the Virginia Chamber of Commerce, and the mayors and city managers of the state's largest cities and urban counties undertook a project to pass legislation offering new directions for the states, cities, and urban regions. After a year-and-a-half program of research, policy development, and negotiation within its membership, the partnership brought forth draft legislation for the 1995/1996 legislative session. An intensive lobbying effort led by a former governor, Linwood Holton, succeeded in passing five bills addressing the Urban Partnership's recommendations. The major piece of legislation, the Regional Competitiveness Act of 1996, closely follows the partnership's policy recommendations. It is remarkable that this radical nontraditional legislation in the contentious area of local government law did not have a sponsor 30 days prior to its passage, yet it passed the House of Delegates 96–4 and the Senate 37–3. Here indeed is a message of hope for coalitions in other states addressing regionalism before state legislatures.

Because Virginia's legislature made an unusual $200 million dollar addition to state formulas for higher education funding in its 1996 session, it limited its initial support for the Regional Competitiveness Act to startup funds. In 1997, the Urban Partnership has set objectives for guiding the rulemaking process for the new statute by the administering agency, the state Department of Housing and Community Development and for raising the funding for the Regional Incentive Funds to $50 million per year.

The success of the Regional Competitiveness Act will be determined by the quality of the regional partnership initiatives that it stimulates around the state. One large urban area, the Hampton Roads area in southeastern Virginia, established its Hampton Roads Partnership soon after the passage of the state legislation. Its agenda includes making its large port the most competitive in the country, and promoting regional approaches to tourism and to attracting a national sports franchise. Other regions are beginning to consider the advantages of establishing regional partnerships that include new stakeholders and that go beyond traditional economic development activities and beyond traditional federal- and state-mandated regional boards and councils for categorical programs. The new statute enables and financially supports voluntary innovations in regional governance in Virginia. It is an experiment in which cities and suburbs and nongovernmental interests are encouraged, with state incentive funds, to move toward regional strategic planning to improve the economic and social well-being of whole regions. It is a very interesting experiment that many promote functional regionalism in areas beyond infrastructure services, and may promote innovations in local government organization without recourse to unpopular consolidations and regional governments.

Notes

1. See, for example, Harry West, "VISION 2020: Key to Regionalism in the Atlanta Region." *The Regionalist*, 1:3, Fall, 1995; Ronald D. McNeil, "Partners in the Marketplace: A New Model of Business-Civic Leadership," *National Civic Review*, 82:2, Summer-Fall, 1995; Allan D. Wallis, "Governance and the Civic Infrastructure of Metropolitan Regions," *National Civic Review*, 80:2, Spring, 1993; Jan Grell and Gary Cappert, "The New Civic Infrastructure: Intersectoral Collaboration and the Decision-Making Process," *National Civic Review*, 80:2, Spring, 1993; John Stuart Hall and Louis F. Weschler, "The Phoenix Futures Forum: Creating Vision, Implanting Community," *National Civic Review*, 80:2, Spring, 1993.

2. The Urban Partnership, the organization that was formed, was sponsored by a coalition of Virginia cities and the Virginia Chamber of Commerce as a two-year project. The partnership's public sector membership includes the following cities and counties: Arlington County, Charlottesville, Chesterfield County, Danville, Fairfax County, Hampton, Hopewell, Lynchburg, Martinsville, Newport News, Norfolk, Portsmouth, Richmond, Roanoke, Roanoke County, Virginia Beach, and Winchester.

3. Title 15.1. Chapter 26.3, Sections 15.1-1227.1 to 15.1-1227.5.

4. Title 15.1. Chapter 26.3, Section 15.1-227.2 Definitions.

5. *Ibid.* Section 15.1-1227.4 Eligibility Criteria for incentive payments.

6. *Ibid.* Section 15.1-1227.4 Eligibility Criteria for incentive payments.

7. *Ibid.* Section 15.1-1227.5 Assignment of weights for functional activities.

8. *Ibid.* Section 15.1-1227.5 Assignment of weights for functional activities.

9. Rusk, David. 1993. *Cities Without Suburbs.* Baltimore: The Johns Hopkins University Press (Distributor).

10. Minutes, Working Group, March/April 1994, Urban Partnership Files.

11. "The Urban Partnership." 1995. *The Notebook.* Richmond, Va.: The Urban Partnership, The Virginia Chamber of Commerce.

12. *Ibid.*

13. Barnes, William and Larry Ledebur. 1993. *Local Economies: The U.S. Common Market of Local Economic Regions.* Washington, D.C.: National League of Cities.

14. Lucy, William H. and David L. Phillips. "Assets, Liabilities, and Economic Performance in Metropolitan Areas in Virginia and the South." Report to the Virginia Center for Urban Development. Virginia Commonwealth University, June, 1995.

15. Lucy, William H. and David L. Phillips. "The Economic Competitiveness of Virginia's Metropolitan Areas." Report to the Virginia Center for Urban Development, Virginia Commonwealth University, 1995.

16. *Ibid.*

17. *Ibid.*

18. The Partnership's legislative proposals may be found in "Draft Legislative Proposals, The Urban Partnership, November 9, 1995," Working Paper, The Urban Partnership, Richmond, Va., November 1995.

CHAPTER 17

Waterfront Planning Along the Hudson River in New Jersey

David Wallace

At a time when examples of regional coordination are hard to find in the U.S., it is reassuring to know that state and local governments and private entities can, in fact, work together. A case in point: The Hudson River waterfront, the narrow strip of land in Manhattan's shadow that within two decades has been transformed from an environmental wasteland to New Jersey's gold coast.

I've been watching the evolution of the New Jersey waterfront with fascination since 1982 when Russell Myers, then the state's parks and forestry director, asked me to redo another consultant's master plan for Liberty State Park. I had been recommended on the basis of our firm's plan for Baltimore's Inner Harbor, which had been judged a success.

A Mess

In the 1970s, the New Jersey waterfront was littered with empty factories and derelict piers. Obsolete rail lines and yards occupied nearly 1,900 acres — almost half of the waterfront region. The shipping indus-

try had moved to Newark Bay in Port Elizabeth.

A series of state initiatives, local redevelopment programs, and a federal harbor cleanup followed. By the time I arrived, the cleared waterfront was becoming a magnet for developers. A 1985 inventory showed that some 33 million square feet of office and commercial space were proposed in seven of the nine waterfront communities, from Edgewater south to Bayonne. In addition, almost 35,500 dwelling units, 3,600 hotel rooms, and 4,500 boat slips were in planning.

Caught unawares, the waterfront communities had no mechanisms to offer a coordinated, regional response to the development pressure — or to ensure public access to the waterfront. Local leaders favored growth but were leery of its consequences. The state's proposal for a regional waterfront authority similar to the Hackensack Meadowlands Commission was greeted unenthusiastically, to say the least.

Originally published as "Riverfront Reborn," *Planning*, Vol. 64, No. 5, May, 1998. Published by the American Planning Association, Chicago, Illinois. Reprinted with permission of the publisher.

The State Acts

It was then that the state came up with three regional initiatives — a regional transportation plan, waterfront zone design guidelines and a waterfront walkway. All three were accepted and alleviated at least some of the problems.

In my view, these initiatives, which worked together to help both local governments and developers, represent the best that can be done in the way of regional planning absent regional authority and in a state where home rule is nothing short of a sacred cow.

The first initiative — the regional transportation plan — was commissioned by the New Jersey Department of Transportation. It called for a north-south waterfront highway connecting the waterfront municipalities to each other and to the interstate highway network.

The southern portion of the waterfront highway, from Jersey City to Bayonne, is already in place, except for two short segments. The 7.5-mile northern section is being built as development proceeds.

The transportation plan also called for a bus and light rail "transitway" (LRT) from Edgewater to Jersey City. As I write, land acquisition is proceeding — for the Hudson-Bergen Light Rail Transit System. The line is being built under an unusual turnkey arrangement by a consortium led by the Raytheon Company for New Jersey Transit.

Coincidentally, it was the transit agency's chief planner, Al Harf, who proposed the line when he worked for Parsons Brinckerhoff Quade & Douglas, which is now in charge of designing it. The current route, however, differs substantially from what Harf initially conceived.

One difference is that the northern segment from Weehawken to Edgewater won't run along the waterfront. Buses will serve that segment. The official reason is that there is more ridership potential in Bergen County. I think there's potential for both bus and rail and hope the northern routing of the LRT will be reconsidered in a later phase.

It's also troubling that the first phase is so short — only seven miles of the 22.6-mile system. But New Jersey Transit has already invested some $66 million in modernizing its three PATH (Port Authority Trans Hudson) stations in Jersey City. And I'm hoping that Phase I will prove politically popular and create a demand for more. But then, I've always been an optimist.

Walking the Waterfront

The second regional initiative was the creation of a regional waterfront zone, within which the Department of Environmental Protection was given power to approve waterfront development permits and to prepare design guidelines. As the third initiative, the environmental protection agency commissioned a waterfront walkway plan. I prepared the plan, which calls for developers to build and pay for a 36-foot-wide walkway, thus guaranteeing public access to the river.

To date, just over half of the 18.6-mile walkway has been built, and another 3.6 miles are committed. My firm has designed three segments — at Liberty State Park and Exchange Place in Jersey City, and at Lincoln Harbor in Weehawken — about three miles in all. We also take credit for the original idea, which came from a similar proposal in our 1966 plan for Lower Manhattan.

But the honor for getting the walkway built goes in large part to William Neyenhouse, who for 10 years has served as the Hudson River Waterfront Coordinator for the coastal resources division of the environmental protection department.

Even though it is being completed in a somewhat piecemeal fashion, the walkway has brought significant continuity to the entire waterfront. It is also part of a regional open space network uniting the waterfront's two outstanding regional facilities, Liberty State Park and the Palisades Interstate Park.

Opportunities

So far, so good. But clearly there are more opportunities for creating memorable urban places along the Hudson waterfront.

Weehawken is one such opportunity. It is at the southern end, where the high cliffs that stretch six miles north to the George Washington Bridge are close to the river.

Most of the communities along this stretch of the waterfront — Edgewater, North Bergen, Guttenberg, West New York, and Weehawken — have been dedicated to keeping building heights below the viewline from the top of the cliffs, which range from 150 to 300 feet. Just west of Edgewater, in Cliffside Park and Fort Lee, 30-story residential towers were built on top of the cliffs, dominating the skyline.

Port Imperial North in West New York is under construction, with a planned build-out of 4,360 residential units. And in Weehawken, the 80-acre Port Imperial South project, now in the planning stage, will include 2,000 new dwelling units, 2 million square feet of office and commercial space, and a ferry terminal. This site is a natural for a real urban center. I'll be watching to see what happens.

Hoboken, at the center of the overall waterfront "opportunity zone," is another city rich in possibilities. Hoboken is very much a brownstone copy of historic Brooklyn across the river, and the city has been slow to allow waterfront development to proceed.

But that's not to say that nothing is happening. Construction has started on a residential complex on the 45-acre site once occupied by the Bethlehem Shipyard. So far,

I'm sorry to report, the slablike buildings being erected at river's edge are not promising. To the south, below Castle Point, the city and the Port Authority of New York and New Jersey have selected developers for a 50-acre mixed-use development. Detailed design is now under way.

In the last few years, Hoboken officials have turned down several dramatic development proposals for waterfront sites, including the ferry terminal and the New Jersey Transit railyard. In this case, the city recognizes that a new master plan is needed so that this opportunity will not be eroded by short-term, uncoordinated actions.

Jersey City also suffers from uncoordinated and incomplete projects. But change here is already dramatic. Over 8 million square feet of office development have been completed in the downtown in the last 10 years, and another 14 million are in the pipeline. Office workers and residents alike have been lured by the convenience of three PATH stations five minutes from Manhattan.

Both the light rail line and the waterfront walkway have been incorporated into Jersey City's current development plans and have influenced the character of the designs significantly. For some years to come, however, until new LRT stations are opened, downtown Jersey City will continue to appear as isolated towers in a sea of parking.

There are hopeful signs. The city is about to embark on a vision process as part of a new master plan (my firm is lead consultant). Our hope is that the plan will provide an overall image to link these disparate projects.

What Might Have Been

It's tempting to speculate about a different outcome: what might have been had New Jersey's waterfront had a regional authority with the power to impose a detailed regional plan like those governing Manhattan's Battery Park City or Baltimore's Inner Harbor. Could there have been an overall urban design vision for the 18.6-mile waterfront?

Of course, in New York City and in Baltimore, only one city was involved — and no private owners. Would it have been possible to come up with a single image that included land uses, densities, design principles, policies regarding affordable housing, public facilities, open space, and the sequence and financing of development? Is it likely that an image bold enough to "stir men's blood," in the time-honored words of Daniel Burnham, could have been agreed upon by nine communities, two counties, multiple egocentric owners and developers, and the general public?

I like to think so, but then, as I said earlier, I am an optimist. Elements of such a plan — the light rail line, the waterfront highway, the walkway, and the design guidelines — are already in place. And maybe that's enough, although a regional authority could have accelerated development and helped finance open space improvements.

A waterfront authority might have helped to ensure economic diversity. As it is now, the waterfront's preponderance of luxury rental units has yielded little in the way of minority population — or of affordable housing. So far, the issue of schools has been largely avoided because of the many one- and two-bedroom apartments. But that situation could change.

Summing up, we see a waterfront region that so far is more suburban than urban, with disconnected projects looking for context. But think what this system could be like with a real regional plan. Maybe it's not too late.

CHAPTER 18

JOINT ECONOMIC DEVELOPMENT PLANNING IN SPRINGFIELD, OHIO

Marya Morris

As part of the GROWING SMART^SM project, American Psychological Association (APA) has been investigating various approaches to addressing regional and interlocal disparities in the capacity to raise revenue. Chapter 14 of the project's *Legislative Guidebook* will offer two models in this area: (1) regional tax-base sharing legislation, in which growth in commercial, industrial, and high-value residential components of the regional property tax base is shared among local governments and (2) a statute permitting voluntary intergovernmental agreements among two or more units of local government to create an economic development zone. These statues are designed to promote common goals and the fiscal health of central cities and their surrounding suburbs.

"The Promise and Politics of Regional Tax Base Sharing," (*Public Investment*, December, 1995) served as the background working paper on which Minnesota State Rep. Myron Orfield based the tax base sharing model legislation. This issue of *Public Investment* describes an Ohio statute that allows cities and townships to create joint economic development districts. It offers case

studies from two such districts in Ohio. The GROWING SMART^SM model legislation for intergovernmental agreements for joint economic development zones, described in a sidebar in this issue, is based in part on the Ohio statute.

Ohio legislation (Ohio Rev. Code Secs. 715.69–715.81) permitting the creation of Joint Economic Development Zones (JEDZs) and Joint Economic Development Districts (JEDDs) aimed at fostering regional economic development and reducing the need for municipal annexation. JEDZs are based on contracts between municipal corporations. JEDDs are based on contracts between a municipal corporation, county, and/or a township.

JEDDs allow municipalities and townships to enter into contracts to share the costs of improvements for areas targeted for economic development. Each contract stipulates the townships' and municipalities' respective contributions of services, money, or equipment to the district. The primary benefit for a township in becoming part of a JEDD is that JEDD contracts permit the district's governing board to levy an income

Originally published as "Joint Economic Development Districts and Zones," *Public Investment*, June, 1996. Published by the American Planning Association, Chicago, Illinois. Reprinted with permission of the publisher.

tax on business profits in the district and on the income of district residents; the revenue is then shared among participating governments. The ability to levy such an income tax is not otherwise available to counties or townships. Imposition of the income tax is subject to a vote by the electors of the district.

When forming a district, participating governments must hold a joint public hearing and make available a description of the proposed district and an economic development plan for the zone that includes a schedule for the provision of any new, expanded, or additional services, facilities, or improvements. Each participating government must also adopt an ordinance or resolution to approve the contract. Once the district is formed, a governing board with representatives of each government is appointed to manage the district.

When originally enacted in 1992, use of the JEDD tool was limited to municipalities and townships within counties that had an adopted charter and to areas surrounding airports owned by a municipal corporation. This limited the use of the JEDDs to Summit County (Ohio's only charter county) and to 21 cities with airports. Springfield was the only city with an airport that applied to create a JEDD in the 12-month window following the passage of the legislation.

Under the original legislation, there were two alternatives for contracts to become valid. The petition method required local governments to file a petition with the legislative authority of the county. The petition had to contain all the information stipulated in the contract (i.e., summary of services to be provided by each participating government, signatures of contracting parties, and signatures of a majority of the property owners and land owners in the district) as well as copies of the ordinance or resolutions. The county legislative body would hold a public hearing, then decide

whether to approve the petition and create the district. Under an alternative method, the participating township's resolution approving the contracts would be subject to a vote in the township election. If the township electors voted to approve the contract, the county legislative body would then meet to approve the contract via a resolution.

In late 1995, the law was amended (House Bill 269 codified at ORC Sec. 715.69) to make the tool available to all counties, municipalities, and townships, although some fairly significant limitations were added. The new rules combine the petition method with the township election method. Any future contracts must be supported by a majority of property owners and business owners in the proposed district and will also be subject to a townshipwide vote in order to be approved.

The composition of the governing boards for future districts will also be different. Instead of being composed of representatives of participating local governments, future boards will have representatives of businesses and employees in the district. Involving the business owners, says state Rep. Kirk Schuring (who sponsored last year's legislation) allows them to "evaluate the proposed district as they would any other business decision." For example they could weigh the benefit of the additional infrastructure in the district with the added cost of the income tax to be levied on district businesses. Ellen Hoover, Springfield's economic development administrator who is overseeing the development of AirParkOhio, says cities will play a much smaller role in districts formed in the future than Akron and Springfield currently play in their districts, given the changes in board composition.

Case Studies

The first two communities to use the joint economic development districts in

Ohio were Akron and Springfield. The Akron districts were a direct attempt to stave off pressure on the city to annex portions of three townships to expand the tax base. In Springfield, the district was formed to launch a new industrial park adjacent to the municipal airport.

Akron Joint Economic Development Districts. In 1994, Akron became the first city in Ohio to form joint economic development districts with adjacent townships when it entered into contracts with Copley, Coventry, and Springfield Townships. David Moore, of the Akron Mayor's Office of Economic Development, said the rationale for creating the districts was a "blending of assets" from each community (i.e., vacant developable land in the township with water and sewer service from the city) and tax-sharing (i.e., property taxes to the township and new income tax revenue to the district and city).

The contracts specify long-term city and township commitments of 99 years with two 50-year renewal periods. They focus on the provision of city water and sewer services to business and residential property within the district. Townships retain autonomous zoning power. They also retain their property tax base. The city, however, receives income tax from businesses and persons employed in the district. The tax revenue generated is initially earmarked by the contract to cover the cost of extending sewer and water service into the township.

Pursuant to the statute, a board of directors was formed of elected officials from each of the townships, the mayor of Akron, and two city council members. The board meets quarterly to consider property owners' petitions for sewer and water service and to act on other business. Presently, the district is moving ahead with designing and constructing sewer and water facilities in

---

FIGURE 1

Elements of the Akron Joint District Contract

1. Name of the district
2. Contracting parties: Participating units of government
3. Purposes: e.g., job creation and preservation; promoting regional cooperation
4. Territory of district: Subject to contract, physical boundaries, affected properties by use
5. District changes: Rules governing addition and removal of areas or properties from the district
6. Terms: Length of contract; rules of termination
7. Contributions to the district: City contributions of infrastructure; mutual aid agreements for police, fire, other
8. Township service area: Residential areas not in the JEDD that have been designated for potential utility tap-on; tap-on fees; water and sewer user fees
9. Ownership of facilities: Specify unit of government that owns water and sewer
10. Board of directors: Powers and duties
11. Income tax: City administration and collection of income tax per agreement with JEDD board; revenues earmarked for city's share of water/sewer design, acquisition, and construction
12. Annexation: City agreement not to annex township land without consent of township; township agrees to oppose annexations, merger, or consolidations that lack city support
13. Other provisions: Defaults and remedies; amendments; binding effect; support of contract; severability; and governing law

areas it determines to be the most suitable for development within the district. Moore says he expects development proposals to begin once the infrastructure is in place.

City of Springfield/AirParkOhio. A second JEDD was formed through a contract between the city of Springfield and Green Township in 1993. The district encompasses the Springfield-Beckley Municipal Airport and the Ohio Air National Guard base. The primary purpose of the district was to assemble AirParkOhio, a new industrial park adjacent to the existing runway and airport terminal. Ellen Hoover says the district promotes economic development of underused city-owned land that will never be needed for airport expansion.

A major hurdle that had to be jumped shortly after the district was formed was a proposal from the federal military Base Realignment and Closure committee to close the Ohio Air National Guard Base in the JEDD and move it to Wright-Patterson Air Force Base nearby. The closure of the National Guard base (which the committee eventually dropped from consideration) would have severely curtailed development potential in the JEDD. And given that the base is the JEDD's largest employer, the city of Springfield's desire to implement an income tax on base employees had to be tabled until the base closure issue was resolved.

Working with the Ohio Department of Development and the Aviation Division of the Ohio Department of Transportation, Hoover has identified several industries to target for location in the district. They include aviation component manufacturers, electronics firms, and the computer and telecommunications industry.

Improvements made to the district since its formation include roadways, electricity, landscaping, and street lighting. The airpark officially opened in the fall of 1994. Hoover is currently working on a marketing agreement for the district with the local chamber of commerce.

Conclusion

Competition for tax base creates intergovernmental conflict through pitched battles over annexation and bidding wars for new and relocating businesses. Local governments that wish to grow continue to annex land from unincorporated land in the county and townships, resulting in a depletion of tax base of those units of government. Townships and unincorporated areas need access to services that cities provide without relinquishing fiscal benefits. In encouraging other states to pursue a joint district program, state Rep. Schuring says that "Ohio is not unique in terms of the urban/suburban rivalry. Joint economic development districts will hopefully enable both communities to get on the same team and work on common goals and objectives."

FIGURE 2
A Model Intergovernmental Agreement Statute for a Joint Economic Development Zone

By Stuart Meck, AICP

The GROWING SMART[SM] *draft model statute provides for a voluntary intergovernmental agreement among two or more units of local government to establish a joint economic development zone. It is based on the Ohio legislation described in this issue and on similar programs in Virginia and Michigan (Code of Va. Ch. 26.2:1 (1994); Mich. Comp. Laws Sec. 124.505 (1991)). Under this model, the zone may be located within the boundaries of one or more local government units. The local governments negotiate what public services and facilities are to be provided to the area included in the zone and which tax and other revenues that result from commercial, industrial, and other development will be shared and in what amounts and proportions. Local governments may address joint planning and administration of development regulations in the agreement. In addition, as a quid pro quo, a municipality may agree not to annex land in an unincorporated area in exchange for sharing revenue. Alternately, a municipality may annex land from the unincorporated area and share the resulting revenues with the county or township.*

The model lists the typical taxes—real property, sales, and income—that states authorize as potential sources of revenue for voluntary sharing. Some states may permit local lodging, restaurant, or specialized sales taxes as well. Because each state has its own suite of taxes and other revenue sources that may be levied by local governments, this model will need to be adapted.

It should be noted that the model does not contemplate extraterritorial taxation. For example, if the state permits municipalities to have local income taxes, and the joint economic development zone is in an unincorporated area, then the city could not impose its local income tax on residents and business in that area. But, if the economic development zone were in the municipality, then the municipality could collect its income tax and share its benefits with the county, township, or the unincorporated unit under a distribution formula contained in the contract.

14-201 Joint Economic Development Zone [Draft Statute Subject to Revision]

(1) Two or more local governments may enter into a contract whereby they agree to share in the costs of improvements and/or services and revenues from tax and other sources for an area located in one or more of the contracting local governments that they designate as a joint economic development zone for the purposes of facilitating new or expanded growth for commercial or industrial development in the state, ensuring the equitable sharing of resources and liabilities among the contracting local governments, and providing an alternative to annexation. The zone created shall be located within the territory of one or more of the contracting local governments and shall consist of all or a portion of such territory.

(2) The contract shall set forth:

   (a) The names of the contracting local governments.

   (b) A legal description of the area to be designated as the joint economic development zone, including a map in sufficient detail to denote the specific boundaries of the area or areas.

FIGURE 2 *(continued)*
A Model Intergovernmental Agreement Statute
for a Joint Economic Development Zone

(c) The amount or nature of the contribution of each contracting local government to the development and operation of the zone. The contributions may be in any form to which the contracting governments agree and may include, but are not limited to, the provision of services, money, real or personal property, facilities, or equipment. The contract shall provide a schedule for the provision of any new, expanded, or additional services and facilities.

(d) Any other terms and conditions pursuant to paragraphs (3), (4), (5), and (7) of this section.

(e) The duration of the contract.

(3) The contract shall set forth the formula or formulas for allocating any tax and other revenue to be shared from the economic development zone and a schedule and method of distribution of the shared revenue, as may be agreed upon by the contracting local governments. Taxes and other revenues to be shared may include:

[Note: The following items are offered as examples of revenues that units of government participating in a joint zone may pool for redistribution.]

[(a) Any [municipal] *or* [local] income tax revenues derived from the income earned by persons employed by businesses located within the economic development zone after it is designated as such by the contracting local governments and from the net profits of such businesses.]

[(b) Any local real property tax revenues derived from commercial and industrial real property located in the economic development zone after it is designated as such by the contracting local governments.]

[(c) Any local revenues resulting from fees, charges, and fines derived from commercial and industrial real property located in the economic development zone after it is designated as such by the contracting local governments.]

[(d) Any local sales tax revenues derived from sales from businesses located in the economic development zone after it is designated as such by the contracting local governments.]

[(e) *Add other taxes that could be shared.*]

(4) The contract may provide for the joint comprehensive planning of the economic development zone and administration of zoning, subdivision, and other land-use regulations, building codes, inspection of public improvements, and other regulatory and proprietary matters that are determined, pursuant to the contract, to be for a public purpose, and to be desirable with respect to the operation of the economic development zone or to facilitate new or expanded economic development, provided that no contract shall exempt the territory within the zone from procedures and processes of land-use regulations applicable pursuant to local regulations or ordinances.

(5) The contract may provide for a waiver of annexation rights pursuant to [*the state*

FIGURE 2 *(continued)*
A Model Intergovernmental Agreement Statute
for a Joint Economic Development Zone

annexation statute] and such other provisions as the contracting local governments deem in their best interests.

(6) Before the legislative authority of any of the contracting local governments enacts an ordinance approving a contract to designate a joint economic development zone, the legislative authority of each of the contracting local governments shall hold a public hearing concerning the zone and contract. Each such legislative authority shall provide at least 30 days' public notice of the time and place of the public hearing in a newspaper of general circulation in the area served by the local governments. The public notice advertising the hearing shall include a statement that a true copy of the contract is available for public inspection in the office of the [clerk of the legislative authority] of each of the contracting local governments. The public hearing shall allow for public comment on the contract. After the public hearings required by this paragraph have been held, the legislative body of each contracting local government may enact an ordinance approving the contract to designate the joint economic development zone. Prior to enactment of the ordinance, the legislative bodies of the contracting local governments may modify the contract as a consequence of comments made at the public hearings or for any other reason without holding additional public hearings.

(7) A contract entered into pursuant to this section may be amended and it may be renewed, canceled, or terminated as provided in or pursuant to the contract. The contract shall continue in existence throughout its term and shall be binding on the contracting parties and on any entities succeeding to such parties, whether by annexation, merger, or otherwise.

(8) Upon the enactment of an ordinance approving a contract to designate a joint economic development zone or any amendments to the contract, the contracting party shall certify a copy of the ordinance and the contract to the director of the [state department of development *or* the state planning agency], who shall maintain a list of local governments in the state that have established joint economic development zones.

Editor's Note

The above figure was excerpted from Chapter 14 of *Growing Smart Legislative Handbook: Model Statutes for Planning and the Management of Change*, 1996. Published by the American Planning Association, Chicago, Ill.

CHAPTER 19

CONSERVATION EASEMENTS ALONG THE MISSISSIPPI RIVER IN WISCONSIN

Brian W. Ohm

Public funding to purchase conservation easements[1] has received increased political acceptance in recent years. Public money to acquire conservation easements was included in many of the programs approved by voters across the United States in November, 1998, as part of a "grassroots rebellion against sprawl" (Meyers, 1999, p. 1). A growing number of programs to purchase conservation easements are being used to preserve agricultural land (American Farmland Trust, 1997; Daniels, 1991; Daniels & Bowers, 1997).

Conservation easements are a less-than-fee, non-possessory interest in a parcel of land recorded by a real estate deed. They are acquired by public agencies or private conservation organizations either through purchase or donation. The holder of the underlying possessory interest retains certain rights to the land. The holder of the easement has the right to prevent certain activities on the land consistent with conservation and aesthetic objectives. Conservation easements may prohibit all ground-disturbing activity on the land or prohibit only certain activities. While some conservation easements are designed to last for a specified term, often the easements are intended as a perpetual restriction on development of the land (Wright, 1994). Because of this perpetual orientation, many conservation organizations see them as an alternative to temporary regulatory tools such as zoning and the uncertainty of the political process governing the use of such tools.

Very little is understood about what "perpetual" means in the context of conservation easements. As a legal term, "perpetual" is defined as "never ceasing; continuous; enduring; lasting; unlimited in respect of time; continuing without intermission or interval" (Black, 1983, p. 595). A common perception is that conservation easements will maintain the status quo for land use (Rodegerdts, 1998). However, measuring what perpetual means in this context is difficult because these programs are a development of recent decades. The earliest purchases of conservation easements were by the federal government in the 1930s when the United States Fish and Wildlife Service pur-

Originally published as "The Purchase of Scenic Easements and Wisconsin's Great River Road: A Progress Report on Perpetuity," *Journal of the American Planning Association*, Vol. 66, No. 2, Spring, 2000. Published by the American Planning Association, Chicago, Illinois. Reprinted with permission of the publisher.

chased easements in Minnesota and North and South Dakota to protect wildlife habitats. During the 1930s and 1940s, the National Park Service purchased conservation easements to protect scenic views along the Blue Ridge Parkway in Virginia and North Carolina, and along the Natchez Trace Parkway in Alabama, Mississippi, and Tennessee. The first major program devoted to purchasing conservation easements on agricultural land to prevent more intensive development was in Suffolk County, New York, in 1974 (Buckland, 1987).[2]

This article examines the first major state-supported program to purchase conservation easements in the United States — Wisconsin's Great River Road project — to provide a framework for understanding the "perpetual" nature of conservation easements. From the early 1950s through the 1960s, the Wisconsin Highway Commission (now the Wisconsin Department of Transportation) purchased scenic easements along the highways adjacent to the Mississippi River, the southwestern border of the state. The oldest easements have been in place for almost 50 years.

Wisconsin had two goals in purchasing scenic easements along the Great River Road during the 1950s and 1960s. One was the desire to permanently preserve the scenic values of the rural landscape along the Road — the Mississippi River on one side and bluffs on the other side, with limited development so as not to obstruct the vistas. A second goal was to avoid the limitations of zoning, by using an alternative tool to promote the public interest in protecting and preserving private lands. These goals are still prominent today in public programs to purchase development rights and in the use of conservation easements by private conservation organizations such as land trusts.

Wisconsin's use of scenic easements to implement the plans for the Great River Road received national attention during the 1960s and 1970s. The scenic easements cap-

tured the interest and enthusiasm of open space advocates in light of a growing national concern over the loss of open space and the destruction of natural resources. Many works lauded the scenic preservation efforts of Wisconsin's Great River Road project. Among them were William H. Whyte's seminal 1959 study for the Urban Land Institute, *Securing Open Space for Urban America: Conservation Easements*, in which Whyte first popularized the use of conservation easements for preserving open space. Whyte's subsequent works also highlighted the Wisconsin Great River Road project (1962, 1968). By the mid 1960s, the State of Wisconsin had more experience than any other state with the use of scenic easements. Several national conferences highlighting its easement program were held in Wisconsin in the 1960s. Preservation efforts in other states, such as the plans for the Brandywine Region in Pennsylvania, attempted to build upon Wisconsin's experiences (Strong, 1975). Influential studies on the use of conservation easements as a technique for the preservation of natural areas by private organizations, such as land trusts, also built on Wisconsin's experiences (Dunham, 1966; Gregory, 1972; Plimpton, 1966).

Early evaluations viewed the use of scenic easements along Wisconsin's Great River Road as a planning success (Coughlin & Plaut, 1978). It is important to follow this work to see how the Great River Road easements have fared 20 years later. In the early 1980s, Strong (1983) recommended an analysis of "older easement programs, such as ... the Great River Road program" (p. 61), but that was never done. The longevity and the early national influence of the Great River Road easements make it a good case study on the issue of perpetuity. The history of this project reveals a variety of issues and concerns that are still shared by conservation easement holders. This history also provides an important context for the purchase of scenic easements along highways as presently authorized in the federal Transportation Equity Act for the 21st Century (1998). Many of the issues related to publicly funded land protection highlighted in this article also apply to private conservation easement holders.

The historical experience of the Great River Road easements shows that while easements can provide long-term protection, issues may arise that create the need to modify or terminate the easements. It is important for easement holders to plan strategically for how they will address these issues. The experiences of the Great River Road project reveal that for conservation easements, the achievement of perpetuity depends on how the easements are written and administered. Easements are meant to provide an alternative to police power regulation; it is important that they do not fall prey to the same limitations.

The research for this article involved analysis of the original planning studies for Wisconsin's Great River Road and other historical information about the project, including the proceedings from the two major conferences on Wisconsin's use of conservation easements held in the 1960s. In addition, the planning literature (both historic and contemporary) and legal literature on conservation easements were reviewed. The research also involved 21 standardized, open-ended telephone interviews conducted in 1998 and 1999. Interviewees included current and retired staff of the Wisconsin Department of Transportation, local planners and zoning administrators, local realtors, and others familiar with the Great River Road project. The interviews focused on the ongoing administration of the scenic easements and how and why decisions were made.

Historical Overview

In 1936, the governor of Missouri recommended the creation of a scenic parkway along the Mississippi River in that state. Interest in the idea of a national parkway through all 10 states along the Mississippi River grew rapidly, and in 1938 those states established the Mississippi River Parkway Planning Commission. In 1939, the Commission asked Congress to authorize a feasibility study of a proposed parkway similar to the Blue Ridge Parkway in Virginia and North Carolina and the Natchez Trace Parkway in Alabama, Mississippi, and Tennessee, both under development at that time. The outbreak of World War II stopped any work on the Mississippi River Parkway (Fisher, 1982).

Planning for the Parkway resumed in 1949, when Congress authorized a study by the National Park Service and the Bureau of Public Roads. In 1951, the two agencies submitted a report to Congress entitled *Parkway for the Mississippi*. The report stated that a new route patterned after the Blue Ridge Parkway was not feasible because of cost and because a new road would duplicate existing highways that already occupied the most desirable scenic locations.

In light of these findings, the report recommended improving existing highways to park-like standards, with new construction where gaps existed to ensure a continuous route along the river. According to the report, "[t]he essence of the parkway concept is to provide a park-like corridor that insulates the motor road from uncontrolled development along the roadsides" (Johnson & Cron, 1958, p. 3). The report recommended against outright purchase of the land because the "high value of the land and improvements" made the cost prohibitive and because of the "maintenance burden" (p. 3). Rather, according to the report, the corridor should consist of scenic easements

under which the State seeks to preserve the existing rural scene by purchasing the owner's right to change the use of the land. By acquiring such scenic controls along the existing highways, it was felt that the roadsides could be cleaned and protected, and thereafter maintained in parkway atmosphere. (p. 3)

Federal funds for the acquisition of scenic easements were not made available until the passage of the Highway Beautification Act of 1965. Nevertheless, Wisconsin began purchasing development rights as part of the Parkway project in 1951— the only Mississippi River state to do so at this early time (Land Economics Studies Unit, 1967).

Detailed plans for the scenic easement acquisitions were not completed until the late 1950s. The Federal Aid Highway Act of 1954 provided planning funds for the project and designated the Mississippi River Parkway as the "Great River Road." The State Highway Commission of Wisconsin requested the federal Bureau of Public Roads to conduct a study of the route for the Great River Road through Wisconsin in accordance with the act. The study findings, entitled *Report on a Recommended Route for the Great River Road (Mississippi River Parkway) Through the State of Wisconsin* (Johnson & Cron), were released in 1958. The study identified the recommended corridor where scenic easements would be used. Since much of the land that would be affected was farmland, the study concluded that scenic easements would serve important aesthetic functions. The easements would "perpetuate the rural scene in substantially its present condition" while allowing landowners to "continue to cultivate and use these lands for agriculture and pasturage but [not] erect unsightly objects such as billboards and utility pole lines, or change the type of use as from agricultural to residential or commercial" (p. 8). In addition, the easements would allow the lands to remain in private ownership to help maintain the local property tax base (Cunningham, 1968; Whyte, 1968).

This study also provided an early argument against zoning as another important reason to support the use of scenic easements in Wisconsin: Zoning was a temporary tool

subject to local politics and was not consistent with the goal of permanent preservation of a scenic corridor. According to the study, if scenic easements are purchased, "they will 'run with the land' and not depend for their permanence and effectiveness upon the actions of zoning boards or other regulatory bodies" (Johnson & Cron, 1958, p. 8). Despite this aversion to zoning, the study still identified scenic easements as "controls ... similar to zoning" (p. 8).

At a 1961 conference on the Great River Road project, one of the attendees questioned why the State was paying for development rights to control land uses rather than zoning the land under the police power. He observed that "more drastic invasions of property rights are accomplished under zoning without payment" (Wisconsin Department of Resource Development, 1961, pp. 111–112) than under the terms of the easements. While other states at this time tied local authority to regulate aesthetics to health and safety issues, in 1955 the Wisconsin Supreme Court became one of the first courts in the nation to hold that zoning could be exercised for purely aesthetic considerations (*State ex rel. Saveland Park Holding Corp. v. Wieland*, 1955).

The problem with zoning for the Great River Road was that the Department did not have authority to zone land, and many of the communities along the Mississippi River did not have zoning ordinances. Rural zoning in Wisconsin had been promoted during the late 1920s as part of a comprehensive strategy to address the socio-economic crisis resulting from the destruction of the forests in northern Wisconsin during the late 1800s and early 1900s (Carstensen, 1958). Because the lands along the Mississippi River had escaped the environmental degradation of northern Wisconsin, the original purpose for rural zoning was not as compelling for this part of the state. Therefore, even though Wisconsin had pioneered the development of rural zoning, most of its rural lands along the Mississippi River remained unzoned during the late 1950s. Indeed, great portions remain unzoned today (Ohm & Schmidke, 1998).

Furthermore, Wisconsin, like many other states, had delegated land use authority to the hundreds of local governments in the state. Wisconsin's purchase of scenic easements beginning in the early 1950s occurred before Wisconsin's other bold experiment, in 1966, with state mandated shoreland zoning, recognized as part of the "Quiet Revolution" in land use control (Bosselman & Callies, 1971). That program, rooted in the state's responsibilities under the Public Trust Doctrine to protect the public interest in the waters of the state, allowed Wisconsin to implement a program seeking to protect its lakes and rivers from adverse development impacts. Efforts to give the Department of Transportation zoning authority to protect the lands along the Mississippi River were made in the late 1950s but failed (Wisconsin Department of Resource Development, 1961). According to the 1958 study, scenic easements could be used whether or not zoning ordinances existed. Therefore, the use of scenic easements was critical to implementing state land use policy along the Great River Road.

By 1961, Wisconsin had used general highway funds to acquire 234 scenic easements covering 1,579 acres along approximately 53 miles of the Great River Road (Jordahl, 1963; Olson, 1965). The early easement acquisitions confirmed that buying a less-than-fee interest was a bargain compared to fee simple purchase. At that time, the average price for easements was $20.66 per acre, in contrast to $41.29 per acre for fee simple acquisitions (Jordahl, 1963). In late 1961, the easement acquisition program was greatly accelerated with the passage of Governor Gaylord Nelson's innovative outdoor recreation and resource development program, a 10-year, $50-million statewide conservation program financed by a tax on

cigarettes. Of the total amount, $2 million was earmarked for acquiring scenic easements along highways throughout the state. Completion of the easement acquisitions along the Great River Road was given top priority (Jordahl, 1963).

By July 1967, Wisconsin had acquired scenic easements along most of the approximately 250 miles of the Great River Road. They covered 6,223 acres and involved 601 parcels (Land Economics Studies Unit, 1967). The department purchased scenic easements only in rural areas because purchases within cities and villages along the route would have been too expensive. The department continued to purchase scenic easements along the Great River Road into the 1970s on a limited basis in conjunction with road improvement projects along the route.

Approximately 90 percent of the Great River Road scenic easements were acquired through negotiation. The remaining ones were acquired by condemnation (Cunningham, 1968). Having the power of condemnation in reserve placed the state in an advantageous position during negotiations. However, the use of condemnation to acquire easements was not without controversy. One challenge to the state's authority to condemn easements resulted in a landmark case decided by the Wisconsin Supreme Court. *Kamrowski v. State* (1966) upheld the state's use of the power of eminent domain to protect scenic values as a legitimate public purpose. According to the court:

> The enjoyment of the scenic beauty by the public which passes along the highway seems to us to be a direct use by the public of the rights in land which have been taken in the form of a scenic easement.... [T]he concept of preserving a scenic corridor along a parkway, with its emphasis upon maintaining a rural scene and preventing unsightly uses is sufficiently definite so that the legislature may be said to have made a meaningful de-

cision in terms of [the] public purpose....
(*Kamrowski v. State*, 1966, p. 797).

The use (or threat of use) of eminent domain is a feature that distinguishes the Great River Road project from more recent programs to purchase development rights, which rely on voluntary sales. Political opposition to the use of eminent domain to acquire scenic easements resulted in the demise of similar resource protection programs elsewhere (Strong, 1975). While the department still occasionally acquires scenic easements elsewhere in the state on a limited basis, it no longer does so by the power of eminent domain. This change in policy is based on the department's decision to limit its use of eminent domain to activities that are more germane to its direct functions, such as acquiring rights of way for building highways (M. Beekman, personal communication, May 6, 1999). However, the use of eminent domain for the Great River Road ensured the inclusion of key properties to complete the parkway corridor, something that voluntary acquisition programs cannot guarantee.

Conservation Easements and the Meaning of Perpetuity

The Wisconsin Department of Transportation still owns all the scenic easements it purchased along the Great River Road in the 1950s and 1960s. Some adaptations to the program have occurred over time and are discussed below. These adaptations provide a basis for more general lessons about the use of conservation easements.

Early Adaptations to Easement Terms

At first, the department acquired uniform easements. They included both sides of the highway to a width of 350 feet from the center line. Within that area, the following provisions applied:

- Single-family resident uses were permitted on lots greater than five acres.
- General farming was permitted except for fur farms or farms for the disposal of garbage or related material.
- Existing commercial and industrial uses could be continued, maintained, and repaired but not expanded or structurally altered.
- Any use incidental to the permitted use on the property was permitted.
- Telephone, telegraph, pipeline, and micro-wave radio relay structures were permitted.
- Signs were not permitted, except for one sign of not more than eight square feet to advertise goods produced and sold on the premises.
- Dumping, disposal, or storage of unsightly material was prohibited.
- Trees or shrubs could not be destroyed, cut, or removed except when necessary in performing a permitted use.

To simplify drafting the agreements, the department developed a two-page form that contained standard terms (Beuscher, 1966).

During the process of implementing the easement program, the department refined the standard easement form to address specific issues that arose under the above terms. Some refinements were meant to address development patterns permitted under the terms of the first easements that had proved undesirable. For example, the Department changed the five-acre lot restriction to permit single-family residents on lots with a minimum frontage of 300 feet. The new spacing provision prevented an excessive number of entrances to the highway, which sprang up as people built on narrow five-acre lots.

Despite the initial objective of standardized easement terms, the department realized that a more flexible approach was appropriate. This flexibility was necessitated in part by the unique nature of the land. For example, protecting the first 350 feet on either side of the highway center line was not always sufficient to protect scenic views, which often encompassed a greater area. Development contrary to the objectives of the scenic easement program occurred outside the easement area. The department departed from the uniform standard to allow for a more individualized approach with easements designed to protect a larger vista, depending on the topography of the property. Often the newer easements covered the entire parcel. As a result, there are differences among the individual easements along the Great River Road, depending on the age and location of the easement.

The standard easement forms were also modified to list only the prohibited uses, not the permitted ones. This change reduced the confusion and administrative burden from people asking the department if they could use their property in a way not expressly permitted in the easement.

Lastly, the original easement forms did not include any affirmative or positive rights. This proved inadequate, as trees and shrubs grew and blocked views that were meant to be preserved. In addition, with the outbreak of Dutch elm disease in Wisconsin, many elm trees died and needed to be removed and replaced. In response to these changes in the natural environment, the easement forms were changed to include positive rights to permit state highway officials to enter the property to plant and/or selectively cut or prune trees and brush to preserve the scenic view and to implement disease prevention measures (Cunningham, 1968).

AMENDMENTS TO
RECORDED EASEMENTS

Once recorded, all easements can be amended to modify the original negotiated terms. Some of the scenic easements along the Great River Road have been modified in response to requests from the landowners. Although the scenic easement documents did not specify an amendment process, the Department of Transportation developed a "variance" process, borrowing from the concepts and language of zoning. These variances represent an ongoing balancing act that occurs between the changing demands of the landowner and the programmatic interests of the department, the easement holder. While the department granted many variances in the early days of the program, today fewer variances are granted. During the past five years, the department has granted approximately four variances (A. Proksch, personal communication, May 12, 1998). The department consistently denies variance for billboards and ones that may create traffic safety problems. However, the department does not maintain accurate data regarding the total number of variance requests and the number and types of variances granted since the inception of the program.

Many of the early variances that were granted related to problematic language in the first easement form. For example, variances were granted to allow residential landowners to cut trees and shrubs to help maintain scenic vistas. As discussed above, the standard form was modified to address these issues for later easements. Unlike amending the text in a zoning ordinance and having that change apply universally to all properties in a district, separate easements are recorded against individual parcels of property, so each easement has to be amended as needs arise. Other early variances addressed property maintenance issues. For example, the prohibition on the expansion or alteration of commercial structures resulted in blighted properties, so the department granted some variances to allow commercial establishments to modernize their buildings.

Other variances reflect a balancing by the department to "alleviate some of the adverse economic effects accruing to commercial property as a result of the easements" in ways that are "not detrimental to the scenic beauty of the area" (Land Economics Studies Unit, 1967, p. 21). Over the years, the department has approved several variances that allow uses not permitted under the easements, including a golf course and a number of commercial and industrial uses such as a bank, a trucking firm, a business park, and a retail distribution center. In exchange for granting variances, the department uses the easement to negotiate landscaping and design changes in an attempt to preserve the scenic quality of the area. The department also negotiates highway access issues to limit the impact of the new development on the parkway.

The variance for the retail distribution center, granted in 1996, provides an illustration of the challenges these easements face. It involved the construction of a 300,000-square-foot distribution center, warehouse, and retail store for a major sporting goods retailer. A very small part of the building infringed upon the easement area. To attract the business to the area, the state provided the largest incentive package ever for southwestern Wisconsin. The City of Prairie du Chien, where the center is located, also created a tax increment finance district to pay for improvements to the site (Gribble, 1996). Although the department did negotiate aesthetic and access changes for this distribution center, the public paid for a development that negatively impacted a resource they had already paid to protect.

The process for granting variances involves review by both the Department of Transportation and Wisconsin's Mississippi River Parkway Commission. The Commission is a 17-member body appointed by the governor that was originally established as part of the initial planning for the Great River Road in 1939. The department's district offices take final action on variance requests after receiving input from the commission.

Neither the department nor the commission have any formal guidelines or criteria for evaluating variance requests. Each request is evaluated on its own merits. The ability to modify easements can introduce a considerable amount of flexibility and discretion into the process of administering easements. With this discretion comes the responsibility to ensure that the variances are consistent with the original objectives of the Great River Road project.

William H. Whyte (1968) summed up those objectives in *The Last Landscape*: "When you drive along the Great River Road you do not feel you are driving on a manicured parkway; you are driving through a real-life countryside, punctuated with real-life towns with their characteristic spatterings of outlying houses...." (p. 293). The scenic easements were not meant to prevent all development, and the continued existence of "real-life towns" is key to the landscape the Great River Road project seeks to preserve. Yet, what these towns look like has not been formally defined. The department evaluates variance requests for consistency with local land use plans. However, evaluating variances against local plans is not possible in the many areas along the Great River Road that do not have plans. Also, for those communities with plans, there is no formal process for evaluating local plans for consistency with the State's Great River Road program.[3] Without design criteria or the use of visual assessment processes, it is difficult to judge whether the variances interfere with the preservation of the rural landscape described by Whyte (Chenoweth, 1991).

Another issue raised by the use of variances is the need to protect the public's investment. With publicly funded programs to purchase development rights, the public has paid for an interest in the land, as opposed to police power regulations, where the public did not pay for the interest acquired. Prior to 1999, the department did not require landowners to buy development rights back as part of the variance process. While the department negotiated some quid pro quo for a few variances in the form of landscaping and/or access restrictions, it is difficult to measure whether those exactions provided adequate compensation for changing the easement terms.

In late 1998, however, with development pressures increasing along the Great River Road, the department determined that landowners requesting variances must buy back the development rights from the department. To place a value on the development rights, the department intends to follow a process similar to its process for selling excess rights of way. The department plans to retain an appraiser to determine a value for the interest and negotiate a price with the landowner. As of October 1999, no variances with repayment had been processed. It is unclear how a loss of scenic value will be accounted for under this process. The department anticipates that requiring repayment will deter most landowners from requesting variances or that they will develop outside the easement area (A. Proksch, personal communication, May 7, 1999).

Requiring repayment will prove contentious. It is difficult for present landowners who may have to pay thousands of dollars for the right to develop their property to feel appeased by the fact that 40 years ago the former property owner received $22 per acre for the easement. Issues of equity will also arise as a third- or fourth-generation owner of land subject to the scenic easement is required to pay for the right to develop while a neighboring landowner with no easement can obtain a rezoning at no cost to allow development. For programs to purchase development rights, these complicating factors evolve over time. The first generation of landowners under the easements are cognizant of the payment received in exchange for the easement. While subsequent owners did not receive a direct payment for the loss of the development rights, in theory this loss would be reflected in a lower cost for the property. Yet, it is unclear whether this is true. Studies have shown that the Great River Road easements did not have a significant negative impact on property values (Land Economics Studies Unit, 1967). There is also the perception among realtors and others that the easements actually enhance property values (G. Lass, personal communication, May 13, 1998; T. Levrich, personal communication, May 15, 1998). Arriving at an acceptable repayment figure poses many challenges.

Embedded in the challenges facing the easements is the difficult nature of private property rights, particularly the economic valuation of property rights (Jacobs, 1999). The easement program removed one of the sticks in the bundle of private property rights. Yet, landowners today raise the same concerns about the easements as they do about uncompensated police power regulations. For example, department officials note that one of the primary reasons for variance requests is that farmers want to modify the easement terms to increase land values so they can sell their land for retirement income (A. Proksch, personal communication, May 12, 1998). Private property rights advocates also pose a challenge to the administration of the Great River Road project. Individual efforts to maximize the economic interests of landowners do not recognize society's interests in their land, particularly when society paid for its interest over 30 years earlier. Even though the public legally owns an interest in much of the land along the Great River Road, the enduring cultural strength of private property rights in that same land poses a challenge to the perpetuity of the easements.

OTHER CHALLENGES TO PERPETUITY

The law also places additional limitations on the perpetual nature of easements. These limitations are briefly outlined below.

To date, they have not been an issue for the Great River Road, but are included here to present a more complete discussion on conservation easements and perpetuity.[4]

The Nature of Conservation Easements. During the development of the Great River Road and continuing today, legal scholars have voiced concern over the use of the term "easement" and the resulting legal uncertainties. At a national conference exploring Wisconsin's experiences with the Great River Road, the late University of Wisconsin Law Professor Jacob Beuscher, a pioneer in land use law, summarized the "very hoary history in Anglo-American law" (1967, p. 51) of easements. Generally, conservation easements are negative easements in gross — a form of easement not universally accepted under common law.[5] Furthermore, conservation easements allow one owner of land to forever bind future owners — a restraint on the transfer of property. The law has historically tried to prevent such restraints (Dana & Ramsey, 1989; Korngold, 1984).

Since the acquisition of the Great River Road scenic easements, most states have responded to the uncertain legal status of conservation easements under common law by creating statutes to expressly enable their use (Bruce & Ely, 1988). To aid in these efforts, the National Conference of Commissioners on Uniform State Laws approved the Uniform Conservation Easement Act in 1981 to provide a model enabling law for states to follow and provide greater certainty to the evolving concept of conservation easements (Gustanski & Squires, 2000). These statutes clarify the right of qualified private organizations, such as land trusts, to hold conservation easements.[6]

Termination of Conservation Easements. None of the easements along the Great River Road have yet been terminated. Nevertheless, the law recognizes several methods to terminate a conservation easement: the public power of eminent domain; foreclosure of a pre-existing lien on the property; marketable title acts, which limit restrictions on property to a certain number of years[7]; the equitable doctrine of changed conditions; release of the easement by its holder; release of the easement by the failure of the holder to enforce the terms of the easement; and merger when the easement holder also acquires the underlying fee interest (Baldwin, 1997; Blackie, 1989; Dana & Ramsey, 1989; Ginsberg, 1988). A court in equity may also imply a "reasonable duration" to terminate the easement or to limit enforcement of the easement if enforcement would do more harm than it would prevent (Korngold, 1984). Some states try to limit by statute the ways in which conservation easements can be terminated. For example, Wisconsin exempts conservation easements from the application of its marketable title act (Wis. Stat. §700.40).

While failure to enforce an easement can lead to its termination, enforcement has not been a major difficulty for the Great River Road. Most easement violations are the result of a misunderstanding rather than willful transgressions (M. Beekman, personal communication, May 11, 1998; Gose, 1966). When the department notifies landowners of easement violations, they usually comply. In the case of sign violations, if the landowner does not comply, the department removes the sign. In one case, the storage of junk has proved to be a persistent problem because of the unwillingness of the property owner to comply and the expense for the department to remove the junk. It remains to be seen whether a future court would consider this a failure to enforce the easement and allow for its termination.

Conclusions

The purchase of perpetual scenic easements to preserve aesthetic values along the 250-mile Great River Road in Wisconsin remains a pioneering effort in resource protection. It provided early support to the proposition that less-than-fee acquisition could work as a planning tool, especially for entities without land use regulatory authority, such as the Wisconsin Department of Transportation and private land trusts. Without purchasing the easements, the department would not have been able to protect the scenic vistas along the Great River Road to the extent that it does. The use of scenic easements is still valued as a successful strategy by those familiar with the program.

The longevity of the Great River Road easements also provides insights into the ability of conservation easements to maintain the status quo forever. While many are intended to be perpetual, conservation easements have inherent limitations and constraints which temper the definition of "perpetuity." First, the law recognizes several methods to terminate easements. Second, there is continuing uncertainty over how courts will interpret conservation easements in the future. Because of these limitations and constraints, conservation easements are not the final step in the protection process. Recording a conservation easement against a parcel of property does not by itself guarantee that the easement will have perpetual duration. A conservation easement holder, public or private, must be cognizant of these potential limitations and continually work to minimize them, or accept them only when there is a rational basis to support their effects. Whether a conservation easement lasts five, 50, or 500 years will depend on how these limitations are applied.

To date, the scenic easements purchased by the Wisconsin Department of Transportation have endured. Their longevity can be attributed to a number of factors, including the limited rights acquired under the easements, low development pressure from the marketplace, and the ongoing commitment of the department to enforce them. The department's experience also shows that flexibility is an important factor in the success of easement programs. Early in the program, the department learned that flexibility is needed in the drafting of easements, to tailor each easement to the unique qualities of individual parcels of property while maintaining the overall objectives of the program. The ability to vary easement terms from parcel to parcel distinguishes easements from the uniformity requirement within zoning districts. Easement purchase programs need to take full advantage of this flexibility.

Flexibility is also important in the long-term management of easements to address issues regarding easement terms that may arise in subsequent years. Because it is difficult to predict the future in an ever-changing natural environment, easement terms may need to be modified to be more or less restrictive. Over the course of decades, or even a few years, words used in the easement may need to be redefined. Land management techniques may change. While these techniques may be easily implemented on public lands in fee ownership, they may be more difficult to use on private lands with conservation easements. Depending on the terms of the easement, the easement holder may not be able to unilaterally make the needed changes. In addition, unforeseen circumstances may arise that need to be addressed, or standards in the easement may prove unworkable. In these cases, the easement may need to be amended.

However, this flexibility must be exercised with care to uphold the long-term objectives of easement purchase programs. The challenge for conservation easement holders is to ensure that any modifications are in the public interest. Years ago, Babcock (1966) pointed out the shortcomings of zoning to resolve conflicts over the use of private lands. Conservation easements are in part an answer to these shortcomings. They reflect a growing public desire for the permanent protection of resources in light of historical legal doctrines and social norms that favor the unrestrained use of land.

Conflicts over the use of private lands will continue, even when those lands are protected by an easement. Conservation easement holders need to devise strategies for addressing these potential conflicts. Continuing communication with affected landowners is essential since the conflicts will be framed by the attitudes and understandings of the landowners. Community education and linkages to community planning initiatives are also needed to make programs relevant for successive generations. In addition, developing a policy framework to provide a rational basis for decisions the easement holder makes about the easements can build political support and help courts understand the context for the use of easements if there is a lawsuit. For programs to purchase conservation easements, this framework may also need to address difficult issues such as whether to allow landowners to buy back development rights and potential inequities of a program that provides financial gain to one landowner and not to future landowners. Resolution of these issues will be key to the continued longevity of easement programs such as the one protecting the scenic beauty of Wisconsin's Great River Road.

Notes

1. Scenic easements are one type of conservation easement. The terms *scenic easements* and *conservation easements* are used interchangeably in this article, which is how those terms appear throughout the history of the Great River Road project. Programs to purchase conservation easements are also referred to as the purchase of development rights.

2. There is a growing body of literature beginning to evaluate the use of programs to purchase development rights in saving farmland. Maynard et al. (1998), Pfeffer and Lapping (1994), and Kline and Wichelns (1994) examined the motives behind programs to purchase development rights for farmland preservation. This research indicates that while these programs may succeed in saving open space, it is too early to tell if they will succeed in keeping agricultural operations viable.

3. Some communities use the easements as the basis for local decision making, thereby limiting requests for variances. In one case, a request to rezone an area to allow a farm equipment/auto repair business was denied because of the easement. The rezoning was approved when the proposed business located outside the easement area.

4. Cheever (1996) addresses the limitations of private land trusts to "lock up" private land forever to prevent future development.

5. Common law generally divides easements into two types: *affirmative* and *negative.* *Affirmative easements* provide the easement holder with a limited right to make use of land owned in fee by someone else. Examples of affirmative easements include highway right of way easements, hunting and fishing rights, and lake access easements. *Negative easements*, not as common as affirmative easements, grant another party the right to prevent a landowner from using his/her land in specified ways. Examples of negative easements recognized by the courts in some states include easements which prohibit blocking solar access, removing lateral support for a building on adjacent property, and obstructing views.

Traditional common law also divides easements into two classes depending on who benefits from the easement: *appurtenant easements* and *easements in gross. Appurtenant easements* are connected with and attached to the ownership of nearby land. An example is a right of way across to one piece of land possessed by the owner of a nearby piece of land. Since the scenic easements along the Great River Road were adjacent to the state-owned highway, they are generally considered to be appurtenant. The land subject to the right of way is known as the *servient estate.* The adjacent land, whose owner gets the benefits of the easement, is known as the *dominant estate.* An *easement in gross*, on the other hand, is generally viewed as a personal interest or right to use another's land without regard to ownership of nearby land. The U.S. courts traditionally disfavor easements in gross. Because they are a personal interest, courts have generally found them to be not inheritable, not assignable, and not extendable beyond the life of the owner.

6. The important role of private organizations in land preservation was recognized at the 1966 national conference on the use of easements along the Great River Road. The conference included a panel discussing nongovernmental easement programs, which agreed on the need for private organizations such as land trusts to assist in conservation efforts. However, the panel concluded that private programs were "definitely of secondary importance to ... public ones in saving landscapes" (Dowling, 1966). Changes in the federal income tax code by the Tax Reform Act of 1976 to allow charitable deductions for donations of conservation easements to private and public organizations have also encouraged their use. Private land trusts have benefited from this provision and filled a need for land preservation not met by government acquisition programs.

7. Many states have marketable title acts which remove encumbrances, such as easements, from the title to real estate after a period of years, often 30, unless the encumbrance is re-recorded. This promotes the marketability of real estate by ensuring that the title is free from defects resulting from antiquated encumbrances.

References

American Farmland Trust. (1997). *Saving American Farmland: What Works*. Northampton, MA: Author.

Babcock, R.F. (1966). *The Zoning Game*. Madison: University of Wisconsin Press.

Baldwin, M.W. (1997). Conservation easements: A viable tool for land preservation. *Land and Water Law Review, 32*, 89–123.

Beuscher, J.H. (1966). *Land Use Controls — Cases and Materials* (4th ed.). Madison, WI: College Printing & Typing.

Beuscher, J.H. (1967). Some legal aspects of scenic easements. In *Scenic Easements in Action: Proceedings of Conference* (pp. 49–59). Madison: University of Wisconsin Law School.

Black, H.C. (1983). *Black's Law Dictionary* (5th ed.). St. Paul, MN: West Publishing.

Blackie, J.A. (1989). Conservation easements and the doctrine of changed conditions. *The Hastings Law Journal, 40*, 1187–1222.

Bosselman, F.P., & Callies, D. (1971). *The Quiet Revolution in Land Use Control*. Washington, DC: U.S. Government Printing Office.

Bruce, J.W., & Ely, J.W. (1988). *The Law of Easements and Licenses in Land*. Boston: Warren, Gorham & Lamont.

Buckland, J.G. (1987). The history and use of purchase of development rights in the United States. *Landscape and Urban Planning, 14*, 237–252.

Carstensen, V. (1958). *Farms or forests: Evolution of a state land policy for northern Wisconsin, 1850–1932*. Madison: University of Wisconsin-Madison.

Cheever, F. (1996). Public good and private magic in the law of land trusts and conservation easements: A happy present and troubled future. *Denver University Law Review, 74*, 1077–1106.

Chenoweth, R. (1991). Landscape simulation and aesthetic policy. *Journal of the Urban and Regional Information Systems Association, 3*(1), 6–13.

Coughlin, R.E., & Plaut, T. (1978). Less-than-fee acquisition for the preservation of open space: Does it work? *Journal of the American Institute of Planners, 44*, 452–462.

Cunningham, R.A. (1968). Scenic easements in the highway beautification program. *Denver Law Review, 45*, 168–266.

Dana, A., & Ramsey, M. (1989). Conservation easements and the common law. *Stanford Environmental Law Journal, 8*(2), 2–45.

Daniels, T.L. (1991). The purchase of development rights: Preserving agricultural land and open space. *Journal of the American Planning Association, 57*, 421–431.

Daniels, T.L., & Bowers, D. (1997). *Holding our ground: Protecting America's farms and farmland*. Washington, DC: Island Press.

Dowling, P.B. (1966). Non-governmental easement programs panel report. In *Scenic Easements in Action: Proceedings of Conference* (pp. C-1–C-10). Madison: University of Wisconsin.

Dunham, A. (1966). *Preservation of Open Space areas: A Study of the Non-Governmental Role*. Chicago: Welfare Council of Metropolitan Chicago.

Federal Aid Highway Act of 1954, ch. 1076, §1(8), 68 Stat. 966 (1954).

Fisher, R.G. (1982). *Wisconsin Great River Road Public Recreational, Cultural and Scientific Amenities Inventory*. La Cross, WI: Mississippi River Regional Planning Commission.

Ginsberg, W.R. (1988). Term and termination: When easements aren't forever. In J. Diehl & T.S. Barrett (eds.), *The Conservation Easement Handbook* (pp. 129–134). San

Francisco: Trust for Public Land; Alexandria, VA: Land Trust Exchange.

Gose, T. (1966). *Workshop Manual for Conference on Scenic Easements in Action*. Madison: University of Wisconsin Law School.

Gregory, D.D. (1972). *The Easement as a Conservation Technique*. Morges, Switzerland: International Union for Conservation of Nature and Natural Resources.

Gribble, R.A. (1996, June 22). Cabela's picks Prairie du Chien. *Wisconsin State Journal* (p. 8B).

Gustanski J.A., & Squires, R.H. (Eds.). (2000). *Protecting the Land: Conservation Easements Past, Present, and Future*. Covelo, CA: Island Press.

Highway Beautification Act of 1965, 79 Stat. 1032 (1965).

Jacobs, H.M. (1999). Fighting over land: America's legacy ... America's future? *Journal of the American Planning Association*, 65 (pp. 141–149).

Johnson, W.A., & Cron, F.W. (1958). *Report on a Recommended Route for the Great River Road (Mississippi River Parkway) through the State of Wisconsin*. Washington, DC: U.S. Department of Commerce, Bureau of Public Roads.

Jordahl, H.C. (1963). Conservation and scenic easements: An experience resume. *Land Economics*, 34, 343–365.

Kamrowski v. State, 31 Wis.2d 256, 142 N.W2d 793, 797 (1966).

Kline, J., & Wichelns, D. (1994). Using referendum data to characterize public support for purchasing development rights to farmland. *Land Economics*, 70, 223–233.

Korngold, G. (1984). Privately held conservation servitudes: A policy analysis in the context of in gross real covenants and easements. *Texas Law Review*, 63, 433–495.

Land Economics Studies Unit, Appraisal Section, Bureau of Right of Way, Division of Highways. (1967). *A Market Study of Properties Covered by Scenic Easements Along the Great River Road in Vernon and Pierce Counties*. Madison: Wisconsin Department of Transportation.

Maynard, L.J., Kelsey, T.W., Lembeck, S.M., & Becker, J.C. (1998). Early experience with Pennsylvania's agricultural conservation easement program. *Journal of Soil and Water Conservation*, 53(2), 106–112.

Meyers, P. (1999). *Livability at the Ballot Box: State and Local Referenda on Parks, Conservation, and Smarter Growth, Election Day 1998.*

Washington, DC: Brookings Institution, Center on Urban and Metropolitan Policy.

Ohm, B.W., & Schmidke, E. (1998). *An Inventory of Land Use Plans in Wisconsin*. Madison: University of Wisconsin-Madison/Extension, Department of Urban & Regional Planning.

Olson, J.A. (1965). Progress and problems in Wisconsin's scenic and conservation easement program. *Wisconsin Law Review 1965*, 352–373.

Pfeffer, M.J., & Lapping, M.B. (1994). Farmland preservation, development rights and the theory of the growth machine: The views of planners. *Journal of Rural Studies*, 10, 223–248.

Plimpton, O.A. (1966). *Conservation Easements: Legal Analysis of Conservation Easements as a Method of Privately Conserving and Preserving Land*. Washington, DC: Nature Conservancy.

Rodegerdts, H.E. (1998). Land trusts and agricultural conservation easements. *Natural Resources and Environment*, 13, 336–340.

State ex rel. Saveland Park Holding Corp. v. Wieland, 269 Wis. 262, 69 N.W.2d 217 (1955).

Strong, A.L. (1975). *Private Property and the Public Interest: The Brandywine Experience*. Baltimore: Johns Hopkins University Press.

Strong, A.L. (1983). Easements as a development control in the United States. *Landscape Planning*, 10, 43–64.

Tax Reform Act of 1976, Pub. L. 94-455, 90 Stat. 1520 (1976).

Transportation Equity Act for the 21st Century, Pub. L. 105-178, 112 Stat. 107 (1998).

Whyte, W.H. (1959). Securing open space for urban America: Conservation easements. (Technical Bulletin 36). Washington, DC: Urban Land Institute.

Whyte, W.H. (1962). *Open Space Action* (Study Report No. 15). Washington, DC: Outdoor Recreation Resources Review Commission.

Whyte, W.H. (1968). *The Last Landscape*. Garden City, NY: Doubleday.

Wisconsin Department of Resource Development. (1961). *Conservation Easements and Open Space Conference* (Summary Report). Madison: Wisconsin Department of Resource Development.

Wisconsin Statutes, § 700.40 (1997).

Wright, J.B. (1994). Designing and applying conservation easements. *Journal of the American Planning Association*, 60, 380–388.

CHAPTER 20

METROPOLITAN GOVERNMENT IN THE TWIN-CITIES AREA OF MINNESOTA

Jim Miara

Suburban sprawl, endless traffic jams, air and water pollution, and dwindling open space are 21st-century evils descending like an implacable plague on major metropolitan centers. After ignoring warning signs that have been mounting for decades, urban planners and public officials everywhere now are scrambling to find short-term and long-range strategies to battle the cumulative effects or uncontrolled growth. And many of them are looking northward for guidance.

Minnesota's Twin Cities area is one of the first U.S. metropolitan regions to formally recognize that haphazard growth is a serious threat to its quality of life and then take steps to combat it. In 1967, the Minnesota legislature created a regional agency called the Metropolitan Council and gave it the authority and tools to help shape the metropolitan area's future.

To advocates of regional planning, the Met Council, as it is called, is a model of enlightened government, with the authority to conduct long-range planning for an area that includes Minneapolis and Saint Paul

and the surrounding seven counties of Anoka, Carver, Dakota, Hennepin, Ramsey, Scott, and Washington. The vast metropolitan region comprises 189 municipalities and 2.4 million residents.

A major weapon in the Met Council's planning arsenal is its ability to review the comprehensive plans of all communities within its jurisdiction to ensure that they are in concert with regional goals. It also has the authority to plan for transportation needs and guide regional development, including air travel; water quality and supply; housing; and parks and open spaces.

Following a 1994 legislative mandate to merge with three other regional agencies, the Met Council gained an operational component, which manages the regional wastewater collection and treatment system, the regional transit system, and the Metropolitan Housing and Redevelopment Authority (HRA). The council — with 3,700 employees and an annual budget of nearly $500 million — is financed with funds from a local property tax, user fees from the wastewater

Originally published as "Council, My Council," *Urban Land*, Vol. 60, No. 4, April, 2001. Published by the Urban Land Institute, Washington, D.C. Reprinted with permission of the publisher.

treatment system, and the transit system, plus supplemental state and federal funds.

The Met Council gained its widespread authority because it was clear that resolving the multifaceted problems created by growth requires comprehensive planning. The development of transportation (highways and airports) must be coordinated with the transit system. Residential development must be channeled to areas where the infrastructure to support it is in place. And all planning must consider environmental and quality-of-life issues.

"The Metropolitan Council seeks to meld three ideas — economic growth, environmental preservation, and fiscal conservatism, which means maximizing use of existing infrastructure," says Ted Mondale, who was appointed chairman of the Met Council in February 1999, by Minnesota Governor Jesse Ventura. "The problem is fairly simple: 500,000 more people are expected to be living in the Minneapolis/Saint Paul metropolitan area by 2020. Mondale said, "How far should the area spread, and will such population growth lead to unprecedented congestion?"

Mondale, the son of former U.S. vice President Walter Mondale and himself a former state senator and candidate for governor of Minnesota, believes it is the Met Council's job to make sure that does not happen.

"The council creates a framework for regionalism. There is a whole set of services that can be done on a regional scale that can't be done at the local level," he says. "We avoid competition [among cities] because we look at development decisions around systems — transportation, parks and open space, and air and water quality."

This regional framework aligns the council's policies and investments for transportation and sewers to support regional growth objectives. In the Twin Cities, the Met Council is using a combination of incentives, seed money, and design tools for communities to serve as smart growth models.

Unique and Controversial

Curtis Johnson, who served as the council's chairman from 1995 to 1999, points out that the Met Council "is an authentic regional government, one of only two in the country." (Portland, Oregon, is the other.) Since 1994, when the Met Council was reconfigured, he says, "It has done a good job of creating an integrated whole. It conducts planning and operations well, which is difficult. The council has done a good job balancing the two, and the synergy created has been effective."

But Johnson, who now runs Citistates, a Minnesota-based consulting firm that provides advice to regional planners, says that the Twin Cities model would be difficult — if not impossible — to duplicate in other areas. In 1967, when the Met Council came into being, the privately owned bus system was languishing; the wastewater treatment system was inadequate, resulting in pollution of local rivers and lakes; and suburbs were mushrooming with haphazard growth, leading to traffic congestion. In other words, conditions were ripe for an expansion of regional responsibility, and local turf wars — the bane of regional governments — were kept to a minimum. In typical Minnesota fashion, no one perceived the council as a threat, even though it added a nonelected layer of government that superseded the authority of local officials.

Sounding like Garrison Keillor of Lake Wobegon on National Public Radio, Johnson says, "The Twin Cities are cursed by an absence of crisis; nothing bad ever happens here. We have steady growth, a diversified economy, and the unemployment rate has been half the national average for ten years. As a result, it's hard to arouse people over problems, particularly long-range problems."

By 1994 it was clear that traffic congestion and pollution needed a regional remedy. Johnson says the Met Council was accepted as a necessary nuisance, even though some elements of the council's charter are highly controversial. The most contentious debate concerns whether the chair and the 16-member board should be elected. Currently, members are appointed and serve at the pleasure of the governor, although they are confirmed by the state senate in consultation with local elected officials. Opponents of the current system note that the regional government in Portland is elected, and the Met Council, which has taxing power and enormous authority, should be, too. "Taxation with representation" is a common cry among those advocating change.

"The Met Council is the only regional planning board in the country that has taxing power," notes Karen Anderson, mayor of Minnetonka, an affluent town of 53,000 located in the western suburbs of Minneapolis. "And there are tax disparities — a 1972 state law provides for sharing of tax proceeds among communities, although the Met Council does not directly administer this program. It's a big deal and people don't like it." Even so, she says that the majority of her constituents support the Met Council in its present form as long as it is monitored closely.

"Minnetonka has always contributed more money than we have gotten in return, but we approve of what the council is doing. We just have to be proactive to make sure there are no greater disparities," says Anderson, who has been in office for seven years. When it comes to the ongoing elected-versus-appointed battle, Anderson, like many in the Twin Cities area, is conflicted. "I have changed my mind several times, but I come back to the appointive system," she says.

Johnson also has come down in favor of the appointive system after initially favoring elections. "I can see it both ways; there are distinct advantages in each," he explains. With an appointed board, he says, it is possible to recruit qualified people who otherwise would not run, and they are more likely to think districtwide. An elected board, on the other hand, would have more legitimacy, and candidates could make the council's agenda part of their campaigns. In the end, he says, "Electing the council is probably not the best idea, but I think elections will be inevitable."

Mondale clearly favors the appointed body. "Elected officials sometimes end up being complaint-takers from constituents. Now, we have a council that is leading, rather than responding to pressure." He also notes that developers, who have enormous interest in the council's decisions, likely would be huge contributors to district campaigns.

The Twin Cities are unique in that all the pluses and minuses of a given metropolitan area are multiplied by two. There are two urban centers, two symphony halls, two downtown arenas, and two rush-hour commuting patterns. Sixty percent of Minnesota's population lives in the Met Council region, and most of the state's cultural and political institutions are located there as well.

Considering the extensive scope of the council's jurisdiction and the fact that it has the third-largest budget of local governments in the state, some Minnesota legislators have voiced concern that it could challenge the legislature's authority. Jim Solem, who served as the Met Council's regional administrator from the time of the merger of public agencies in 1994 until last year, points out that even though the council is not elected, it is extremely sensitive to the need to build support for its actions — in the districts, in the legislature, and, most important, with the governor.

"The first thing the council has to do is sell the governor," Solem explains. "Fortunately, the current governor [Jesse Ventura] is very supportive. When he was running for office, he questioned the need for the council, but now he is very supportive."

Indeed, Ventura is so convinced of the council's value that he has given Mondale cabinet-level status.

Regional Planning Successes

Both its opponents and its supporters agree that, over the past seven years, the Met Council has made progress in several key areas. For example, the rivers, lakes, and streams are cleaner. As Johnson, the former council chair, says, "Today, you can fall into the Mississippi without taking a toxic bath. You couldn't ten years ago." Also, urban services are delivered more efficiently and cost-effectively than they were before. Furthermore, rural areas and the nationally acclaimed Twin Cities regional park system have been protected and the number of affordable housing units has increased significantly.

Most observers consider reform of the region's wastewater treatment management system as one of the council's most significant accomplishments. Administered by local boards prior to 1967, the multiple and antiquated wastewater treatment systems strained under the pressure of the suburban population spurt of the 1950s and 1960s. The region's many waterways were being polluted, endangering the quality of life considered to be one of the Twin Cities's major assets. "One of the reasons we supported the creation of the Met Council," says Mayor Anderson, "was [because] Lake Minnetonka was suffering pollution due to the many western suburbs that had poor wastewater treatment systems. Something had to be done."

When the Met Council was created, however, changes came quickly. From 1970 to 1985, some 33 smaller wastewater treatment plants scattered across the region were consolidated into a regional system of nine larger and more efficient plants. More system improvements were made, and in the late 1990s, facing strong opposition from unions, the council nevertheless restructured the workforce. As a result, the operating budget was reduced by $20 million per year over three years. At the same time, it made repairs to the system, started construction of new wastewater treatment plants, and reduced rates for local communities. "It was no longer a situation where a small local board got overwhelmed by unions," explains Solem, who as regional administrator was in the thick of the battle. "The council initiated competition and set cost parameters. There was a little fuss and feathers along the way, but we made the changes."

Transportation

In the 1940s, the Twin Cities region bustled with public rail transportation. Mass transit was so good, in fact, that some urban historians contend that the easy access to rail transport made feasible the development of low-density, single-family homes, which fostered suburban sprawl. But as the popularity of the automobile began to grow in the 1950s, the Twin Cities, like most other metropolitan areas, shifted focus from mass-transit systems to superhighways. As a result, much of the old rail system was neglected and eventually removed. Today, virtually none of the old rail lines are in service.

The Met Council has begun to reverse the situation. In January, ground broke on the $675 million Hiawatha Light-Rail Transit Line, which will extend 11.6 miles from downtown Minneapolis to the Minneapolis/ Saint Paul International Airport. Scheduled to open in 2004, the Hiawatha Line is expected eventually to carry 24,800 passengers a day.

"Once this is up and running, there will be an uncritical rush for everyone to have their own line," says Mondale. "It's a high-quality amenity. When there's a big snowstorm, would you like to get to the office in 12 minutes or sit in traffic for a couple of hours?" Adds Todd Paulson, a Met Council board member from Brooklyn Center, "We weren't just breaking ground on a light-rail system, we were breaking ground on regional planning. We are integrating the transit system with community redevelopment, affordable housing, and environmental protection. All the elements have to be coordinated."

Light rail also is a catalyst for development. Mary Hill Smith, a council member representing the western suburbs of Minneapolis and the chairwoman of the council's transportation committee, outlined how integrating the transit system with community redevelopment, affordable housing, and environmental protection is part of the transportation investment. "All elements are interrelated in terms of policies and investments," she says.

Not everyone has welcomed the prospect of the new rail service, however. More than 150 community meetings have addressed abutters' concerns about the Hiawatha Line's disruptive effects. "The light-rail line will affect a lot of people, so we needed to build a consensus," explains Natalio Diaz, the Met Council's transportation planning director. "It required a lot of dialog and education. We tried to make it explicit that transportation systems are integral to growth."

Smart Growth

Expressed in the simplest terms, says Mondale, the Met Council's goal is to preserve the area's quality of life through smart growth. A no-growth strategy is impossible and uncontrolled growth creates chaos; the only logical alternative, therefore, is to guide growth in directions acceptable to the community.

In an address to a conference on smart growth last year, Mondale said, "We've had a debate in our region for a long time about whether we want to be Mayberry or whether we want to be New York City. If we continue where we're going, we're going to be L.A. or Atlanta, and that's not the kind of place we want to be. The smart growth approach is the way to get out of that either/or debate."

In 2000, the Met Council launched a regional initiative called Smart Growth Twin Cities that engages regional residents in the urban design process by asking them to voice their thoughts about how they want the Twin Cities to look in the future. With a grant from the McKnight Foundation, the council hired Calthrope Associates, a San Francisco, California-based urban design firm, to facilitate the process.

In workshops to be held this spring, residents will consider development preferences for local sites. In fall 2001, the council will host regional workshops considering issues such as the environmental and economic impacts of current and planned growth and debate alternative land use plans. Six test "opportunity sites" have already been chosen. The Met Council hopes these sites will allow for compact, efficient development "that is walkable and transit-friendly and will serve as models for other communities planning smart growth." Residents will participate in small teams of business people, city officials, and developers to create detailed, feasible plans. Local officials have welcomed the initiative. "This gives us a wonderful opportunity to work with our citizens to see where our future may go," says Mayor Myrna Kragness of Brooklyn Center, one of the opportunity site host communities.

The Livable Communities Act, passed by the state legislature in 1995 and coauthored by then state senator Ted Mondale, has become one of the Met Council's most effective tools in implementing smart growth policies. The law authorizes the council to provide grants to communities to develop projects that include a mix of housing and create a community that is more walkable and transit-oriented while preserving green space. Other goals include expanding affordable housing and cleaning up polluted sites for redevelopment to accommodate housing, business, and jobs. Last year, the Met Council awarded $19.2 million to 24 communities and two counties for smart growth projects.

The livable communities program has garnered commitment from communities for an estimated 76,000 units of affordable housing by 2010. About 16,000 units have been built to date by participating communities.

"When we passed the Livable Communities Act in 1995, people thought we were speaking Chinese," recalls Mondale. "We had to look for development sites to clean up, but now we have hundreds of applications. Communities are seeing how they can revive used lands and turn them into vibrant community centers."

In keeping with the council's incentives philosophy, new grant criteria now before the council call for expansion of affordable housing by giving participating cities and counties a chance to earn a higher priority for regional investments in community development, transportation, and environmental projects.

"The council is committed to a regional growth strategy that sustains this region's competitive advantage in the future. We do this by making connections among jobs, housing, transportation, land use, and our region's environmental assets," add Mondale.

Eye to the Future

In the end, proponents of the Met Council say, the objective is to prepare for the half-million new residents who will inhabit the Twin Cities region in just 20 years — and to do it in a way that preserves the area's cherished quality of life. Accomplishing this requires a comprehensive approach that factors in variables such as economic and social vitality, the best use of land and resources, and the preservation of parks, waterways, and other environmental amenities. At the same time, growth should take place in a way that enhances the urban centers and older neighborhoods.

"The future of the Twin Cities," says Mondale, "depends on the strength of the whole, not just some of its parts. I think the Met Council is on the verge of building a consensus — and it is happening before we reach a crisis point. Florida started taking action only after the Everglades were seriously harmed. Maryland moved only after the Chesapeake Bay was polluted. We want to do things before anything here collapses."

CHAPTER 21

REGIONAL PLANNING AND GROWTH MANAGEMENT IN PORTLAND, OREGON

R. Bruce Stephenson

Portland is a premier "green city" whose quality of life is consistently ranked among the highest in the United States (Chapman & Starker, 1987; Friedman, 1993; Partners for Livable Communities, 1994). In an era when government planning is viewed as a problem, not a solution, Portland provides a rare model for melding environmental protection and a booming economy (Artibise, Moudon, & Seltzer, 1997; Easterbrook, 1995; Egan, 1996). "Even more shocking," wrote columnist E.J. Dionne, Jr., "the planning system — in place since 1973 — is popular" (Dionne, Jr., 1997, p. A27). Yet, even in this planning Mecca, half a century lapsed before citizens moved toward the regional city Lewis Mumford had envisioned. Exploring the slow realization of Mumford's vision not only opens another chapter in Portland's planning history (Abbott, 1983; Blackford, 1993; MacColl, 1979); it may also help other metropolitan regions trying to replicate the Oregon growth management model.

Portland lines both sides of the Willamette River just south of its juncture with the Columbia River. The surrounding landscape is a scenic mix of bucolic farmland, evergreen forests, and commanding mountain peaks. Historically, Portland's economy centered on timber and agriculture, which made the landscape a common bond in the life of residents and a central concern for numerous plans (Artibise, Moudon, & Seltzer, 1997). The longstanding effort to systematically preserve the northern Willamette Valley's scenic and productive landscape is due, in part, to a "moralistic political culture" (Abbott, 1994, p. 207) that values the public good over the individual. Since 1970, Portlanders have generally accepted the notion that government should enforce a system of public planning and land-use controls to guide private land developers toward collective goals (Abbott, 1994). While a unique political culture underlies Portland's growth management system, good fortune has also contributed.

The creation of Forest Park, the largest wilderness preserve in an American city, typifies the Portland experience. In 1903, John Olmsted, Frederick Law Olmsted's

Originally published as "A Vision of Green: Lewis Mumford's Legacy in Portland, Oregon," *Journal of the American Planning Association*, Vol. 65, No. 3, Summer, 1999. Published by the American Planning Association, Chicago, Illinois. Reprinted with permission of the publisher.

stepson, recommended establishing a linear park along the Tualatin Ridge on the west side of Portland. The Parks Board executed only a portion of the Olmsted plan, and almost all of the Tualatin Ridge remained in private hands. In 1915, subdividers platted 1,400 acres along the ridge and investors were soon secured. Road building, however, proved too difficult on the steep slopes and the project collapsed. The city gained title to the property, but Olmsted's proposal remained buried until the city hired Robert Moses in 1943 to delineate public projects for postwar development. Moses rejuvenated the idea of a "Forest Park," recommending "that the steep wooded hillsides located on the westerly border of the city be placed in public ownership" (Moses, 1943, p. 38). After the war, a "Committee of Fifty" championed Moses' proposal and, in September 1948, the City Council dedicated 4,200 acres to create Forest Park (Houle, 1988). Today this 5,000-acre preserve lies in the midst of one of the nation's faster growing urban regions, a product of vision, perseverance, and luck. Like the Olmsted blueprint for Forest Park, Lewis Mumford's summons for a green, regional city waited for decades until finally resurrected in the late 1980s.

Lewis Mumford's Vision of Green

In his first book, *The Story of Utopias* (1922), Mumford introduced the concept of *regionalism*, a philosophic template to guide modern city-building around the constructs of nature (Luccarelli, 1995; Thomas, 1990). All individuals and societies hold utopian notions of a better life, but without a vision that incorporates limits as well as aspirations, he wrote, "the outlook for our civilization is almost as dismal as Herr Spengler finds it in *Der Untergang des Abendlandes*" (Mumford, 1922, p. 268). Science and tech-

nology were remaking the world, but Mumford feared that if these forces were not channeled into "human patterns," individuals would be cut off from nature and become as standardized as the modern city's growing proliferation of machines. He advocated regional surveys as the means to focus scientific studies on the needs of the local community, while the Garden City concept provided the model for building *utopias*—"good places" that "spring out of the realities of our environment" (Mumford, 1922, p. 307).

In 1927, in his keynote address at the National City Planning Conference, Mumford challenged the nation's planners to adopt a regional perspective. He chastised the profession's bent for viewing cities as machines designed for production rather than biological organisms capable of reproduction. "City planning can do nothing on this basis which cannot be done just as well as a matter of engineering technique, and just as blindly from the social standpoint, in the ... municipal engineer's office" (Mumford, 1927, p. 47). Unless planners recognized regional environmental constraints, cities would pass "the limits of functional size and use" (p. 48). Mumford recounted a sequence of deterioration that occurred when past urban civilizations exceeded natural limits. Periods of excessive growth were followed by ecological catastrophe and then the collapse of cities and civilization. The "necropolis" or dead city, Mumford cautioned, was the fate of any society that promoted unlimited growth (p. 48). Another decade elapsed, however, until his ideas gained national attention.

In 1938, Mumford's career reached its apex. After a grueling two-year writing schedule, he published *The Culture of Cities* to laudatory reviews. In this rich study, Mumford analyzed the evolution of the modern city and critiqued American civilization. The world's first consumer economy had no bounds. Given the capabilities of modern technology, the nation's rapid urbanization posed a special problem: America's frontier heritage had created a culture that excelled at exploiting nature's bounty, but in their fervor Americans had failed to construct stable or well-designed communities. The accelerated expansion of urban America during the 1920s testified to the efficiency of mass production techniques, but standardized projects followed a factory-style regimen that lacked personal or cultural functions. Just as the factory was designed to assemble and mobilize workers, the modern city was becoming a center for assembling and mobilizing consumers. Since his first book, Mumford had written of urban dwellers evolving into robots, removed from nature, dependent upon artificial means for survival, and programmed to consume. In *The Culture of Cities*, he argued that the city was no longer a place to live, but a place to buy. "A rootless world removed from the sources of life: a Plutonian world, in which living forms become frozen into metal: cities … defiling their own nest, reaching into the sky after the moon: more paper profits, more vicarious substitutes for life" (Mumford, 1938b, p. 255).

In 1938, Mumford's appearance on the cover of *Time* not only attested to his stature as a writer, but to his growing influence in the ongoing experiments to restructure American life. In contrast to most of the intellectual left, Mumford's vision of a better society was tinted with green rather than red. His environmentalism had a revolutionary edge, as he pushed "to transcend the machine, and to create a new biological and social environment" (Mumford, 1938b, p. 492). But he eschewed radical change for an orderly transformation that would bring urban civilization into harmony with evolutionary and organic patterns (Luccarelli, 1995; Miller, 1989). The New Deal greenbelt towns outside Milwaukee, Cincinnati, and Washington, DC, put Mumford's theories to the test and, at the same time, augmented his stature as America's leading urbanist.

Regional Planning in Portland

The acclaim that greeted *The Culture of Cities* afforded Mumford the luxury to travel and explore new possibilities. Out of a flood of offers, he accepted requests from Honolulu and the Northwest Regional Council (NRC), a nonprofit regional planning group, to work as a consultant for the first time (Miller, 1989). *The Culture of Cities* was "causing young men to see visions and old men to dream dreams," the NRC's Ben Kizer wrote to Mumford. After this "tremendous task of composing *The Culture of Cities*, new scenes, new aspects of human effort and human folly might rest and refresh the spirit" (Kizer, 1938, p. 4). The opportunity to visit a region long associated with Eden attracted the weary author. The offer to study "what the government is doing with the Columbia, that great river of power, beauty and greatness" (p.3) ensured his services.

In 1937, the opening of the Bonneville Dam had given regional planning its first foothold in Portland (Robbins, 1997). "The Bonneville Dam was … a fine piece of planning," Earl Riley, Portland commissioner and future mayor, stated in his address to the 1937 Oregon Planning Conference (Oregon State Planning Board, 1937, p. 15). The 300 planning advocates gathered in Portland were united by the belief that the new energy source offered the means to stimulate the economy and reduce "haphazard growth" (p. 17). A wave of migration from the Dust Bowl had diminished the supply of affordable land, but with the Bonneville complex, stated Walter Blucher, executive director of the American Society of Planning Offices, "new growth … can be the deliverance or the destruction of the area, depending on how it is controlled.... This is the only place in the United States new enough so that you can make it become a land flowing with milk and honey.... I hope you won't spoil it" (p. 18).

That summer, Portland's Reed College hosted a follow-up meeting to discuss creating an agency for disseminating research on regional issues and coordinating planning efforts. The mix of academics, planners, and resource managers agreed that "only an impartial agency, free from political influence, and financially independent of special interest groups could fill the need" (NRC, 1943, p. 8). A steering committee organized the NRC's first conference and garnered a 3-year, $74,000 Rockefeller Foundation grant to establish a three-person staff in Portland (NRC, 1943).

After the NRC opened its new office, Kizer wrote Mumford imploring him "to make a swift reconnaissance of this region ... and discuss our plans with us, criticizing and helping us develop them" (Kizer, 1938, p. 2). It was a unique opportunity. In *The Culture of Cities* Mumford had concentrated on replanning mature regions, but "here," as Kizer put it was "a new land, with new possibilities of development, with virgin resources" (p. 2). Mumford agreed to spend two weeks touring the Northwest and to deliver a series of lectures on the prospects for regional planning.

Like many before him, the worldly traveler was transfixed by Oregon's landscape. "What I have seen with my eyes has been fabulously beautiful: the Great Douglas firs" and the "snow swept crest of Mt. Hood, rising above rim after rim of stark mountains" (Mumford, 1938d, p. 3). The logging operations, however, amounted to a "massacre" (Mumford, 1938e, p. 2). The wasteful practices of these "hard-bitten businessmen" did not stem from greed, Mumford believed, but from the desire for power: "for nothing testifies to power like the ability to destroy" (p. 2).

The picturesque Columbia River Gorge east of Portland especially intrigued him. The "abrupt rocks and water falls" reminded him of the "great Chinese paintings of the classic era. Esthetically, perhaps, the greatest landscape I have ever seen," he wrote, "surpassing in intensity even ... Hawaii" (Mumford, 1938d, pp. 3–4). Encroaching industrial development, however, marred this natural masterpiece. This preyed on Mumford. A local historian wrote that his response, delivered to Portland's City Club, "set the narrow-minded business community on their ear" (DeMarco, 1991, p. 129).

In his speech to the City Club, Mumford proposed that Portlanders could "do a job of city planning like nowhere else in the world" (Mumford, 1938a, p. 26). But after encountering the "neglect in letting this fine land with its wonderful scenic beauty get away from you, it made me wonder," he asked, "if you are good enough to have it in your possession? Have you enough intelligence, imagination, and cooperation among you to make the best use of these opportunities?" (p. 26). He summoned business leaders to "control more vigorously" (p. 26) the land along the Columbia because industry had already decimated some of the most scenic sites.

After this engagement, Mumford's trip devolved into a fast-paced, perfunctory exercise, "even speaking, God save me," he confided in a personal letter, "to the [Seattle] Chamber of Commerce!" (Mumford, 1938e, p. 3). "Out of it all much will ... come" (p. 3), but he was unsuited for the "role of honored authority" (Mumford, 1938c, p. 2). While this role was gratifying, he felt rushed, "empty," and yearned for the "whole life" (p. 2). "A week of rest on my native soil," he wrote a friend, "will cause me to put forth green shoots again" (Mumford, 1938d. p. 5).

Regional Planning
in the Northwest

Mumford's "green shoots" sprouted when he penned *Regional Planning in the Northwest* that fall. The 20-page memorandum outlined an alternative to the "false ambitions and stultifying slogans" that constituted Portland's "melancholy plan" (Mumford, 1939a, p. 2). He advocated a "change of direction" (p. 3) in planning to coincide with the new power-generating capacity of the Bonneville complex. Mumford adhered to an "energy utopianism," a belief that once regions switched energy sources, the potential for change would dramatically accelerate. In the Northwest, the new power system was the means to decentralize population into garden cities and reduce pollution in city centers (White, 1995).

Mumford envisioned Portland branching into a series of "urban inter-region[s]" (Mumford, 1939a, p. 11) that balanced function and aesthetics. He recommended greening the city's central core and enhancing the industrial and cultural base of smaller towns to foster the "reforestation" of urban culture and stem "social erosion" (p. 20). Directing growth into a system of interconnected "greenbelt towns" would ease congestion, while new development would spread around, not over, the Willamette Valley's fertile land and scenic sites. Funds spent on "urban rehabilitation" and garden city design, Mumford concluded, "would obviate the very need for grandiose engineering experiments to which we are all by sheer inertia and fashion, too easily committed" (p. 19).

To institute this vision, a "regional authority" needed "to plan, to zone, to purchase and to dispose of land" (Mumford, 1939a, pp. 14–15). Its "first duty" would be to channel development "into points of maximum advantage ... without infringing upon the original beauties of nature" (p. 13). The authority should also "carry out the de-

tails" of planning and have the power to override "short-sighted local opposition" (p. 15). These "collective democratic controls" would inhibit property rights, but Mumford forecasted corresponding reductions in "disorder ... foul building practices, ... duplicated railroad systems, abandoned logging towns, and dead mining camps" (p. 7). In addition, greenbelt towns with affordable housing and integrated transportation systems would "provide a special invitation to settlement by new industries" (p. 11).

Mumford remained a utopian at heart. "What Christianity expressed in terms of heaven," he pictured "in terms of daily living" (Mumford, 1938b, p. 378). He sought to revive the "organic community" (Blake, 1990, p. 200), a traditional form balancing work, nature, and civic responsibility, in a region blessed with a landscape of "overpowering beauty" (Mumford, 1939a, p. 1). A renaissance would ensue, he hoped, once nature became an active component of culture, and culture, in turn, harmonized around nature. Once "people ... know in detail where they live and how they live; they will be united by a common feeling for their landscape, their literature, and their language" (Mumford, 1938b, p. 386). Then the northern Willamette Valley would offer a place to live Mumford's cherished "good life,"[1] rather than merely pursuing the goods of life.

The NRC printed 1,500 copies of *Regional Planning in the Northwest* and circulated all but 20. Mumford anticipated returning to Portland in May 1940, to deliver the commencement address at Reed College and to re-examine the region. He cancelled the engagement, however, because his interest in planning and architecture seemed "the most pusillanimous act in the world" with the threat of "Hitlerism triumphant" (Mumford, 1939b, pp. 1–2). In a "world ... getting blacker" (p. 1), Mumford turned his attention to preparing the nation for a monumental crusade.

Mumford never returned to Portland,

and the immediate impact of his work was negligible. The weakness of *Regional Planning in the Northwest*, like all Mumford's writing on regional planning, was his politics. His goal was a society of cultured citizens, but experts had to direct the "groping intelligence and under-lying desires of the majority" (Blake, 1990, p. 283) towards new ideals. Politics for Mumford, Casey Blake writes, "rested on demonstration, not argument, on expert guidance, not popular participation, and on assent, not consensus" (p. 283). The NRC promoted Mumford's vision, but it never moved beyond academia and New Deal agencies. By 1943 the NRC ceased operations because it failed to gain backing from the private sector. That same year, at the urging of business leaders, the City hired New York's Robert Moses (who labeled Mumford "an outspoken revolutionary" [Caro, 1975, p. 471]) to plan Portland's postwar transition (Abbott, 1993).

For the most part, Moses' plan reiterated projects, such as Olmsted's Forest Park proposal, outlined in earlier plans. He did, however, expand the role of public facilities and the auto (MacColl, 1979). "What triumphed in wartime Portland was a conception of planning as a prelude to civil engineering," wrote Carl Abbott (1983, p. 144). Rather than Mumford's complex of garden cities, Robert Moses' "engineered city" would guide planners in Portland after World War II.

The "Oregon Experiment" in Portland

In the decade after 1945, planning rarely moved beyond the realm of traffic engineering or public works in greater Portland. Except for Forest Park, Moses' major civic improvements were never realized, and the quest for suburban land often made design guidelines superfluous. For instance, grocer Fred Meyer, the region's leading retailer, moved his projects outside of Portland if they were constrained by planning regulations. The region's rapid suburban growth paralleled the national experience, but a distinct uneasiness also took hold. "Jerked by the war from an Arcadian existence among flowers and firs, it looks back longingly…" Richard Neuberger wrote in his exposé on Portland for the *Saturday Evening Post* (1947, p. 23). Residents wanted "their Eden undisturbed" (p. 23) and in the midst of an economic boom this gave the city "a split personality" (p. 23), according to the future Oregon senator. While Neuberger expressed Portlanders' reluctance to see their city become "a swashbuckling, industrial giant" (p. 23), the threat of urban sprawl would later engender similar feelings.

In 1969, exploding urban growth in the Willamette Valley pushed Governor Tom McCall to make land use planning a "statewide, not merely local, concern" (MacColl, 1995, p. 205). Urban pollution, the loss of rich farmland to "leap-frog" subdivisions, and a fear that the state's renowned "livability" was in decline all fueled Oregon's planning revolution (Abbott, 1983; MacColl, 1995). McCall, a maverick Republican, voiced the concerns of both the rural and urban constituents who "thought land was too valuable" to let "the ticky-tacky treadmill of development" destroy Oregon's natural resources (Walth, 1995, p. 246). During his first term (1966–1970), McCall pushed Oregon into the forefront of environmental reform, and, in 1969, Senate Bill 10 established the nation's first comprehensive planning act. In his second term (1970–1974), McCall renewed his planning crusade in the opening address to the 1973 State Legislature. The former journalist touched a common nerve among Oregonians, especially those west of the Cascades, by denouncing the "coastal condomania and the ravenous rampage of suburbia in the Willamette Valley" (DeGrove, 1984, p. 237). Compiling plans was not enough to rein in the "grasping wastrels of the land," who "mock Oregon's status as the environmental model for the nation" (p. 237). The Legislature followed McCall's lead and in 1973 passed Senate Bill 100 (SB 100), which required local governments to formulate comprehensive plans that met state-mandated goals.

The new act led to the establishment of statewide goals, one of which required designated territorial limits for each city. In Portland the regional Metropolitan Services District (Metro) was directed to manage and design an Urban Growth Boundary (UGB), encompassing 24 cities and portions of three counties.[2] The implementation of SB 100 coincided with a deep recession in the Oregon economy. During this period of slowed growth, consensus building in Portland faced relatively little pressure from development interests. In 1978 voters approved a new charter that gave Metro formal powers for regional planning. This referendum made Metro the nation's only directly elected regional government, consisting of a 12-member board and an executive officer (DeGrove, 1992; Poulsen, 1987). A year later, the State accepted Metro's UGB (which contained 364 square miles), and Portland would become the one American metropolis that could be described, in James Kunstler's words, as "Lewis Mumford's dream come true" (Kunstler, 1993, p. 205).

SB 100 revolutionized the planning process, but a number of obstacles remained before Portland could become the green city Mumford had envisioned. The UGB protected farmlands and forests from urban encroachment, but within the UGB little had been done to safeguard the natural landscape. Goal Five, one of the 14 state goals for planning, requires local governments "to conserve open space and protect natural and historic resources for future generations" (Oregon State Planning Goals, 1994, p. 300). SB 100, however, failed to require standardized inventories or methods of data collection, resulting in plans of wildly divergent quality. Goal Five also orders a "balancing" between economic and environmental factors in the review of development proposals, but without guidelines, local governments showed broad discretion in their decisions. Planning departments often relied on volunteers to inventory natural areas and even monitor sites after conditions were placed on development projects in environmentally sensitive areas.

Metropolitan Greenspaces: Renewing the Vision

As Portland's economy surged to life in the late 1980s, growth pressures mounted and Goal 5 became the rallying point for activists seeking to protect the region's natural beauty and ecology (Ketcham, 1994). Portland Audubon, the region's most influential environmental organization, took the lead in inventorying natural areas for Goal 5. In the early 1980s, Mike Houck, Audubon's urban naturalist, noticed that the remaining natural corridors matched many sites identified in the Forty-Mile Loop Trust's plan to complete the Olmsteads' original system of parkways. Houck, however, could barely pursue this finding because of his time commitments as head of a coalition trying to protect the region's remaining natural areas.[3]

In 1983, the Clackamas County Commission sold Deep Creek Park, a 76-acre wilderness, to a logging company for $400,000. The Commission claimed the park represented a "luxury" (Kohler, 1983, p. D1) the County could no longer afford, and proceeds from the sale funded improvements for the County's remaining parks. After this defeat, Houck realized that Portland's "green city" status did not immunize citizens from the contentious land use issues that drive local politics throughout the United States (M.C. Houck, personal communication, April 24, 1995).

The next year, Oaks Bottom, a 160-acre wetland on the Willamette River, seemed destined for a similar fate. Portland had acquired the willow and cottonwood swamp 25 years earlier to create a park in a heavily developed area, but the city was considering turning the site into either a motocross course or a yacht harbor. Houck employed a campaign of stealth and education to keep Oaks Bottom natural. First, he made 40 "Oaks Bottom Wildlife Refuge" signs and placed them throughout the property. Then, at countless public meetings, Houck's advocacy inspired conservationists, key politicians, and even reluctant business interests to believe that this riparian wetland represented a "providential gift" (Collins, 1990, p. 14). The persuasive naturalist also led scores of field and canoe trips to introduce citizens and politicians to the 140 species of birds nesting near the central city. In 1988, Mayor Bud Clark, who became a heron enthusiast after a Houck canoe trip, led the City Council in designating Oaks Bottom as a wildlife refuge (Pierce, 1990).

After this victory, a local foundation awarded Houck a grant to set up a Metropolitan Wildlife Refuge System. For citizens intent on preserving urban natural areas, Houck was a "Modern-day Moses" (Collins, 1990, p. 14) with a vision of "the promised land of Portland's future" (p. 14). Houck, however, made it clear that before attempting to secure the future, civic leaders needed to revisit the past. In a speech to the City Club in 1989, he called on his audience to renew an old mission, not invent a new one. Natural corridors were essential for enhancing biodiversity, but as Olmsted and Mumford argued, an interconnected system of natural landscapes also enhanced *human* life (Houck, 1989). In an age of communal dissolution, greenways offered a means, Houck argued, "to link people together. We need to cultivate — or renew — a feeling of the landscape. We need to rediscover what living here means to us on an intuitive, visceral level" (Collins, 1990, p. 11).

After Houck's address, Metro's planning staff investigated linking the region's natural areas with a series of greenways. Metro had shown little interest in open-space planning until a 1986 study found that local governments had generally failed to address the acquisition of wilderness preserves or to inventory natural areas. In 1989, Metro completed a regional park study which found that "there was no regional coordination in natural area parks and preserves" (Metro, 1992, p. 42). This problem manifested itself when a revitalized economy spurred growth rates in the late 1980s. By 1990, only Orlando and Atlanta, among metropolitan areas with populations over one million, were growing faster than Portland. In 1990, Metro projected 500,000 new residents by 2010, which would push the region's population to 1.7 million. Caught off guard by the population surge, residents feared that "the region's unique identity" and its "livability" would be "compromised" (Houck & Poracsky, 1994, p. 254).

In response to these concerns, Metro hired Joseph Poracsky, a geography professor at Portland State University, to map the region's natural lands.[4] The study team mapped 3,600 natural sites totalling 119,000 acres in a 602-square-mile area. After Poracsky found that only 8.5 percent of the natural land acreage was protected, he co-wrote a position paper, *Recommendations for a Regional System of Natural Areas*, that set the guidelines for what became a Metro initiative, Metropolitan Greenspaces (Houck & Poracsky, 1994).

Metro worked closely with Houck in promoting its new program. The agency provided Houck with office space to conduct public outreach and network development after he helped the agency obtain a $1.1-million grant from the Interior Department to establish the Greenspaces Program, one of two national demonstration projects.

Houck remained on loan from Audubon and the Wetlands Conservancy from 1989 to 1992. He maintained his independence from Metro so that he could continue to serve as an advocate and critic of the Greenspaces Program (Howe, 1998). In 1991, the first Greenspaces brochure introduced the concept of linking "a mosaic of natural areas into greenspaces, preserving wildlife habitat and crafting greenways for animals, plants, and people" (Metro, 1991). Metro staff also traced the genesis of this initiative to the Olmsteds and Lewis Mumford:

> These wild lands are our legacy, remnants of the native landscape enjoyed by past generations. But very little remains. The metropolitan area's burgeoning population ... could result in the extinction of our most wondrous experiences. Nearly a century ago, the Olmsteds, the renowned landscape architects, proposed for us an ambitious scheme of interconnected parks. Three decades later, planning visionary Lewis Mumford advocated a natural areas system for the region.... Metropolitan Greenspaces is that renewed vision. (Metro, 1991)

In their advocacy of greenspaces, some enthusiasts lost track of time and history. After nearby Vancouver, Washington, decided to design a greenway system in conjunction with Portland, the project coordinator claimed his inspiration came from "Lewis Mumford, Portland planner, the first to have a dream of a regional system of greenways back in 1903" (Richards, 1991, p. B2). Even if planners had difficulty distinguishing between Olmsted and Mumford, they had finally come to appreciate their solutions for protecting and enhancing the region's natural beauty.

In 1992, Metro published *A Guidebook for Maintaining and Enhancing Greater Portland's Special Sense of Place* (Ribe, 1992), crafted by a team from the University of Oregon's School of Landscape Architecture. The study reprinted Mumford's challenge to the City Club, and followed his recommen-

dation to design a "new urban pattern ... providing a proper distribution" of the three essential landscapes: "the primitive, the rural, and the urban" (Mumford, 1939a, pp. 18–19). The guidebook presented 10 illustrated planning principles to "harmonize growth patterns with regional landforms" (Ribe, 1992, p. 5). The team also recommended a slow expansion of the UGB to ensure that future development followed "quality growth patterns" (p. 51).

That July, Metro completed the Greenspaces Master Plan. Based on the discipline of landscape ecology, the plan sought to protect and restore the "green infrastructure" through land acquisition and regulation (Metro, 1992). It took three more years of consensus building, however, before voters passed a $138.8-million bond measure to fund a natural land acquisition program.[5] In 1992 voters also approved a home rule charter for Metro that gave it a new political legitimacy, including the authority to write functional plans to which City and County plans had to conform.

In 1994, the Metro Council adopted the *Region 2040* concept to "set the course" (Metro, 1995, p. 1) for regional planning over a half century. In the future, the region's development would follow a more compact form to lessen dependence on the automobile and to preserve open space networks. In 1995, the Council debated three growth concepts to guide *Region 2040*: Expand the UGB by 25 percent; keep the UGB intact and funnel development into centers and corridors with high transit use; or channel new growth into satellite cities outside the UGB (Metro, 1994). The Metro Council rejected the Mumfordian concept of satellite cities and voted to focus development within a single UGB. Although part of his plan was ignored, "the revival of interest in regional land use planning indicates the continuation of Mumford's legacy: the importance of reorienting 'place' as a means of social and environmental reform," writes one Mumford scholar (Luccarelli, 1995, p. 220). Toward this end, activists have embraced Mumford's vision to move their community in a new direction. Perhaps more than his plan, it is Mumford's conception of life connected to community and nature that led Neil Goldschmidt, former Portland mayor and governor of Oregon, to conclude that "Portland is a better city thanks in large part to the wisdom and foresight of Lewis Mumford" (Haar & Kayden, 1982, p. 16).

Today, Metro oversees an evolving, regional city: Wilderness and agricultural greenbelts mark growth boundaries; coherent architecture defines commercial centers; 140 miles of trails and greenways connect natural lands and neighborhoods; and a system of buses, trolleys, and light rail lines offers transportation alternatives to the automobile. By the end of 1997, Metro had acquired half the lands listed on the 1995 bond measure while using only one third of the approved revenues (Hunsberger, 1998). The amenities of this green city are matched by its "silicon forest's" lucrative economic landscape. Portland offers an evolving prototype in a nation struggling to accommodate growth (DeGrove, 1994). But even here, half a century elapsed before regional planning took hold, and questions about its viability remain.

The economic dynamism of the region's silicon forest and its pleasing lifestyle are spurring a heavy in-migration that is unlikely to slow in the foreseeable future. At the same time, development interests are demanding the expansion of the UGB to counter rising urban land values (Ehrenhalt, 1997).[6] The increase in land values has placed open space at a premium, and despite Metro's land acquisition program, these sites are being lost at an unprecedented rate. According to Howe (1998), "the fact that no one can say just how much has been lost highlights a fundamental weakness in Metro's planning agenda" (p. 67).

In part, Metro is a victim of its own success. The progress made in land acquisition could lead to the perception that natural resource protection is a moot point, when, in fact, Metro is struggling to implement the Metropolitan Greenspaces Plan. In *Region 2040*, planners designated 16,000 acres of environmentally sensitive land as unbuildable. Yet, until Metro adopted provisions for protecting floodplains and water quality (Title 3 of the Urban Growth Management Function Plan) in June 1998, there were no regulatory means to enforce this directive, and local governments were given 18 months to realign their plans to fit Metro's vision. Since 1990, 1,100 housing units have been constructed on floodplains within the UGB. With the region's development pressures, construction on sensitive habitats will continue unless funds and technical assistance are invested to implement the Metropolitan Greenspaces Plan. "Metropolitan Portland faces the very real prospect," Howe (1998) contends, "of becoming a densely developed region that is devoid of wildlife and subject to the vagaries of nature including floods and mudslides" (p. 71).

The problem plaguing Metro parallels the inherent weakness of Mumford's regionalism: Regional planning postulated by experts cannot succeed without a reciprocal effort at the local level. Activists such as Mike Houck helped Metro set a new agenda, but the Portland model will remain in question until the "critical problem," which Mumford identified in 1939, becomes more central to the local and regional planning process. "The critical problem is redistributing population in places of maximum advantage for life: in sites that are physically healthy and stimulating, with a sufficient underpinning of natural resources, with a sufficient supply of social facilities and cultural institutions" (Mumford, 1939a, p. 18).

Despite its limitations, Mumford's genius remains relevant because he tied human well-being to the mystery of life. He floated many thoughtful abstractions, but his basic theorem never extended too far from reality. In an age devoted to consumption, technology, and engineering, Mumford advocated the art of design to solve the complex problems of urbanization and to initiate a renewal of American culture. Communities designed around the constructs of nature can sustain ecological health while humans confront a complexity, balance, and force they can neither replicate nor fully comprehend. In its essence, Mumford's conception of regional planning offers the "myth of life" (Williams, 1990, p. 45). This option still remains viable, Mumford wrote in his first book, provided "we ignore all fake utopias and social myths that have proved either so sterile or disastrous" (Mumford, 1922, p. 300).

Notes

1. Mumford's concept of the "good life" came from the tradition of public humanism dating back to Aristotle. "'Men come together in cities," said Aristotle, "in order to live: they remain together to live the good life" (Mumford, 1938b, p. 492).

2. Regional planning reappeared in Portland in 1957 when planners and office-holders in the three metropolitan counties in Oregon (Multnomah, Clackamas, and Washington) and Clark County, Washington, formed the voluntary Portland Metropolitan Planning Commission (1957–1966). The Commission's cooperative efforts garnered federal funds for studies, but it remained primarily a research organization with little power. For more on the history of regional planning in Portland, see Poulsen (1987) and DeGrove (1992).

3. Houck and Esther Lev were instrumental in organizing the Friends and Advocates of Urban Natural Areas (FAUNA). Members represented watershed protection groups advocating the preservation and enhancement of open spaces and fish and wildlife habitat in the areas where they lived. Houck also was responsible for organizing four "Country in the City" symposiums at Portland State University between 1988 and 1991. Over 2,000 people listened to experts

in the fields of ecology, recreation, planning, and landscape architecture share their knowledge of how to design programs to preserve and enhance urban natural areas.

4. Natural areas were defined as self-sustaining plant and animal communities largely devoid of man-made structures. "Working landscapes" such as tree plantations, golf courses, and agricultural areas were not included.

5. In November 1992, a referendum to secure $200 million in general obligation bonds for acquiring sites identified in the Metropolitan Greenspaces Plan failed. After the defeat, Metro initiated a $138.8-million bond campaign for land acquisition. The late Bill Naito, a leading developer, headed a "blue ribbon" committee to promote the initiative. This time the acquisition sites were listed and prioritized on the ballot. The measure passed in 1995 with over 60 percent of the vote.

6. In 1997, Metro voted to designate as urban reserves 18,000 acres of land outside the UGB (equivalent to 8 percent of the land within the current boundary). The urban reserves will be incorporated into the UGB in the near future; 5,359 acres were so added in December 1998, to comply with state law requiring that UGBs contain a 20-year supply of buildable land. For more on this issue, see Egan (1996) and Ehrenhalt (1997).

References

Abbott, C. (1983). *Portland: Planning, politics, and growth in a twentieth century city*. Lincoln, NE: University of Nebraska Press.

Abbott, C. (1993). *The metropolitan frontier: Cities in the modern American West*. Tucson, AZ: University of Arizona Press.

Abbott, C. (1994). The Oregon planning style. In C. Abbott, D. Howe, & S. Adler (Eds.), *Planning the Oregon way: A twenty-year evaluation* (pp. 51–84). Corvallis, OR: Oregon State University Press.

Artibise, A., Moudon, A.V., & Seltzer, E. (1997). Cascadia: An emerging regional model. In R. Geddes (Ed.), *Cities in our future* (pp. 149–174). Washington, DC: Island Press.

Blackford, M.G. (1993). *The lost dream: Businessmen and city planning on the Pacific Coast, 1890–1920*. Columbus, OH: Ohio State University Press.

Blake, C.N. (1990). *Beloved community: The cul-*

tural criticism of Randolph Bourne, Van Wyck Brooks, Waldo Frank, and Lewis Mumford. Chapel Hill, NC: University of North Carolina Press.

Broder, D. (1998, July 15). Pioneering livability. The Oregonian, p. M2.

Caro, R.A. (1975). The power broker: Robert Moses and the fall of New York. New York: Random House.

Chapman, N.J., & Starker, J. (1987). Portland: The most livable city? In L. Price (Ed.), Portland's changing landscapes. (pp. 191–207). Portland, OR: Portland State University Press.

Collins, C. (1990, August 26). The greening of Portland. The Oregonian, pp. 10–17.

DeGrove, J. (1984). Land, growth, and politics. Chicago: American Planning Association Press.

DeGrove, J. (1992). The new frontier for land policy: Planning and growth management in the United States. Cambridge, MA: Lincoln Land Institute.

DeGrove, J. (1994). Following in Oregon's footsteps: The impact of Oregon's growth management strategy on other states. In C. Abbott, D. Howe, & S. Adler (Eds.), Planning the Oregon way: A twenty-year evaluation (pp. 227–244). Corvallis, OR: Oregon State University Press.

DeMarco, G. (1991). A short history of Portland. Portland, OR: Lexikos.

Dionne, E.J., Jr. (1997, March 21). Government planning that keeps Portland green. The Washington Post, p. A27.

Easterbrook, G. (1995). A moment on the earth: The coming age of environmental optimism. New York: Viking.

Egan, T. (1996, December 30). Drawing the hard line on urban sprawl. New York Times, pp. A1, A14.

Ehrenhalt, A. (1997, May). The great wall of Portland. Governing, 10, 20–24.

Friedman, E.S. (1993). The facts of life in Portland, Oregon. Portland, OR: Portland Possibilities.

Haar, C.M., & Kayden, J.S. (1982). A tribute to Lewis Mumford. Cambridge, MA: Lincoln Land Institute.

Houck, M.C. (1989, October 13). Protecting our urban wild lands, renewing a vision. Address to the City Club of Portland.

Houck, M.C., & Poracsky, J. (1994). The Portland metropolitan urban natural resources program. In R. Platt (Ed.), The ecological

city: Preserving and restoring urban biodiversity (pp. 251–267). Amherst, MA: University of Massachusetts Press.

Howe, D. (1998). Metropolitan Portland's greenspaces program. In Creating sustainable places symposium (pp. 67–71). Tempe, AZ: Hershberger Center for Design Excellence, Arizona State University.

Houle, M.C. (1988). One city's wilderness: Portland's Forest Park. Portland, OR: Oregon Historical Society.

Hunsberger, B. (1998, January 12). Metro gives itself an "A" for land buys. The Oregonian, p. E1.

Ketcham, P. (1994). To save or to pave: Planning for the protection of urban natural areas. Portland, OR: Portland Audubon Society.

Kizer, B. (1938, May 17). Kizer to Lewis Mumford. Lewis Mumford Papers, University of Pennsylvania Special Collections.

Kohler, V. (1983, April 29). Clackamas County sells 76-acre Deep Creek Park. The Oregonian, p. D1.

Kunstler, J.H. (1993). The geography of nowhere. New York: Simon and Schuster.

Luccarelli, M. (1995). Lewis Mumford and the ecological region. New York: Guilford Press.

MacColl, E.K. (1979). The growth of a city: Power and politics in Portland, Oregon 1915–1950. Portland, OR: The Georgian Press.

MacColl, E.K. (1995). The battle to control land use: Oregon's unique law of 1973. In R. Lowitt (Ed.), Politics in the postwar West (pp. 203–220). Norman, OK: University of Oklahoma Press.

Metro. (1991). Metropolitan greenspaces. [Brochure]. Portland, OR: Author.

Metro. (1992). Metropolitan greenspaces plan. Portland, OR: Author.

Metro. (1994). Concepts for growth, Portland, OR: Author.

Metro. (1995, Spring/Summer). To the citizens of the region. 2040 Framework. 1. Portland, OR: Author.

Miller, D.L. (1989). Lewis Mumford: A life. New York: Weidenfeld and Nicolson.

Mumford, L. (1992). The story of utopias. New York: Boni and Liveright.

Mumford, L. (1927). The next twenty years in city planning. Proceedings of the nineteenth national city planning conference (pp. 45–58). Washington, DC: American Institute of City Planning.

Mumford, L. (1938a, July 22). Are you good

enough for Oregon? *Portland City Club Bulletin*, 18, 26.

Mumford, L. (1938b). *The culture of cities*. New York: Harcourt, Brace, and Company.

Mumford, L. (1938c, July 3). Mumford to Sophia Mumford. Lewis Mumford Papers, University of Pennsylvania Special Collections.

Mumford, L. (1938d, July 17). Mumford to Josephine Strongin. Lewis Mumford Papers, University of Pennsylvania Special Collections.

Mumford, L. (1938e, July 27). Mumford to Josephine Strongin. Lewis Mumford Papers, University of Pennsylvania Special Collections.

Mumford, L. (1939a). *Regional planning in the Pacific Northwest: A memorandum*. Portland, OR: Northwest Regional Council.

Mumford, L. (1939b, September 4). Mumford to Josephine Strongin. Lewis Mumford Papers, University of Pennsylvania Special Collections.

Neuberger, R.E. (1947, March 1). The cities of America: Portland, Oregon. *The Saturday Evening Post*, 219, 22–24, 104–108.

Northwest Regional Council. (1943). *A summary of the history of the Northwest Regional Council*. Portland, OR: Author.

Oregon State Planning Board. (1937). *Proceedings of the Oregon planning conference*. Portland, OR: Author.

Oregon state planning goals. (1994). In C. Abbott, D. Howe, & S. Adler (Eds.), *Planning the Oregon way: A twenty-year evaluation* (pp. 300–304). Corvallis, OR: Oregon State University Press.

Partners for Livable Communities. (1994). *America's most livable communities*. Washington, DC: Author.

Pierce, N. (1990, April 29). Portland pioneers urban natural areas. *The Oregonian*, p. M2.

Poulsen, T.M. (1987). Shaping and planning Portland's metropolitan development. In L. Price (Ed.), *Portland's changing landscapes* (pp. 86–98). Portland, OR: Portland State University Press.

Ribe, R. (1992). *Ten essentials for a quality regional landscape: A guidebook for enhancing greater Portland's special sense of place*. Portland, OR: Metro.

Richards, L. (1991, December 24). Dream taking shape as network of green. *The Oregonian*, p. B2.

Robbins, W.G. (1997). *Landscapes of promise: The Oregon story 1800–1940*. Seattle: University of Washington Press.

Thomas, J.L. (1990). Lewis Mumford, Benton MacKaye, and the regional vision. In T.P. Hughes & A.C. Hughes (Eds.), *Lewis Mumford: Public intellectual* (pp. 66–99). New York: Oxford University Press.

Walth, B. (1995). *Fire at Eden's gate: Tom McCall and the Oregon story*. Portland, OR: Oregon Historical Society.

White, R. (1995). *The organic machine. The remaking of the Columbia River*. New York: Hill and Wang.

Williams, R. (1990). Mumford as Historian of Technology. In T.P. Hughes & A.C. Hughes (Eds.), *Lewis Mumford: Public intellectual* (pp. 43–65). New York: Oxford University Press.

CHAPTER 22

REVENUE SHARING AND URBAN GROWTH IN THE DENVER, COLORADO, METRO AREA

Richard M. Sheehan

Colorado has been experiencing enormous growth throughout the state and particularly in the Denver-metro area. In 1994, the governor started his "Smart Growth Initiative." This program included organizing a summit of more than 1,000 people who discussed the creation of local councils to develop regional plans to deal with this growth. The group assigned to the Denver-metro region joined with the Denver Regional Council of Governments (DRCOG) plan, which was already in progress. DRCOG, consisting of eight counties and 41 municipalities, was developing a plan to face the anticipated population growth of nearly 700,000 over the next two decades. DRCOG's *Metro Visions 2020* is a 25-year comprehensive plan designed to guide the development in these jurisdictions and examine issues such as transportation, air quality, water quality, and urban sprawl.[1] It was in this environment that the issues of urban planning crossed paths with the existence of local government competition for retail sales revenues.

In Colorado, urban sprawl has financially impacted local governments. To meet growth-financing needs and infrastructure demands, municipalities and counties often "face off" against one another to get more revenue into their own operating budgets. Local government revenues are collected at the local level in Colorado to allow for more autonomous decisions regarding the use of these resources. In contrast, in some state systems, the state government acts as a central collection source that distributes revenues based upon a formula or population base.

Colorado's revenue collection structure does not automatically encourage cooperation among jurisdictions and often results in a struggle to gain revenue share. For the Denver-metro area, this struggle can produce inconsistent "flagpole" annexation (an attempt by municipal government to annex

Originally published as "Revenue Sharing and Urban Growth Agreements," *Government Finance Review*, Vol. 14, No. 2, April, 1998. Reprinted with permission of the Government Finance Officers Association, published of *Government Finance Review*, 180 N. Michigan Ave., Suite 800, Chicago, IL USA 60601 (312/977-9700; fax: 312/977-4806; e-mail: GFR@gfoa.org). Annual subscription: $30.

around residential development in the shape of a flagpole in order to gain property having retail sales) and undesirable urban planning as cities fight for a piece of the revenue pie. Inspired by "Smart Growth" and *Metro Vision 2020* planning, the Metro Mayors' Caucus initiated a task force to seek and study alternative solutions. The task force's goal is to identify tools that have been successfully employed in the past and to create models for voluntary agreements that reduce competition and increase cooperation between local governments around retail development. One common tool used by governments in the Denver-metro area has been a number of revenue-sharing agreements; other tools include county planning restrictions, comprehensive planning agreements including "development phasing," and creative alternatives such as transferring development rights.

Metro Mayors' Task Force

In an effort to seek our methods used to discourage competition between cities, the task force examined several regional revenue-sharing efforts as well as other methods used to increase cooperation and control the type of development in growing surrounding areas. Among these were:

- The Boulder Chamber of Commerce was encouraging the city of Boulder to consider an Intergovernmental Agreement (IGA) with its outlying cities. This agreement, although unsuccessful, would turn revenues over to adjacent cities in hopes of encouraging growth outside of Boulder's boundary. It was also the goal of Boulder to control development along its central access road of US 36 and to slow the growth of inner-city traffic congestion.
- Two cities outside Boulder, Superior and Louisville, recently achieved success in creating an IGA to share revenues and avoid a legal entanglement. The goal of the IGA is to discuss the determination of 80 acres based upon land-use and serviceability issues rather than solely on revenue sharing.
- To control unincorporated development, Adams County, just northeast of Denver, is negotiating intergovernmental agreements to encourage development within municipal boundaries. The county hopes that by having an IGA it will not be forced into providing expensive infrastructure before its time.
- Thornton and Westminster, cities on the northern border of Denver, in 1986 developed an IGA designed to define a "sphere of influence" related to revenues generated on the Interstate 25 corridor.
- During what was called the "annexation wars" of the 1980s, officials of Brighton and Commerce City developed an IGA, which defined the boundaries of two cities along a major access road that the cities believe will one day be a thriving commercial district generated by development around Denver International Airport.

These models represent the Denver-metro area's effort to meet urban growth financing needs and attempts at minimizing urban sprawl before the infrastructure and municipal government are there to support it.

The Metro Mayors' Caucus Task Force, while exploring these projects, has stirred up a debate centered on sales tax collection policy and its impact on development: Is the current sales tax collection policy of Colorado creating uneven urban sprawl and encouraging unincorporated municipal-like communities, or would such haphazard development occur anyway? Should revenue-sharing agreements be used to curb the cost to local governments as they attempt to meet financing and infrastructure needs or should a more comprehensive approach be initiated to limit urban area growth in counties altogether?

The following sections of this chapter summarize five studies by the Metro Mayors' Revenue Sharing Task Force, providing examples of attempts by local government leaders to avoid a centralized state collection system with the use of revenue-sharing agreements and comprehensive land-use planning. These models have proven effective in developing cooperative approaches to what might otherwise be a divisive situation between local government entities. It is in these trenches that the battle will be won or lost to preserve autonomy and keep local sales tax control.

Boulder Regional Tax-sharing Plan

In 1995, the Boulder Chamber of Commerce recommended a regional sharing effort. After determining a base-year level of revenues, each city would share in the incremental growth of sales tax revenues based upon an allocation formula of population or existing retail share. Large cities might receive less sales tax than previously but still increase revenues based on their population. Smaller cities would have substantial gains, which would allow them time to develop income from market sources other than retail, such as manufacturing, tourism, service firms, or construction.

In theory, by equalizing sales tax revenue distribution, policy decisions would shift towards planning that focuses on neighborhood characteristics, land-use decisions, and environmental concerns rather than on the struggle to gain retail market share to meet short-term budgetary needs.[2] This attempt to create a revenue-sharing

agreement was abandoned in 1997, as it became too difficult to gain a consensus in the political climate of the time. As growth continued, outlying cities around Boulder saw enough development in their jurisdictions to discourage continued dialogue of the IGA.

Tax Sharing for Two Cities

As a result of territorial battles around Boulder, the cities of Superior and Louisville entered into a revenue-sharing agreement. This agreement, ratified by citizens in the November 1997 election, concentrated more on land-use issues and serviceability than on urban growth. Superior and Louisville are separated by US 36, which forms a natural boundary; however, because 80 acres on the south (Superior) side of US 36 were included in the Louisville city limit, property owners of this region made two attempts to file with the court to disconnect from the city of Louisville. Rather than battle it out in court, the two communities entered into a revenue-sharing agreement through which the property would become a part of Superior, and Superior would collect any retail taxes generated from any development. In return, the city of Louisville would receive 50 percent of the retail sales tax revenues, and Superior allowed Louisville to include an additional parcel in its natural boundary north of US 36. Superior experienced some complication in implementing the agreement, as it had to accommodate three special districts inside its borders that also were counting on future revenues generated from any retail development. The agreement was careful to include specific provisions dealing with utility sales tax, tax rate changes, and how the collection process would work within statewide law. Although forced by legal concerns, this model emphasizes the need to take a proactive posture when competitive issues arise.

Adams County: Growth Policies

The Adams County approach to revenue equalization is tied to its comprehensive planning process. Adams County and its constituent cities — Arvada, Aurora, Bennett, Brighton, Bloomfield, Commerce City, Federal Heights, Northglenn, Thornton, and Westminster — are developing growth-related policies within a county wide comprehensive plan which uses a tiered system designed to phase in urban-level development in three tiers: the next five years, by the year 2020, and post-2020. The goal for these local governments is to promote contiguity, infrastructure compatibility, and formal integration of their comprehensive plan. This effort is supported by government officials in the area who generally believe that urban-level growth belongs in municipalities where services can be provided in a more cost-effective manner. Adams County officials hope to achieve this goal by a series of intergovernmental agreements.

If the comprehensive plan is adopted in Adams County, urban development during the next five years that occurs in unincorporated areas would be required to meet city development standards and be subject to city review. This is designed to discourage development efforts that historically have played cities and counties off against one another. With this policy, cities must annex development within their individual urban growth boundaries. By the year 2020, comprehensive planning will be done in concert with urban centers and the county to insure consistency between individual plans. These are lofty goals, but if the spirit to cooperate remains, Adams County might have a model other local area governments can adapt rather than "duking it out" over limited resources.

Westminster-Thornton IGA

Another case in point is the "sphere of influence" revenue-sharing agreement between Thornton and Westminster, two cities just north of Denver. For Thornton and Westminster the issue was boundaries.[3] The city of Thornton was considering the annexation of land west of I-25. The city of Westminster, however, viewed that same territory as "sacred ground" and it expected to annex one day. The two city managers met to discuss the development of an agreement that would outline boundaries and set the stage for future development in the area. The discussion evolved into a 10-page IGA that included a requirement for a cooperative master plan, outlined consistency in building codes, and suggested the kinds of public service to be provided. Most importantly, a revenue-sharing formula was agreed upon. This agreement, believed by some to have curtailed development in the I-25 corridor, has yet to reach fruition, as build-out has not occurred. The city manager stated that the reason development has not occurred is not the existence of the intergovernmental agreement, but rather because there is "a lack of roof tops" in the area — once there is more housing, retail development will follow. Both mayors felt that this agreement allowed the governments to retain control over development in the area, and they believe that it removed the pressure from the two cities to compete for sales revenues. As a model to potentially follow, other cities — Commerce City and Brighton, for example — were influenced by the Thornton/Westminster agreement.

Boundary Line Agreement

In February of 1989, Brighton and Commerce City both wanted to stake claim to certain potential annexation areas. Some property owners were petitioning one city to be included in its boundary while the other city was concerned that if it did not act quickly, it might miss out on an opportunity to expand its borders and achieve potential sales tax revenue from what looked to be an area of future retail development as an outgrowth of Denver International Airport.

A good line of communication existed between the two municipalities, and avenues existed for increased cooperation — the Adams County Council of Governments (ADCOG), for example. With a cooperative environment in place, and a willingness of both parties to seek a "win-win" scenario, Brighton and Commerce City developed a revenue-sharing agreement that included land-use issues and boundary specifications. This agreement carefully described the use of debt for infrastructure and the pledging of revenues.

With the state legislature closely watching these "annexation wars," the two cities developed a model that other municipalities could follow. One of the terms of the agreement required that a joint plan be prepared as a guide for the development of land and the provision of public services and that it include design standards and land-use criteria. A truly cooperative venture now gives both cities the ability to control development and insure a steady proportionate revenue stream. In addition, their government officials do not have to concern themselves with developers trying to pit one city against the other to gain tax advantages.

Future of Revenue Sharing

The next areas of study for the Revenue Sharing Task Force include investigating a regional agreement to limit urban-level development to municipalities and promoting a dialogue between cities and counties. Cooperative agreements of this type are being explored by Boulder, Adams, and Larimer counties.

Other alternatives to development phasing include encouraging developers to build in a city. To encourage density in the city rather than in potentially agricultural or unincorporated areas, in Boulder County a property owner can sell his/her right to build at a certain density level and grant that right to an owner of a parcel of land inside the city. The opportunity to sell this right (like a mineral right) encourages the owner not to sell to developers and to keep the land rural in nature; yet the owner may "profit" by not selling. In turn, property owners inside the city boundary, who cannot build high-density property due to historical zoning restrictions, now can purchase this right and increase their profit margin by developing more units and therefore selling more units.[4]

Jefferson County, also concerned about this urban sprawl into unincorporated areas, recently put together a task force to address this issue. This task force will examine the need for a tax increase or new taxes, cutbacks in services, and incorporation or annexation of incorporated areas. The commissioners have seen financial forecasts that suggest the county's tax base cannot support what are essentially municipal services that are incurred by the unincorporated areas and to which the rest of the county is contributing financially. Whether statewide law changes are necessary or a spirit of brotherhood among local governments must continue, solutions to this issue are not easily found.

Whether these models work or lead to statewide policy changes, the issue behind these cooperative plans and revenue-sharing models is clear: Philosophically, economic development in a community needs to be based on desired characteristics and local community needs, rather than on short-term revenue gains; in practice, however, sales tax policy in Colorado is one of the driving forces that often prevents this type of development from happening. The communities in the Denver-metro area have seen the result of this retail competition and re-distribution of wealth in the financial misfortunes of two major shopping malls in the region.

Local communities like Adams County, nevertheless, have found ways and created models to benefit the citizens through comprehensive land-use planning. Local governments have kept their autonomy and avoided a centralized state collection system with the use of revenue-sharing agreements, in the cases of Louisville/Superior and Westminster/Thornton. Competition, although healthy to an economy, can be crippling to a community government that relies on retail sales taxes. Cooperation between com-munities continues to hold the key; if answers cannot be found at the local level, statewide solutions may become the only alternative.

Notes

1. Metro Vision 2020 Implementation Strategy: Economic Development/Regional Tax Policy, DRCOG, May 1996.
2. Clark, Tom, *Colorado Real Estate Journal*, "Regional Tax Sharing," July 1995.
3. Intergovernmental Agreement between the City of Thornton and the City of Westminster, January 1996.
4. Boulder County Transferred Development Rights, April 1995.

CHAPTER 23

FISCAL REGIONALISM IN ALLEGHENY COUNTY, PENNSYLVANIA

Brian K. Jensen and James W. Turner

Since the decline of the steel industry, Allegheny County, Pennsylvania, and the Greater Pittsburgh area have struggled to provide an attractive quality of life and a competitive tax environment to residents. To accomplish this goal, in 1994, Allegheny County implemented Act 77, one of the largest tax redistribution mechanisms in the country. As a result of that act, the Pennsylvania State Treasury will distribute more than $144 million in revenues collected through a one percent county-wide local option sales tax for the support of regional assets and tax relief to the county and its 128[1] municipalities this year.

Act 77 had three essential goals: 1) to supplement funding sources to local assets; 2) to promote intergovernmental cooperation; and 3) to provide tax relief to local municipalities. Act 77 has successfully addressed these goals. First, sales tax proceeds support regional assets like libraries, stadiums, parks, museums, the zoo, conservatory and aviary, and a variety of cultural and performing arts groups. Second, Act 77 has promoted intergovernmental cooperation by helping to fund the county's eight councils of governments.

This article will focus on the third goal of Act 77 — providing new revenues to local government for tax relief. Act 77 has successfully shifted burdens away from high property and "nuisance" taxes and onto the sales tax. The act's allocation formula tends to redistribute money from richer to poorer municipalities. Additionally, Act 77 provides tax relief for low-income senior citizens.

The benefits of the sales tax have been widespread and significant. A prominent civic leader has called Act 77 the single greatest change ever to Allegheny County's governance system. While implementation of the sales tax was a long and intricate process, requiring the efforts and active support of numerous experts and civic agencies, stakeholders, and elected official leadership, its numerous and obvious benefits make the Act 77 model one well worth consideration by other jurisdictions.

Originally published as "Act 77: Revenue Sharing in Allegheny County," *Government Finance Review*, Vol. 16, No. 6, December, 2000. Reprinted with permission of the Government Finance Officers Association, published of *Government Finance Review*, 180 N. Michigan Ave., Suite 800, Chicago, IL USA 60601 (312/977-9700); fax: 312/977-4806; e-mail: GFR@gfoa.org). Annual subscription: $30.

Background

A number of factors contributed to the decision to seek a local option sales tax. First, in 1990, civic leaders in the Pittsburgh region came to the discouraging conclusion that the financial support mechanism for the region's most popular assets was on shaky ground. The City of Pittsburgh, suffering from economic decline, sharp population loss, and ever-tighter budgets, had historically been the sole underwriter for the zoo, conservatory, and aviary even though the majority of visitors came increasingly from outside the city. Likewise, the city provided the only public subsidy to Three Rivers Stadium (home of the city's professional baseball and football teams) even though city residents accounted for fewer than one-sixth of attendees of Pittsburgh Pirates games.

A report by the Pennsylvania Economy League, Inc., (PEL) a non-profit, non-partisan local government research and policy analysis organization, found that the zoo, conservatory, and aviary had been unable to close the gap between their ongoing needs and available public financing. The report recommended the creation of a special county taxing district to support the zoo, conservatory, aviary, and other regional assets through a local option sales tax.[2] An earlier PEL report had come to the similar conclusion that those city facilities generated less than 25 percent of their total operating costs while city subsidies made up the bulk of the difference. The report recommended that Allegheny County help support the assets since non-city residents were their predominant users.[3]

Second, at the same time that local leaders were questioning the fairness and practicality of continued city funding for regional assets, the Pittsburgh region's economic base of heavy industry had severely eroded. A number of towns formerly dependent on the steel industry were suffering from economic dislocation and had begun to fail financially. The fiscal disparity between the county's wealthier and poorer municipalities had been growing since the early 1980s. Civic leaders wanted a local means of providing financial assistance to poorer municipalities.

Finally, local municipalities, and the City of Pittsburgh and Allegheny County in particular, had overly relied on several tax sources that diminished regional competitiveness. The city amusement tax rate was considerably higher than similar taxes in other cities, and was seen as a deterrent to increased performances and ticket sales. The city's and county's personal property taxes also were seen as uncompetitive. In addition to eliminating administratively expensive "nuisance" taxes (such as per capita taxes), civic leaders hoped to lower real estate taxes.

The Sales Tax Solution

In late 1991, Pittsburgh's mayor asked the Allegheny Conference on Community Development, a leading regional civic agency, to engage the private-sector leadership in undertaking the task of rectifying the regional assets funding problem. The Allegheny Conference, using its time-tested skills at encouraging private/public collaboration, advanced special legislation in 1993 that authorized the county to implement a one percent local option sales tax.

The sales tax was a good solution to the city's and county's numerous problems. First, the sales tax is arguably fairer than property or per capita taxes. While often viewed as regressive, Pennsylvania exempts the necessities of food and clothing from the sales tax, thus lessening the impact on the poor. Second, the sales tax generates new, out-of-county revenues. It has been estimated that non-residents generate about one of every four Allegheny County sales tax dollars. The sales tax was uniquely positioned to derive revenue for the regional assets from a significant population of non-county users.

On Dec. 14, 1993, the General Assembly passed Act 77. The act authorized the Allegheny County Board of Commissioners to adopt an ordinance establishing a one percent local option sales tax. The board exercised this authority on March 31, 1994. The law divided sales tax proceeds into two parts: 0.5 percent would support the creation of the Allegheny Regional Asset District (ARAD) for assistance to the county's various regional assets, while the other 0.5 percent would fund tax reform. The ARAD has already been discussed widely elsewhere.[4] The remainder of this article will focus on the tax reform and briefly touch on the intergovernmental cooperation elements of Act 77.

Tax-base Sharing

One of Act 77's key elements was its redistributive nature. Of total tax proceeds, projected to be about $144.3 million in 2000, half is allocated to ARAD for support of regional assets while the other half, more than $72 million, is distributed between the county and its municipalities.

Half of the amount allocated for redistribution, or 0.25 percent of the total, goes directly to Allegheny County. As a result of the elimination of the personal property tax, sales tax proceeds are the county's only tax revenue other than real estate and a relatively small hotel/motel tax. The sales tax is projected to generate more than $36 million in revenue for the county this year, nearly six percent of its total revenue. The sales tax has significantly broadened and diversified the county's revenue base.

The State Treasury allocates the remaining 0.25 percent among the 128 municipalities each month. Pittsburgh will get about $19.3 million and the remaining municipalities will get about $16.7 million this

year. In 1998, sales tax distributions comprised 2.2 percent of total municipal revenues in Allegheny County. By the end of this year, nearly $200 million will have been redistributed among the county's municipalities since the sales tax was implemented.

The sales tax has been a growing source of revenue, profiting from a strong retail economy and increasingly thorough collections since its inception. In the first full year of the sales tax, about $52.8 million was available for redistribution to the county and local governments.[5] Sales tax growth has averaged 6.6 percent annually. The projected $72 million distribution this year is a 37 percent increase over 1995.

The formula used to determine municipal distributions, while accounting for tax effort, is weighted to favor poorer municipalities. The weighting is a product of relative per capita market values of real property. Each municipality's percentage of distribution is the ratio of its weighted tax revenue to total weighted tax revenues. The state calculates a municipality's weighted tax revenue by dividing its total tax revenue by the ratio of its per capita market value of taxable real property to that of all county municipalities in aggregate. At a given level of tax revenue, lower market value ratios generate higher weighted tax revenues.

Positive Impact

The salutary effects of the distributions to the county's poor municipalities have been considerable. Braddock Borough, for example, once hosted a vibrant steel industry and numerous steel-related jobs. With a reduction in population of 72 percent since 1950, the decline of heavy industry severely reduced its ability to pay for municipal services. Braddock has had one of the highest municipal real estate tax rates and one of the lowest per capita real estate tax yields in Allegheny County for decades. In 1998, its market value ratio to that of Allegheny County was 0.29. It was declared distressed under a state financial recovery program in 1988 and continues to be one of the county's most financially distressed municipalities.

In 1998, the $149,000 in sales tax revenues allocated to Braddock accounted for nearly 9 percent of its total revenues. It was the equivalent of 15 mills of real estate tax — more than a third of the borough's real estate tax amount. In terms of impact on the expenditure budget, sales tax revenues were enough to cover its street department costs.

Sales tax distributions have had similar beneficial effects in the county's other hard-pressed towns, allowing them to hold down property tax rates and increase municipal services. PEL's municipal financial distress index demonstrates clearly the redistributive nature of the allocations. The median per capita 1994–2000 allocation for the county's 14 most stressed municipalities was $158 compared to $69 for the 11 least stressed and $94 for all municipalities.

Tax Reductions Mandated

A key goal of Act 77 was to reduce or eliminate taxes that contributed to an uncompetitive climate relative to other regions of the country by replacing them with a sales tax. As a condition for receiving sales tax proceeds, Act 77 required all recipients, beginning in 1995, to eliminate or reduce a variety of taxes.

The law mandated that Allegheny County eliminate its 4 mill personal property tax for the first full calendar year in which disbursements were received. The city also was obligated to eliminate its personal property tax, levied at a rate of 4 mills, for the first year.[6] Repeal of the county's and city's personal property taxes resulted in $18 million in tax reductions.

The city also was obligated in the first year to reduce its amusement tax from 10

percent to an amount not to exceed 5 percent. This $6 million tax reduction has benefited event patrons through lower ticket prices and increased use of city venues for sports, performing arts, and entertainment events.

The county's other 127 municipalities besides Pittsburgh, upon adoption of a resolution urging the county to create the ARAD and adopt the sales tax, also were eligible for sales tax distributions. As a condition of receiving sales tax proceeds, these municipalities were required to use at least two-thirds of their disbursements in the first year for tax reductions. Thirteen municipalities eliminated their $5 to $10 per capita taxes. Three municipalities reduced their earned income tax rates.

The greatest tax reduction impact, however, resulted from lowering real estate tax rates. Sales tax distributions and support for county-funded regional assets allowed Allegheny County to reduce its 36.5 mill real property tax rate by 5 mills in 1995 and by an additional 2 mills in 1996, a 20 percent reduction.[7]

Of the county's 127 municipalities other than Pittsburgh, all but 12 reduced real estate tax rates, some by nearly 18 percent.[8] While the average municipal tax cut was 1.6 mills, municipalities collectively cut more than 180 mills. Sales tax support allowed real property owners to pay about $7.1 million less in municipal and $62.1 million less in county real estate taxes in 1995.

In addition to general tax cuts, Act 77 required the county, city, and other municipalities to provide tax relief for low-income seniors. Nearly all municipalities piggybacked on the county's program that froze property assessments at the 1993 level for elderly, long-time property owners with low incomes.

Tax Reductions Remain

Critics of Act 77 claimed that the tax cuts mandated during the first year of distributions would soon evaporate as municipalities, always looking for extra revenues, would reinstitute the taxes they eliminated and ratchet their property tax rates back up again. But this has not been the case.

Municipalities on the whole, although not required to maintain the tax cuts, have not reinstituted former taxes nor raised rates to recapture foregone revenues. The 13 municipalities that eliminated their per capita taxes in 1995 have not restored them. Three additional municipalities eliminated their per capita taxes and have not restored them. The three municipalities that reduced their earned income tax rates have not raised them back again, and in fact, two cut their rates even further since 1995. Neither the City of Pittsburgh, the Pittsburgh School District, nor Allegheny County have reinstated their personal income taxes.

Finally, of the 115 municipalities that reduced real estate tax rates in 1995, 86 continued to levy property taxes in 2000 at rates below 1994 levels. Of those 86, 22 municipalities actually reduced their rates in subsequent years to levels below their initial 1995 cut. One municipality that did not change its property tax rate in 1995 has since reduced it below the 1994 level. Allegheny County has not raised its property tax rate since its large cuts in 1995 and 1996. The tax cuts induced by Act 77 have become a permanent part of the Allegheny County local tax landscape.

Commercial Activity Unharmed

Another criticism of Act 77 has been that a higher sales tax will induce shoppers to avoid making purchases in Allegheny County and force them over the borders into neighboring counties. Act 77, however, was designed to mitigate against such a problem. Sales taxes on big-ticket items, such as motor vehicle sales, are tracked to the county of the purchaser, not the location of the dealership. An Allegheny County resident purchasing a car in Westmoreland County still pay 7 percent sales tax on the purchase, with 6 percent kept by the state and 1 percent divided between ARAD and tax relief to Allegheny County and its municipalities. Similarly, the higher sales tax rate is no deterrent for a Washington County resident to shop for a car in Allegheny County because he or she would only pay 6 percent on the purchase.

Neither analysis of county business patterns nor survey research has demonstrated suppression of commercial activity in Allegheny County, nor are increases in commercial activity apparent in neighboring counties as a result of the sales tax. A PEL analysis of comparative retail trade growth for selected SIC categories in Allegheny County and five surrounding counties demonstrated no dampening of the Allegheny County retail economy relative to its neighbors since the introduction of the 1 percent local option sales tax.

Additionally, a survey of retail-oriented businesses and management organizations along both sides of the Allegheny County border concluded that shoppers place a higher value on time, than on sales tax differentials. Few Allegheny County businesses reported a negative impact on sales because of the additional tax. Likewise, businesses just across the county line did not report increased activity as a result of shoppers avoiding the higher Allegheny County sales tax.

Intergovernmental Cooperation

Another important, but often downplayed, element of the local government assistance portion of Act 77 is its mandatory contributions to councils of governments or other intergovernmental entities or agreements. Beginning with the second year of disbursements, Act 77 has required each municipality, with the exception of Pittsburgh and Allegheny County, to annually contribute 25 percent of any sales tax increase over the previous year's distribution to the council of governments of which it is a member or to some other intergovernmental arrangement. This provision has channeled more than $1.1 million to the eight Allegheny County councils of governments and other intergovernmental efforts since 1996. This year, sales tax increase contributions will comprise as much as 7.25 percent of some COG's total revenues.

Conclusion

Act 77 has strengthened southwestern Pennsylvania in a number of ways. In addition to the improved quality of life as a result of ARAD, the law's local tax relief and local government assistance features have mitigated the county's noncompetitive tax environment and have shifted tax burdens to a significant degree onto residents of other counties and regions. Mandatory allocations to councils of governments and other intergovernmental activities reduce inefficiencies, strengthen local governance and further enhance the region's competitiveness. The redistributive nature of Act 77 has helped to "level the playing field" for Allegheny County's financially weaker municipalities.

Tax base sharing has proved successful in Allegheny County. In considering Act 77 as a model for redistributing taxes to support their goals, other regions should engage a reputable public policy expert to assess potential benefits and limitations. It will be crucial to line up civic agency and stakeholder support and to foster active buy-in from elected official "champions" at both the local and state levels. They should then prepare for a long campaign. The benefits will be well worth the trouble, though, for by spreading the wealth, Act 77 has enhanced Allegheny County's future.

Notes

1. Allegheny County has 128 municipalities wholly within its boundaries. Two other municipalities that lie predominately in neighboring counties have small parts that cross over into Allegheny County. Those two municipalities do not receive sales tax distributions.

2. Pennsylvania Economy League, Inc., Western Division, *Regional Asset Nature of the Pittsburgh Zoo, Phipps Conservatory, and the Pittsburgh Aviary*, (Pittsburgh: Pennsylvania Economy League, Inc., Western Division, October, 1990), pp. 36–38.

3. Pennsylvania Economy League, Inc., Western Division, *Pittsburgh: A Regional City with a Local Tax Base*, (Pittsburgh: Pennsylvania Economy League, Inc., Western Division, October, 1982), xx–xxii.

4. See *Government Finance Review*, June 1995, pp. 19–22.

5. Sales taxes were first collected in 1994 but only during the last four months of the year, generating $14.2 million for redistribution.

6. Act 77 provided for the City of Pittsburgh to reimburse the Pittsburgh School District for any loss of revenue resulting from the repeal of the school district's 4 mill personal property tax. The school district chose to eliminate its personal property tax, and the city has reimbursed it annually since then. Repeal of the school district personal property taxes resulted in $4 million in tax reductions.

7. The newly elected Allegheny County Board of Commissioners cut an additional 4.3 mils in 1996, but this tax cut was not offset by sales tax distributions or support for regional assets.

8. Eight of the 12 that did not cut property taxes either eliminated their per capita taxes and/or reduced their earned income tax rates. Four municipalities, because of exceptional financial circumstances, offered no tax reductions.

CHAPTER 24

FINANCING ARTS AND CULTURAL ORGANIZATIONS IN THE DENVER, COLORADO, REGION

Jane Hansberry

On Nov. 8, 1988, during the worst regional recession in decades, citizens in metropolitan Denver, Colorado, voted three-to-one to increase their sales tax to support the region's scientific and cultural facilities. That day marked the beginning of a new division of local government in Colorado — the Scientific and Cultural Facilities District (SCFD).

The 1988 vote was an extraordinary event for three reasons. First, it was counterintuitive that citizens would vote for a tax increase in such bad economic times. Second, it was a vote to provide public support for arts and cultural organizations at a time when many pundits doubted the public's willingness to support culture with tax dollars. Third, the vote established a regional basis for supporting cultural organizations, many of which were located in the core city. The region that was created comprised Denver and the five surrounding suburban counties.

Background

Several events led to the November 1988 vote to support the scientific cultural facilities. First and foremost was the loss of state funds to the institutions. As a result, trustees developed a legislative strategy, and a bill outlining the cultural district was introduced into the state legislature. Then, cultural organizations launched a campaign to sell the cultural tax.

Loss of State Funds

In 1982, the City of Denver's major cultural institutions, namely the Denver Art Museum, the Denver Zoo, the Denver Botanic Gardens, and the Denver Museum of Nature and Science (referred to hereafter as the "Big Four"), lost the state funding they had enjoyed for half a century. The City and County of Denver (Denver is a

Originally published as "Denver's Scientific and Cultural Facilities District: A Case Study in Regionalism," *Government Finance Review*, Vol. 16, No. 6, December, 2000. Reprinted with permission of the Government Finance Officers Association, published of *Government Finance Review*, 180 N. Michigan Ave., Suite 800, Chicago, IL USA 60601 (312/977-9700; fax: 312/977-4806; e-mail: GFR@gfoa.org). Annual subscription: $30.

combined city/county jurisdiction) already provided nearly half these institutions' annual budgets, and they were unable to make up the shortfall. Denver was experiencing a loss of revenue and population to the suburbs that exacerbated a regional and statewide recession and population emigration.

The institutions were forced to seek new sources of funding. They set up foundations and raised fees, but neither of these strategies, nor others that they employed, were able to mitigate the loss of state funds. In fact, the strategies of new and increased fees had driven attendance down, furthering financial losses and curtailing planned exhibits and programming.

A Strategy Takes Hold

In 1983, faced with rapidly deteriorating finances, the trustees of the four institutions began to discuss and explore their options. A chance encounter between a Denver Art Museum trustee and a trustee from the St. Louis Art Museum would prove fortuitous. From this meeting, the Denver trustee learned of the St. Louis Metropolitan Zoological Park and Museum District, which were created in 1971 through a referendum. The St. Louis District provided a regional base of support for the city's museums and zoos with property tax revenues. The Denver trustee took hold of the idea as a possible framework for how the Denver cultural organizations might proceed.[1] A regional funding base would provide a more equitable basis of financial support than reliance on the City and County of Denver alone. Surveys of attendance and membership rosters supported this plan by indicating that the majority of visitors to the four cultural institutions were residents of suburban counties outside of Denver.

From 1983 to 1986 when the first enabling legislation for the creation of a tax district was proposed, trustees from the Big

Four institutions worked through political and legislative strategies. In the past, these institutions had viewed each other as competitors and had very little history of collaboration. They had learned, however, that the best legislative and political case could be made together, and not as separate entities.

The strategy was to find legislators willing to sponsor enabling legislation for a Denver metro-area sales tax district encompassing Denver and the surrounding suburban counties — Adams, Arapahoe, Boulder, Douglas, and Jefferson. These were the same boundaries as the Regional Transportation District and would prove to be a boost for the cultural district concept because a "regional footprint" already was established.

The proposed rate of .1 percent sales tax would raise $13 million. The plan was to direct 75 percent of the revenue to the Big Four, and give the remaining 25 percent of the revenue to the six counties' boards of county commissioners (and Denver City Council) for a locally controlled distribution to smaller cultural organizations in each county. A proposed selling point would be the lean administrative structure, which allocated less than 1 percent of revenues to administration of the tax. The tax would be created by the legislature and ratified by a vote of the citizens in the six-county region.

The Legislature

In January 1986, a bill outlining the cultural district was introduced. Initial debate centered on the questions of whether public funding for culture was an appropriate use of taxes and what percentage of the tax burden should be shouldered by Denver and by the suburbs. However, the discussion soon became argumentative even within the cultural community. With the introduction of the legislation, the entire cultural community became aware of the Big Four's plans.

The major performing arts organizations, not included in the legislation as drafted, argued that they had been left out, while the smaller cultural organizations at the county level argued that, since they were written into the legislation, they wanted some input as to the shape of the proposed district.

These intra-cultural community arguments took place during the Colorado State Senate Local Government Committee hearings on the bill. The committee told the factions to go away and work through their issues and come back in two weeks. Despite the compromise solution hammered out at that time, the bill died when it was sent to the House side for review, mainly because of the infighting among the various cultural organizations.

Regrouping for Success. The group was convinced that it needed to hire professional political talent to develop and implement a legislative agenda. A political consultant was hired in 1986 for the task of "herding the cultural cats" and cultivating new legislation for 1987. The efforts proved successful. House Bill 1138 was introduced in the 1987 session. It encompassed the framework for the creation of a six-county district that would collect and distribute a 10th of a percent sales tax to three "tiers" of cultural organizations: 1) The Big Four, 2) the major performing arts organizations, and 3) the smaller cultural institutions. In April 1987, the legislation passed and was signed into law by the governor on May 22.

The Campaign

The campaign to promote the cultural tax that ensued is remembered for its creativity, focus on message, and penetration of the region. Polling indicated that the campaign would be best served by focusing on the most popular institutions, such as the zoo. The campaign highlighted the benefits of supporting cultural organizations, arguing that culture was not only good for the individual, but it was also good for the community's quality of life and economic well-being.

The cultural organizations provided the bulk of the campaign funding (approximately $750,000) as well as its labor power. They also provided resources for the look and feel of the campaign's collateral pieces and ads. A particularly effective television ad was one in which a small boy is kept from entering a museum wing by a guard who says, "Sorry, son, this exhibit is closed." Another campaign asset was the late actor Raymond Burr, a great friend to Denver, who appeared in public service announcements on behalf of the cultural tax.

On Nov. 8, 1988, when more than a half million voters voted yes (by a ratio of three-to-one) to create the new tax, they were also saying yes to a regional system of supporting culture.

Creating a New District

As prescribed by the enabling legislation, the Scientific and Cultural Facilities District (SCFD) had a board of directors in place at the time of the vote. Each county appoints a representative to the board to serve for no more than two consecutive three-year terms. In five of the counties, these appointments are made by the boards of county commissioners, and in Denver, the appointment is made by Denver City Council. In addition, the governor appoints three members of the board, who are also term-limited to no more than two terms, for a total of nine board members.

The board's duties as outlined in the enabling legislation include: hiring staff; providing for the distribution of SCFD tax funds and the reporting and review of those funds, and calling for and administering an election for the renewal of the tax.

The initial SCFD tax had a sunset of

June 30, 1996, unless otherwise renewed. On Nov. 4, 1994, the voters renewed the SCFD through June 30, 2006.

The enabling legislation provided the SCFD distribution formula of 65 percent to the Big Four or "Tier I," 25 percent to the mid-sized performing and exhibiting organizations or "Tier II," and 10 percent to the smaller cultural groups operating at the county level (the "Tier III" organizations). These percentages were adjusted in the 1994 renewal to 59, 28, and 13 percent respectively, to reflect changes in audience and changes in the number of Tier II and III organizations.

Although the SCFD statute provided a framework for the district, the policy and procedural work necessary to implement the statute was considerable. An example of this work was the process undertaken to develop the Tier II accounting and auditing procedures. Unlike the Tier I organizations which are named in the statute, Tier II organizations are only functionally described in the statute. In order to qualify for Tier II status, an organization must meet the statute's primary purpose test, be a non-profit organization or agency of local government, have a minimum operating budget of $700,000 (in subsequent legislation this number was adjusted for inflation), and provide public benefit. Once an organization met these requirements, they provided an audit of their previous year's attendance and their previous year's operating budget. This information would be a part of their Tier II certification process and would determine how much of the Tier II funds each organization would receive, according to a formula that averaged the attendance and budget figures and then proportioned that average against the projected Tier II total funds.

The income side of the equation proved to be a relatively straightforward auditing process; the attendance side of the equation proved more challenging. The SCFD Board brought the auditors of the likely Tier II organizations together to work with them on devising workable auditing practices for auditing attendance. The questions that were addressed included how to handle classes that the organizations might sponsor, that is, how to weight a class series of two sessions as compared with a series of 10 sessions. Another question surrounded whether or not the number of tickets sold or the number of tickets actually used should be the base for auditing.

The class-session question was answered by counting each individual session of a class or workshop series. The ticket question was answered by auditing the number of tickets sold. It was also necessary to understand the differences in ticketing policies and operations of the exhibiting organizations as contrasted with the performing organizations. The work of the organizations' independent auditors was an integral part of the SCFD Tier II auditing and certification procedures, and established early on the district's style of working directly with the field, and not developing policy and/or procedure in isolation.

The Tier II formula provides that the larger organizations receive more funding, per the intent of the statute that the SCFD would reinforce the public's support as expressed through their patronage and attendance. And though it is a "the-rich-get-richer" formula, there have been new entrants to Tier II nearly every year, with the number growing from seven organizations in 1989, to 19 in 1999.

Tier III — The Wild Card

The Tier I organizations were named in the statute and the probable Tier II organizations were well known. In that first year of funds distribution, though, no one knew what to expect from Tier III. Just as with Tier II, Tier III was described in the statute, and eligibility criteria was outlined. An organization needed to have the statutory primary purpose, be a non-profit organization or agency of local government, and provide public benefit. In short, provide all of the criteria of Tier II, with the exception of the $700,000 budget threshold.

By statute, each county appointed a cultural council whose job it was to oversee the distribution of Tier III funds. Those six councils worked with the district to develop application and grant making protocols and procedures. The district board understood that beyond statutory compliance, each county was free to develop rules of procedure and policies appropriate for their county's resources and needs. Like Tier II, Tier III has grown; from 1989 to 1999, the number of Tier III organizations grew from 159, to just greater than 300.

The impact of Tier III funds on local government has been substantial. Because local government agencies are statutorily eligible to receive SCFD funds, many municipalities have been able to expand their arts and cultural commissions' programming. A number of these municipal arts and cultural commissions also provide a re-granting function to small cultural organizations and a nexus of information and referrals for those small cultural organizations. The City of Brighton, for example, developed an Arts and Culture Department in 1995 that has sponsored an annual "CultureFest," celebrating the many cultures of the local people; "Brass Blast" bringing the best of brass to perform in Brighton; and "Art Awakenings," designed to inspire all citizens to celebrate their creativity through the arts.

Since the Vote

Since the SCFD began, its revenues and distributions have grown from $14.9 million in 1989 to just more than $33 million in 1999. The number of institutions receiving funding has doubled to more than 300. The region's economy has recovered from the depths of the recession of the 1980s and is now thriving. Concerns about growth management and infrastructure capacity have replaced those of job loss, office vacancy rates, and population emigration.

The SCFD also has become a part of the regional landscape. Since the initial voter approval in 1988, SCFD was re-authorized by voters in 1994, thus fulfilling the "sunset" provision in the enabling legislation. Another reauthorization vote will be held sometime before 2006.

In November 1998, the Scientific and Cultural Facilities District celebrated its 10th anniversary by throwing a "Community Thank You Celebration." More than 45,000 people throughout metro Denver enjoyed free programming at 90 venues throughout the region.

The long hours spent creating the district and working the campaigns (for initial approval and renewal) have forged strong bonds within the cultural community. For instance, in 1990, after market research demonstrated that the major performing arts organizations collectively were only reaching 11 percent of metro households, those organizations came together and pooled a portion of their SCFD funds to create joint marketing and public relations programs. Donor and subscriber lists were shared and merged. Joint campaigns to "discover yourself in the arts" were launched. The guiding principle of the cooperation of these institutions is "to do together what we cannot do singly, reflecting, perhaps, the very spirit of regional cooperation that created the district itself. The results of these campaigns have been dramatic; there has been a marked increase in participation in arts and cultural events in the past decade.

The Public Benefits

In 1999, according to "The Economic and Social Impact of the Scientific and Cultural Facilities District" study produced by Deloitte and Touche and the Colorado Business Committee for the Arts, total attendance at SCFD organizations was 9.3 million visits. (Those visits consisted of approximately 7.1 million paid, 1.8 million free, and 440,000 reduced rate admissions.) In contrast, the combined home-game attendance of the Denver Broncos professional football team, Denver Nuggets basketball team, Denver Avalanche hockey team, and Colorado Rockies baseball team was 5.8 million visitors.

There is a recognition on the part of the cultural organizations that receiving SCFD funds translates into a higher level of responsibility to the community. The entire cultural community has pitched in to supplement arts and science education in schools by providing school tours, school contacts, and after-school programs. In 1999, SCFD organizations provided 2,700 programs to underserved populations including children at or below the poverty level, people of diverse ethnic backgrounds, the elderly, and people with disabilities. In addition, more than 489,000 people enrolled in paid and free courses offered by SCFD organizations.[2]

The economic impact and benefits of the SCFD are as impressive as the social impacts. The same study reports an estimated $844 million in gross economic impact when the operating expenditures, capital expenditures, and audience ancillary spending by patrons of the organizations are totaled. Of that figure, the impact of cultural patrons who came from outside Colorado and stayed overnight was more than $130 million. Throughout 1999, SCFD organizations employed nearly 7,000 people and paid more than $15 million in payroll, seat, and sales taxes.[3]

Economic Development

Since the SCFD was created in 1988, Pittsburgh, Kansas City, and Salt Lake City have created cultural districts, each tailored to the resources and needs of their respective regions. Other urban areas and regions are studying the issue as public support of culture is increasingly seen as an investment in a region's present and future quality of life. There is a growing awareness of the role that the arts and culture play in developing an educated workforce, and, on the other side of that coin, in attracting an educated workforce.

More and more evidence is indicating that the arts are a fundamental part of education. In one state study, reading comprehension was shown to improve when children took drama classes in addition to their regular classes. In a study that included multiple cities, at-risk children who participated in an arts program consistently scored higher in core subjects than children not placed in the program.[4]

It has been demonstrated that quality accessible cultural amenities are considered by businesses to be a prerequisite for attraction and retention of qualified employees. As technology increases the mobility of the workforce and allows for "virtual" industry structures, there will be concomitant changes in the nature of labor recruitment. The traditional model of attracting residents to a city or town based on employment opportunities may be shifting. In the future, the quality of life that states and communities provide will become an increasingly important element in attracting residents.[5]

The essential ingredient for the formation of cultural tax districts remains the development of public support for the concept and for raising taxes to fund it. This support may be more readily available than is commonly known. A 1996 Louis Harris survey on the arts showed that by a three-to-one margin U.S. citizens are strongly in favor of supporting arts and cultural organizations with taxes. The survey showed that 67 percent of Americans support local government arts agencies giving financial support to the arts, 63 percent believe that state governments should fund the arts, and 57 percent support federal support of the arts.[6] These numbers should be encouraging for regions contemplating an increase in the support of their arts and cultural institutions through a regional mechanism.

The Greater Denver Chamber of Commerce launched the "Year of Regional Cooperation" this year. The theme's goal is to continue reaching out to other public, private, and nonprofit-sector organizations to look for regional solutions for future regional issues and challenges.

Notes

1. McCarthy, Mike, "A Short History of the Scientific and Cultural Facilities District," produced on behalf of the Scientific and Cultural Facilities District, 1993, p. 4.

2. The Economic and Social Impact of the Scientific and Cultural Facilities District," study conducted by Deloitte and Touche and the Colorado Business Committee for the Arts, Denver, Colo. October 2000.

3. Ibid. p. 4.

4. "Eloquent Evidence: Arts at the Core of Learning," National Assembly of State Arts Agencies, 1998.

5. National Survey: Business Support to the Arts 1998, Business Committee for the Arts, Inc. 1999.

6. The Washington Post, Friday, June 21, 1996.

CHAPTER 25

REGIONAL GROWTH MANAGEMENT SYSTEMS IN SEVEN STATES

Benjamin G. Hitchings

Across the United States, regional land use patterns are shaping the local quality of life. The challenge many regions face is to help local governments work together to address growth issues effectively while respecting political traditions that favor local control. Regional growth management frameworks in the United States exist along a continuum, with differing levels of authority vested at the regional level. This article describes a typology for classifying these systems as *ad hoc, advisory, supervisory,* or *authoritative*. Brief case histories from selected regions across the county illustrate the continuum.

The most significant advances in recent years are the continued evolution of the Metropolitan Service District in Portland, Oregon and the emergency of moderate alternatives in San Diego and Seattle that combine regional oversight with local responsibility for implementing a regional growth strategy.

As local governments seek to mitigate the downsides of the low-density post–World War II suburban growth, those jurisdictions that establish land use controls in

isolation risk simply deflecting new development to outlying jurisdictions (Downs 1994) that often have fewer resources to manage it. In so doing, they risk accelerating the degradation of important regional systems such as watersheds, airsheds, and transportation networks. In the search for new mechanisms to shape regional development patterns and advance common regional interests, metropolitan areas can learn much from existing efforts. By classifying the range of regional growth management systems in the U.S., this article seeks to clarify the present alternatives and spark future innovations.

A Continuum of Approaches

Regional cooperation can take many different forms, including joint services delivery by local governments, cooperative research and development by private firms, and infrastructure development initiatives sponsored by nonprofits (Nunn and Rosentraub, 1997). However, both managing growth and shaping land use patterns on a

Originally published as "A Typology of Regional Growth Management Systems," *The Regionalist*, Vol. 3, No. 1/2, Fall, 1998. Published by the National Association of Regional Councils, Washington, D.C. Reprinted with permission of the publisher.

regional level must involve government since the rules that govern the land development process are drafted and implemented through government.

A number of states and/or local governments cede varying degrees of land use planning and decision-making authority to the regional level to help local communities pursue their common interest in the physical development of their region. The resulting systems for managing development at a regional scale exist along a continuum, with differing amounts of power vested in the regional body.

At one end of the continuum are communities that take an *ad hoc* approach to addressing regional growth issues. In this arrangement, local governments may work together to confront specific land use issues such as protecting water supply watersheds or siting a regional airport, but they have no updated written plan in place for coordinating the future physical development of the region as a whole. These places may have a voluntary council of governments that provides a forum for discussing issues of regional concern but has insufficient resources or authority to draft a current regional plan or require regional coordination (Figure 1).

The next group of regions is categorized as having an *advisory* system to growth management. These metropolitan areas have drafted regional plans, but have little or no means for implementing them. As a result, they must rely on voluntary action by local governments to realize the regional vision.

Next in the continuum are regional bodies with supervisory powers that administer a regional growth strategy developed with the local jurisdictions. Responsibility for implementing the strategy lies with local communities, while the regional body oversees compliance and tracks the progress made toward realizing the goals of the regional plan. This explicit implementation responsibility distinguishes the supervisory framework from the advisory one.

FIGURE 1

A Typology of Regional Growth Systems in the United States

Classification	Examples
Ad Hoc	Research Triangle, North Carolina
	Many other regions
Advisory	Denver, Colorado
	Atlanta, Georgia
Supervisory	San Diego, California
	Seattle, Washington
Authoritative	Minneapolis–St. Paul, Minnesota
	Portland, Oregon

The other end of the continuum is marked by regions that have statutory authority to develop a regional growth strategy and oversee its implementation. In such *authoritative* systems, the regional body can require changes in the plans and development codes of local communities to ensure that these documents are consistent with the regional strategy.

A System of Classification

Previous typologies have tried to classify approaches to regionalism in one of three ways:

- across issues (Seltzer 1995, Robinson and Hodge 1998);
- across sectors (Downs 1994); or
- across both issues and sectors (Walker 1987, Nunn and Rosentraub 1997).

Works by Ndubisi and Dyer (1992) and Downs (1994) both examine the regional role in managing development. The former looks at regional councils in the context of state land-use programs, while the latter pans across sectors in search of the most promising regional approach.

The typology presented in this article

takes a different approach, specifically examining the relationship between local governments and the regional council on the assertion that how this relationship is structured fundamentally influences the chances for success in addressing regional development issues.

This typology classifies regions into four categories based on three factors (Figure 2a):

1. Whether the region has a current regional plan.

2. Whether the regional council has been given the responsibility to oversee local government compliance with the regional plan to help ensure its implementation.

3. What authority the regional council has to manage land use across the region by requiring changes in local land use plans and development codes to ensure consistency with the regional plan.

These latter tools, more than any others, provide a mechanism for promoting regional coordination.

Local governments can pursue a *de facto* local growth management framework in the absence of an adopted local plan since they have land-use control and taxing and spending authority and therefore can guide growth using their development codes, fiscal policies, and capital improvements programs. This is not generally possible for regional councils, which typically lack land use authority and often are limited in their control over regional infrastructure decisions. As a result, a regional growth management system is generally effective to the extent that it coordinates and enforces the myriad local plans and development codes and guides collective local decisions such as how to spend regional transportation funds.

Four Broad Categories

Therefore, this typology classifies a regional growth management system as *ad hoc* if the region does not have a current regional

---

FIGURE 2a

Key Features of Selected Regional Growth Systems: Deciding Factors in Classification

Region	Has Current Regional Plan	Administers Regional Implementation Strategy	Can Require Changes in Plans or Other Codes
Ad Hoc			
Research Triange, N.C.			
Many Other Regions			
Advisory			
Denver, Colo.	x		
Atlanta, Ga.	x		
Supervisory			
San Diego, Calif.	x	x	
Seattle, Wash.	x	x	
Authoritative			
Twin Cities, Minn.	x	x	x
Portland, Ore.	x	x	x

FIGURE 2b
Features of Selected Regional Growth Management Systems: Supporting Factors[1] in Classification

Region	Plan Review Authority Local Plans	Dev. of Reg. Impact	Regional Revenue Sharing	Selection of Governing Board	Financial Investment Reg. Planning
Ad Hoc					
Research Triangle, N.C.				Locally delegated	Low
Many Other Regions					
Advisory					
Denver, Colo.				Locally delegated	Low
Atlanta, Ga.	x	x		Locally delegated	Medium-low
Supervisory					
San Diego, Calif.				Locally delegated	Medium
Seattle, Wash.	x			Locally delegated	Medium
Authoritative					
Twin Cities, Minn.	x	x	x	Appointed	Medium-high
Portland, Ore.	x			Directly elected	High

development plan. If it has a plan but no regional oversight authority, it is classified as *advisory*. If it has a plan and administers a regional implementation strategy developed jointly with the local governments, it is categorized as *supervisory*. If it has a plan and the ability to require and enforce modifications in local plans and codes to ensure consistency with the regional plan, it is classified as *authoritative*.

The typology becomes more precise through use of five additional factors to determine where a region falls within each of the four broad categories (Figure 2b). These measures have been selected for their usefulness in implementing a regional development plan, fostering regional cooperation, and building the political will to advance common regional interests. They include:

1. The regional body's relative control over the development of regional infrastructure systems. Such influence can be used to guide growth on a regional level and promote local compliance with regional plans. Examples include direct management of infrastructure systems such as wastewater collection and treatment, as well as planning and permitting for these systems. Another source of influence is whether the regional council serves as the Metropolitan Planning Organization responsible for helping local governments prioritize the allocation of federal funds for transportation projects in the region.

2. The extent of the regional body's plan-review authority. Does the body have the authority to review local comprehensive plans for consistency with a regional plan? Does it review proposed developments of regional impact? Such authorities systematize the process of ensuring local coordination with a regional plan.

3. The extent of regional revenue sharing. Do local communities in the region pool sales tax revenues and/or property tax base to reduce competition for new tax base and promote greater regional cooperation? Such a mechanism can make a regional plan widely acceptable even if it calls for an uneven distribution of new development and resource protection areas (Orfield 1997).

4. The manner in which members of

the regional body's governing board are selected. Are they locally elected public officials sent as delegates by each community? Representatives directly elected by the voters in the region? Or members appointed by the governor? If a public decision maker is elected or appointed regionally, that person may be more likely to take positions that are in the best interest of the region as a whole, as opposed to a local delegate whose primary responsibility is to his or her local community (Orfield 1997).

5. The region's annual per capita financial investment in regional land use planning. More resources per capita should enable a regional body to work more closely with local jurisdictions to develop and implement an effective strategy for managing regional development. In addition, the relative certainty of the funding is important, with more stable sources such as a regional tax base and mandatory annual contributions from local governments improving the ability of regional councils to provide long-term coordination of regional development activities. This level of financial investment has been ranked as *low*, *medium*, or *high* for the purposes of this study based on research conducted by the Greater Triangle Regional Council (1998).

Depending on the situation, the presence of one or several of these factors can justify classifying the growth management framework in a region as "enhanced" within its category. What follows are the results of this analysis for seven regions, including a brief description of each system and a discussion of how it fits into the typology. Together, these examples encompass the range of regional growth management systems presently in use in the United States.

Case Studies

REGIONS WITH AN *AD HOC* APPROACH

Perhaps the most common approach to managing growth on a regional scale in the Untied States is the *ad hoc* arrangement. A typical example is the Research Triangle Region of North Carolina.

Research Triangle, North Carolina: One of 18 regional councils in North Carolina, the Triangle J Council of Governments (TJCOG) serves as the regional forum for a six-county area that includes 30 municipalities. It conducts planning and research, and provides programs and services to communities throughout the region. Participation by local governments is voluntary, and members pay annual dues based on population (TJCOG 1997).

The organization is governed by a board composed of one local elected official from each member jurisdiction. It has no direct control over regional infrastructure and no authority to review local plans. Regional transportation planning is carried out by two separate federally-designated Metropolitan Planning Organizations (neither of which is TJCOG), the state Department of Transportation, and a regional transit authority.

No revenues are shared on a regional level, although a portion of sales tax revenues are pooled on a statewide basis and distributed based on population. In comparison with the other regions examined in this study, the Research Triangle's investment in regional planning is *low*, with TJCOG spending an average of 30 cents per capita on regional land use planning in fiscal year 1996-97 (GTRC 1998).

In 1969, TJCOG's predecessor, the Research Triangle Regional Planning Commission, produced a regional development guide that included maps and a discussion of the development issues facing the region (Research Triangle Regional Planning Commission, 1969). This document has never been updated and is not current. As a result, efforts to coordinate land use activities throughout the region have taken place strictly on an *ad hoc* basis, as defined in the classification scheme. Communities have worked together to site a regional airport, develop watershed protection measures, and establish a buffer along the Interstate 40 corridor, the region's "Main Street."

Now, a coalition of leaders from the business community, government, academic institutions, and civic organizations called the Greater Triangle Regional Council (GTRC) has sponsored an examination of possible future development patterns in an effort to build cooperation on regional growth issues. It remains to be seen what form, if any, such cooperation might take, and whether it will be enough to address the issues the Research Triangle Region faces as it grows by a projected 600,000 new residents over the next generation.

REGIONS WITH AN
ADVISORY FRAMEWORK

Some regions have established an advisory system of regional growth management that includes the development of a regional plan but lacks a binding mechanism for implementing it.

Denver, Colorado: With 436,000 new jobs and 770,000 new residents expected by the year 2020, Denver is projected to grow at a pace similar to the Research Triangle Region (Denver Regional Council of Governments, 1997). Working through the Denver Regional Council of Governments (DRCOG), communities in the metropolitan area are now developing a regional framework for managing this growth.

DRCOG serves an eight-county region with just over 2 million residents. It is the state-designated regional planning commission charged with the task of drafting a plan for the physical development of the region and serves as the federally-designated Metropolitan Planning Organization responsible

for regional transportation planning. Participating jurisdictions pay annual dues based on population and tax base. Decisions are made by a board consisting of delegates from each of the member governments (Knight 1997).

DRCOG has no authority to review local plans and does not oversee any mechanism for sharing revenues on a regional level. Its spending on regional land use planning amounted to $0.32 per capita in fiscal year 1996, giving it a *low* ranking on financial investment compared with the other metropolitan areas in this study (GTRC 1998).

The Metro Vision 2020 Plan approved by the DRCOG Board of Directors in the spring of 1997 sets policy objectives for six core elements related to growth and quality of life in the region, providing the basis for more detailed plans for regional development, regional transportation, and clean water (DRCOG 1997). A key goal seeks to contain the region's growth to a 700-square-mile area. This provision helps phase growth outward instead of allowing it to leapfrog to distant rural areas (DRCOG 1997). DRCOG worked closely with local governments and recently drafted an interim growth map covering 731 square miles (DRCOG 1998). This is out of a 5,075 square mile region.

Other Metro Vision 2020 implementation efforts include: encouraging local communities to develop comprehensive plans that are consistent with the regional plan; identifying regional centers for mixed-use development; and integrating the Metro Vision 2020 Plan with the regional transportation, water quality, and air quality plans (DRCOG 1997).

In addition, DRCOG has created a new point system for prioritizing transportation projects for federal funding. Under the proposed arrangement, 5 percent of the total points would go to projects that support urban centers and the voluntary urban growth boundaries. The new formula is scheduled to be implemented in two years (Broderick 1998).

Local governments are responsible for carrying out the Metro Vision 2020 Plan, since the document establishes that all implementation strategies be voluntary (DRCOG 1997). It is not clear how far they will progress toward realizing their common vision, however, in the absence of any mutually binding agreement.

Atlanta, Georgia: Local governments are responsible for implementing the Atlanta area regional plan. However, as a result of several state laws, the Atlanta Regional Commission (ARC) is authorized to conduct a number of functions that help promote regional coordination.

The ARC provides regional planning and inter-governmental coordination to a 10-county region containing 3 million people. Strictly an advisory agency, the ARC plans for job training, transportation, and aging needs in the region, as well as for land use, environmental protection, and economic development. The organization is governed by a board composed of 23 local public officials and 15 private citizens. Local government membership in the ARC is mandatory, and each jurisdiction pays annual dues of $0.80 per capita (Georgia 1989).

The ARC has no direct control over regional infrastructure, and no system of regional revenue sharing has been established. Its per capita spending on regional land use planning amounted to $0.63 in fiscal year 1997, giving it a *medium-low* ranking (GTRC 1998).

One major function the ARC undertakes is drafting a regional plan (West 1995). Phase I of this plan, VISION 2020, generated a shared vision for the region and set regional benchmarks. Phase II of the process, titled "Detailing the Vision," involves producing a development plan, a transportation plan, and a water supply plan for the region. Phase II includes analyzing different future regional development options.

The need to comply with federal air quality standards may spur implementation of the regional plan. The region has been downgraded to severe non-attainment for ground-level ozone pollution and must develop a regional transportation plan by 2005 that will bring it into compliance. As part of this process, the federal government has frozen federal funding for many new road projects (Goldberg 1998).

The ARC performs other planning functions. Under the provisions of the Georgia Planning Act of 1989, it reviews Developments of Regional Impact (DRIs) based on a range of factors, makes non-binding rulings on whether the DRI projects are in the best interest of the state, and reviews local comprehensive plans for compliance with state planning standards established under the act (ARC 1987). In addition, the ARC exercises planning and project review authority for proposed developments along the Chattahoochee River, which provides more than 65 percent of the region's drinking water, to ensure compliance with development restrictions in the corridor (ARC 1987).

Together, the regional plan, the DRI process, the consistency review, and the project review responsibilities along the Chattahoochee River give the ARC significant ability to coordinate planning efforts throughout the region. These measures are no substitute for the authority to require local consistency with the regional plan, and the Atlanta regional growth management framework still falls into the *advisory* category. Because of these added planning responsibilities and its significant financial commitment to regional planning, the Atlanta approach represents an enhanced *advisory* system.

REGIONS WITH A SUPERVISORY FRAMEWORK

Two regions in the United States are helping to define a new middle ground in the regional growth management continuum. Local governments in both San Diego, California, and Seattle, Washington, have worked in their regions to develop regional growth strategies. In addition, they have given their regional planning bodies some authority to administer their strategies and encourage local communities to implement them, creating a *supervisory* system of regional growth management. Each region, however, is taking a slightly different approach to this task.

San Diego, California: To help protect the quality of life as the region grows, the 18 cities within the County of San Diego all voluntarily participate in the San Diego Association of Governments (SANDAG). Formed in 1980, this association conducts regional planning for transportation, growth management, environmental management, and criminal justice. Member governments pay annual dues and receive votes on the governing board based on a weighted formula.

SANDAG does not have direct control over any regional infrastructure systems and, to date, no system of regional revenue sharing has been established. Its financial investment in regional planning is ranked as *medium*, based on spending of 93 cents per capita on regional land use planning in fiscal year 1997. However, thanks to voters, it possesses an unusual tool for coordinating land use planning in the region.

Concerned about the increasing impacts of growth on the region, citizens passed their own ballot initiative in 1988 requiring the formulation of a plan to manage development on a regional level. All 18 municipalities and San Diego County were required to participate in the plan development process and comply with the resulting growth management framework, known as the Regional Growth Management Strategy (Detwiler 1992). This document includes measurable standards and objectives for nine quality of life factors including air quality, open space protection, housing, and eco-

nomic prosperity (SANDAG 1993). SANDAG is responsible for overseeing compliance with the Regional Growth Strategy.

Under the procedure developed jointly by the local governments in the region, every two years each jurisdiction must conduct a *self-certification* review process using a SANDAG checklist to determine whether its general plan is consistent with the Regional Growth Strategy. The major inducement to comply with the Regional Growth Strategy provisions is peer pressure. One jurisdiction can challenge the compliance claims of another, triggering an examination by the Review Board and possible mediation through SANDAG's conflict resolution process.

At present, SANDAG has no authority to review and verify the self-certification findings submitted or offer incentives for compliance. Instead, it simply performs an administrative function, issuing a compilation of the local government findings (Baldwin 1997). Researchers Judith Gruber and Michael Neuman note that the resulting system of regional growth management "sets standards that each community has to meet, but decisions about how to meet them remain local." (Gruber and Neuman 1993, 96)

Do local governments follow through on their commitment? So far, local communities have undergone three cycles of self-certification and a number are still working to achieve consistency with the Regional Growth Strategy (SANDAG 1996). To date, no jurisdiction has challenged the self-certification findings of another. The local review process has received little public attention, with minimal debate at the public meeting that each community must hold before it can certify that its general plan and ordinances are consistent with the Regional Growth Strategy. Since its inception, though, the strategy has helped focus the attention of public officials on regional growth issues.

To date, the overall success is mixed. By requiring local jurisdictions systematically to compare their plans and codes to the shared regional goals on a regular basis, the self-certification process has improved regional coordination. However, so far, the mechanisms created to promote implementation of the strategy have had a minimal impact on the land use plans and policies of the local jurisdictions.

In addition, no monitoring system has been established to measure the region's progress toward achieving the quality-of-life improvements called for in the strategy (Baldwin 1997). The region has moved slowly toward greater consistency in its policies and does not yet know what the impact of this movement has been.

Seattle, Washington: Seattle has crafted a regional growth management framework largely through consensus-building with local governments. But unlike San Diego, Seattle has the ability to impose financial sanctions if local jurisdictions do not develop plans that are consistent with the regional transportation plan. The organization that administers this system is the Puget Sound Regional Council (PSRC).

The PSRC has no service provision responsibilities and instead functions strictly as a planning body. In addition, it has no direct control over regional infrastructure systems and administers no form of regional revenue sharing. However, it does have significant regional plan development and local plan review authority. It derives much of its authority from an Interlocal Agreement signed by its member governments. This document created the organization and outlined its major functions, including maintaining an updated regional growth strategy, developing a regional database, and providing technical assistance to local governments (PSRC 1991).

In addition, the PSRC ensures local compliance with the state Growth Management Act and serves as the federally-designated agency in charge of regional transportation planning. Membership in the PSRC presently includes four counties and

64 municipalities, as well as three port authorities and two state agencies. The organization is governed by its Executive Board and its General Assembly. Representatives from member governments, seated in numbers approximately proportional to member jurisdictions' populations, constitute the General Assembly. A per capita spending rate of 97 cents on regional land use planning in fiscal year 1997 gives it a *medium* ranking (GTRC 1998).

In an effort to shape growth in the region over the next generation, the PSRC's predecessor and local governments developed a strategy in 1990 for growth management, economic development, and transportation in the four-county area. This VISION 2020 document was updated in 1995 with extensive public input and calls for locating new development in urban growth areas that can be more efficiently furnished with public services (PSRC 1995). PSRC staff are now developing a performance monitoring program to gauge progress toward implementing the plan.

Another major function of the PSRC is to review local comprehensive plans throughout the region. The agency does so in three ways, including providing consultation on local comprehensive plans, upon request, to strengthen coordination with regional plans; systematically examining county wide and multicounty planning policies to ensure compliance with state law; and systematically reviewing local comprehensive plans and county wide planning policies to ensure consistency with the Regional Transportation Plan and compliance with the State Growth Management Act (PSDRC 1996).

An appeals process is available if local governments disagree with the results of this latter consistency review. In some states, such a review is conducted for the entire comprehensive plan. In this case, however, it only applies to the transportation component of the plan (PSRC 1996). Under state law, if the PSRC deems that local plans are not consistent with the regional transportation plan, it can withhold federal transportation funds. However, it prefers to work cooperatively with local governments, giving them a chance to review PSRC's findings and revise their plans and codes before any money is withheld. Planners feel the program has been very successful from a policy perspective, with local policies largely consistent with regional policies (Piro 1998). Now the challenge is to implement these measures.

One factor that has strengthened the PSRC's ability to coordinate planning throughout the region is the growth management framework established by the state. Passed in 1990, the Growth Management Act requires communities in larger and faster-growing counties to develop comprehensive plans that are consistent with 13 state planning goals.

Spurred by the state growth management law and a desire to promote their common interest, local governments in the Seattle region have created a system that verges on authoritative, with the regional council empowered by the state to withhold federal transportation funds. Yet, through careful negotiation, the PSRC has succeeded in promoting consistency in a nonconfrontational manner. This could provide a new model for regions that are hesitant to develop a system that is truly authoritative.

REGIONS WITH AN
AUTHORITATIVE FRAMEWORK

Two regional bodies in the United States have statutory authority to require changes in local plans if these documents contradict regional goals.

Minneapolis–St. Paul, Minnesota: First created to address the problem of failing septic tanks, the Metropolitan Council has developed into one of the most influential regional councils in the country. Directed by a 17-member board chosen by the governor, the Met Council serves seven

counties and 186 cities and townships with a combined population of 2.4 million people. Its primary function is to draft plans for the different regional infrastructure systems, including transportation facilities, sewers, parks, and airports. In addition, it operates the regional wastewater treatment system and the regional transit system. In fiscal year 1997, it spent $2.08 per capita on regional land use planning, giving it a *medium-high* ranking (GTRC 1998).

Thanks to a law passed in 1971, the Met Council also administers a system of regional tax-base sharing that pools 40 percent of the commercial and industrial tax-base growth above the 1971 base from each jurisdiction and reallocates it to local jurisdictions through a formula based on population and assessed value. A 1995 analysis of the program by the Met Council found that the program had narrowed the disparity between the communities with the highest and lowest commercial and industrial tax base per capita from 17-to-1, down to 4-to-1 (Metropolitan Council 1995).

A 1976 state law requires all communities in the Twin Cities area to draft comprehensive plans and submit them to the Met Council for review. The Met Council then makes sure they are consistent with its metropolitan system plans and other adopted plans, as well as with the plans of other jurisdictions (Metropolitan Council, Jan./Feb. 1997). It can require a local government to "modify any comprehensive plan or part thereof which may have a substantial impact on or contain a substantial departure from metropolitan systems plans." (Minnesota Statutes 1997) This provision gives the Met Council authoritative power. It constitutes a more comprehensive mandate than Seattle's authorization to review local plans for consistency with the regional transportation plan and one that is completely absent from the San Diego system of self-certification.

However, as Minnesota state legislator

Myron Orfield notes, "Under a system of self-imposed restraint, the council will require a plan amendment only when the local comprehensive plan imposes a burden on a metropolitan system that 'threatens its capacity'—a fairly cataclysmic event." (Orfield 1997, 177) As a result, the regional growth management framework in the Twin Cities could be termed nominally *authoritative*.

While the Met Council is cautious about using its legislated authority to require revisions in local plans, it is not shy about using its control over sewer permits and transportation investments to pressure local jurisdictions to comply with the regional plan. As a result of these measures, 93 percent of the development in the region between 1980 and 1990 took place in areas where it was planned to go, saving an estimated $1 billion in infrastructure costs in the process (Met Council, Jan./Feb. 1997).

More growth is anticipated in the future, with the region projected to add an additional 650,000 people by the year 2020. To discuss this challenge, the Met Council sponsored public debates on the region's future during the mid–1990s. The resulting regional growth strategy, Metro 2040, calls for the efficient provision of regional services, reinvestment in the urban core, protection of rural areas and agricultural lands, and an adequate supply of affordable housing. To accomplish these goals, the strategy seeks to guide growth to a municipal urban service area and rural growth centers, while establishing a permanent rural area with an average density of one unit per 10 acres and a permanent agricultural area with a minimum lot size of one unit per 40 acres (Metropolitan Council 1996).

The Met Council is implementing the growth strategy by means of its regional transportation and water resources management plans, which direct public investments in sewer and transportation facilities. Local communities help this effort when they revise their local comprehensive plans (Met Council, Jan./Feb. 1997). This effort is enhanced by a 1995 amendment to the Metropolitan Land Planning Act, which obligates local governments to include an implementation plan in their local comprehensive plans and requires them to adopt local land use regulations, fiscal measures, or capital improvements programs that are consistent with the plan (Minnesota Statutes 1997). Other initiatives also support the strategy. The Livable Communities Act passed by the state legislature in 1996 provides funds for affordable housing, the development of mixed-use, pedestrian-friendly communities, and the cleanup and redevelopment of contaminated lands (Metropolitan Council 1998).

A shift from its present policy regarding the use of its statutory authority to require changes in local plans might well require a change in the manner in which the council is selected. The present system of gubernatorial appointment makes the council beholden to the governor, and according to critics such as Myron Orfield, prevents it from developing the political will to fully use its legislated power (Orfield 1997). Until it does, the Twin Cities system of regional growth management will remain classified as nominally *authoritative*.

Portland, Oregon: In contrast with the Twin Cities, the regional growth management framework in the Portland region is functionally *authoritative*. Here, the Metropolitan Service District (METRO) combines regional planning, regional service provision, and land use management authority to maintain the environmental quality of life in the region. METRO is the only directly elected regional body in the country, composed of an executive officer and a seven-member council. It is augmented by an advisory board of local officials called the METRO Policy Advisory Committee (MPAC).

METRO's primary function is regional land use and transportation planning. In addition, it manages regional parks and green spaces, solid waste disposal, and a number of civic facilities including the METRO Zoo and the Oregon Convention Center. It also oversees the region's urban growth area sized to accommodate new development in the region over the next 20 years and protect rural land uses outside the line. The urban growth area represents 363 square miles out of the region's 3,069. In fiscal year 1996-97, it spent $3 per capita on regional land use planning, giving it a *high* ranking (GTRC 1998).

In 1992, voters passed a home rule charter for METRO giving it new financing powers and requiring a Regional Framework Plan, completed in December 1997, to accommodate growth in the region over the next 50 years. To implement the new plan, METRO has the power to draft specific standards which must be followed by the three counties and 24 cities in the region. Examples include minimum development densities, floodplain protection measures, affordable housing objectives, and transportation performance standards. In addition, each community is responsible for accommodating a portion of the regional population and job growth over the next 20 years (Metropolitan Council 1996).

Local governments must amend their comprehensive plans and development codes to comply with these standards, and then submit them to METRO for verification. Those that fail to do so are subject to a conflict resolution process, followed by possible legal action and a reduction in regional transportation funding, among other measures (METRO 1996). In contrast to San Diego's dispute resolution process, METRO makes the final decision in disputed cases on whether to require a local government to change its comprehensive plan (METRO 1995). This gives METRO a level of authority over land use issues that is unique in the United States.

One key to the Portland system is that,

like Seattle, it operates within a state growth management framework. Passed in 1973, the Oregon Land Use Act requires every city and county in the state to draft a comprehensive plan for its community. Each plan is then reviewed by the state for consistency with 19 state planning goals. Furthermore, communities must ensure that their development codes are consistent with their plans (Oregon 1990).

These measures, combined with substantial investments in public transit, have succeeded in minimizing leapfrog development and providing greater certainty about where and when development can occur. A regional approach to regional problems and an authoritative growth management framework are the basis for this success.

Conclusion

As regions across the United States grapple with growth and explore ways to manage it, a fundamental measure of success will be whether their growth management systems succeed in shaping regional development patterns. The categories presented in this chapter provide differing prospects for achieving this objective. The *ad hoc* approach affords the possibility of cooperating on certain mutually agreeable regional problems, but provides no framework for addressing regional development issues in a comprehensive, coordinated, and ongoing manner.

The advisory framework can generate a common vision for the future physical development of a region, but does not provide the means to pursue this vision in a systematic and sustained way.

The evidence provided by the regions studied in this chapter suggests that only when regions develop a *supervisory* or an *authoritative* framework and maintain it over a significant period of time can they truly begin to shape development patterns on a regional scale, not just in particular corridors or sectors as might be possible with major regional infrastructure investments.

Portland is one region which has achieved some success at this endeavor. Here, a regional growth management system has been in place long enough and with the requisite authority to curtail leapfrog development and spur redevelopment in downtown Portland. Considerable efforts are now underway to promote more compact development within the urban growth area.

Minneapolis–St. Paul has had more limited success molding growth. The region has managed to expand urban services in an orderly manner, hold down the cost of public sewer service, and maintain a relatively vital urban core (Davis 1998). Yet low-density development continues to spread at a rapid pace outside of the urban services area and the density of new residential development inside the boundary is about two-thirds that of new projects in the Portland region, leading to escalating automobile travel and traffic congestion (Metropolitan Council, Sept./Oct. 1997). While the Metropolitan Council appears to have the legislative authority to take stronger measures, an ongoing challenge has been finding the political basis to do so.

Perhaps the most promising approach for regions reluctant or unable to establish an *authoritative* system is to develop a *supervisory* framework. Seattle has made substantial progress toward building such a system of regional coordination. Thanks to diplomatic enforcement of state law and a commitment on the part of local governments, the Puget Sound Regional Council has been successful in coordinating regional transportation planning and associated land use planning on a policy level. Time will tell if this system is able to influence regional development patterns.

Although it was initiated earlier than Seattle's, the system in San Diego has been slower to develop. While substantial investments in transit and a region-wide effort to protect endangered species habitat are helping to implement the regional growth strategy, the region is still working to coordinate local and regional growth policies. San Diego's experience suggests that once a mutually agreed-upon regional plan has been developed, a binding agreement among local jurisdictions is needed for the system to be successful.

The language of the voter initiative that spawned the regional planning framework calls for the cities and the county in the region to "participate in the formulation of, and ... comply with the adopted regional growth management plan." (SANDAG 1993) In addition, it says that the "Regional Board [SANDAG] shall have the authority to require that the county and the cities adopt the necessary legislation to implement the regional growth management plan." (SANDAG 1993) Theoretically, then, SANDAG should have the authority to oversee the implementation of the regional growth management plan, but to date, it lacks this power.

The experiences of Seattle and San Diego highlight the fact that the supervisory framework is still evolving. While it holds considerable promise, it is as yet unproven in its ability to shape regional development patterns. A key to realizing this potential is the establishment of a binding mechanism to ensure the long-term group discipline necessary to implement a regional plan.

This feature is absent in both Atlanta and Denver. While Atlanta has a number of legislatively authorized planning functions vested at the regional level, unabated sprawl in the region indicates that the system to date has not been sufficiently potent to counteract many of the downsides of growth. In Denver, local jurisdictions have recently agreed to an interim urban growth boundary in an effort to minimize leapfrog development and help implement the Metro Vision 2020 plan.

Key questions remain, however, such as whether local jurisdictions will stay committed to the boundary over the long term, whether the standards associated with the boundary are sufficient to prevent sprawling development outside of it, and how the region develops inside these borders.

Regions that want to move to a supervisory or authoritative system might take note of how regional councils in the past have been empowered to coordinate regional development activities. Generally, this authority has come from either:

- The state, through state legislation.
- Local governments, through an interlocal agreement.
- Voters, through an initiative or referendum.

Building support for at least one of these actions, then, is a critical task to developing a supervisory or authoritative system. Certain common elements are essential to garnering this support in each case, such as widespread public sentiment that unmanaged growth is compromising the local quality of life. However, additional factors are also important.

At the state level, advocates of state planning legislation might take heed of recent trends in such initiatives and move toward more incentive-based programs to build the necessary support.

A hybrid of the Maryland Smart Growth approach has potential. To receive state funding under the Maryland law for new transportation facilities and certain housing projects, water and wastewater facilities, and economic development projects, jurisdictions must designate growth areas that meet certain standards. Existing municipalities and enterprise zones are automatically eligible. Local governments can identify additional growth areas provided they are developed to specified infrastructure and density standards (Maryland Senate Bill 389).

States that wish to establish a similar system might first require the local governments in a metropolitan region to develop a common regional plan and implementation strategy. Short of this, states might provide regions access to a special infrastructure fund if they can demonstrate a certain level of regional cooperation on land use issues. The regional Competitiveness Act, passed in Virginia in 1996, provides an example of this kind of legislation (Richman and Oliver, Spring 1997).

In the absence of state legislation, local governments may find it difficult to support a regional growth framework without some regional system of revenue sharing to help balance the benefits and burdens of the growth strategy developed. The tax-base sharing program in the Minneapolis–St. Paul region remains the most instructive model in the United States and has been credited with defusing excessive local competition for new commercial and industrial development sufficiently for individual communities to consider regional land use initiatives.

If the politics can't be worked out at the local government level, citizens may try to spur action directly through the local initiative process, if one has been authorized in the state. Here in particular, a well-developed sense of regional citizenship and an understanding of the regional nature of growth issues are crucial. While regional civic organizations have an important role to play in each approach, they are especially important in this latter case to mobilize widespread support among voters. With a better understanding of the institutional framework needed to develop effective regional growth management systems, metropolitan areas can more readily improve their ability to grow on their own terms.

References

Atlanta Regional Commission. 1997. *Strategy '97: Atlanta Regional Commission 1997 Work Program and Budget.*

Atlanta Regional Commission. 1995. *A Community's Vision Takes Flight— VISION 2020: Key Initiatives for the Future.*

Atlanta Regional Commission. 1987. *Review of Area Plans — Administrative Report.*

Atlanta Regional Commission. 1987. *Metropolitan River Protection Act Review — Administrative Manual.*

Baldwin, Susan, senior land use planner, San Diego Association of Governments. September 5, 1997. Personal communication with Benjamin Hitchings.

Broderick, Bill, planner II, Denver Regional Council of Governments. December 11, 1997 and February 27, 1998. Personal communication with Benjamin Hitchings.

Davis, Bob, senior planner, Metropolitan Council. July 31, 1997 and March 2, 1998. Personal communication with Benjamin Hitchings.

Denver Regional Council of Governments. 1998. "Special Feature: Interim Urban Growth Boundary." *Regional Report.*

Denver Regional Council of Governments. 1997. *Metro Vision 2020 Plan.*

Detwiler, Peter M. 1992. "Is Cooperation Enough? A Review of San Diego's Latest Growth Management Program." Chapter 4 in *State and Regional Initiatives for Managing Development*, Douglas R. Porter, ed. Washington, D.C.: The Urban Land Institute.

Downs Anthony. 1994. *New Visions for Metropolitan America.* Washington, D.C. and Cambridge, Mass.: The Brookings Institution and the Lincoln Institute of Land Policy.

Georgia Official Code. 1989. *Annotated Section 50-8-80.* Atlanta Regional Commission.

Goldberg, David. July 1998. "Heads Up, Atlanta. It's Clean Air Time." *Planning*, Vol. 64, No. 7: 20–23.

Greater Triangle Regional Council. 1998. *Spending Comparison on Regional Land Use Planning.*

Gruber, Judith E. and Michael Neuman. 1993. "San Diego Regional Growth Management Strategy." Case 3 in *Coordinating Growth: Environmental Management Through Consensus Building*, Judith Innes, ed.

Knight, Audrey, principal regional planner, Denver Regional Council of Governments. November 24, 1997. Personal communication with Benjamin Hitchings.

Maryland. 1997, *Senate Bill 389: "Smart Growth" and Neighborhood Conservation.*

Metropolitan Council (Twin Cities). 1998. *1997 Annual Report.*

Metropolitan Council (Twin Cities). 1997. *Local Planning Handbook.*

Metropolitan Council (Twin Cities). Jan./Feb. 1997. *Council Directions.*

Metropolitan Council (Twin Cities). Sept./Oct. 1997. *Council Directions.*

Metropolitan Council (Twin Cities). 1996. *Regional Blueprint.*

Metropolitan Council (Twin Cities). 1995. *Regional Update: Tax-Base Sharing in the Twin Cities Metropolitan Area.*

Metropolitan Service District [METRO (Portland)]. December 1997. *Regional Framework Plan.*

Metropolitan Service District [METRO (Portland)]. 1996. *Urban Growth Management Functional Plan.*

Metropolitan Service District [METRO (Portland)]. 1995. *Regional Urban Growth Goals and Objectives.*

Minnesota Statutes. 1997. *Section 473.175: Review of Comprehensive Plans.*

Minnesota Statutes. 1997. *Section 473.864: Plans and Programs; Adoption; Amendment.*

Ndubisi, Forster and Mary Dyer. Fall 1992. "The Role of Regional Entities in Formulating and Implementing Statewide Growth Policies." *State and Local Government Review*, Vol. 24, No. 3: 117–127.

Nunn, Samuel and Mark S. Rosentraub. Spring 1997. "Dimensions of Interjurisdictional Cooperation." *Journal of the American Planning Association*, Vol. 63, No. 2: 205–219.

Oregon Land Conservation and Development Commission. 1990. *Oregon's Statewide Planning Goals.*

Orfield, Myron. 1997. *Metropolitics: A Regional Agenda for Community and Stability.* Washington, D.C., and Cambridge, Mass.: The Brookings Institution and the Lincoln Institute of Land Policy.

Piro, Rocky, senior planner, Puget Sound Regional Council. September 8, 1998. Personal communication with Benjamin Hitchings.

Puget Sound Regional Council. 1996. *Puget Sound Regional Council Adopted Policy and Plan Review Process.*

Puget Sound Regional Council. 1995. *VISION 2020: 1995 Update.*

Puget Sound Regional Council. March 13, 1991. *Resolution A-91-01: Framework Plan, Interlocal Agreement.*

Research Triangle Regional Planning Commission. 1969. *1969 Research Triangle Region Development Guide.*

Rhea, Beverly, review coordinator, Review Process Division, Atlanta Regional Commission. June 30, 1997. Personal communication with Benjamin Hitchings.

Richman, Roger and James B. Oliver, Jr. Spring 1997. "The Urban Partnership and the Development of Virginia's New Regional Competitiveness Act." *The Regionalist*, Vol. 2, No. 1: 3–19.

Robinson, Ira M. and Gerald Hodge. May 1998. *Canadian Regional Planning at 50: Growing Pains.* Plan Canada: 10–14.

San Diego Association of Governments. July 18, 1996. *Regional Growth Management Strategy Self-Certification Status Report for 1994-95.*

San Diego Association of Governments. 1993. *Regional Growth Management Strategy.*

Seltzer, Ethan. Feb. 1995. "Responsibilities to Our Regions." *IGA/APA Intergovernmental Affairs Division Newsletter*, No. 43: 1, 10–13.

Triangle J Council of Governments. 1997. *Growing with the Region: 1996-1997 Annual Report.*

Triangle J Council of Governments. 1996. *Budget: Fiscal Year 1996/97.*

Walker, David B. 1987. "Snow White and the 17 Dwarfs: From Metro Cooperation to Governance." *National Civic Review*, Vol. 76.

West, Harry. Fall 1995. "VISION 2020: Key to Regionalism in the Atlanta Region." *The Regionalist*, Vol. 1, No. 3: 33–41.

CHAPTER 26

The City of DeBary Contracts for Services with Volusia County, Florida

Matt Greeson

One of the greatest challenges facing local, state and federal governments these days is the issue of "intergovernmental relations." Modern local governments are struggling to find innovative ways to work effectively with other cities, counties, special districts, and higher levels of government. In Florida, the city of DeBary and the County of Volusia are demonstrating that city-county cooperation can pay off.

When the city of DeBary incorporated in 1993, its leaders were challenged with planning for the delivery of municipal services to DeBary's 16,000 residents. The community clearly demanded a high level of service, a low tax rate, and a large degree of self-governance through a responsive city government. The city's leaders made an important strategic decision. Rather than developing the city's own capacity to deliver municipal services by hiring staff and purchasing capital equipment, the city negotiated an agreement with Volusia County to continue delivering the majority of services to its residents. After three years since De-Bary's incorporation, the relationship between the city and Volusia County contin-

ues to flourish. The city of DeBary contracts with Volusia County for the provision of police, fire, public works, parks and recreation, finance, and growth management services. As a result of the contract relationship, DeBary's city hall operates with a staff of only three full-time employees and the city has no long-term personnel costs overburdening their budget. The city takes advantage of the economies of scale provided by the presence of a county government already equipped with the staff, equipment and knowledge of providing services to De-Bary's residents.

DeBary's residents benefit the most. They enjoy the benefit of a low tax rate, a highly accessible city staff, and no reductions in the levels of service provided prior to incorporation. The success of this relationship can be attributed to several factors. The first was a recognition by the original DeBary City Council and other community leaders that hiring the staff necessary to begin delivering their own services would require them to incur costly personnel and capital expenses and would result in unwanted budget increases.

Originally published as "The City of DeBary and Volusia County: An Intergovernmental Relations Story," *Quality Cities*, Vol. 70, No. 9, March, 1997. Published by the Florida League of Cities. Reprinted with permission of the publisher.

Secondly, Volusia County government has demonstrated a strong commitment to continuing the delivery of services to DeBary's residents and helping one of Florida's newest municipalities succeed in every way possible. The contract relationship with DeBary has permitted county government to maintain relatively the same staff levels and revenue stream that DeBary previously generated as part of the county's Municipal Services District tax. Additionally, DeBary's focus on outsourcing services through interlocal agreements has required the county government to respond to DeBary, "the client," in a more entrepreneurial fashion. This has been done through quarterly reports and the institution of performance measures to ensure accountability.

The third and most important factor has been the presence of a high level of trust and communication among city and county officials. As many cities and counties throughout Florida struggle to deal with issues of regional concern, DeBary and Volusia County have maintained open and honest communications regarding the quality of services being provided and the nature of the contract relationship. County council member Patricia Northey from Deltona pointed out that "there is a high level of trust between the elected leadership of DeBary and the county and a high level of trust at the staff level." She stated "if you don't have trust it won't work; trust is the key element."

This trust has been cultivated through constant communication. Volusia County communicates with its customer, the city of DeBary, through a variety of mediums. DeBary's staff is connected to all county officials through the county's e-mail system, and can also view DeBary's financial status and related expenditures through the county's financial status and related expenditures through the county's financial system, and shares Geographic Information System (GIS) information. DeBary City Manager, Bob Mauney, attributes the success of the

contracts partly to constant communication. He said that "the feedback loop has been put in place and is constantly massaged." He commended the county for adopting an approach that focuses on customer satisfaction and pointed out that DeBary "determined the level of satisfaction of DeBary's citizens with county services in the beginning and translated it into a contractual relationship." The end product has been a satisfied customer and citizenry.

Volusia County's successful relationship with the city of DeBary has provided it with additional opportunities to continue delivering services to Southwest Volusia. When DeBary's neighbor, now the city of Deltona, incorporated last year, it chose to contract with the county for delivery of services to its almost 60,000 residents. Arguably, the county's partnership with the city of Deltona would probably have been more difficult to develop had Volusia County not already successfully developed a contract with DeBary. The DeBary experience has positioned county government to be a more effective provider of municipal services to all of its clients, including Deltona.

The DeBary–Volusia County case represents a departure from the traditional concept of municipal service delivery. In the State of Florida, municipal services are often delivered through myriad governmental organizations, including counties, cities, and special districts. Unfortunately, service delivery is not always coordinated to reduce duplication. However, the nexus of interlocal agreements between Volusia County and the cities of DeBary and Deltona creates a new possibility for the future of service delivery systems in Florida. The outsourcing of services, whether to a county government, another city or a private sector entity, allows governments to maintain contractual control of the quality of the service and also guarantees the ability for citizens to provide input through the democratic process. If coordinated properly, this method can prevent or eliminate any duplication of services and save taxpayers dollars.

Volusia County's situation is unique. To have two incorporations in one region of a county within such a short period of time is rare. This situation allowed Volusia to develop a new system, based on outsourcing and contractual relationships. This was accomplished in the absence of traditional road blocks to service delivery reform. The same progressive spirit that motivated two of Southwest Volusia's communities to incorporate has also led to open-minded consideration of this innovative new approach. While changes are inevitable, the strong ties that have been developed will ensure that long-term alterations to Volusia's service delivery system will occur in a well planned and coordinated fashion.

Chapter 27

The Cities of Greensboro and High Point Share Services with Guilford County, North Carolina

Tara L. Humphries

Two heads may be better than one, but two (or more) departments doing the same job doesn't make sense, Guilford County and its municipalities agreed. Together they formed the Guilford County Intergovernmental Shared Service Initiative to search for more cooperative ways to do things all the governments needed. The result will be reduced cost and/or increased service to town, city and county residents.

The shared services project began in 1994 at the request of the county officials. Some cooperative ventures already had a successful track record, such as a joint municipality-county property tax collection program begun in 1993.

The city councils of Greensboro and High Point each met with the Guilford Board of County Commissioners and discussed areas of potential cooperation. The groups narrowed their list to 10: countywide comprehensive planning, parks and recreation, law enforcement, printing, radio communications, animal control, solid waste management, purchasing, libraries, and employee training.

Next, the elected and appointed officials from these three local governments shared their ideas with representatives of the counties' four smaller municipalities: Jamestown, Stokesdale, Gibsonville and Whitsett. The smaller communities were particularly interested in cooperative ventures in purchasing, training and land-use planning.

Jamestown has been sharing services with its neighboring cities and the county since at least 1981, said Town Manager John J. Frezell. Working together wherever they can makes sense because "it saves money all the way around," he said.

His town buys its water from High Point and Greensboro and is a partner with High Point in a sewage treatment plant. Police service is contracted out to the sheriff's department, which means that Jamestown has access to resources such as a crime lab it couldn't afford on its own. The pendulum swings the other way during snow, and

Originally published as "Guilford Governments Look for Ways to Cooperate for Efficiency and Economy," *Southern City*, Vol. 66, No. 1, January, 1996. Published by the North Carolina League of Municipalities, Raleigh, North Carolina. Reprinted with permission of the publisher.

Jamestown uses its snow removing equipment to clean all the roads into High Point and Greensboro and then lends its plows to the big cities.

The local government staffs continue to identify additional ways to cooperate within the 10 general areas. "I think it is a good beginning for looking at efficiency and cost-saving," said High Point Mayor Becky Smothers. "You have to have compatible systems and services, to have maximum gain, and in some ways we don't have that now."

Making Progress

Countywide Comprehensive Planning: The governments adopted a framework, timetable and budget for a two-year comprehensive planning process for policy development. The long-range planning project, called Forecast 2015, involves representatives of all the county's governments and more than 100 residents participating in focus groups.

Animal Control: Greensboro, High Point and Guilford County created and adopted a single animal control ordinance and consolidated animal control functions under the county animal shelter.

Parks and Recreation: Guilford County decided to continue to contract park operations out to the cities of High Point and Greensboro rather than form its own parks and recreation department.

Solid Waste Management: Greensboro, High Point and Guilford are working toward a single, county-wide solid waste management plan and have invited the smaller municipalities to join the effort.

Law Enforcement: The county and cities are looking at shared support services, particularly to reduce the backlog of warrants.

Purchasing: The governments already cooperate in fuel dispensing, vehicle purchasing, telephone communications and tire recycling. The next step is combined contracts. "The best way to save money is on big purchases. On things we all buy, we need to consolidate into one bid," explained Charlie Martin, High Point's purchasing director.

Printing: Guilford County closed its print shop and now contracts with Greensboro and High Point municipal printing facilities.

Libraries: Little progress has been made on a feasibility study of merging existing municipal systems into a single county system.

Radio communications: Greensboro and Guilford jointly contracted for the construction of an 800 MHz emergency communications system compatible with High Point's system. The new system will be capable of serving all governments in the county.

Employee Training: Greensboro and Guilford are working on a program to share training personnel and programs. Some courses have been offered to employees of both.

"In all of these, there is a willingness to discuss ways we can work together, and there are a lot of ways we can cooperate," commented Martin. "When you gain efficiency, you reduce cost, and it has got to end with savings for the taxpaying citizen."

Editor's Note: In July 1995, Guilford County received the National Association of Counties 1995 Achievement Award and made presentations on the cooperative effort at both the NACO conference and the International City/County Management Association Annual Conference held in September 1995.

CHAPTER 28

BUILDING REGIONAL LEADERSHIP IN THE ATLANTA, GEORGIA, AREA

Harry West

The Genesis of VISION 2020

VISION 2020 recognizes that the face of leadership has changed drastically in Atlanta. The region ranks as one of the nation's most successful economic centers with excellent prospects for the future. Historically, a strong sense of community purpose has driven this success. During the 1960s and earlier, a small group of influential business leaders based in downtown were able to rally the entire community around bold initiatives to take Atlanta to the next visionary plateau. Public officials, executives, and civic leaders worked together to make Atlanta "the city too busy to hate," a major league city, and the world's next international city. During the 1970s and 1980s, in particular, the region attracted an influx of newcomers from diverse backgrounds. It also saw the emergence of influential commercial centers throughout the suburbs. These two trends combined to transform the region's population and its leadership structure.

In the late 1980s the Atlanta Regional Commission (ARC) faced a series of controversial issues ranging from a second air-port plan to proposals for stronger growth management. It became clear that residents did not share a common vision of the future and that the region's splintered leadership too often acted at cross purposes. Beyond these pressing problems, ARC members recognized that new and emerging societal, economic, and technological trends were reweaving the very fabric of regional communities across America. This new era, vastly different from the past, renders many old assumptions obsolete. Now and in the future, innovation, collaboration, and inclusion are cardinal to meeting the growing challenges and opportunities facing the nation's urban centers.

As a regional planning body made primarily of key local elected officials, ARC's leadership recognized that ARC had gone about as far as it could alone. They explored ways to involve others from the business, civic, and non-profit sectors in a common quest to develop a world class region. In 1991 ARC's board and staff undertook concurrent efforts to design a regional leadership program and develop a visioning project that embraced the entire regional community.

Originally published as "VISION 2020: Key to Regionalism in the Atlanta Region," *The Regionalist*, Vol. 1, No. 3, Fall, 1995. Published by the National Association of Regional Councils, Washington, D.C. Reprinted with permission of the publisher.

Building Regional Leadership

First ARC gained the support of the Metro Business Forum to establish a Regional Leadership Institute (RLI) that would bring together leaders from all sectors in all areas of the Atlanta region. The Forum is an umbrella organization of chambers of commerce in seven of the region's 10 counties, and its members include the chief executive and top leaders from each chamber board. In 1991 it was chaired by George Busbee, Georgia's governor from 1975 to 1983, who quickly became a champion of the RLI and later was a member RLI's second class.

The Metro Business Forum and ARC joined forces as co-sponsors of RLI, with both organizations contributing seed capital to get the first program underway in September of 1991. Since then ARC staff has coordinated recruitment and program development for six RLI classes. More than 250 leaders have completed an intensive, one-week program of classes and team-building exercises. Each year a distinguished faculty of regional and national experts gives participants a broad view of the region's problems, issues, and challenges. The educational program is paired with opportunities to share and learn from each others' experiences.

Upon completion of RLI, participants can choose to join the Regional Leadership Foundation, a membership organization for graduates of RLI. Created in 1994, its mission is to act as a springboard for leaders to work together to help resolve regional issues. The ultimate goal of both RLI and RLF is creation of a regional network of leaders who view themselves as a civic force for positive change in the region.

Phase I: Creating a Shared Community Vision

Initially, VISION 2020 focused on creating a shared community vision for the At-

lanta region's development through the year 2020. This first phase involved two years of intensive research and unprecedented community outreach by ARC and its community partners, including the Regional Leadership Institute. It began in July of 1991 when ARC staff completed the first draft of a prospectus outlining a multi-year visioning process. In October 1991, with the backing of ARC's board and encouragement from community leaders, ARC began to build a steering committee to lead this project. Former Governor George Busbee agreed to chair the steering committee and personally recruit its members. Also in October 1991, ARC contracted with a public relations firm to assist with initial communications support materials and strategies for the VISION 2020 project.

In December of 1991, a press conference in midtown Atlanta announced the formation of VISION 2020 and its steering committee of illustrious business and community leaders. Governor Busbee and other members of the steering committee were instrumental in helping ARC secure funding for the exceptional costs of VISION 2020. ARC contributed all staff resources as part of related projects financed with local dues. In early 1992, the Georgia Power Foundation contributed a start-up grant of $75,000 to VISION 2020. Subsequently, the Robert W. Woodruff Foundation awarded a grant of $625,000 to carry Phase I to completion over a three-year period.

To begin the process, ARC engaged an independent research firm to conduct a Delphi survey of regional and national experts on a variety of critical issues and trends relevant to the long-term development of the region. In May 1992, ARC used its annual Outlook Conference as the first public event to showcase VISION 2020. It attracted more than 800 public and private leaders, more than double the number attending the conference in prior years. Outlook '92 released the results of the Delphi survey and featured keynote speaker Glen Heimstra, a leading futurist and strategic change consultant from Seattle. He made a compelling case for the power and importance of vision and challenged attendees to create their preferred future for the Atlanta region.

During the summer of 1992, the VISION 2020 steering committee worked with others in the community including the Regional Leadership Institute, the ARC board, city and county managers, local planning directors, and local finance directors to develop draft "future statements." This work outlined what might happen if the region does nothing to change its current course and what it could become with ambitious intervention.

In October 1992, more than 500 citizens — including elected officials, private citizens, business leaders, high school students, and experts from a variety of fields — attended a VISION 2020 Regional Congress. The purpose of the congress was to bring together a cross-section of the region's citizens to react to the initial future statements and to begin building a vision for the future. Attendance, interest, and participation exceeded all expectations. Those present engaged in lively and thoughtful discussions in both plenary and break-out sessions focused on different aspects of the region's future. The Institute of Community and Area Development at the University of Georgia facilitated the Regional Congress and most of the meetings of the steering committee and other groups during 1992 and early 1993.

Phase I: Community Outreach

In late 1992, ARC selected the public relations firm of Pringle Dixon Pringle to help carry out the heart of the VISION 2020 project, a public outreach campaign to involve the entire regional community in creating a shared vision of the future. ARC based its choice on several factors, including Pringle Dixon Pringle's track record for successfully executing community service projects — such as the campaign that revived Zoo Atlanta and the "Pennies from Heaven" fundraising campaign for The Atlanta Project. In addition, the firm's bid, the lowest of all the bids, reflected a great deal of pro bono work they and their subcontractors committed to VISION 2020.

The public outreach campaign ran from January to May 1993. Its primary purpose was to inform citizens about their future options and alert them to the opportunity to help mold the future of their region. It focused on two key public involvement programs. The first was the creation of the VISION 2020 Speaker's Bureau. Speakers drawn primarily from the steering committee and members of RLI delivered more than 100 presentations to civic, community, business, and government organizations, including public housing tenant associations and homeless shelters. Members of RLI also sponsored a series of 23 community forums in strategic locations throughout the region. These forums provided more than 2,000 grassroots citizens an opportunity for direct involvement in formulating the vision for their future.

In March, local network affiliate WAGA-TV broadcast a live townhall meeting to hundreds of thousands of viewers during prime time on a Thursday evening. More than 300 citizens participated in the studio audience and two satellite locations. Local business and civic leaders authored a series of seven guest editorials on VISION 2020 issues published by the *Atlanta Journal and Constitution*. A special VISION 2020 program involved hundreds of youth through Junior Achievement. Other activities included an array of radio and television interviews, public service announcements, and free billboard advertising.

The townhall meeting publicized a special newspaper supplement and public opinion survey, which ran in the *Atlanta Journal and Constitution* on the following Sunday. In addition, the supplement and survey ran in the *Atlanta Tribune*, in Chinese in the *Chinese World Journal*, and in Spanish in *Mundo Hispanico*. The *Atlanta Journal and Constitution* also delivered the survey, along with an excerpt of the supplement, as part of its REACH edition targeted to nonsubscribers. Combined, these newspapers reached more than 1.5 million people with information exploring the issues and decisions facing the region. ARC staff and VISION 2020 volunteers also delivered copies directly to hard-to-reach audiences including non–English speaking citizens and homeless persons.

The community's contribution to this first phase in cash and pro bono contributions totaled more than $2 million, not counting donations of thousands of hours of time.

The Shared Vision Unveiled

ARC staff carefully studied and synthesized all data, ideas, and suggestions received through this massive outreach effort. The most stunning discovery of Phase I was the common values shared by citizens from different cultures and income levels. VISION 2020 found that all people are interested in the same basics for their families and communities. These simple but profound elements include a sense of personal safety; a strong education system; job opportunities; a clean environment; cooperation among governments, chambers of commerce, and other institutions; and harmony among people of different races and cultures.

Finally, after months of outreach efforts and comments from thousands of citizens, "A Shared Vision for the Atlanta Region" was complete and ready for its unveiling at ARC's Outlook '93 Conference in May

1993. The 1,200 people who attended viewed the vision through a printed report and a video produced with the help of WAGA-TV. Futurist Glen Heimstra again addressed the Outlook participants, this time in a video message, encouraging them to help take part in making the vision a reality. He congratulated the community on completing the monumental task of creating a vision but reminded the crowd that the really hard work was still ahead — implementation.

Phase II: Making the Vision a Reality

Phase I focused on giving every person in the Atlanta region an opportunity to voice their opinions, hopes, and dreams about the future. That was no easy feat since the region's 10 counties of 3,000 square miles are home to almost 3 million people. Building a shared vision for future development is an unusual and laudable accomplishment. However, bringing life to that vision is the truly difficult part. The purpose of Phase II was to involve a diverse cross-section of the community in creating initiatives and action steps as well as to acquire community support to take that vision to reality.

Phase II began with a search for a method to build community consensus on a way to implement the community's vision. The method chosen was the collaborative process developed by the National Civic League (NCL), headquartered in Denver. In June of 1993, ARC sponsored three two-day training sessions on community collaboration for 150 key regional leaders. The training, led by NCL staff, helped to prepare a core group of people to lead the implementation process using a method of collaboration and cooperation.

With this training as a starting point, the VISION 2020 steering committee began work on Phase II in the fall of 1993. They first established initiating committees around 10 key issues that regional citizens considered critical to the future. For each committee, they selected 10 to 15 individuals based on their diverse perspectives related to each issue. The issues covered the spectrum, including diversity, economic development, education, environment, governance, health, housing, human services, public safety, and transportation.

In January 1994, Chris Gates, now president of NCL, conducted several training sessions for the initiating committees. During the same visit, he delivered the keynote address for a VISION 2020 breakfast at the Atlanta History Center to kickoff the work of the 10 initiating committees. He explained NCL's model and its strategic purpose of bringing diverse perspectives and intellect from all areas of the community to bear on building better communities.

Over four to five months, the 10 committees adapted the NCL model to deal most effectively with local views and concerns about their specific issue areas. They also identified and recruited about 100 people with diverse perspectives from all parts of the region to serve on each of the 10 groups. Their charge was to examine the community's vision and create action plans to address the critical issues. To assist the work of the collaboratives, ARC contracted with a local firm, Leadership Strategies, Inc., to help ARC staff adapt the NCL model, to manage the process, to train ARC staff and community volunteers in facilitation techniques, and to provide a core group of professionals to serve as lead facilitators of the VISION 2020 collaboratives.

The Outlook '94 Conference in May launched the collaborative process and released ARC's 2020 baseline forecasts of population and jobs. In collaboration with the Georgia Tech Research Institute, ARC produced an innovative, award-winning video that combined motivational messages with computer visualization of the small area

forecasts and selected region-shaping development policies. The community would now have a chance to alter those forecasts through "trend-bending" action plans. By June, all 10 VISION 2020 collaboratives had begun their year-long task of determining what barriers stand in the way and what actions are critical to achieving the community's shared vision for the future. Nearly 1,000 citizens met at least once a month, sometimes more often, to finish this critical work.

Leadership is the single most important factor in this community collaborative process. The initiating committees recognized this by carefully selecting and recruiting widely respected leaders who could provide strong but inclusive leadership to chair each collaborative. Their official duties went beyond simply chairing meetings to include planning each meeting in detail, adjusting the process as needed, and encouraging members to stay involved. They also organized committees to work in the following areas: research, to bring needed information to the deliberations; membership, to be certain that all concerned perspectives were at the table; and outreach, to involve others and gain community awareness and acceptance of recommendations emerging from the collaborative.

Phase II: Community Outreach

While they worked, the VISION 2020 collaboratives reached out to the larger community to check their work, refine their directions, and build civic will for needed changes. Outreach included speaking engagements, community forums, guest editorials, and many other activities. VISION 2020 held another Regional Congress in February of 1995 to report progress and to involve the larger community. WAGA-TV again produced and aired a live television townhall meeting to discuss critical issues facing youth in the future. The education collaborative involved every school in the Atlanta region in a project called "The Future through Young Eyes." Students discussed the future and contributed art, poetry, essays, and videos depicting the world they envision in the next century.

On Sunday, June 25, 1995, a special 16-page newspaper supplement, called "The Regional Dialogue," appeared in the *Atlanta Journal and Constitution*. The supplement focused on efforts by VISION 2020, the Regional Leadership Institute, and the United Way of Metropolitan Atlanta to involve citizens in creating a great future. It featured a second public opinion survey to test ideas emerging from the VISION 2020 deliberations.

The special insert was a gift to the community provided by a partnership of the *Atlanta Journal and Constitution*, the *Clayton News Daily* (a suburban daily), and Southeast Newsprint. This was the first time known that two competing newspapers have partnered in a joint community service project of this scale. Southeast Newsprint donated the 41 tons of paper needed to print "The Regional Dialogue." The supplement and survey, which reached hundreds of thousands of citizens, represented pro bono contributions of more than $300,000 in services, newsprint and donated space.

Bringing It All Together

It became apparent early on that the 10 VISION 2020 collaboratives would need to address the cross-cutting and duplicative issues shared among them. In May of 1995, leadership from each collaborative met to synthesize the work of all 10. Altogether, 11 major sets of actions emerged from the collaborative process. These groups of initiatives addressed topics from transportation and land use to cultural arts.

In June 1995, ARC held a celebration breakfast to present the synthesized initiatives of all 10 VISION 2020 collaboratives. As a small token of appreciation, participants received VISION 2020 lapel pins to signify the work accomplished and to remind the community of the challenges and opportunities that lie ahead. The celebration breakfast launched the work of action planning teams formed to work through July to put the final touches on the 11 sets of initiatives. The action planning teams completed initial implementation plans on schedule for a total of 41 initiatives.

ARC's 1995 Outlook Conference on Sept. 8 unveiled the results of the four-year VISION 2020 process. The report, "A Community's Vision Takes Flight," set forth the framework for accomplishing the 41 initiatives. A standard format outlined the purpose of each initiative, key action steps, the lead organization and other partners, a generalized description of timing and resource requirements, and a contact for additional information. In December, ARC will publish a comprehensive report covering milestones of all 10 community collaboratives and, when available, more detailed and updated action plans. Both reports are, however, simply snapshots of works in progress. Together they give leaders and citizens a clear and executable plan for achieving the region's full potential in the future.

To assure that the plans lead to action, VISION 2020 established an implementation committee composed of all collaborative chairs and two representatives each from the VISION 2020 steering committee, the Regional Leadership Foundation, and the Atlanta Regional Commission Board. The 23-member committee, chaired by George Busbee, began work in July to give direction to the action planning teams and to oversee and monitor production of the VISION 2020 framework plan released in September. The implementation committee, for at least the next year or two, will approve and coordinate organizations to lead implementation of specific initiatives and foster interest in those initiatives that falter. This committee anticipates setting a sunset date for its transitional work after they have determined, in concert with the regional community, the best way to assure the long-term success of VISION 2020.

At the same time, ARC's board passed a resolution accepting the work of and affirming its commitment to VISION 2020. The resolution also recognizes ARC's responsibility to assist other organizations involved in implementing key initiatives and to monitor and report on implementation activities. As part of this process, ARC is taking the lead on a set of VISION 2020 benchmarks to provide an annual picture of regional well-being and to measure progress toward achieving the goals of VISION 2020. The benchmarks will alert regional citizens to the need for change when trends take a negative turn, and they will serve as milestones for community celebration when targets are achieved. Finally, to provide a guide for other regions, ARC has contracted with an independent consultant to document and evaluate the VISION 2020 process. The chief purposes are to determine lessons learned, thank participants, and elicit ideas on future directions for VISION 2020.

Funding Phase II and Beyond

ARC returned to the foundation and corporate community to fund the second phase of VISION 2020. In early 1994, the Robert W. Woodruff Foundation offered VISION 2020 another generous donation to help fund this effort. At that time, the Phase II budget for exceptional out-of-pocket costs exceeded $1 million. Foundation managers supported the budget but felt that Phase I had generated sufficient interest and support for ARC to seek corporate and community funding as well. The Woodruff Foundation donated $500,000

for Phase II and offered an additional challenge grant of $250,000 to be matched by corporate funding.

During the first half of 1994, ARC staff explored a number of corporate solicitation strategies with members of the VISION 2020 steering committee and ARC's board. Under the leadership of board member John Williams, chairman and CEO of Post Properties, ARC prepared a comprehensive prospectus covering not only VISION 2020 activities but also other unfunded projects identified as imperative by the VISION 2020 process. Following the advice of experienced fundraising professionals and volunteers, ARC staff produced a set of support materials that spelled out the tangible end products of this work program and the benefits of specific interest to regional businesses. The identity chosen for the fundraising campaign was "MISSION 2020: to move the region from vision to reality."

Other preparations included developing a list of businesses considered to be good prospects for ARC's fundraising. The list featured many of the region's responsible corporate citizens and others whose interests match ARC's mission and the objectives of MISSION 2020. Starting with the most promising prospects, Mr. Williams or Governor Busbee made appointments and visited targeted corporations and foundations with ARC's director to make the case for MISSION 2020 and ask for a specific level of funding. Prior to the appointment ARC sent personalized letters introducing MISSION 2020. Then during the visit, the ARC delegation presented each prospect a set of prestige-quality printed materials to support their personal appeal. By the end of 1994, the Woodruff challenge grant was matched by corporate contributions totaling almost $1 million from Georgia Power, UPS, NationsBank, Trust Company Bank, Wachovia Bank of Georgia, Post Properties, BellSouth, and Georgia Pacific.

ARC's preparation for this fundraising

program began several years ago with early efforts to involve the private sector in its annual Outlook Conferences, the regional Leadership Institute, expanded committees of the board, and other outreach efforts. Beyond preparation, once again *leadership* was the key to ARC's success in its maiden voyage into corporate funding. Although ARC carefully targeted businesses who knew and appreciated ARC's mission, every contributor was clearly most influenced by the personal testimonial made by either Governor Busbee or Mr. Williams.

To reinforce the confidence of contributors, ARC committed to keep separate accounts of these private sector funds and established a board of trustees to oversee the expenditure of funds and completion of the work program. Once the agency has a proven track record for performance, private sector funding of portions of ARC's ongoing work program may become routine.

In Conclusion

The release of the VISION 2020 plan serves as a beginning for long-term positive change in the Atlanta region. Prominent agencies and corporations have taken the lead on some initiatives, while teams of community leaders are pushing others forward. United Way has opened its planning process to its entire donor community using survey and outreach methods that mirror VISION 2020's. The agency also is committed to integrating VISION 2020 concerns and initiatives into its strategic plan. United Way serves as an outstanding example of many new partnerships formed to work on either specific VISION 2020 initiatives or complementary community efforts.

The four-year project has endeavored to tap the community's vision, energy, and commitment to excellence. It has produced a cadre of leaders interested in making this community the best it can be. Barriers are beginning to come down. Strangers are becoming friends. Relationships are forming that will help Atlanta compete as one cohesive region in the global economy of the 21st century. Most importantly, VISION 2020 has helped to build a new civic infrastructure and contributed to a systemic change in community decision making in the Atlanta region.

Through VISION 2020 the community has begun work on a set of benchmarks to measure how well the vision is doing. The benchmarks will serve as only one of many ways that VISION 2020 will keep the community informed on regional progress and persistent problems. What happens from this point forward represents the true test of VISION 2020's effectiveness. Hopefully, VISION 2020 will signal the end of complacency and herald the arrival of a sharp sense of urgency. Ultimately, VISION 2020's success will mean that the entire regional community works together, not only to plan for the distant future but also to accomplish the important trend-bending actions needed today.

CHAPTER 29

PROMOTING REGIONAL GOVERNANCE IN THE BALTIMORE, MARYLAND, AREA

The Greater Baltimore Committee

This chapter proposes a new vision for the Baltimore region. To achieve that vision will require sustained, regional leadership and bold action. We need to start thinking and acting like a region if we are to be successful in the future. The Greater Baltimore Committee (GBC) is convinced that the result will be a healthy and vigorous community that can complete successfully in the global economy of the 21st century. The alternative would be decline throughout the region and the spread of social and economic problems. The choice is clear.

The Baltimore Region

Ever since its founding in 1955, the GBC has been concerned about both the competitiveness and the quality of life of the Baltimore region. Yet, even the GBC, a regional organization by virtue of its membership and its mission statement, has largely focused on the condition of individual jurisdictions and particularly on Baltimore. As an organization of corporate and civic leaders, we have concluded that an exclusive focus on individual jurisdictions is no longer in the best interests of either the region or its individual jurisdictions. While we may, at times, become involved in policy issues that are predominantly local, we believe it's time to start thinking outside the lines as well.

The reasons for thinking about regionalism, for not having our alternatives limited by existing political boundaries, are strong and compelling and growing by the day. The motivation comes from both problems and opportunities.

Many of the problems are already apparent. For example, we can readily see that older, inner-ring suburban neighborhoods in Baltimore County are facing social and economic problems that we formerly associated with inner city neighborhoods. As is the case in many areas of the country, we can expect those problems to continue to spread outward, unless we figure out how to deal with them.

If you make a list of the major issues facing any particular jurisdiction, you are

Originally published as "One Region, One Future: A Report on Regionalism" *The Regionalist*, Vol. 2, No. 2, Summer, 1997. Published by the National Association of Regional Councils, Washington, D.C. Reprinted with permission of the publisher.

likely to conclude both that a similar list exists for other jurisdictions and that the solutions cannot possibly be effective unless they are undertaken on a broader basis. How about crime? Criminals are not limited by political boundaries. Efforts to reduce crime shouldn't be either. Similarly, environmental quality and the threats to it have nothing to do with artificial lines on a map.

The failures of the Baltimore city schools have a direct impact on the quality of the workforce available to employers throughout the region.

Even the relative success of high-growth suburban areas may be misleading. A growing number of studies, as well as examples from other parts of the country, show that overall economic prosperity and growth are less in regions with declining central cities than in regions where the central city, as well as the suburbs, is flourishing. Although many seem reluctant to accept the fact, we really are all in this together. For the GBC, regionalism is very much about a dynamic, competitive, and productive business climate for all the citizens of the metropolitan area.

A Global Economy

Regionalism is also about opportunity. In a world of rapid and dramatic change, the most significant development may well be the emergence of the global economy. The term is no longer one only for futurists, but describes a reality we are facing today. Our economic partners and competitors are no longer just our neighbors or some nearby states. Our goods and services can be offered to a world market, but they face serious price and quality competition. The stakes are very high. Winners will grow and prosper and losers will face declining standards of living and quality of life.

The point is that we are a region, like it or not. The question is whether we will be

---

A Report Adopted by the Greater Baltimore Committee Board of Directors.

The Greater Baltimore Committee (GBC), composed of business and civic leaders from the Baltimore region, established a committee, the Policy Study Group on Regionalism, in September 1996, to examine key issues related to the health and competitiveness of the Baltimore region and to make recommendations to the GBC Board of Directors. The report printed here was unanimously adopted by the GBC board in April 1997, and was highlighted at the GBC's Annual Meeting in May 1977. GBC's chair is Frank Bramble, president and CEO of First Maryland Bancorp.

The president of the GBC is Donald Hutchinson. The GBC's regionalism initiative is directed by GBC vice president Laslo Boyd, a member of the Board of Trustees of the Institute for The Regional Community. The 23-member Policy Study Group on regionalism was chaired by Mark K. Joseph, chairman of the Shelter Group, and Carl Stearn, president and CEO of Provident Bankshares Corporation.

Copies of the "One Region, One Future" can be obtained by writing to the attention of Laslo Boyd, Vice President, Greater Baltimore Committee, 111 South Calvert St., Suite 1500, Baltimore, Maryland 21202.

---

a competitive region. To compete successfully, not only with Phoenix and Jacksonville, but also with Frankfurt and Osaka, we will have to grow and also to attract businesses that find in Baltimore the resource base that they need and the quality of life that they want. This is why the quality of *all* our schools is important. This is why public safety *throughout* the region is important.

Regions are becoming the primary economic competitors in the new global economy. In part, this is the case because regions are natural economic areas, as opposed to political jurisdictions, which are totally arbitrary. Additionally, regions have the ability to develop the scale of economic activity and the clusters of industries that can support and reinforce each other. For example, one of the key industries for Maryland's economic future is biotechnology. Looking at a map, it is very clear that the biotechnology companies and the various interrelated enterprises, such as research universities, are spread throughout the region, and operate with no regard to the political boundaries that may separate them.

The Baltimore region faces the paradoxical situation that the jurisdiction with the most problems has the least capacity to deal with them. Addressing the social and economic problems that are, at the moment, largely concentrated in Baltimore city is essential to the long-term vitality of the entire region. Baltimore city will not be able to develop successful responses to the problems it faces on its own. Moreover, research by urban experts demonstrates that efforts like the Empowerment Zone, that focus exclusively on the city without considering the interdependence of the entire region, are not likely to reverse major trends.

We need to find policies and mechanisms and partnerships that bring the resources and capabilities of the entire region to bear on a set of problems that ultimately affect every single person living and working in the entire area. A number of other organizations and individuals are thinking about and talking about similar questions. That's a very positive sign, because our ability to develop new approaches to some very old problems will require the participation of the corporate, nonprofit, civic, and political communities.

Getting to the Solutions

What are the solutions? In the next section of this chapter, we make a number of specific recommendations. None is short-term or easy to achieve. All will require education and discussion and the development of political support. We have looked at the experience of other regions, but ultimately we must devise a solution that works for the Baltimore area and that is the product of a process that involves the different parts of our community.

One qualification is in order, however. When we talk about regionalism and thinking outside of the lines, that does not mean we are advocating the elimination or redrawing of the political boundaries of this region. In many respects, we already have one of the best approaches to local government with our county system, which is far better than many areas of the country that have literally hundreds of units of local government in their metropolitan areas.

The question, rather, is how we can cooperate to find solutions that work for our problems, regardless of where in the region they are. The result will be a healthier and more competitive region which will benefit all of us.

The Choices We Face

The GBC regional strategy results from a careful and thorough examination of both our region and the experiences of other areas. That process has led us to five fundamental propositions that form the basis for the recommendations that follow.

1. Regions with declining core areas do less well overall than regions with healthy and viable cores. There is growing evidence from all over the country for this conclusion. The point, and it is central to our whole effort, is that there are real and serious adverse consequences for apparently thriving suburban areas if the central city is in decline. For one, the problems always spread. Building walls or digging moats does not work. Neither does moving farther and farther out from the central city. Secondly, the resources of a viable central city are a key part of the attractiveness of a region and cannot be replaced. Efforts at replicating such resources absorb enormous public costs and end up making the region less competitive.

2. The city and the counties of the Baltimore region are growing increasingly interdependent. We think that this interdependence is the fundamental fact of life in the emerging global economy. Moreover, as we examine the social and economic trends within our region, it is clear that our futures are linked together. Many in the Baltimore region have not recognized this fact or have tried to resist it, but the evidence is overwhelming.

The first step in building a workable regional agenda to make this a viable, competitive region is to get people throughout the region to recognize this interdependence. We believe that our five fundamental points are connected. If we see ourselves as being tied together and having a common fate, then we can start working to develop the policy solutions to benefit the region as a whole and the political will to implement those policies.

We use the term "regionalism" throughout this report to refer to the view that all of us in the Baltimore region have an interdependent future and to the goal of developing regional policy approaches to deal with the key issues that affect all of us. We are talking about "governance," working together in partnerships and in collaboration, rather than about how we organize or structure our governments in the region.

3. Despite significant successes, Baltimore city will not be able to reverse trends in population loss and increase in poverty by itself. We have seen a series of

studies over the years, from Peter Szanton to Neal Peirce to David Rusk to Myron Orfield, which all come to the same conclusion.[1] The data and trends are alarming and getting worse. Population and jobs and fiscal capacity are all declining. Concentration of poverty and crime rates and failures of the education system are all increasing. That many other cities are facing the same problems, and not solving them either, is of little comfort.

We believe that Baltimore's condition will not be improved by any of the traditional means that cities have employed in the past. Those approaches, whether in the form of financial aid for the city or innovative programs to deal with a specific issue, have, for the most part, treated symptoms rather than fundamental causes. While it is possible to point to successes, the city has been unable, on its own, to reverse the overall trends.

4. Social and economic problems are not limited to Baltimore city and are increasing and spreading to other parts of the Baltimore region. Inner-ring suburbs and other older communities are experiencing problems associated with poverty and aging infrastructure similar to what Baltimore city has confronted. Concerns about drug use, public safety, and quality of schools, among other issues, are not limited even to those areas, but can be seen throughout the region.

The point is that the beneficiaries of regional cooperation and problem solving are all of the jurisdictions and residents of the region. Similarly, the consequences of inaction will affect the entire region.

5. Finally, we need to acknowledge that race relations is one of the key issues that we must confront. At the very least, perceptions about race impede solutions to many of the problems facing the region. In the opinion of some, racial attitudes are one of the causes of those problems. The data on those problems, particularly with respect to poverty, reflect sharp distinctions by race. If we are to work together as a region, we cannot allow ourselves to be divided by race. That is a challenge that runs throughout all the issues facing us.

Recommendations

The GBC has concluded that concentration of poverty, extreme wealth disparities, and the consequent declining fiscal capacity are fundamental issues that need to be addressed directly if the region is to be viable and competitive in the 21st century global economy. Policy recommendations that address these issues directly will require time, persistence and political skill.

The political challenge in pursuing these policy recommendations is formidable. We must get beyond immediate negative reactions and engage in a process that has as its objective the long-term viability of the entire region. That is an undertaking that will test our resolve and commitment, but is, we believe, worth the effort.

The GBC endorses the following initiatives:

1. Regional growth management policies that lead to redevelopment and reinvestment in older neighborhoods and reduce the infrastructure costs to the governments and taxpayers of the region.

Encouraging reinvestment in older areas, whether Baltimore city, inner-ring suburbs, or other communities, is essential if we are to have a healthy region. A thoughtful growth management approach for the region is one of the important tools for bringing about revitalization of the older communities.

The evidence is clear. Places that have gotten serious about growth management have stimulated reinvestment in their central cities and older suburbs at the same time that they have attracted investment and growth because they were appealing places to live and work. Portland, Oregon is a national success story with the most advanced growth management policies in the country. The key element in that policy is the determination of an urban growth boundary line. Future development areas are concentrated inside of the line while growth outside the urban boundary is limited. While the details of the planning process have evolved since its inception in 1973, the patterns of development in the Portland area have consumed land at a rate roughly equivalent to the population growth and have fostered significant reinvestment in the older downtown areas. By contrast, the proportion of land consumption to population growth in the Baltimore area from 1960 to 1990 was approximately five to one.

A Portland-style growth management approach for Baltimore would promote redevelopment of Baltimore city and inner-ring suburbs, reduce the overall infrastructure costs for the region, and preserve agricultural and park lands.

2. Policies that result in a system of tax base sharing in the region. Any system should focus on the growth in tax base and could draw upon a number of different models that have been adopted across the country. Tax base sharing and revenue sharing are not new in this country. The relationships between the federal government and the states and between Maryland and its local governments are filled with examples. Moreover, in Maryland's system of large county governments, there is a form of implicit revenue sharing that takes place between different sections of the same county.

The best-known regional example in the country is in the Twin Cities area. Under a Minnesota law that went into effect in 1975, 40 percent of the *increase* in the assessed value of commercial and industrial property in the Twin Cities area is placed into a common pool to be redistributed to all 187 municipalities in the region, based upon a formula that includes both population and comparative property wealth. The total pool as of 1995 was $241 million. The goal of the program has been to reduce fiscal disparities among jurisdictions. The Minnesota program has benefitted large numbers of political jurisdictions in that region.

The goals of a tax base sharing system for the Baltimore region could be to reduce fiscal disparities, to lessen the competitive disadvantage of any area with a disproportionately high tax rate in attracting and retaining businesses and residents, and to finance a fair-share housing program for the region.

A system that shared the *growth* in the commercial and industrial tax base would create a shared interest in economic development anywhere in the region. Such an approach would also lessen the incentives for costly and unproductive competition within the region.

There are a number of variations of this approach. Allegheny County, Pennsylvania has created a Regional Asset District that shares a 1 percent sales tax in the region to support cultural facilities and reduction of other taxes. The Dayton, Ohio area has a voluntary tax base sharing system to support economic development projects as well as for revenue redistribution, although the total revenues shared are not large. The Denver, Colorado region has a Scientific and Cultural Facilities District that shares a one-tenth of one percent regional sales tax.

3. A policy for developing affordable housing throughout the metropolitan area. A key goal of this policy should be to avoid creating concentrations of people living in poverty. The national model most often cited exists in Maryland. Montgomery County passed legislation in 1975 requiring developers of new housing to include moderately priced units. Under the Moderately Priced Dwelling Unit policy (MPDU), any new housing development of at least 50 units must include up to 15 percent moderately priced units. Of that 15 percent, the

county's Housing Opportunities Commission can purchase up to one-third for low income residents. The program has produced more than 10,000 units of moderate and low income housing that are distributed across the county.

The Montgomery County MPDU model could serve as the basis for an affordable housing policy for the Baltimore region. This approach would require either a collaborative agreement among housing agencies or some sort of areawide housing agency, as well as a financing mechanism.

Conclusion

These recommendations go to the core of the GBC's mission "to improve the business climate of the Greater Baltimore Region by organizing its corporate and civic leadership to develop solutions to the problems that affect the region's competitiveness and viability."

The GBC is making a long-term commitment to advocating for, and supporting regional approaches to, economic and social issues in the Baltimore metropolitan area. Regionalism will be on the GBC work plan and at the top of its agenda for the next decade and beyond.

In addition to advocating for specific policies, the GBC will be actively engaged in the educational campaign that will be needed to build support for regionalism in general, as well as for those specific policies. An important starting point is to enhance current areas of regional cooperation. The GBC, through its organizational activities, as well as through the efforts of its individual members, will seek ways to raise the visibility of regional issues and to facilitate discussion among different groups and individuals about regional solutions.

None of our recommendations will be accomplished easily or quickly. That the ultimate objectives are long term does not mean, however, that we should not be actively pursuing them immediately and identifying interim and short-term steps that move the Baltimore region in the right direction. If we do not start working on these hard issues now, we will find ourselves in another decade facing even more difficult problems.

As a region, we have the resources to compete successfully with any place. But we must develop a regional framework for success.

With well-focused, effective regional teamwork on key public policy issues that relate directly to our business climate, Greater Baltimore can be a global business leader. Without it, we risk placing ourselves, and our children, at a serious competitive disadvantage.

Notes

1. Orfield, Myron. 1996. *Metropolitics: A Regional Agenda for Community and Stability.* Washington, D.C.: The Brookings Institution and the Lincoln Institute of Land Policy.

2. Peirce, Neal, et al. 1993. "Baltimore Breaking the Boundaries," in *Citistates: How Urban America Can Prosper in a Competitive World.* Washington, D.C.: Seven Locks Press. Originally published as a special section of *The Baltimore Sun,* May 6, 1991.

3. Rusk, David. 1996. *Baltimore Unbound: A Strategy for Regional Renewal.* Baltimore: The Hopkins University Press.

4. Szanton, Peter L. 1986. *Baltimore 2000: A Choice of Futures.* A Report to the Morris Goldseker Foundation.

CHAPTER 30

REGIONAL INITIATIVES AMONG FRAGMENTED GOVERNMENTS IN THE DAYTON-SPRINGFIELD, OHIO, METROPOLITAN AREA

Mary Ellen Mazey

Metropolitan regions across the United States increasingly face the challenge of competing in a globalized economy. This challenge of globalization is handicapped by features unique to the American landscape, from chaotic governmental structure to stringent environmental quality goals to even the social inequality manifested between the central cities and suburbs. Furthermore, problems compounded by regional fragmentation are faced by the larger metropolitan areas, such as Los Angeles, Chicago, and Philadelphia. Although at a different scale, medium-sized metropolitan areas must seek to resolve similar issues and problems. One such case is the metropolitan area of Dayton-Springfield, Ohio, located in southwestern Ohio and the subject of this case study on regionalism.

The Dayton-Springfield Metropolitan Area is a four-county region of approximately 1 million people who live in a highly decentralized environment. A 1990 ranking of 100 largest cities in the country found that the Dayton region was the eighth most decentralized metropolitan area. The decentralization rating measures the percent of the total metropolitan population that resides in the central city as compared to the suburbs. Of the region's nearly 1 million population, only 183,000, or approximately 20 percent, lived in the core central city. The other 80 percent live in the nearly 160–170 general purpose governments and 50 school districts, plus 30 chambers of commerce served by the region. Of the four counties composing the metropolitan area, Montgomery County, where Dayton is located, composed only slightly more than one-half of the region's population. Therefore, this proliferation of governments scattered throughout four counties poses problems to regionalism efforts.

The fragmentation has prompted numerous regional efforts to be put forward from various segments of the community. This research analyzes a number of the past efforts along with some of the newest ven-

Originally published as "Creating Regionalism Amid Fragmentation," *The Regionalist*, Vol. 2, No. 2, Summer, 1997. Published by the National Association of Regional Councils, Washington, D.C. Reprinted with permission of the publisher.

tures. These efforts are evaluated based upon factors the literature indicates are needed for success.

The New Regionalism Movement

The new regionalism movement of the late 1980s and 1990s has grown out of the unsuccessful federal public policies, such as the Federal Housing Administration (FHA), the Veterans Administration (VA), the National Defense Highway Act, and the U.S. Supreme Court decision on busing. The FHA and VA programs promoted segregated neighborhoods with a value and philosophy in the real estate market that fostered segregation. By providing low interest loans that spurred suburban housing development, the white middle class fled the central city to live the American dream. The real estate industry reaped the profit of this migration and benefitted greatly from keeping the suburbs segregated and land and housing values inflated.

The cheap cost of energy, providing inexpensive transportation costs, and the proliferation of the automobile worked as "pull" factors to spur the population migration from America's central cities to the suburbs. Added to this was the Supreme Court decision to institute busing which worked as a "push" factor to enhance the migration to the suburbs and exacerbate the problems associated with segregation. The federal government also subsidized the movement by giving a tax deduction on abandoned buildings and tax credits to new plants and equipment. With the building of industry in the suburbs, this, in turn, encouraged the migration of jobs to these outlying areas.

Therefore, the competitive advantage of the central city was being destroyed as government policies worked to foster decentralization and development in the sub-

urbs. A further consequence of these policies was the federal government subsidizing of residential living and jobs for the middle class in the suburbs, while the central cities were becoming enclaves of poverty. This latter conclusion has been well documented in the urban studies literature since the 1960s and more recently in Judd and Swanstrom's work (Judd and Swanstrom, 1994).

Given these public policy developments, by 1980 twice as many people nationwide were commuting from suburb to suburb rather than from suburb to the central city. This has led to a greater polarization in the population of metropolitan areas at a time when urban researchers such as Neal Peirce and others have indicated that metropolitan regions will be the basic units for the global economic competition. David Rusk, in his book, *Cities Without Suburbs*, finds that the more successful cities across the United States are the ones that are elastic and have the ability to expand through annexation or some other means. Those cities that are inelastic, such as Dayton, Ohio, that have not expanded their geographical size, have become surrounded by incorporated suburbs.

In addition, Rusk asserts that cities where the median income of the central city is less that 66 percent of the suburbs have an ever-increasing gap as socioeconomic disparities of the region's population increases. Dayton has a median income which is less than 66 percent of the suburban areas (Rusk, 1993, pp. 46–47). In fact, Dayton ranks sixth when the poverty rates of the 100 largest cities are compared. If Dayton is to compete globally, Rusk's findings would suggest that the region must surmount its inelasticity to move toward a more regional framework.

The literature on the new regionalism movement indicates that successful regional efforts build on a strategic planning process that sets a common vision and goals, upon which various sectors of the community — public, private, and nonprofit — can reach a consensus (Wallis, 1994).

In fact, Allan Wallis, fresh from a long-term study of regional cooperation, writes that it is best not to invent new organizations but rather build on the strengths of existing organizations in order to foster regional initiatives (Wallis, 1994, p. 458). This paper will analyze the degree to which the Dayton area has followed the guidelines of Wallis as it has ventured forth on a number of regional endeavors.

These regional efforts include a strategic regional planning assessment initiated by the business community in 1987, a regional strategic planning process undertaken in 1989, a countywide volunteer tax-sharing program initiated in 1989, a collective attempt in 1989 to offer fire services more efficiently, and, finally, initiatives targeted to coordinate economic development strategies with the creation of new organizations in 1995. These efforts will first be discussed on an individual basis and then analyzed in terms of their collective impact.

Historical Aspect of Regionalism

By the mid–1980s, the Dayton area, like other communities across the country, became increasingly concerned about its ability to compete economically with other metropolitan areas. A group of CEOs from major corporations and the presidents of the three major higher education institutions in the region met on a weekly basis to discuss items of common interest. This group, known as the Dayton Area Progress Council, commissioned a study by two Wright State University economists to interview the key business leaders in the region to determine the region's strengths, weaknesses, and opportunities. The conclusion of the study indicated that, historically, the region had

been strong in manufacturing. It is the country's second largest employment center of General Motors. In addition, it caters to advanced technology through Wright Patterson Air Force Base, which is the Air Force's center of research and development.

However, the business community's report also stated that, even with these economic strengths and opportunities, the region's greatest weakness was its political fragmentation and its inability to work together for the "good of the whole." Therefore, the recommendation from the report was to create a regional strategic plan to assist in resolving this fragmentation and infighting (Community Factors Study, 1987). Out of this recommendation, the Dayton Area Chamber of Commerce, which at the time viewed itself as a regional entity (its mission has changed after a problem with expenditure of public funding in 1993), commissioned the Center for Urban and Public Affairs at Wright State University to undertake a regional strategic planning process. This effort encompassed a year-long process of meetings of a 60-member steering committee composed of community leaders from all different segments of the region. Nine task forces met to discuss issues and set a regional agenda in the following substantive areas: education, economic development, technology and innovation, regional cooperation, infrastructure, resource enhancement, environment, transportation, and human relations/human needs.

A Regional Vision

The outcome of this effort was a regional vision with a target of 12 immediate major objectives. The report also recommended the creation of a regional leadership network to pursue these and other regional objectives. Such a network was composed of leaders of the public, private, and nonprofit sectors and was called the Challenge 95

Leadership Network. As a volunteer group with only minimal funding contributed by the four counties in the region, this regional effort continued through 1995 with the logistical support of Wright State University. However, since 1995 a number of new regional organizations have been created. These new organizations have led to newly created regional entities with paid staff.

First, out of the Challenge 95 Leadership Network grew a volunteer group of county commissioners from four of the region's counties (the four were involved in Challenge 95 but an additional county of the Metropolitan Statistical Area chose not to participate). This group, known as the County Caucus, was able to forge its resources to create a joint economic development office known as the Regional Office of Economic Development, which, in turn, worked in partnership with a group of economic development practitioners known as the 170-75 Development Association. This group had been initiated during the time the regional strategic planning process was being undertaken and continued as a minimal-fee membership group of economic development practitioners and private sector members who generally came from small companies and sought a place to network.

The purpose of the 170-75 Development Association, in conjunction with the new Regional Office of Economic Development, was to work on collective marketing, site selection, business retention and expansion, and information gathering and dissemination. The public sector provides the office's entire financial support and a board representing the county commissioners of the participating counties oversees the new office. The staff includes a director, an economic development practitioner and a secretary.

A second regional group, the Regional Economic Strategies Forum, has formed since the Challenge 95 Leadership Network completed its work. This group sees its position as being a public educator. It holds public forums and meetings, disseminates a regional economic profile and markets specific economic strategies. This group does not have a full-time staff but utilizes two economics professors, one from Wright State University and one from the University of Dayton, to provide it with guidance and direction. This group is led by a state senator from the region.

Private Sector Initiatives

In addition to these two public sector-driven regional efforts, the private sector has developed its share of new initiatives. Since 1987, when the first regional assessment was commissioned by the business community, three new organizations have been formed to promote private sector agendas.

The Area Progress Council, mentioned earlier, continues to meet monthly to remain educated on important regional issues, but has no paid staff. A spin-off business group, known as the Dayton Business Committee, is composed of the 15 CEOs of the major large-scale corporations located primarily in the region's central core county. This group meets on a regular basis and has a paid staff of two — executive director and secretary. During the time of the regional strategic planning process, Challenge 95, this group became very concerned about the decline of downtown Dayton. It assisted in the creation of the Downtown Dayton Partnership, a not-for-profit corporation focused on the economic development of downtown Dayton. This entity was funded for three years by two governmental bodies, the City of Dayton and Montgomery County, but now has formed a special tax district to support it through the year 2000, with only downtown Dayton as its geographical boundaries. However, it has a core group of highly-paid professional staff people.

A third group, created and staffed in

1995, is the Miami Valley Economic Development Coalition with a purpose to develop the region's core strengths, including the Air Force Base and its spin-off industries and the automotive industry. This group has also taken charge of the region's lobbying effort at the state and federal levels of government. This entity has a director, one professional staffer and a secretary.

Finally, a recent regional effort, begun in 1989 as the regional strategic planning process was taking place, was the creation of a study committee by local fire officials to determine how their services could be offered more efficiently on a regional scale. This effort included representatives from the fire and emergency medical providers (75 members) from four of the region's counties. The group first studied the present situation and then evolved into a new study group consisting of township trustees and administrators, city managers, mayors, and Wright State University. This group spent 14 months studying the reports of the previous group and hiring an outside consultant for recommendations. The group decided that even though there would be a cost-savings benefit to merge all 33 fire departments, this could not be implemented for political reasons. Instead, a new council of governments known as the Miami Valley Fire/EMS Alliance was created and funded.

The alliance represents 20 fire departments and 27 local governments and is funded on a $.24 per capita fee from the participating fire departments. This funding supports the office and staff which opened in 1995. This alliance can already report a savings for its members in shared purchasing programs. With eight standing committees, the organization is working to increase the efficiency and effectiveness of its members. Its number one issue is to eliminate duplication of service.

This group had a track record on which to build because the fire service had joined together in the past to create collaborative programs, such as the Dayton Regional Hazardous Materials Response Team, the Technical Rescue Response Team, and the Automatic Mutual Aid Response Program. The Alliance also benefits from its executive director's track record. He has been the fire chief of both the central city of Dayton and a major growing suburb in one of the outlying counties, which gives him credibility to work with the fire chiefs and city managers from throughout the region. In an odd twist, the Air Force Base's own fire department is prohibited from joining a regional cost-saving effort due to federal regulations.

Continued Support to Existing Councils

Given these new initiatives that recently have been created and implemented to build regionalism in the Dayton-Springfield area, it is interesting to note that the region continues to support two prior existing councils of governments. One, the Miami Valley Regional Planning Commission (MVRPC), rose to national prominence in the 1970s for instituting a regional fair-share housing plan linked to federal funds and its ability to provide A-95 review. This organization has downsized, but still is in existence and is primarily providing members with services. The ISTEA (Intermodal Surface Transportation Efficiency Act) legislation revitalized it since it is the region's major transportation planning body.

In addition to MVRPC, the suburban governments created a council of governments, the Miami Valley Cable Council, to serve as a negotiator of their cable franchise fees. However, this organization has grown in functions and now coordinates training for the employees of suburban governments, plus houses their multijurisdictional crime prevention effort. Again, both of these councils of governments are primarily dependent on public funding for support and do not have a focused regional agenda.

ED/GE Program

The private sector's major regional unit prior to 1993 was the Dayton Area Chamber of Commerce. That organization was reorganized after the problems mentioned previously, and a number of its officials were forced to resign. Now the organization has new leadership and seems to be functioning with a more focused agenda. In 1989, it was the key organization that worked with the core county's (Montgomery) elected body to create the Economic Development/Government Equity (ED/GE) which is a volunteer tax-sharing program among the 33 different governmental units in Montgomery County, including the central city of Dayton. This one county regional effort was based on a carrot-and-stick approach to involvement and long-term participation.

The county commission has set aside $5 million annually for economic development projects, but in order to participate in the competition to receive these funds, a government must agree to put the new tax dollars earned from the economic development effort into a government equity tax-sharing pool. However, in order for the county to get the governments to join the tax-sharing fund, they guaranteed that no government would ever have more of their tax dollars go into government equity than they received from the economic development competition. The private sector was very supportive of this program and supported an increase in the county sales tax in order to fund it. A board composed of elected officials and private sector leadership decides on the allocation of the economic development funds.

Therefore, the private sector now has a role in making decisions on the county's tax dollars. This program is still relatively new with only about five years of allocation and tax sharing having taken place. The amount of tax dollars that has actually been shared between governmental jurisdictions is small, but at least communities are working together cooperatively on the program. The program was only instituted for 10 years, but, based on its successes thus far, it will in all likelihood be renewed for 10 more years.

Evaluation of Regional Initiatives

As stated previously, the Dayton area is extremely decentralized and governmentally fragmented. It is not surprising that the regionalism generated from the existing metropolitan region is equally fragmented. In fact, a common problem cited is lack of leadership for a unified regional area. Presently, different organizations and individuals want to be in control of the power and resources on a regional scale. Groups, especially the business community, keep creating regional leadership control mechanisms that only serve to feed a more uncontrollable situation. With such fragmentation, the region continues to decline economically, when compared to other metropolitan regions across the country, and it continues to foster greater economic disparity particularly between the central city and suburbs.

However, given the degree of fragmentation, the Dayton region should pride itself upon the amount of risk-taking and major regional cooperative initiatives it has undertaken in such a short time frame during the past 10 years. The volunteer tax-sharing program and the Miami Valley Fire Alliance are models for generating regional cooperation among governments, enhancing and saving tax dollars, and generating an awareness of the problems of the core central city. As long as these efforts produce results, they will continue.

However, the public and private sectors

need to question how many different orga-nizations they feel are essential to support regional economic development efforts. The more such organizations that are created to focus upon the entire region or any part of it, such as downtown Dayton, the more difficult it becomes to coordinate and sus-tain a return on the costs of staff and facil-ities. If the private sector is supporting mul-tiple economic development organizations, where will they find the funds to focus on regional concerns such as the high poverty rate in the core city? Most of the new orga-nizations have small staffs, but additional re-sources were needed to fund the efforts. In addition, as was stated earlier, Wallis con-tends that regional efforts should build on the resources and efforts of existing organi-zations. Therefore, the Dayton area should question its affinity to create new regional entities.

In the future, the region needs to ex-amine what other states have accomplished regionally. Ohio, with seven major cities, is often referred to as the state of city-states, and all of Ohio's city-states have experi-enced their new growth on the metropoli-tan periphery rather than near the urban core. Thus, the economic disparity within the metropolitan regions only continues to increase.

A number of states are addressing these disparities. For example, Oregon has adopted a statewide land use plan and mandates that regional plans be created in conformity to the statewide plan. Implementation of this mandate has created a unique governmental body in the Portland Metropolitan Area. With the adoption of the Metro Charter, Portland changed its rather traditional council of governments into a regionally elected body. This Metropolitan Service District was given the power in its charter to:

1. Develop and adopt a 50-year com-prehensive vision for the region by 1995.

2. Adopt a regional framework plan

for regional transportation and mass transit systems, management and amendment of the urban growth boundary, and other re-gional matters such as housing densities, water resources, and storage by 1997. This regional plan complies with statewide plan-ning goals and requires that local compre-hensive plans and implementing regulations comply with the regional framework plan within three years after its adoption (Metro Charter, 1992).

Such a coordinated intergovernmental approach gives regionalism the political le-gitimacy it needs to act with legal authority between the state government and the mul-tiplicity of local governments in the metro-politan area. Anthony Downs, in his book *New Visions for Metropolitan America*, advo-cates the creation of urban growth bound-aries as a means to control urban sprawl and foster the development of a functioning metropolitan governmental/planning frame-work. Without such a growth boundary in operation, the problems the Dayton area and other Ohio cities have developed will continue and exacerbate in the future, while all the time and financial resources spent on regional efforts really become nothing more than rhetoric, persuasion to cooperate for the good of the whole metropolitan area, or development of regional marketing mecha-nism.

Recommendations for Future Urban/Metropolitan Development

As the Dayton-Springfield Metropoli-tan region and other metropolitan regions throughout Ohio and the rest of the nation move forward, it is incumbent upon them to initiate and implement policies that will fos-ter regionalism. To institute public policies that will ultimately change the development of metropolitan areas and work toward a less segregated metropolitan environment with fewer spatial disparities, the following 12 recommendations are proposed, based upon others' work in regionalism:

1. Create a metropolitan growth boundary through a regional land use planning process, which is mandated by state government, that requires conformity of all local governments.

2. Designate an agency at the metropolitan level to plan and manage all federal aid entering a metropolitan region, with the exception being that paid directly to individuals.

3. Work to modify current federal policies such as the capital gains tax and home mortgage deduction that place central cities at a disadvantage and encourage the metropolitan population to decentralize.

4. Support Brownfield legislation in order to make central cities more competitive with suburbs for development.

5. Eliminate tax abatement policies that promote competition between central cities and suburbia.

6. Establish a regional mechanism that concentrates jobs in designated nodes such as the downtown.

7. Intersperse higher-density housing, both single-family and multi-family, with low-density development.

8. Create a job information network throughout the metropolitan area with information centers in blighted city neighborhoods.

9. Reduce the number of school districts in order to create more administrative efficiency and increase the number of frontline employees to work with students.

10. Make available comprehensive social services through the school system for child development.

11. Develop more school-to-work programs that enhance workforce skill development.

12. Develop incentives for more training programs for the underskilled and underemployed and link these programs directly to job opportunities.

These 12 recommendations seek to address the regional problems that have been created through years of public policies that have directly exacerbated the central city/suburban situation. The recommendations are intended to address the issues in multiple domains from the federal to state to local governments. The recommendations transcend traditional regional land-use planning, and they focus on the creation of a labor force that serves an entire metropolitan area and knows no political boundaries. By providing assistance to individual needs, the region will develop a productive citizenry for future economic, social, and governmental needs.

References

Blair, John and Robert Premus. 1987. *Community Factors Study*. Wright State University, Dayton, Ohio.

Downs, Anthony. 1994. *New Visions for Metropolitan America*. Washington, D.C.: The Brookings Institution.

Judd, D., and T. Swanstrom. 1994. *City Politics: Private Power and Public Policy*. New York: Harper Collins College Publishers.

Mazey, Mary Ellen. 1991. "Creating A Model for Regional Cooperation Through Citizen Participation." *National Civic Review*, (Spring).

Metro Charter. 1992. Metro Charter Committee, "Portland Metropolitan Service District."

Rusk, David. 1993. *Cities Without Suburbs*. Baltimore, Maryland: Johns Hopkins University Press.

Wallis, Allan. 1994. "Inventing Regionalism: A Two Phase Approach." *National Civic Review*, (Fall-Winter), 447–468.

CHAPTER 31

MAKING THE CASE FOR REGIONAL COOPERATION IN THE GREATER PHILADELPHIA, PENNSYLVANIA, REGION

Theodore Hershberg

Will metropolitan Philadelphia be better off in the global economy if the city at the core of the region collapses? If you live in the suburbs, do you believe that what happens to Philadelphia is without significant consequence for you and the community in which you reside?

Let us be clear about the argument. It is not that the suburban communities surrounding a failed Philadelphia will be wiped out by virtue of their proximity to ground zero in an atomic blast. They won't. But suburban residents are wrong if they think they won't suffer any fallout. The fact is they have a compelling economic interest in Philadelphia's viability.

Ample evidence documents that suburbs surrounding healthy central cities are better off than those surrounding unhealthy ones, and proof is mounting that regions — not cities or counties — will be the preeminent competitive units of the global economy. The issue is not whether the city and suburbs are tied together in a regional economy — they are — but how to ensure that the region will prosper in the future.

The fear and frustration felt by so many suburbanites about the problems of big cities is understandable, but their economic interests are not well served by turning their backs and ignoring the troubles next door. Such a course guarantees that problems will grow, opportunities will be lost, and, in the long run, everyone will be worse off. The time has come to recognize the mutual interests across the region and to begin a rational dialogue about what is required to work with each other to shape a prosperous future.

Regional cooperation spins on two axes, not one. Although the focus of this chapter is on the more familiar and difficult city-to-suburb relationships, suburb-to-suburb cooperation remains an important part of the larger challenge facing the region. Southeastern Pennsylvania has 239 municipalities and 63 school districts. These units of government offer citizens highly-valued local control, but they also give rise to a cloud of parochialism that obscures the necessity for change that is demanded by

Originally published as "The Case for Regional Cooperation," *The Regionalist*, Vol. 1, No. 3, Fall, 1995. Published by the National Association of Regional Councils, Washington, D.C. Reprinted with permission of the publisher.

the competitiveness of the new global economy.

New Global Economic Realities

There is an apocryphal story about an American in the 1930s who grew weary with the world rushing off to war. To get away from the madness, he sold all his possessions in the states and bought a piece of land on a remote South Pacific isle known for its beauty and tranquillity. Unfortunately, he settled on Guadalcanal, the site, as World War II buffs know, of the fiercest fighting in the Pacific Theater. The moral of the story is that the past is not always a useful guide for the future.

The global economy ensures the future will differ from the past. International trade, which equaled only 11 percent of America's gross national product (GNP) in 1960, reached 25 percent in 1990 and is growing rapidly. Already 25 percent of agricultural produce is exported, 30 percent of autos sold in America are produced by foreign manufacturers, 40 percent of corporate profits among Fortune 500 companies and 20 percent overall are derived from international activities, and 40 percent of all commercial loans in the United States are made by foreign banks. Ten percent of American pension funds, $500 billion, are invested in Asian companies alone.

Many Americans, particularly those in leadership positions who came of age between 1945 and 1970, still do not fully understand the nature of this change. The subconscious assumptions they hold about America's place in the world order were formed when we were the world's undisputed leader after World War II decimated the economies of our friends and enemies alike. In the late 1940s, America's GNP was half of the world's; in 1950, American per capital GNP was four times that of West Germany and fifteen times that of Japan.

But world dominance was temporary, and it gave way rapidly in the years following 1970. By the late 1980s, America accounted for only 23 percent of the world's GNP, and by 1990, Japan's per capita GNP slightly exceeded America's. Since 1970, dominance has been lost in industries that were once synonymous with America — steel, machine tools, chemicals, and autos — while consumer electronics has been virtually wiped out.

As the rest of the developed world caught up with us in these difficult decades, the lives of working men and women were affected. Real wages have been flat since 1970: only the top 20 percent of American male workers have improved their standing, 20 percent were stagnant, and 60 percent actually experienced a decline. Our standard of living did not fall at the same time, largely because women entered the labor force in record numbers, but absent polygamy there will be no third spouse to send into the labor force to bail us out in the future. Moreover, since 1989, even median *household* income has fallen despite the fact that Americans now work longer hours and a greater proportion now hold at least two jobs than in the last half century. According to Lester Thurow (1995), income inequality also is growing — among men working full time the earnings gap between the top and bottom quintiles doubled in the last 25 years — and the distribution of wealth is worsening, with the share of wealth held today by the top 1 percent of the population — more than 40 percent — rising to what it was in the late 1920s. Although these troubling statistics result from many factors, including new labor-saving technologies and the decline of unions, it is clear that America must adapt to the competitive challenges of the global economy.

The global economy has already affected the lives of all Americans in powerful ways, and its impact will increase as barriers to free trade continue to fall, global capital markets become more fluid, and telecommunication technologies accelerate the flow of information. If we understand the future, we greatly increase our chances of successfully adapting to the changes it will bring.

The Regional Implications of the Global Economy

The starting point is to recognize that the competitive unit of the global economy is the *region*—not the city, suburb, or county. Victor Petrella, director of science and technology forecasting for the European Union, believes:

> Within 50 years, such nation states as Germany, Italy, the United States, and Japan will no longer be the most relevant socioeconomic entities and the ultimate political configuration. Instead, areas like Orange County, California; Osaka, Japan; the Lyon region of France; or Germany's Ruhrgebiet will acquire predominant socioeconomic status. The real decision-making power of the future ... will be transnational companies in alliance with city-regional governments (quoted from Toffler and Toffler 1993).

Kenichi Ohmae (1995), former senior partner at McKinsey & Company and leader of a Japanese reform movement, put it this way in his new study, *The End of the Nation State*:

> The noise you hear rumbling in the distance is the sound of the later 20th century's primary engine of economic prosperity—the region-state—stirring to life. No longer will managers organize the international activities of their companies on the basis of national borders. Region-states have become the primary units of economic activity. It is through these region-states that participation in the global economy actually takes place.

Neal Peirce, nationally syndicated columnist and, with Curtis Johnson and John Stuart Hall (1993), coauthor of *Citi-states: How Urban America Can Prosper in a Competitive World*, contends, "Only when the central city and its surrounding counties work together will they be able to compete effectively. It won't be America versus Japan or Germany, but Greater Philadelphia versus metropolitan Tokyo or Stuttgart."

It is not difficult to understand why this is true. Only regions have the necessary scale and diversity to compete in the global marketplace. Only regions have an asset profile capable of projecting overall strength, in sharp contrast to the much less attractive profiles of individual counties or cities that lack either key infrastructure or a sufficiently skilled labor force.

Regions, moreover, are the geographic units in which we create our goods and services. We hire from a regional *labor force*. We count on a regional *transportation system* to move the people and materials involved in their production. We rely on a regional *infrastructure* to keep the bridges and roads intact and our sewers and pipelines functioning. We live in a regional *environment* whose water and air do not recognize political boundaries.

Finally, although most people don't realize it, regions have always been the geographic units of economic competition. The national economy is a set of summary statistics drawn from the performance of distinct regional economies.

The global economy has important implications for regions. Let us consider three: develop human resources, lower the costs of goods and services, and use scarce investment capital wisely.

Develop Human Resources

The source of comparative advantage in the future will be human capital. Future competition, argues Lester Thurow (1992) in *Head to Head: The Coming Economic Battle among Japan, Europe, and America*, will be characterized by competition over seven "brain intensive" industries — computers and software, robotics and machine tools, civilian aviation, microelectronics, materials sciences, biotechnology, and telecommunications — that offer high paying jobs to their workers and bring prosperity and world prestige to their countries. But even jobs requiring lower skills will be far more demanding than in the past. While only 30 percent of the jobs in the year 2000 will require college degrees, fully 89 percent will require post-secondary training.

Employers may recruit their top managers from a national labor pool, but they must rely on the regional labor force for the lion's share of their workers. If the region's schools and training institutes are not producing workers with adequate skills, the premium that employers will have to pay to attract qualified labor from outside the region will erode their competitiveness. Even though big corporations have the resources to compensate by retraining their workers, such a strategy unavoidably adds to their costs. Small businesses, utterly dependent on the quality of local institutions, lack even this option.

The central argument of *America's Choice: High Skills or Low Wages*, the report of the Commission on the Skills of the American Workforce (1990), was summarized by William Brock, a commission co-chair and former U.S. labor secretary. If companies in every country in the world can now buy "idiot-proof machinery" to compensate for workers with terribly deficient skills, and if there are people elsewhere in the world who will work for $5 per day with the same equipment as Americans who want $10 or $15 per hour, then we cannot compete on the basis of wage. We can compete only on the basis of skill.

Suburban schools generally have lower dropout rates, better achievement scores, and higher college enrollment rates than city schools, but there should be no comfort in this comparison. Nor does it matter if our schools are somewhat better than they were 20 years ago. The appropriate comparisons are first to schools in the rest of the developed world, and the results are sobering.

On average, American students are measurably far behind students in other nations — their future competitors — in math, science, and critical thinking skills. Only the top 10 to 20 percent of our children can be considered truly competitive.

The second comparison — how does the human capital of our children match up with the skill requirements of twenty-first century jobs — is equally troubling. Of new entrants to the nation's labor force between 1985 and 2000, roughly 80 percent have the skills for only the bottom 40 percent of the jobs, and only 5 percent have the skills for the top 40 percent of the jobs.

As corporate leaders well understand, America cannot succeed in the global economy unless every able-bodied citizen has the skills required by the demanding jobs of the new economy. The results of the recent *National Adult Literacy Survey* (Kirsh et al. 1993) are shocking: half the adult population in the United States is ill-equipped for the job requirements of the 21st century global economy. Although this makes clear that the challenge is national rather than solely urban, the fact remains that great efforts to improve human capital must be made in our cities. Here is where a disproportionate number of the fastest growing segment of new labor-force entrants — immigrants and minorities — reside, which means they are attending some of the nation's worst schools and living in some of our worst environments.

The cost of supporting people who are unable to contribute to the economy — those without skills, on welfare, or in prison — will hold us down just as surely as a weight tied to a kite's tail. The suburbs cannot be sealed off from the city or the world. The future standard of living of the children of the *haves* will be determined to a significant extent by the productivity of the children of the *have-nots.*

The region — city and suburbs together — must work to adopt rigorous academic performance standards for its students and schools, benchmarked against the toughest in the developed world; greatly expand training for high school graduates not going to college; make admission to its colleges and universities far more demanding; and increase the availability of advanced on-the-job training in the work place.

Lower the Costs of Goods and Services

The good news is that the global economy means vast new markets; with 5.5 billion people, the world has more than 20 times the population of the United States. The bad news is that our goods and services must now compete with those from firms around the world. As the latest round of corporate downsizing suggests, the competition is fierce, in part because of a dramatic shift that is making commodities out of what used to be specialized products. A decade ago an IBM personal computer was unique. Today many manufacturers produce high quality clones, making computers a commodity, like so much rice, wheat, and potatoes. The result in industry after industry is rapidly falling prices, and the message is clear: firms that can keep costs down will remain competitive; others will fade away.

Grasping how global competition differs from domestic competition is absolutely essential. For 30 years, critics have pointed out the inefficiency of duplicated services, facilities, and personnel that result from too many local governments. Others have lamented the inadequate management of re-

gional resources such as labor force, transportation, infrastructure, and environment. But despite the higher costs resulting from inefficiencies found outside the firm and beyond the direct control of company managers, reformers found few supporters.

These inefficiencies did not matter very much when the competition was *domestic,* for two reasons. First, the inefficiencies noted above did not cut into profit margins because producers passed their costs to their customers as higher prices. Second, since all domestic producers did the same thing, no one derived competitive advantage.

But when the competition is *international*— and for whatever reasons the prices of foreign goods and services are lower than our own — inefficiencies that spring from domestic practices undercut our competitiveness. Thirty years ago, 20 percent of General Motors' assembly line workers were illiterate, but it didn't matter, as David Osborne and Ted Gaebler (1992) remind us, because 20 percent of Ford's and Chrysler's workers were illiterate as well. Today, when 100 percent of Toyota's workers are literate, it matters a great deal. When voters understand that to maintain the competitiveness of American goods and services in a global economy, the choice is either to lower their wages or to find ways outside their firms of more efficiently reducing costs and managing resources, they will, not surprisingly, choose the latter. Behaviors and governance structures considered sacrosanct today, I contend, will change far more rapidly than most people currently think.

The time has come to scrutinize a host of current behaviors. In metropolitan Philadelphia, for example, fiscal policy, land use, growth management, and zoning decisions are being made by municipalities — 239 in Southeastern Pennsylvania and 100 in southern New Jersey — rather than at the level of multiple municipalities, the county, or the region. But the response should not assume that the regional scale is automatically best. Rather, the political smog that obscures our choices should be blown away by an objective cost-benefit analysis to determine what size "service shed"—on a geographic scale—is appropriate for what service and, for that matter, whether government should produce the service or contract it out to the private sector. The issue before us, as Richard Nathan (1994) has argued, is not *structural*—requiring the consolidation of local governments into larger units, but *functional*—offering services at the most efficient geographic scale.

Use Scarce Investment Capital More Productively

When crime, drugs, homelessness, and other social problems spill over into adjacent suburban communities, the response of those who can afford it has been to move even farther away to more pristine areas at the peripheries of our regions. This process is embedded in the concentric rings of growth that emanate outward from our central cities.

Very troubling signs in the older, inner-ring suburbs suggest that the pace of out-migration and other indicators of deterioration—job loss, housing depreciation, drugs, crime, and related social problems—are accelerating faster than in the central cities they surround. The reason is that these small communities lack the basic resources the big cities use to slow down and mediate the process of decline. These inner-ring communities do not have large central business districts generating substantial tax revenues to underwrite essential services in the neighborhoods; they do not have large police forces to maintain safety and a sense of social order as the crime rate climbs; and they do not have the sizable public and not-for-profit human and social service agencies to address the needs of the poor and disadvantaged.

This out-migration from the cities and the inner-ring suburbs leads to new development in the exurbs requiring new roads and highways, water mains and sewer lines, schools and libraries, homes and shopping centers, and offices and sports complexes. When this happens, we end up spending our scarce investment dollars redundantly because we are essentially duplicating an infrastructure that already exists in older suburbs and central cities. Such growth also often represents a highly inefficient use of land. In southeastern Pennsylvania between 1970 and 1995, for example, while population declined by 140,000, one-quarter of the region's prime farmland was lost to development.

This redundant spending imposes heavy opportunity costs because these dollars are not available for vital investments in productivity. To improve our competitive position in the global economy, America's regions would be far wiser to undertake more cost-effective development by adopting metropolitan growth rings, increasing residential and job densities in existing suburbs and cities, and investing the savings in research and development, plant and equipment, and human capital. The current practice of redundant spending is akin to eating our seed corn. America can ill afford public policy that leads to throw-away cities, throw-away suburbs, and throw-away people.

"It's the economy, stupid" read the now famous sign on James Carville's wall, announcing the central message for the 1992 Clinton presidential campaign. For those of us who want to see our metropolitan areas prosper in the 21st century, the sign should be amended to read "It's the *global* economy, stupid!" In sum, the global economy has forever changed the rules of competition. Either we adapt intelligently, or we face a significant deterioration in our standard of living and an increasingly worrisome unequal distribution of wealth within our regions that threaten the stability of our democracy.

Economic Linkages Between the City and the Suburbs

The nation's economy is an aggregation of metropolitan economies in which the fortunes of the cities and suburbs are intertwined. Here are just a few examples of the economic linkages that bind them together. We'll first consider relationships between cities and suburbs in general and then review some of the specific linkages between Philadelphia and the surrounding suburban counties.

DETROIT AND ITS SUBURBS

Skeptics about regional cooperation often pose the "Detroit question": if cities and suburbs are so interdependent, then why are Detroit's suburbs doing well while the city is an economic wasteland? While the Detroit suburbs are doing well relative to the city, it turns out this is a misleading comparison. According to a Philadelphia Federal Reserve Bank study (Voith 1992) of 28 metropolitan areas in the Northeast and Midwest, the better off the central city is, the better off its suburbs are. The Detroit suburbs have experienced considerably slower job, population, and income growth than the suburbs surrounding healthier central cities. For example, although the population of the Detroit suburbs grew 2 percent between 1980 and 1990, the average for the northeastern suburbs studied for that period was almost 7 percent.

NATIONAL LEAGUE OF CITIES

In its recent study, *All in It Together: Cities, Suburbs, and Local Economic Regions* (Ledebur and Barnes 1993), the National League of Cities documents that in each of the 25 metropolitan areas with the most rapidly growing suburbs, central city in-

comes also increased from 1979 to 1989. "No suburb in this high growth set experienced income growth without corresponding growth in their central city.... For every $1 increase in central city household incomes, suburban household incomes increase by $1.12." Cities and suburbs are not two distinct economies, the report concludes, "but a single highly interdependent economy.... Their fortunes [are] inextricably intertwined. Cities and suburbs grow or decline together."

CITIES WITHOUT SUBURBS

In *Cities without Suburbs*, David Rusk (1993), former mayor of Albuquerque, New Mexico, describes a fascinating set of differences between *elastic* cities (those that have been able to annex or merge with their suburbs so they are "without" suburbs) and *inelastic* cities (those whose growth stopped at their historic political boundaries and therefore are surrounded by suburbs). In elastic cities, income distributions are more equal, poverty is less concentrated, crime rates are lower, residential segregation is lower, and schools are less segregated. By contrast, Rusk argues, inelastic cities like Philadelphia "are programmed to fail." He does not write off the Philadelphias of the world, however, because he believes public policies promoting regional responses can produce greater social and economic equity.

CITISTATES

In *Citistates: How Urban America Can Prosper in a Competitive World*, Peirce, Johnson, and Hall (1993) argue that the true economic units of the global economy are *citistates*, a new name for metropolitan areas. With the end of the Cold War, the battleground of the future will be economic, not military, a shift that will diminish the role of nations and enhance the importance of regions. Based on case studies of metropolitan areas that included Baltimore, Dallas, Phoenix, and Seattle, Peirce contends that only when the central city and the surrounding suburban communities work together will they be in a position to compete effectively against the metropolitan economies of Frankfurt, Milan, and Osaka. Peirce urges metropolitan residents to recognize the indivisibility of the citistate, find a niche for the region in the global economy, focus on workforce preparedness, plan for a multicultural future, fight for fiscal equity, and build a sense of regional citizenship.

The consequences of continued urban decline will be felt well beyond city borders. A 10 percent decline in the value of real estate in just nine of America's largest cities would mean losses of $160 billion, reports Joseph Gyourko (Gyourko and Summers 1994), real estate professor at the University of Pennsylvania's Wharton School. This amount roughly equals the cost of the entire savings and loan bailout. A great many suburbanites — shareholders in the banks, insurance companies, and pension funds that own these properties — would be among the losers.

The evidence from around the nation, then, is compelling, but does it hold true for southeastern Pennsylvania? Despite the striking growth of the suburbs in past decades, research done here strongly suggests that many economic ties bind Bucks, Chester, Delaware, Montgomery, and Philadelphia Counties together.

COMMUTING PATTERNS IN METROPOLITAN PHILADELPHIA

Although most people live and work in a single county and suburb-to-suburb commuting is on the rise, a great many people cross Philadelphia's borders as part of the journey to work. Each day 395,000 commuters are on the move in and out of the city. Fifteen percent of suburban residents come into the city (down from 20 percent in 1980), and altogether, Philadelphia imports almost one-third of its labor force.

Meanwhile, 20 percent of city residents commute to jobs in the suburban counties (up from 15 percent in 1980). These commuting patterns are important linkages between the city and surrounding counties that are experienced by real people in very real ways.

PURCHASES OF GOODS AND SERVICES

A 1991 survey of more than 1,000 area firms conducted by the Center for Greater Philadelphia revealed that despite considerable suburban economic growth, the region's economy remains tightly integrated. For example, nearly 20 percent of all goods and services purchased by firms in Bucks, Chester, and Delaware Counties are acquired from Philadelphia firms. Overall, when direct and indirect purchases are considered together, roughly one-quarter of Southeastern Pennsylvania's $110 billion gross metropolitan product in 1991 was a function of city-county business transactions.

BEST-CASE AND WORST-CASE SCENARIOS FOR THE YEAR 2000

When Philadelphia was at the brink of bankruptcy in 1991, leaders of the Pennsylvania General Assembly asked the Center for Greater Philadelphia to consider the question "what would happen to the suburbs if the city went down the tubes?"

Two regional job scenarios were constructed for the Sixth Southeastern Pennsylvania State Legislators' Conference (Hershberg 1991). The *worst case* was based on the 1970s when the city lost 40 percent of its manufacturing jobs, 18 percent of its total jobs, and 13 percent of its population. The *best case*, was based on the 1980s when the city ended the decade with roughly the same number of jobs it had at its start and population loss slowed to less than half the prior decade's rate.

The difference between these two scenarios in the year 2000 is 268,000 fewer jobs in Bucks, Chester, Delaware, and Montgomery Counties and 178,000 fewer jobs in Philadelphia. This would represent a loss to the region of $11.6 billion in wages and a loss to the state treasury of $585 million in personal income, corporate net income, and sales taxes (in 1990 dollars).

IT WON'T BE A ZERO-SUM GAME

Nor would Philadelphia's deterioration be a zero-sum game for Pennsylvania in which city jobs move to the suburbs and the state treasury breaks even because only the location of economic activity changes. Although many city firms would move to the suburbs, some would close rather than relocate, others would downsize, and still others would leave the region entirely. One study of manufacturing firms in the 1970s estimated that at least 30 percent of jobs eliminated in the city did not relocate. Such losses are shared by everyone.

SUBURBAN HOUSING VALUES ARE AFFECTED BY PHILADELPHIA'S ECONOMY AND ACCESS TO COMMUTER RAIL

Another glimpse into the integrated regional economy comes from the work of Richard Voith (1993), senior economist at the Federal Reserve Bank of Philadelphia. Voith set out to learn whether access to commuter rail service in the suburban counties boosts home values. In a careful study that controlled for access to highways and the quality of homes, Voith found that residences in neighborhoods with rail service — about 258,500 owner-occupied houses — enjoy a premium of 6.4 percent in housing values over those areas without service. This amounts to $1.45 billion in the value of residential real estate over the five-county region. In examining the value of homes in Montgomery County located near commuter rail lines, Voith found that prices fell in the 1970s as the city's manufacturing economy collapsed and rose sharply in the mid–1980s when the Philadelphia economy, especially downtown jobs, rebounded.

Good Things Happen When the City and Suburbs Cooperate

The case for regional cooperation is solid. Intense new competition in the global economy makes regions the strategic units of future economic competition. Moreover, economic linkages between the city and the suburbs make cooperative strategies in everyone's self-interest. But there is a third basis for this approach, and that is, simply put, good things happen when the city and the suburbs cooperate. Let's consider three of the leading achievements of regional cooperation in Southeastern Pennsylvania in the last decade.

REGIONAL SUCCESS STORIES

Pennsylvania Convention Center: The new center, the most important economic development project in Philadelphia's modern history, functions as the cornerstone of an ambitious, multi-pronged effort to make Philadelphia a "Destination City" in the burgeoning global hospitality industry. The suburban counties are now working with the city to develop a regional tourism strategy. The $525 million facility was made possible with a contribution of $185 million from the Commonwealth of Pennsylvania, an investment that required cooperation between political leaders from both parties across the region.

Philadelphia Regional Port Authority (PRPA): In 1990, the General Assembly created the PRPA, a partnership between the state and Bucks, Delaware, and Philadelphia Counties. PRPA has been a "win-win" proposition: the city was freed from a multimillion drain on its annual budget; $60 million was made available for port capital and marketing projects, including Philadelphia's first intermodal facility; and PRPA was in-strumental in attracting a new rail line to the region. The port's competitive position will be greatly improved by the recent affili-ation of PRPA and the South Jersey Port Corporation under the auspices of the Delaware River Port Authority.

SEPTA Capital Funding. In a historic breakthrough in 1991, the Pennsylvania General Assembly provided a source of pre-dictable capital funding for all 37 of the commonwealth's mass transit agencies. Nu-merous studies have documented the significant impact the Southeastern Penn-sylvania Transportation Authority (SEPTA) has on the region's economy, and the guar-antee of a reliable funding stream allows SEPTA to continue its rebuilding process. Once the region's leaders reached consensus on ensuring SEPTA's future capital needs, the debate between city and suburbs gave way to the search for a politically viable funding formula.

SOUTHEASTERN PENNSYLVANIA COMMANDS CONSIDERABLE STATE POWER

The reason good things like these can happen when city and suburban state lead-ers cooperate is that southeastern Pennsyl-vania is the most powerful region in the state. John Stauffer, the former majority leader of the Pennsylvania State Senate from Chester County, recognized this at the first regionwide conference of elected officials in 1985 when he said, "If we in Southeastern Pennsylvania ever flexed our political mus-cle on *both* sides of the aisle, we'd be a for-midable force to be reckoned with in Har-risburg."

While Bucks, Chester, Delaware, Montgomery, and Philadelphia Counties are only five of the state's 67 counties, they ac-count for 31 percent of the state's popula-tion, 33 percent of its jobs, and 36 percent of its income. The five counties, moreover, are home to many leaders of the General As-sembly. As of November 1995, these include House Speaker Matthew Ryan (R–Delaware County); House Majority Leader John Perzel (R–Philadelphia); Senate Majority Leader Joseph Loeper (R–Delaware County); and all four appropriations com-mittee chairmen — Rep. Dwight Evans (D–Philadelphia), Sen. Vincent Fumo (D–Philadelphia), Rep. Joseph Pitts (R–Chester County), and Sen. Richard Tilghman (R–Montgomery County).

Philadelphia Rebounds

The 1990s are critical years for Phila-delphia and the region. The decade began with a national recession, which in con-junction with an accumulated deficit of $250 million, brought the City of Philadel-phia to the brink of bankruptcy. But in November 1991, Edward G. Rendell won election as the city's new mayor and has led Philadelphia in a remarkable come-back.

Central to his success was a political al-liance with John Street, president of the Philadelphia City Council. This partnership has meant that for the first time since 1980, the city's mayor and city council have worked in tandem to promote Philadelphia's best interests. Since Rendell is white and Street is African-American, it has also meant that highly divisive racial politics have been avoided in a city where whites and non-whites share political power.

Working together, Rendell and Street produced a five-year fiscal plan that won ap-proval from the Pennsylvania Intergovern-mental Cooperation Authority, the fiscal oversight committee created by the state with the power to issue bonds on Philadel-phia's behalf. Bankruptcy was avoided, bud-gets were balanced, and new labor contracts containing remarkable wage, health benefits, and work rule concessions were signed with all four of the city's municipal labor unions.

The public financial markets have responded by buying Philadelphia's bonds at low, prevailing market rates of interest. In 1995, the city reported an $80 million surplus, and Rendell was reelected by a 77 percent margin.

The restoration of Philadelphia's fiscal image has been paralleled by other events with high national visibility:

- Metropolitan Philadelphia was ranked third in overall livability by the 1993 *Places Rated Almanac*.
- *Fortune* magazine rated Philadelphia among the 10 "Best Cities for Knowledge Workers" (November 15, 1993).
- FBI statistics documented that the Philadelphia region is the safest of the 12 largest U.S. metropolitan areas.

The city's long-term economic prospects hold real promise. The city and region have considerable strength in higher education, with 80 institutions granting degrees in higher learning and 50,000 college graduates annually. The region has enormous strengths in health care, medical education and research, biotechnology, and pharmaceuticals. Organized venture capital companies can now be found throughout the region, and they support synergies among universities, entrepreneurs, and the growing base of companies in what promoters call "Medical Valley" and "America's High-Tech Mainstreet."

The $525 million Pennsylvania Convention Center opened in downtown Philadelphia in 1993, and by all measures is living up to its advance billing as the anchor institution for the city's growing hospitality industry that promises to become a major sector of its economy. Efforts valued at several hundred million dollars are now underway to develop the *Avenue of the Arts* on South and North Broad Street as lively settings for the performing arts, and entertainment-based development is proceeding smartly on the Delaware River waterfront. Along with the city's unique comparative advantage as the birthplace of American democracy, these multiple developments are helping transform Philadelphia into an exciting "Destination City" in a global economy marked by extensive travel, tourism and trade.

SERIOUS SOCIAL PROBLEMS REMAIN

Despite these strengths and the mayor's *Economic Stimulus Plan*, Philadelphia's prospects are not without serious threats. The city's tax base has eroded precipitously, as Philadelphia lost 10 percent of its jobs between 1990 and 1993. Although the city added jobs in 1994, other significant weaknesses endure. One family in five is mired in poverty, and unemployment, particularly for nonwhites, remains high. The 1980s saw the rise of new and costly social problems, including AIDS, homelessness, and the crack epidemic. The condition of public housing is disgraceful, and the past performance of public schools has been dismal (although it is gratifying to see the efforts of the new school superintendent, David Hornbeck, to implement fundamental reform through his "Children Achieving" agenda).

So it can be argued that despite all the positive trends described above, Philadelphia and America's other big cities are on greased skids. What distinguishes one from the other is the angle of descent. Aid is needed at least to help level the fiscal playing field so that cities can stabilize their revenues by holding on to their job and population base. But without intervention from federal and state governments, America in the long run may well lose all its big cities, Philadelphia included. The time has come to get the suburbs involved.

Toward a Dialogue Between the City and the Suburbs

If I've convinced you that the region's best chance for success in the global economy requires city-suburb cooperation, it should also be clear that the counties' and state's best interests are to help Philadelphia survive in the face of declining federal aid, an eroding local tax base, and mounting social problems. Philadelphia's neighboring suburban counties can help in three important ways.

First, modest county funds are needed for varied *regional* projects. Bucks, Chester, Delaware, Montgomery, and Philadelphia Counties should undertake joint strategic planning, expand regional marketing strategies, embrace tax base sharing for *new* economic development, promote regional tourism, dedicate funds for the region's arts and cultural institutions, protect open space, and create a regional airport authority. While the details and the politics behind each initiative differ, they share the common notion that regional opportunities require regional responses.

This agenda was advanced by the 2,000 business, civic, and political leaders, as well as concerned citizens, who gathered at the Call to Action Conference on May 25, 1995, which was organized by the University of Pennsylvania's Center for Greater Philadelphia, the Greater Philadelphia Chamber of Commerce, and Greater Philadelphia First. They heard addresses by Pennsylvania Governor Tom Ridge, Philadelphia Mayor Ed Rendell, and Neal R. Peirce and considered 89 regional initiatives collected in the *Greater Philadelphia Investment Portfolio*.

Second, Philadelphia will need political support from suburban legislators in the General Assembly to provide additional state funding for the social costs associated with the support of the disadvantaged. Fairness dictates that these costs should be shared more equitably by citizens across the Commonwealth. These disadvantaged people are Pennsylvanians, not just Philadelphians, and their problems are not of the city's making. To overcome the perception that "giving additional funding to Philadel-

phia is like throwing the money down a hole," most Philadelphians would likely accept some form of state control over social programs in return for adequate state aid to meet needs. Neither economic nor moral ends are served by balancing the city's budget on the backs of the poor or by driving Philadelphia into bankruptcy in a futile attempt to meet social needs beyond its fiscal capacity. Cities cannot solve social problems because they cannot redistribute income without driving out businesses and middle-income taxpayers.

The devolution of federal authority to the states in the form of block grants also presents an excellent opportunity for the states to stimulate regional approaches. Instead of distributing all block-grant funds directly to individual counties, states would reserve portions only for counties that joined together as regions and submitted strategic plans defining how they would allocate funds for health care, welfare, job training, education, environment, and the like. In *New Visions for Metropolitan America*, Anthony Downs (1994) calls for the creation of "regional allocation agencies" to decide how such funds would be spent. Their members could be popularly elected as in Portland, Oregon, or appointed by the governor and the state legislature as in the Minneapolis-St. Paul area, or designated by local governments.

Third, and perhaps most importantly, political leverage from the suburban counties is needed to help the city continue government reform and to use more effectively the large sums of money it already spends on education and government operations.

I am not suggesting that the suburbs should come to the table with a blank check — that would be both counterproductive and politically impossible. But the time has come to begin a candid dialogue about what can be done to keep central cities like Philadelphia fiscally stable and economically viable. Voters in the city and suburbs must ask Republicans and Democrats to stop the histrionics and get on with the difficult task of finding solutions because partisan politics is now a luxury neither the region nor the nation can afford.

If suburban residents believe state funds have been put to poor use in Philadelphia, this is the moment to sit down and agree on the changes that need to be made to use these funds more effectively. If further aid is required in the city, suburban political support could be conditioned on the adoption of fundamental reforms. A possible model is the Wharton Real Estate Center's "New Urban Strategy," which proposes no new net funding for urban America. However, Joseph Gyourko and Anita Summers (1994) argue that cities that undertake serious reform should be rewarded with additional dollars, while those that refuse to make the tough political choices should receive fewer dollars. In short, many desired changes in cities may prove impossible without this new politics of leverage from the suburbs.

Although there is no line item in the federal budget for "cities," as HUD secretary Henry Cisneros (1995) has pointed out, the aggregate impact of the cuts proposed by Congress for Medicaid, food stamps, welfare, Head Start, education, job training, mass transit, and the earned income tax credit will have a devastating impact on urban America because this is where those in poverty and with low incomes disproportionately reside. Suburban leaders need to understand that these cuts will further destabilize the cities they surround, with serious consequences for their communities as well.

We also must not become captives of our own language. Words such as *city* and *suburbs* suggest monoliths where none exist; they give rise to false but powerful images of we/they and us/them. The images are reinforced with census data, and the political numbers favor the suburbs: Nationwide one-quarter of Americans live in cities and one-half live in suburbs.

Yet many older, inner-ring suburban communities more closely resemble the cities than they do the affluent suburbs where the wealthiest 20 percent of Americans live. During the 1980s, these older, inner-ring suburbs generally lost population, had little or no job growth, saw housing values stagnate or decline, and watched urban social problems such as homelessness, crime, and drugs spill over into their communities. The city-suburb duality distorts reality, buttresses partisan approaches, and complicates the cooperative arrangements that should follow economic self-interest.

Not too long ago *regional cooperation* was an oxymoron, but efforts by a great many people and organizations in the last decade have made it a strategy taken seriously by business, civic and political leaders. Although substantial progress has been made, much of what remains to be done will be more controversial. When asked to move in these more difficult directions, elected officials in the city and suburbs first look over their shoulders to see if their constituents are behind them. For those of us who believe in regional cooperation, it is time to build a host of parades.

Of course the barriers of race, class and politics that divide the city and suburbs are formidable. But we must accept the fact the global economy is putting Americans on the same team. The economic realities of the 1990s make clear that we are in this together and that cities and suburbs must work cooperatively. In our region people must recognize that Philadelphia bashing is *old* politics. The failure to respond to the fiscal factors that undermine the city's competitiveness is *old* economics. It is time to change. It is time for city dwellers and suburbanites to develop a quid pro quo — to ask what they expect from each other and to explore what they will do if each fulfills the respective commitments.

Although a compelling argument based on morality and social justice can be made to bring the city and suburbs together, the case presented here is based on economic self-interest. This is not an exercise in what we *should* be doing but in what we *have* to do to be competitive in the global economy.

Lest this task seem overwhelming, it is good to recall in closing that truly radical changes can occur: the Soviet Union has collapsed, the Berlin Wall has come down and the Germanys have united, Arabs and Israelis are making peace, and black and white South Africans are peacefully building a new nation together. Surely we can have regional cooperation in metropolitan Philadelphia.

References

Cisneros, Henry G. 1995. Aid to the Cities Is Being Chopped into Little Pieces by Republicans. *Philadelphia Inquirer*, Oct. 4, Op-Ed.

Commission on the Skills of the American Workforce. 1990. *America's Choice: High Skills or Low Wages*. Rochester, NY: National Center on Education and the Economy.

Downs, Anthony. 1994. *New Visions for Metropolitan America*. Washington, D.C. and Cambridge, Mass.: The Brookings Institution and the Lincoln Institute of Land Policy.

Gyourko, Joseph, and Anita A. Summers. 1994. Working towards a New Urban Strategy for America's Larger Cities: The Role of an Urban Audit. Wharton Real Estate Center, University of Pennsylvania.

Hershberg, Theodore. 1991. At the Crossroads: The Consequences for the City, Region and Commonwealth of Economic Stability or Decline in Philadelphia. Pre-conference report for the Sixth Annual Southeastern Pennsylvania State Legislators' Conference, Center for Greater Philadelphia.

Kirsh, Irwin S., Ann Jungeblut, Lynn Jenkins, and Andrew Kolstad. 1993. *Adult Literacy in America: A First Look at the Results of the National Adult Literacy Survey*. Washington, D.C.: National Center for Education Statistics.

Ledebur, Larry C., and William R. Barnes. 1993. *All in It Together: Cities, Suburbs and Local Economic Regions*. National League of Cities.

Nathan, Richard P. 1994. Reinventing Regionalism. Keynote Address for the Regional Plan Association Meeting, April 26. New York

Ohmae, Kenichi. 1995. *The End of the Nation State: The Rise of Regional Economies*. New York: Free Press.

Osborne, David, and Ted Gaebler. 1992. *Reinventing Government: How the Entrepreneurial Spirit Is Transforming the Public Sector*. New York: Addison-Wesley Publishing Company, Inc.

Peirce, Neal R., with Curtis Johnson and John Stuart Hall. 1993. *Citistates: How Urban America Can Prosper in a Competitive World*. Washington, D.C.: Seven Locks Press.

Rusk, David. 1993. *Cities without Suburbs*. Baltimore: Johns Hopkins University Press.

Thurow, Lester. 1992. *Head to Head: The Coming Economic Battle among Japan, Europe, and America*. New York: Morrow.

_____. 1995. How Much Inequality Can a Democracy Take? *The New York Times Magazine*, Nov. 19.

Toffler, Alvin, and Heidi Toffler. 1993. Societies at Hyper-Speed. *The New York Times*, Oct. 31, Op-Ed.

_____. 1993. Changing Capitalization of CBD-Oriented Transportation Systems. *Journal of Urban Economics* 33.

PART III

The Future of Regionalism

CHAPTER 32

TRENDS IN REGIONAL GOVERNANCE

Allan D. Wallis

Attempts to achieve regional governance have been concentrated in three distinct but overlapping waves. The first wave consisted largely of reform efforts focusing on structural arrangements aimed at reinforcing the hegemony of central cities. A second wave emerged, overtaking the first, as the dominance of central cities gave way to a polycentric constellation of robust suburbs. In this wave the goal of regionalism shifted from enhancing central cities to preserving them, while concern over formal restructuring was replaced by an emphasis on process with the objective of coordination. Whereas the first wave relied on the political power of central cities over suburbs and the singular economic significance of large central cities to their state's economy, the politics of the second wave were played out through the system of federalism, specifically in the form of top-down mandates.

But all of the efforts of the second wave to will regionalism into existence could not reverse the declining fortunes of cities and force a marriage in which suburbs saw no advantage. By the early 1980s, even its advocates seemed willing to concede that regional governance was a moribund cause. But today that perception is being reversed.

From Atlanta to Seattle and Houston to Albany, serious investigations and experiments designed to strengthen regionalism are on the rise. Expectations that central cities were destined to wither away have been replaced by a new appreciation of the complex complementarity between central-city and suburban economies.

Political conditions suggesting strong regionalism was infeasible have been replaced by new realities fueling the third wave. These realities consist of a set of *capacity* factors offering new possibilities for achieving governance and a set of *demand* factors providing increased justification for regionalism.

Capacity factors. New capacities for governance have emerged in at least three areas: 1) significantly increased and direct involvement of the private and nonprofit sectors on a regional scale; 2) a new type of elected leadership that is more willing to negotiate and partner in efforts to build a metropolitan community; and 3) increasing use of facilitated decision-making processes to help establish shared visions, resolve conflicts and develop consensus regarding regional interests.

With respect to the involvement of the

Originally published as "The Third Wave: Current Trends in Regional Governance," *National Civic Review*, Vol. 83, No. 3, Summer-Fall, 1994. Published by the National Civic League, Denver, Colorado. Reprinted with permission of the publisher.

private, or for-profit sector, during the 1970s public-private partnerships became an important alternative approach to central-city and especially downtown revitalization. Under the Carter administration Urban Development Action Grants (UDAGs) were awarded to promote cross-sectoral partnerships. Attempts to establish a metro-wide vision with strong sponsorship from the private sector also became more common in the 1970s, following the lead of Goals for Dallas, initiated after the assassination of President Kennedy. These types of partnership activities have broadened in scope and assumed more of a metropolitan scale from the 1980s to the present. In general, the private sector in many regions has reorganized, moving out of the smoke-filled back rooms where mayors were once selected, to the sponsorship of highly visible organizations designed to plan and promote regional economic development.

During this same period the number of government partnerships with nonprofits grew significantly, especially in the area of human service delivery. With regard to social problems emerging during the 1980s — such as the precipitous rise in homelessness and emergence of the AIDS epidemic — nonprofits were heavily relied upon to formulate early responses and ultimately partner with the public sector in providing more structured programs. And in areas where federal support was significantly reduced during the 1980s — such as community development — local governments have turned to nonprofits to help fill the gap.[1] Of equal significance, such partnerships have provided a more legitimate and effective way for government to invest in community redevelopment.

An important factor in promoting the development of partnerships is a new willingness on the part of big-city mayors to think in terms of metropolitan cooperation, notably in the expansion of airport and port facilities, and joint ventures.[2] This shift in leadership style has been coupled with an enhanced capacity among city administrations to deal with the complexities of joint ventures, often through the creation of urban development authorities.

The character of gubernatorial leadership has also changed, with greater emphasis displayed in the areas of entrepreneurship and facilitation. For example, Governor Keane of New Jersey established a regionally based growth-management process involving negotiated inter-local agreements (cross acceptance). Bruce Babbitt, while Governor of Arizona, established a ground water management system fostering a regulated market for agricultural and urban water users in rapidly developing central Arizona, which includes the Phoenix metro area.

Finally, new capacity for regional governance has emerged through the application of facilitated decision-making processes. Negotiation has become more commonplace in attempts to reduce gridlock and red tape. Strategic planning and visioning have replaced traditional master planning as methods for building consensus and mobilizing resources on a regional basis. Improved data analysis also has served to support decision making and efforts to improve coordination.

Capacity and characteristics of governance. While attempts to achieve regional governance during the first two waves focused primarily on relations among units and levels of government, the new capacities for governance described above have spawned a third wave of efforts, which are distinguished by at least five characteristics:

• *Governance vs. Government.* Advocates of regionalism today tend to speak in terms of governance rather than government. The change in terminology reflects a shift in focus from formal structural arrangements to informal structures and processes for setting policy and mobilizing action.[3] In part, de-emphasizing government recognizes that the public opposes reforms that would effectively create a new layer of government.

• *Cross-Sectoral vs. Uni-Sectoral.* Responsibility for achieving effective regionalism no longer is viewed as primarily falling to the public sector. As the change in terminology from government to governance implies, it is an effort requiring the active involvement of the for-profit and nonprofit sectors, frequently working together with the public sector. Each sector has unique capacities and specific areas of legitimacy. Cross-sectoral arrangements make it possible to combine these in ways that allow for a far more effective mobilization of effort.

• *Collaboration vs. Coordination.* A major objective of regionalism in the past was improved coordination of public sector planning and action. Today, the cross-sectoral character of regional governance stresses collaboration over coordination. The objective is not simply to know what others re doing, but to develop arrangements that mobilize the unique capacities and legitimacy of *each* sector working together to accomplish specific tasks of regional scope.

• *Process vs. Structure.* The importance of collaboration places new emphasis on process over formal structural arrangements. While process in the past has served the objectives of data analysis and planning, the processes employed today focus on developing a regional vision and goals, formation of consensus among critical stakeholders, and ultimately, mobilization of resources to meet objectives.

• *Networks vs. Formal Structures.* The increased emphasis placed on collaboration and process is also indicative of the fact that regionalism today operates through network-like organizations as opposed to formal structures. Organizations in a network at any one time reflect the specific task or project being undertaken. Nevertheless, such networks tend to have a stable core of stakeholders who share significant interest in specific strategic arenas.

Demand factors and regional alliances. Increasing governance capacity in itself does not give rise to regionalism. Rather, the motivation for change comes from a set of demand factors which are fundamentally restructuring life in metropolitan areas. The factors — discussed in the first article in this series ["Evolving Structures and Challenges of Regional Governance," NATIONAL CIVIC REVIEW, Winter-Spring 1994, pp. 40–53] — fall into three strategic arenas: 1) economic development, specifically within the context of global economic competitiveness; 2) allocative concerns related to service delivery, infrastructure development and now, most urgently, environmental protection; and 3) redistributive issues, particularly as aggravated by municipal fiscal disparities.

To varying degrees these demand factors were present in the first two waves of regionalism, but approached in fundamentally different ways. Where the first wave attempted to address all three areas simultaneously by calling for the expansion of general government on a regional scale, during the second wave there were concerted efforts to coordinate policies roughly in terms of each of the strategic areas described here. Moreover, requirements for public participation introduced at that time attempted to bring a broader range of interest groups into the governance process. Although these attempts fell far short of their objectives, they provided an important foundation for current efforts.

In the third wave attempts to achieve regional governance are being led largely by cross-sectoral coalitions or alliances whose interests tend to fall largely within a specific strategic arena. Private corporations, for example, are primarily concerned with economic development, but their interest clearly spills over into concerns over infrastructure, affordable housing, public education and issues in other arenas. Likewise, nonprofits engaged in human service delivery advocacy tend to focus on social equity. Government operates in all three arenas, but particular agencies tend to concentrate on specific ones.

By forming an alliance, participating interest groups acquire a scope of influence, range of expertise and legitimacy that they would lack on their own. At the same time they must be willing to share power and resources. Consequently, what ultimately holds an alliance together is perceived mutual interest.[4]

Although alliances often form to address a single project or need (e.g., rallying support for a new convention center), there is often a good deal of stability in relationships among participants. Consequently, over a course of decades an alliance may create several different structures to meet specific needs or changing conditions, but with the same core of key participants involved in each.

Examples of Regionalism in the Third Wave

With these general characteristics in mind it is useful to briefly consider several examples of regionalism under the third wave. These examples are first discussed in terms of the strategic arenas in which they arise, and then in terms of the metropolitan areas where such activities appear to be most concentrated.

Economic development. Competitiveness in a global economy is a major development and revitalization of many regional alliances. Some of these alliances are expansions, in both territory and mission, of traditional chambers (e.g., Seattle, Detroit, Hartford). Several, however, are independently organized associations (Cleveland, Houston, Orlando, Philadelphia, Pittsburgh). All have agendas requiring involvement with the public sector, but only some include public sector members. Although

their focus is essentially business-oriented, this interest is often broadly defined to include involvement in planning and developing major infrastructure improvements (e.g., ports and airports), work force preparedness, and the efficiency of local government operations.

It is typical for these alliances to engage in strategic planning with an emphasis on market opportunities for their region. But the way they pursue identified objectives often is quite different. Some organizations feel that it is both appropriate and necessary to try to influence public policy (e.g., municipal fiscal practices, school reform, etc.), whereas others choose to focus on specific projects with clear but narrow economic development impacts (e.g., ball parks, convention centers).

It is not surprising that some of the strongest economic development partnerships have emerged in regions which suffered early and significant economic restructuring challenges, notably the northeast and industrial midwest. But these partnerships also have developed more recently in sunbelt regions with the objective of increasing economic competitiveness. Moreover, with the decline of military procurements, sunbelt regions that benefited significantly from the Reagan build-up have shown increased interest in public-private alliances that can help achieve diversification of their exogenous economies. The Allegheny Alliance, Cleveland Tomorrow and Greater Philadelphia First exemplify strong partnerships emerging from longstanding challenges of industrial restructuring. The Houston Partnership and Seattle's Trade and Development Alliance are characteristic of efforts in the sunbelt.

• *Allegheny Conference on Community Development (ACCD).* Established in 1943 by industrialist Richard King Mellon, the focus of ACCD for several decades was economic development supporting the region's industrial base. Although designed to function as a public-private partnership, ACCD initially was dominated by the private sector.[5]

The rapid decline of steel manufacturing in the region from the 1970s into the 1980s redirected ACCD's interests toward development of a new economic base anchored in high technology. As part of this shift, nonprofit institutions, especially the region's major research universities, have become important partners. In 1985 ACCD helped secure state funding to implement Strategy 21, an economic plan for bringing the region into the 21st century.

Another recent ACCD effort is a collaboration with the Allegheny County Private Industry Council (PIC) supporting a regional jobs training strategy designed to improve coordination among area job programs, communication and improved efficiency in the use of federal funds. ACCD also has worked with the Community College of Allegheny County in establishing a "Customized Job Training Program." Finally, ACCD created the Pittsburgh Seed Fund, a nonprofit agency designed to leverage investments in small, start-up companies by providing them with seed funding.

• *Cleveland Tomorrow.* Founded in 1982, Cleveland Tomorrow (CT) is a nonprofit association whose membership consists of about 50 of the region's largest corporations. CT provides a forum in which corporate leaders can view the region's economic climate and propose initiatives to improve it. CT has produced three strategic plans based on detailed economic analysis.

While CT initially concerned itself with broad policy areas affecting the region's business climate, its efforts currently are directed toward specific projects which it believes will have strategic impact (e.g., the Gateway Stadium/Arena, Playhouse Square, and the Rock and Roll Hall of Fame). However, CT partners with other regional organizations which are more exclusively focused on public policy and civic issues (e.g., the Cleveland Round Table, which provides a

forum to address inter-racial and ethnic tension; Build-Up Greater Cleveland, which engages in infrastructure planning and prioritization).

It is important to note that the establishment of CT was aided significantly by the decision of the George Gund Foundation to support a $600,000 study of Cleveland's regional economy by McKinsey and Company. Gund subsequently contributed $200,000 to help establish CT. Economic analysis of the region's economy has also benefited from an initiative by the region's other major foundation, the Cleveland Foundation, which sponsored a study by RAND. That analysis led to establishment of the Regional Economic Issues Program, now housed at Case Western University.[6]

• *Greater Philadelphia First.* Greater Philadelphia First (GPF), established in the early 1980s, is an association of about 30 corporate CEOs organized to advance the interests of both business and the broader region. Each member firm contributes at least $50,000 to the organization's support. GPF grew out of an early effort — the Greater Philadelphia Movement, established in 1949 — which became dormant by the early 1960s.

Through GPF, individual board members take on leadership roles where their guidance can make a difference to the region's economy and quality of life. GPF has a number of standing committees addressing major regional issues such as government and public policy, economic development, and public education and employment opportunities.

In pursuing specific initiatives, GPF works with and through a number of affiliates including the Greater Philadelphia Economic Coalition, the Greater Philadelphia International Network, PhilaPride, and the Committee to Support the Philadelphia Public Schools. A major GPF initiative, which has recently come to fruition, is the new downtown convention center.

• *Greater Houston Partnership.* The partnership evolved in 1989 out of the Houston Economic Development Council (HEDC), which was established by the Houston Chamber of Commerce five years earlier. Where HEDC focused on attracting new corporations that could diversify the region's economic base, the partnership has adopted a broader mission to "promote, support and improve the economic activity, business climate, job creation, and quality of life throughout the seven-county Houston region."

The work of the partnership is carried out by four principal members: the Houston World Trade Association, which provides services and networking for international business development; the chamber of commerce, devoted to the development of regional systems; HEDC which now specializes in target markets, sales and business development; and the partnership Shared Services, which conducts research supporting the work of the other three partners.[7]

The partnership has more than 4,000 member companies. It is essentially a private sector coalition whose relationship with the public sector consists of contracts. It also lobbies actively for state legislative support of projects it deems important to the region's economy.

Although the partnership engages in strategic planning, it tries to focus on specific projects. In world trade, for example, the partnership secured establishment of a satellite of the U.S. Export-Import Bank, through which it helps to arrange loans to local companies for export finance. Through this division, the partnership conducts export seminars and hosts trade delegations to the city.

• *Trade Development Alliance of Greater Seattle.* Established in 1991, the Trade Development Alliance is a collaboration of the Port of Seattle, King County, the City of Seattle, the Greater Seattle Chamber of Commerce, and organized labor. The alliance's membership includes over 160 companies.

The mission of the alliance is to promote Greater Seattle as one of North America's premier international gateways and commercial centers. Toward this end, the alliance has developed a promotional plan to enhance the identity of the Puget Sound region in targeted world markets. It is also working to develop export trade business for agricultural producers in rural eastern Washington.

It is perhaps telling that some of the alliance's early activities were organizing visits to Europe for metro area delegations. The former director of the Port of Seattle was from Rotterdam. His experience there impressed Puget Sound leaders with the importance of developing stronger public-private partnerships around trade issues. Gary Severson, chair of the Alliance, observes that "global competition and the growing importance of the metropolitan economy are rendering the old adversarial styles ineffective and obsolete…. The Trade Development Alliance is grounded in the notion that it is time to cooperate rather than compete for scarce local resources."[8]

Between August and December of 1993 the alliance conducted a Regional Economic Strategy Project. The project analyzed strategic economic opportunities, identified strategies, evaluated institutional capacity to carry out strategies, and then developed an implementation plan.

• *The Economic Development Equity Fund (EDGE).* Dayton, Ohio has weathered major economic restructuring. Once the automotive tire capitol of the world, no such manufacturing occurs there today. Nevertheless, some communities in the region of Montgomery County are faring better than others in making the transition.

In 1991, Montgomery County established a voluntary revenue-sharing program designed to assist communities in maintaining and improving their economic health.[9]

Funds from the program can be used to expand and establish commercial, industrial and research facilities, and create and preserve job and employment opportunities. Within such developments, EDGE funds are employed significantly to support development of infrastructure improvements necessary to implement projects. Up to 10 percent of the funds are available annually for special projects, such as conducting research and designing strategies to take advantage of evolving economic opportunities.

The equity fund is derived from a share of increased property and tax revenues generated by economic development among participating communities of the county. The fund specifically targets cooperative economic development efforts among local communities. At the time the fund was established it was expected to generate $5 million annually, for a total of $50 million over its authorized life.

Although all of the efforts introduced above are local initiatives, there have been some important federal and state programs addressing economic development on a regional scale. The Job Training Partnership Act of 1982 (JTPA) is designed to support regionally-based public-private partnerships for job training. Only a few states have attempted to tie JTPA to a broader, coordinated agenda of regional economic development.

Oregon, for example, has combined JTPA with its benchmarks agenda, established in 1991. The agenda sets measurable standards for evaluating state progress toward achieving defined objectives. As part of this effort the legislature created the Work Force Quality Council and assigned it the task of coordinating job-training and placement programs. The council successfully recommended that the state's existing JTPA councils be replaced by State Job Training Coordinating Committees. Each region has a work force committee responsible for preparing annual strategic plans for achieving benchmark objectives. They also establish service-delivery agreements designed to coordinate employment, job-training, education, and job-placement services.

Other states with strong growth-management programs — notably Washington and Georgia — have incorporated economic development objectives into that program. As a result, the potential exists for reinforcing both regional governance capacity and effectiveness.

Infrastructure, services and environment. Construction of new infrastructure, provision of such services as garbage collection and law enforcement, and environmental protection are widely viewed as government responsibilities. The ability of government to meet demands in these areas increasingly has fallen prey to gridlock generated by multiple and often conflicting interests: Communities that see new infrastructure as LULUs (locally undesirable land-uses); environmentalists who fear further degradation of air, water and wetlands; and social equity advocates who feel that the poor get a disproportionate share of landfills and power plants.

Local governments also produce gridlock by fighting against each other for limited funds. Rather than advancing shared priorities, individual jurisdictions build fragmented, uncoordinated or duplicative systems. Failure of local governments to agree on a single system or plan results in situations where highway capacity abruptly changes at county lines or transit systems end in the middle of commuter sheds. Being able to move beyond gridlock and toward creation of integrated and appropriate systems is an ever more pressing challenge for regional governance.

This challenge is especially urgent in high-growth regions where there is strong demand for new infrastructure and service capacity at the urban fringe, but where public sentiment also supports strong limits on public spending and/or effective measures for environmental protection. Placing stiff exactions on new development has provided some resources for local communities, but these are increasingly and successfully being challenged in court. Declining central cities are caught in a similar bind between growing demand and diminishing resources. They must restore crumbling infrastructure with a faltering tax base. In both declining and growing regions new federal mandates for clean air and water place even greater fiscal demands on system maintenance and development.

During the 1970s and 1980s the challenge of meeting demands in this strategic arena motivated development of thousands of interlocal agreements.[10] These succeeded in realizing some coordination and increased efficiency, but had little if any effect in achieving the degree of coordination in land-use development necessary to assure adequate and efficient infrastructure development and service delivery.

Although the belief that new growth will eventually pay its way has been largely discredited today, the idea that regional cooperation is essential to preserving and enhancing the quality of life continues to be a tough sell. Nevertheless, there are several notable developments in regional governance in this arena. Some regions — such as Cleveland and Philadelphia — have organized alliances designed to coordinate infrastructure and/or service planning, and to lobby for their funding support. Some states — notably Florida, New Jersey and Washington — have tied new land development to regional planning that requires demonstration of the capacity to provide supporting infrastructure and services. The federal government, as well as the State of California, have established new programs requiring closer linkage between transportation planning and attainment of clean air objectives. Some of these efforts are briefly described here:

• *Build-Up Greater Cleveland.* Cleve-land, like most major cities, has suffered from crumbling, aged infrastructure. In 1981 the Growth Association (chamber of commerce) conducted a survey of members asking how they thought the region's economic competitiveness could be improved. Their priority response was improving the area's infrastructure. The association approached the region's major foundations, which indicated willingness to help establish a Community Capital Investment Strategy — later renamed Build-Up Greater Cleveland — if local governments would agree to cooperate by coordinating their efforts and providing support for half of any administrative costs.

The city and county were quick to acknowledge their competition for state money and federal funds allocated by the state. It made more political sense to approach state agencies and the legislature with a set of regionally prioritized projects. The objective of Build-Up Greater Cleveland is to convene a forum in which local government, along with corporate and other community interests, can analyze, prioritize and lobby for infrastructure improvements. The result has been effective leveraging of local funds to secure more state and federal funding.

• *SEPTA, Philadelphia.* Government subsidies for mass transit are essential in making multi-modal commuting viable. But declining federal funds for mass transit beginning in the early 1980s left many regions scrambling to provide support for their operating agencies. Mass transit not only assists in maintaining the economic competitiveness of central cities — where automobile commuting times can be a locational disincentive — but provides a basis for reverse commuting that can help provide inner-city residents with access to suburban jobs.

For years the transportation funding priorities of Philadelphia and its suburbs were at odds. As such, state legislators found it easy to ignore budget requests for the Southeast Pennsylvania Transportation Authority (SEPTA), the region's mass transit agency. In the late 1980s the region's local governments — so often at odds — began to achieve consensus regarding the importance of supporting mass transit. They effectively lobbied the Pennsylvania General Assembly, which passed legislation in 1991 providing a predictable source of funding for all 37 of the Commonwealth's mass transit agencies.

• *Metropolitan planning organizations and ISTEA/CAA.* The type of regionally based prioritization of infrastructure development evident in Build-Up Greater Cleveland and the SEPTA lobbying effort may be stimulated elsewhere by the passage of the Intermodal Surface Transportation and Efficiency Act of 1991 (ISTEA). Whereas prioritization of transportation project funding had previously been controlled by states through their Departments of Transportation (DOTs), under ISTEA, regionally based Metropolitan Planning Organizations (MPOs) now have greater authority.[11] This includes new opportunities to move funds between modes, for example, from highways to transit.

One of the central factors that will drive MPO prioritization decisions are requirements of the Clean Air Act of 1990 (CAA) requiring metropolitan areas that fail to attain federal air standards to employ measures bringing themselves into compliance. Such measures include mandates that companies with over 100 employees establish programs reducing the amount of single-passenger work commuting. In addition, no federal money can be used for highway improvements that further deteriorate air quality. Moreover, federal transportation funds may be withheld from non-attainment regions, and even the entire state in which regions continue to be non-attaining.

Some MPOs seem well positioned to use ISTEA/CAA requirements to enhance their capacity to achieve more effective infrastructure planning. For example, the Southern California Association of Governments (SCAG) has reorganized its vast region into 18 sub-regions, each engaged in planning efforts to address both transportation and land-use issues. Restructuring into sub-regions allows for greater participation and presumably stronger citizen support for the resulting plan. SCAG's efforts also benefit from California laws imposing high air-quality standards, while providing special funds to engage in congestion-mitigation planning.

New Jersey has established Transportation Development Districts (TDDs) in areas currently experiencing or anticipating significant traffic congestion. The state's DOT can establish voluntary TDDs comprising all municipalities and counties in the district as well as the DOT. The TDD develops a transportation improvement plan, establishing goals and priorities. The plan provides for the assessment of a special fee (exaction) on any new development placing an additional burden on the transportation system.

The SCAG and TDD examples suggest that the potential of ISTEA/CAA to stimulate regional governance is enhanced by state requirements that provide for a more direct connection between transportation planning, air quality and land-use planning. Without a specific requirement to coordinate land-use planning, ISTEA/CAA requirements are likely to prove difficult to achieve and may have only minor effects on stimulating genuine regional governance.

• *Regionally-based state growth management.* Coordination between land-use and transportation planning is a direct and significant objective of growth-management programs established in Florida, New Jersey and Washington State. In Florida, a 1985 omnibus growth-management act requires local governments to demonstrate that they have existing infrastructure capacity capable of supporting the level of new development that they approve. This so-called "concurrency" requirement is being used to encourage more compact development and improve coordination of transportation and land use on a regional basis. Special scrutiny is given to large-scale developments with regional impacts (DRIs). The state can withhold a variety of revenue-sharing funds from communities failing to meet concurrency requirements.

New Jersey passed a state planning act in 1986. Unlike Florida's approach, which has often been regarded as top-down because it mandates local conformance with state planning goals, the approach in New Jersey is to structure growth management from the local level up. Counties and their municipalities must work out compatible plans that advance certain state objectives. Key among these are: 1) To capitalize on existing infrastructure while preserving open space by directing new development to areas which already are urban or urbanizing. 2) To achieve fair-share housing objectives by assuring the equitable provision of affordable housing throughout metropolitan regions. New Jersey's bottom-up approach to growth management is based on a "cross-acceptance" process that encourages the local governments of a region to negotiate solutions to incompatibilities among their plans.

Washington State passed growth-management legislation in 1990. As in the case of Florida and New Jersey, improving efficiency in infrastructure development and environmental protection were important factors motivating passage of the law. The law has concurrency requirements similar to Florida's, but dealing only with transportation infrastructure. In addition, it requires that urban growth areas (UGAs) be established on a metropolitan basis (e.g., the Puget Sound region). Urban services are not provided to development outside of the UGA. Significantly, a growth management in Washington provides for dispute resolution, especially around issues concerning where boundaries of the UGA are set.

In all of the states cited here there have been attempts to create a capacity for resolving intergovernmental disputes arising over growth management through the use of mediation. Florida has moved gradually but significantly in this direction, New Jersey makes the approach part of plan development and Washington State embraces mediation as part of an ongoing growth-management system. These states also have included significant provisions for public participation in plan development and oversight during implementation.[12]

• *Metropolitan Council of the Twin Cities.* Several bills were introduced during the 1993-1994 session of the Minnesota legislature designed to change the governance and scope of responsibilities of the metropolitan council (Met). Whereas the council was previously charged with waste water permitting and planning, as well as review of large-scale projects of regional impact, under new legislation it absorbs operating responsibilities for regional transit, transportation and waste water services. These functions significantly increase the responsibilities, and potentially the capacity, of Met to help coordinate regional development.

A criticism of the previous council was that it had weak leadership which failed to fully employ the powers available to it. A bill introduced by Representative Myron Orfield that would have established direct election of council commissioners was defeated by one vote. Instead, the appointment of commissioners was changed to make them more directly accountable to the governor, at whose pleasure they serve.

Another bill which passed the legislature but was vetoed by Governor Carlson would have given Met responsibility for establishing a comprehensive housing choice allotment system through which cities and towns in the metropolitan region would be required to meet quotas for supplying their fair share of the region's affordable housing demand. Met would have authority to impose penalties on localities failing to meet their housing mandate. In place of this stronger measure the governor was willing to sign a bill requiring Met to study housing rehabilitation and redevelopment costs and benefits.

By the end of the session, Met's responsibilities were enhanced in the area of infrastructure development but not in areas concerning social equity, notably housing. The degree to which Met will be willing to act stridently in shaping regional development through infrastructure planning depends significantly on the quality of appointments made by the governor rather than by direct vote of the citizens. Nevertheless, Met remains one of the strongest regional authorities in the United States.

Social equity and fiscal disparity. Since the late 1960s, cities have relied increasingly on the federal, and later the state governments, to solve problems arising from social inequities and fiscal disparities. Now that both levels of government are faced with reduced resources — if not staggering deficits — the burden of redistribution falls increasingly to local governments making-up the metropolitan community. If it is true that the economic prosperity of the suburbs is linked to the health of their central cities, then finding ways to share redistributional burdens on a fair-share basis is essential to the well-being of all.

Part of the burden to be distributed consists of assuring that suburban municipalities provide their fair share of the region's demand for affordable housing. Another consists of organizing regional transportation so that inner-city households have access to suburban jobs. Burden sharing also consists of coordinating responses to such crises as homelessness and the growth in AIDS cases, so that the limited resources available to address such problems can be employed more efficiently.

Clearly these challenges do not fall to the public sector alone. Nonprofits play a major role in the delivery of human services and they too must learn to organize regionally. Business can also help develop a regional response, especially in such areas of direct concern as the supply of affordable housing and transportation for the work force.

• *The Atlanta Project.* The Atlanta Project (TAP) was initiated in November of 1991 by former President Jimmy Carter.[13] TAP's goal is to reduce social problems associated with poverty, including teen pregnancy, childhood immunization, school dropout rates, crime and violence.

TAP is organized into 20 clusters, most of which are centered around and operate within high schools. These clusters cover much of the City of Atlanta and spread into adjacent areas of three counties. Each cluster has a local coordinator and stakeholder steering committee which are responsible for planning and implementing cluster-specific projects. The work of clusters is supported by a Collaboration Center which offers sophisticated computer-aided technical assistance, as well as assistance in fund raising and communications. Support is also offered to clusters through a Resource Center, consisting of a core group providing expert assistance as well as leadership to TAP-wide initiatives.

Funding for TAP has come primarily from industry and foundations. But the program also is concerned with mobilizing and coordinating existing public programs. Toward this end, President Carter conceived of the project as providing a means of cutting through bureaucratic red tape in order to mobilize public resources more effectively.

• *Federation for Community Planning, Cleveland.* Established in 1914 as an arm of Cleveland's United Way, since 1960 the federation has served as an independent regional forum for analyzing human service needs and mobilizing public and private resources to address unmet demands. It operates on an endowment large enough to generate several million dollars of income annually.

The federation conducts an annual health and human services institute, attracting as many as 2,000 volunteers who break into workshops to analyze specific problems and design responses. For example, when the issue of homelessness emerged, a federation task force developed a multi-front approach which resulted in establishment of an affordable housing trust fund supported by contributions from state and local governments. The federation also facilitated establishment of a coalition of city, county and some suburban municipalities which developed a coordinated approach to providing emergency shelter for the homeless in the region.

• *Regional Fair Housing Compact Pilot Program, Connecticut.* In 1988, the Connecticut legislature passed an innovative bill creating a pilot program to develop voluntary, regional fair-share housing compacts.[14] The need for affordable housing was to be balanced against environmental, economic, transportation, and infrastructure constraints. The legislation requires that each compact be developed by consensus and enjoy the unanimous support of the negotiating committee. Once consensus exists on the committee, the compact must be ratified by the governing body of each municipality.

Two regions were selected to pilot the program, one of which was the Hartford Capitol Region, which consists of an area of concentrated poverty in the central city surrounded by very affluent suburbs. This effort resulted in the Capitol Region Fair Housing Compact on Affordable Housing, which developed a plan to create between 5,000 and 6,421 local units of affordable housing over five years.

It is important to note that Connecticut has created sticks as well as carrots in its effort to generate affordable housing. The legislature established specific inclusionary zoning requirements, which it subsequently

backed up with an appeals procedure that allows developers to challenge denial of a development permit for an affordable housing project in communities that have not met their fair-share obligation. Other states also have inclusionary or "anti-snob" zoning requirements.

• *East Suburban Council for Open Communities, Cuyahoga County, Ohio.* Out-migration patterns of central-city residents usually result in older suburbs adjacent to central-city black neighborhoods becoming increasingly black and segregated. In Cleveland the pattern of out-migration has been eastward, and by the early 1980s two of the city's inner-ring suburbs had changed from predominantly white to more than 80 percent black. The racial shift has resulted in declining home prices and a weakened tax base.

Over 25 years ago, the inner-ring suburb of Shaker Heights initiated a program — with help from a local foundation and through its own housing office — to try to curb "tipping," whereby a community's racial composition is reversed. The city's objective was to maintain racial balance by offering low-interest mortgages to both black and white families in order to maintain racial balance in Shaker Heights neighborhoods threatened by tipping.[15]

In the early 1980s Shaker Heights successfully expanded its program with the inclusion of several additional inter-ring suburbs to the north and east. These local initiatives were organized into the East Suburban Council for Open Communities (ESCOC). In the mid–1980s ESCOC's ability to maintain racial balance was significantly enhanced by an allocation of mortgage money from the Ohio Housing Finance Agency.

ESCOC's integration maintenance program does more than provide mortgage support, it also helps black families moving into predominantly white neighborhoods make a successful transition. This includes diversity training in the elementary schools, and helping families establish networks of support services in their new communities. What is especially impressive about ESCOC is that it is a local initiative. Local leadership, both elected and in the nonprofit community, created and sustained the program, and then marshalled state funds to help expand and sustain the effort. Unfortunately, ESCOC recently lost its state support, and the program's future has become uncertain.

• *Scientific and Cultural Facilities District, Denver.* The City and County of Denver operates many of the major cultural and scientific facilities of its region: the zoo, Museum of Natural History, botanical gardens, the Denver Museum of Art, and the Performing Arts Center. For many years these facilities received state operating subsidies in recognition of the fact that they are important statewide assets. In fact, a survey of patrons found that most were residents of the suburbs and other areas of the state.

In 1982 the legislature ended its support, forcing these facilities to charge admission fees. Throughout the 1980s, city support for these institutions also was drastically reduced. In 1988 a referendum was put before the voters of the six-county metropolitan area to support creation of a Scientific and Cultural Facilities District (SCFD), that would levy a one-tenth of one percent sales tax. The referendum passed in all counties, and the tax currently produces $14 million per year.

Creating the SCFD required cooperation of the major institutions, which had no previous history of working together. It also involved formulating a distribution policy, which assures that all of the participating counties receive some funds to support their own arts and scientific facilities.

The model used successfully to establish the SCFD has been replicated more recently with establishment of a baseball stadium district to construct and operate a stadium for the Colorado Rockies expansion team. Again, suburban voters perceived that a Denver-based facility was of regional significance, and they agreed to support it with a special levy.

• *Title I Metropolitan Councils serving persons with AIDS (PWAs).* When AIDS first emerged in the United States n the late 1970s its occurrence was believed to be rare and essentially confined to the gay male community. Within a few years the spread of infection was having significant impact on public hospitals and support services, making it clear that a systemic response was required.

In 1990 Congress passed the Ryan B. White CARE Act providing significant funds for AIDS prevention and services. Title I of the Act supports programs in metropolitan areas having at least 2,000 PWAs. Under Title I a governor is required to establish a council which makes recommendations on the disbursement of funds. The law specifies that such councils have memberships representative of a cross-section of key interests, including a specific percentage of PWAs. These governing councils also include representatives of the nonprofit sector and local governments in the designated region.

Title I councils conduct an annual needs assessment which often includes evaluation of consumer satisfaction with services received. As a result, councils are able to plan and monitor the utilization of funds on a regional basis. In many metropolitan areas putting together effective councils and developing adequate delivery systems has been a struggle, but overall development of this approach provides an important model for metro-wide cooperation in responding to a major human service challenge.

• *Coalitions addressing regional racial issues.* Race, especially when combined with class, has been a key factor dividing regions. Practices of racial steering, red-lining, and the discriminatory use of zoning combine to aggravate divisions. Several metropolitan areas have assembled coalitions dedicated to addressing problems of racial tension.

One example is the Greater Philadelphia Urban Affairs Coalition, a nonprofit organization addressing social equity issues in the metro area. The coalition has three primary objectives: To improve the quality of life of the disadvantaged; to bring together diverse elements of the community; and to help strengthen the central city of the region. The coalition places strong emphasis on building community empowerment. It provides administrative support for over 30 affiliated programs covering such areas as AIDS education, homelessness, empowerment training, and public advocacy.

Another example is the Cleveland Round Table. In the early 1980s racial tensions in Cleveland, as in many other cities, produced a powder keg situation ready to ignite into riots. In fact, riots had occurred in the late 1960s. With financial support from some local corporations, the Cleveland Round Table was established to provide a forum in which issues of racial tension could be addressed. What started out as a discussion group later adopted a project orientation, including task forces to improve public education and police relations with minority communities. Although initially city-based, the Round Table also has been broadening its scope to address regional needs. For example, it is participating in development of the Cuyahoga Plan, which addresses fair-share housing objectives throughout the county.

Regions and Civic Infrastructure

The examples presented here suggest a proliferation of regional organizations, many of them cross-sectoral, designed to address issues of specific strategic significance. As indicated earlier, both capacity and demand factors help to account for the development of these organizational alliances. But even though these factors apply to virtually all metropolitan areas, it is important to observe that certain regions have an overall greater concentration of such efforts while many regions have only limited efforts in narrow areas of strategic interest. But why such uneven development?

One explanation is that regional governance efforts are likely to be concentrated in older declining regions which have had to adjust to major transformations in their economy (e.g., Cleveland and Pittsburgh). But other cities experiencing equally radical change — such as Detroit and Buffalo — evidence considerably less regionally organized economic development activity. The fact that a region faces an economic crisis is not sufficient in itself to produce an effective structure of cooperation.

The age of a region might also be expected to influence its level of collaborative activity, but the previous example suggests this is not a credible explanation. Some older regions have strong capacity while others are relatively weak, and indeed suffer from a long history of inter-local antagonisms. By contrast, some younger regions — such as Seattle and Portland — have developed exemplary regional governance efforts.

Although other factors could be considered, the single most significant one appears to be the presence of a strong regional civic infrastructure.[16] This infrastructure consists of a rich network of organizational affiliations within each sector — public, private and nonprofit — as well as networks crossing sectors. The member organizations of a network not only communicate, they share norms and trust one another.

The civic infrastructure as a whole provides a region with important capacities. First, the ability to perceive threat; to realize, for example, that its economic base is declining. Second, the ability to recognize opportunity; for example, that nonprofit research activity might provide a new economic base. Third, the ability to mobilize resources commanded by each of the sectors in order to advance desired regional objectives. Fragmentation of a region, in this regard, does not focus on the fact that it has too many governments, but that it cannot perceive, think and act as a whole.

In terms of the organizations composing a network, it is important to note that they often have considerable history and demonstrated capacity in adjusting to change. For example, strong regional business alliances have had to deal with changes such as a transforming economic base and globalization of corporations, often resulting in local corporations being absorbed by an international corporation with headquarters elsewhere. In Cleveland, for example, Standard Oil was taken over by British Petroleum, but BP remains a strong participant in local economic development issues through its membership in such alliances as Cleveland Tomorrow. In the case of Cleveland, continuity of local corporate law firms helps provide institutional memory and a basis of shared norms and trust, even when corporate ownership changes hands.

Many regions have not been as fortunate as Cleveland. They have lost major corporate headquarters and find it difficult to bring key private sector interests into partnerships. But in several cases diminished private sector alliances have been replaced by nonprofit partnerships, notably universities and medical centers. Here the challenge has been to create networks among nonprofits, which often have no prior history of acting as an alliance, much less one of regional scope. Again, regions with a tradition of working through partnerships — of engaging their civic infrastructure — seem to be more successful in making the transition.

Another important factor in achieving successful transformation is the presence of large, sophisticated, regionally focused foundations. In Cleveland, the Gund and Cleveland Foundations have been active partici-

pants in helping to shape development in their region; likewise for McKnight and Dayton-Hudson in the Twin Cities. These foundations often help fund the creation and operation of alliances, and they frequently make development of an alliance a requirement for receiving a grant. Regions with younger foundation communities often lack the capacity to play such a catalytic role. But national foundations — such as Ford, Pew and Carnegie — have worked to develop local foundations, by networking them in large projects that include development of civic infrastructure.

Conclusion

In summary, the majority of governance efforts in the third wave rest on a foundation of regional civic infrastructure. Tapping into this capacity is essential to creating effective governance, but it won't be easy, especially in regions which have weak capacity.

The challenge here is analogous to trying to achieve effective community redevelopment in inner-city neighborhoods. Communities with a strong civic infrastructure — comprising local institutions networking with each other, sharing norms, and operating in an environment of mutual trust — are much easier for foundations and government programs to work with than those with a weak or fractured civic tradition.

The third wave has now developed sufficient momentum that an increasing number of state and federal programs, as well as national foundation efforts, have been structured to incorporate the capacity of regional civic infrastructure (e.g., ISTEA/ CAA, state-wide growth management, Title I of CARE and others). But for the most part, this capacity has not been adequately recognized, and far too much of the debate over regional governance continues to focus on solutions from the first and second waves.

The challenge is to seize the possibilities offered by the most promising developments in the third wave, fashioning them into a more intentional and comprehensive approach to governance.

Notes

1. Lester M. Salamon and A.J. Abramson, *The Federal Budget and the Nonprofit Sector* (Washington, D.C.: Urban Institute Press, 1982).

2. D. Judd and M. Parkinson, eds., "Leadership and Urban Regeneration," *Urban Affairs Annual Review*, Vol. 37 (Newbury Park, Calif.: Russell Sage, 1990).

3. The change in emphasis from government to governance is well expressed by Ostrom, Bish and Ostrom in their *Local Government in the United States* (San Francisco, Calif.: Institute for Contemporary Studies, 1988): "We need to recognize, then, that local government in a democratic society cannot be confined only to what transpires in particular corporate entities or agencies identified as units of government. This is why it may be more useful to refer to "governance structures" than "governments." We can then appreciate that something viewed as a process of government (governance) requires reference to a much larger universe of discourse than do units of government as such." (p. 212).

4. For development of this point, see, J.M. Bryson and R.C. Einsweiler, *Shared Power* (Lanham, Md.: University Press of America, 1991).

5. See, A.M. Sbragia, "Pittsburgh's 'Third Way': The Nonprofit Sector as a Key to Urban Regeneration," in Judd and Parkinson, 1990.

6. Diana Tittle, *Rebuilding Cleveland: The Cleveland Foundation and its Evolving Urban Strategy* (Columbus: Ohio State University Press, 1992), pp. 266–267.

7. See, Robert E. Parker and Joe R. Feagin, "A Better Business Climate in Houston," in Judd and Parkinson, 1990.

8. Address by Gary Severson, chair of the Alliance, to the annual meeting of the National Association of Regional Councils, June 22, 1993, Portland, Oregon.

9. In many ways, the fund operates like Minnesota's Fiscal Disparities Act (1974). However, it has a narrower and more specific focus, limited to directing funds to be redistributed for the purpose of stimulating economic development.

10. E. Shanahan, "Going It Jointly: Regional Solutions for Local Problems," *Governing*, August 1991, pp. 70–76.

11. Metropolitan areas with populations over 50,000 are required to have an MPO.

12. For further discussion of state growth management, see, John DeGrove, *Planning and Growth Management in the States* (Cambridge, Mass.: Lincoln Institute of Land Policy, 1993).

13. For additional information, see, *Because There is Hope: Gearing Up to Renew Urban America* (Atlanta, Ga.: The Atlanta Project, 1993).

14. Based on "Consensus-Based Planning Helps Transcend NIMBYism," by Susan L. Podziba, in *Landlines*, published by the Lincoln Institute of Land Policy. For a richer discussion of this effort, see, Lawrence Susskind and Susan L. Podziba, *Affordable Housing Mediation* (Cambridge, Mass.: Lincoln Institute of Land Policy, 1990).

15. In 1988, ESCOC received a Ford Foundation Innovation Award. A case study of the program provides details on its development. See, "'Integration Incentive' in Suburban Cleveland" (Case Program, Kennedy School of Government, Harvard University, case number C16-89-877.0).

16. See, Allan D. Wallis, "Governance and the Civic Infrastructure of Metropolitan Regions," *National Civic Review*, 82:2, Spring 1993, pp. 125–139; Robert D. Putnam, "What Makes Democracy Work?," *National Civic Review*, 82:2, Spring 1993, pp. 101–107.

CHAPTER 33

REGIONAL GOVERNANCE
AND REGIONAL COUNCILS

J. Eugene Grigsby III

Data from the 1990 census indicate that the United States had 39 metropolitan areas of at least 1 million people. The combined population of these areas was 124.8 million, or approximately half of the nation's total population. In 1950, there were only 14 metropolitan areas of this size, and their total population was about 45 million, which was less than 30 percent of the nation's total. Thus, in a span of 40 short years, a significant proportion of the country's population steadily migrated from small towns and rural settings to more densely populated urban centers.

During this same 40-year period, two significant shifts were also occurring within these metropolitan areas. The first involved middle- and upper-income whites migrating away from central city areas to suburban locations. This resulted in an increasing number of low-income minorities, particularly African Americans, being confined to central cities. The second shift taking place during this period was the deindustrialization of the economies in many of these areas, resulting in an exodus of jobs from central cities to suburban locations.

The rapid population growth followed by population redistribution and economic restructuring have given rise to what is often referred to as "urban problems": traffic congestion, smog, polluted water, urban development encroaching on open space, crime, poorly funded school systems, and increasingly low income minority populations trapped in decaying inner-city locations.

It is within this context — rapid metropolitan growth and metropolitan restructuring — that planners and elected officials have sought to develop and implement strategies designed to: 1) induce growth and manage it simultaneously by focusing on infrastructure capacity, 2) respond more effectively to growing social service demands through coordinated delivery systems, and 3) seek ways to be competitive in a rapidly changing economic climate while not exacerbating inequalities between the poor and those with means.

Regional councils have emerged as one of the mechanisms thought capable of meeting challenges posed by these changing conditions. While the success of regional organizations in effectively meeting these challenges has been mixed, there is little doubt that the changing dynamics which metropolitan areas will continue to face will demand more regional approaches to problem

From *National Civic Review*, Vol. 85, No. 2, Spring-Summer, 1996. Published by the National Civic League, Denver, Colorado. Reprinted with permission of the publisher.

solving. In the past, the federal government has been the primary driver behind formulating regional strategies. In the future, it will be states prompted by the private sector and community-based groups who forge the types of partnerships required for regional organizations to become more effective.

The Role of the Federal Government

In the 1950s, few people ever heard of regional councils because there were fewer than 50 nationwide. The number of regional councils reached a peak high of 669 in 1976.[1] The primary factor accounting for this rapid growth in the number of regional councils was the federal government.

During the 1960s, the federal government offered many incentives to local jurisdictions to create and or enhance the position of regional councils. This was achieved by making additional funding available through categorical grant programs and giving preferential treatment in legislation or regulations to regional councils as eligible recipients. The federal government also required the preparation of a regional plan, or formation of a regional planning agency as a pre-condition for receipt of certain types of funds. The objective of coordination was first introduced in 1959 under Section 701 of the Housing Act as amended. Greater emphasis was added in Section 204 of the Demonstration Cities and Metropolitan Development Act, which established a regional review requirement for projects proposed under 30 different federal grant and loan programs. The Intergovernmental Cooperation Act of 1968 and OMB's associated A-95 grant-review procedures extended coordination requirements to 50 federal programs, and in 1971 it was further expanded to cover almost 100 federal programs.[2]

By the mid–1960s, federal government promotion of regional planning rapidly accelerated. In addition to the extension of Section 701, new legislation authorized regional conservation and development districts. In 1962, Metropolitan Planning Organizations (MPOs) for comprehensive transportation planning were initiated and required, where feasible, to plan for entire urban areas on an inter-jurisdictional basis. In 1965, economic development districts were authorized, and local development district legislation followed in 1966. The number of federal grant programs supporting state and local planning efforts increased from nine in 1964 to 160 by 1977.[3]

In a 1992 article in the *National Civic Review*, Patricia S. Atkins and Laura Wilson-Gentry suggest that the cumulative effect of these 1960s era federal programs was the widespread use of regional councils for comprehensive land-use and economic development planning.[4]

It should be noted, however, that not all councils during this era were initially formed to function as coordinating agencies, a number of them were first created as single-purpose organizations and later emerged into a broader coordinating entity. The Metropolitan Council of the Twin Cities, for example, was established in 1967 to address a water-pollution crisis, and the catalytic agent in creating Seattle's Metro was pollution in Lake Washington.[5] Over time these single-purpose agencies have evolved into multi-service agencies which combine planning and operating responsibilities, often by absorbing existing single-purpose organizations.[6]

In the 1970s, the focus of regional organizations broadened to include efforts at coordinating fragmented human services delivery systems. Amendments to existing legislation created Criminal Justice Coordination Councils (CJCCs) to administer comprehensive regional law enforcement and criminal justice programs. In 1973, legislation was passed allowing "prime sponsor" designations for regional councils and other entities to provide job training and employment improvement for the unemployed and underemployed. Areawide agencies on aging (AAAs) were also authorized by legislation in 1973 to provide comprehensive, coordinated social service networks for the elderly. Legislation passed in 1975 created Health Systems Agencies (HSAs) designed to enhance economies of scale and quality in regional health services delivery systems, and authorized social service agencies to extend a wide selection of social services to the eligible poor.[7]

Even though much emphasis was focused on coordinating human services programs during the 1970s, physical and economic planning programs, initiated in the 1960s were also augmented by federal legislation during this period. New pollution-mitigation initiatives in coastal zone management, resources planning, and noise pollution control legislation were enacted in 1972, and legislation related to disaster assistance planning passed in 1974. In 1976, solid waste management planning was created. In 1977 came water pollution control legislation, followed by air pollution control with Air Quality Control Regions (AQCRs) and airport systems planning was authorized.[8]

By the end of the 1970s, there were nearly 48 federal programs which required a regional plan or regional planning organization as a condition of funding, or which gave preference to regional councils within any pool of eligible recipients. Thus, the very essence of regional councils was derived from the strong push of federal policy decisions. But there were signs that things were beginning to change. The U.S. Advisory Commission on Intergovernmental Relations turned from being a champion of strong regional governance to an advocate of public choice with its tacit acceptance that fragmentation is good.[9]

Too much reliance on federal funding,

however, ultimately proved to be the Achilles' heel of regional councils. The dependence of most regional councils on the federal government was significant by the close of the 1970s. According to a 1989 report by Richard Hartman, three-fourths of their budgets came from federal programs.[10]

Turning Off the Federal Spigot

As a part of his campaign strategy, Ronald Reagan promised that if elected, his administration would place more control and authority in the hands of states and reduce the size of the federal budget. Once elected, Reagan moved with all deliberate speed to implement his earlier promises. Reduction in federal spending was felt almost immediately by the nation's regional councils. The number of regional councils declined from a high of 669 in 1976, to 529 in 1991. Staff sizes dropped from an average of 21 in 1977, to 17 in 1988. The number of federal programs administered by regional councils averaged around four from 1977 to 1983, but decreased to 2.5 by 1988. The federal contribution to the regional council budget, as a share of the total budget, plummeted from 75 percent in 1977 to 45 percent in 1988.[11]

The federal government shifted the locus of regionalism to the state—through block grants and changed categorical grants—permitting much discretion as to how regional councils should be used. The transfer of the A-95 review-and-comment responsibilities to the states was accomplished through Executive Order 12372. This shift enabled states to accomplish intergovernmental review of federal project applications, with the option of deferring participation, or, if maintained, doing so without the regional council as the mechanism. By 1992, 10 states, Alaska, Idaho, Kansas, Louisiana, Minnesota, Montana, Nebraska, Oregon, Pennsylvania, and Virginia conducted reviews without the benefit of a regional process.[12] The federal government was rapidly distancing itself from sub-state regional agencies by establishing the state as the preeminent connection. By 1991, only 13 of the 48 federal programs promoting sub-state regionalism that were founded in the 1970s were still funded. The only new federally sponsored legislation which still promotes a strong role for metropolitan planning councils has been the Intermodal Surface Transportation Efficiency Act (ISTEA) which was enacted into law in late 1991.

Because of the reduction of federal monies during the 1980s, regional councils found that they had to diversify their activities, shift from federally mandated comprehensive planning to membership and contract services, become more attuned to customer preferences, enhance their coordination with state policy and administrative cost concerns, establish active advocacy agendas in the state capitals, do more with less funding, and learn how to compete with an expanded pool of recipients of federal funds.[13]

While it is true that much of this shift resulted from direct reduction in federal expenditures, other forces were also in play, influencing this change in strategy. The strongest was the growth of suburban areas as the new locus of power. This shift increasingly called into question the necessity for having a suburban-urban linkage. The majority of metropolitan growth which occurred during the decade of the 1980s occurred in non-central city locations. At the same time, industrial restructuring meant a greater decentralization of the work place, with more new jobs being created outside of central city areas. In a sense, one could argue that the initial strength of the federal government's support for regional councils emanated from the strength of central city elected officials. By the same token, the rapid disengagement of the federal govern-

ment during the 1980s reflects the shifting of power from central city constituents to the emerging suburban constituent base. Ironically, constrained resources at the metropolitan level resulting from both a nationwide recession and global competition may once again focus more attention on regional councils as viable entities for addressing urban problems. Only this time, the federal government will not be the dominant player.

Emerging New Directions

Some scholars have suggested that regional councils as we know them today are not inevitable beyond the 1990s. From their perspective, what is more likely to emerge are increasingly effective integrated networks of intercommunity problem-solving and service delivery mechanisms.[14] There seems to be growing evidence that this view may prevail.

Allan Wallis, for example, identifies two strategic arenas in which these new networks, or alliances as he calls them, will occur. The first arena is economic development. Competition in the global economy is forcing these regional alliances to take place. Examples include Seattle, Detroit, Hartford, Cleveland, Houston, Orlando, Philadelphia, and Pittsburgh.[15] Capitalizing on the work initiated by RLA, a public/private/nonprofit partnership created in 1992, the city of Los Angeles is currently engaged in creating alliances to focus on what the city has identified as major regional growth sectors. Common to these efforts is an agenda requiring public sector participation but with a focus that is primarily business oriented. Typical of these efforts is the attempt to engage in strategic planning explicitly designed to capitalize on growing market opportunities.

The second strategic arena identified by Wallis is social equity and fiscal disparity. Here the questions are what constitutes fair share, whether or not a focus of the planning process should be on redistribution, and of course who pays and who benefits. For Wallis, it is nonprofits who must play a major role in resolving these dilemmas. According to him, providing solutions to these problems cannot fall solely on the shoulders of the public sector. A number of different efforts such as the Atlanta Project, the Federation of Community Planning in Cleveland, the Regional Fair Housing Compact Pilot Program in Connecticut, the East Suburban Council for Open Communities in Ohio, and the Scientific and Cultural Facilities District in Denver are identified as examples of how the non-profit sector and business together can help to develop a regional response to these problems.[16]

Much of the strategy being designed to foster economic development and social equity hinges on the question of whether or not prosperity can exist within suburban locations independent of healthy central cities. Few doubt that major inequities continue to exist between these two geographic locations. What to do about these disparities has been a continuing dilemma since the early days of regional councils. On the one hand, there are the regional economic growth proponents who argue that if you grow the region, then you will lessen the inequalities. Advocates of this position seem to agree that less centralization and less federal involvement will enable this regional economic growth to take place. There is growing empirical evidence that this may not necessarily be the case.

David Rusk, for example, described cities as either elastic or inelastic.[17] He finds that elastic cities "capture" suburban growth and inelastic cities "contribute" to suburban growth. Furthermore, elastic cities tend to expand their city limits, while inelastic cities do not. Not a new finding but one which should be upper-most in our thinking, is that racial prejudice continues to shape city growth patterns. Based upon Rusk's criteria, inelastic areas are more segregated. He also found that city-suburban income gaps were more critical a problem than overall income levels in metropolitan areas (a finding similar to that of Myron Orfeld),[18] and that poverty is more concentrated in inelastic cities than in elastic cities. Most important is his finding that the smaller the income gap between city and suburb, the greater the economic progress for the entire metropolitan community.

Rusk's findings are also interesting relative to their implications for future regional problem solving efforts. For example, he found that fragmented local government fosters segregation, and unified local government promotes integration. Dispersed and fragmented public education is more segregated than centralized and unified public education.

Rusk's findings, as well as those of Neal Peirce,[19] and Oliver Byrum,[20] suggest regional decision making is critical, and more of it, not less, is better. Furthermore, his findings suggest that no matter how regional councils evolve, two critical issues will have to be addressed: 1) How to assure that future suburban growth does not occur at the expense of central city areas; and 2) How to facilitate growth and development while simultaneously narrowing the gap between the poor and the non-poor.

Strategies for the Future

It should be fairly evident at this point that the role that regional councils play has changed significantly over the past 30 years. In the coming years, they undoubtedly will undergo even more changes. John Kirlin,[21] and Allan Wallis[22] both seem to agree that one of the central thrusts of the new change will be a shift from the concept of metropolitan government as a separate entity to a focus on governance. This belief is supported by a number of recent surveys which indicate that while there is some general support for regional government, most respondents question the ability of regional government to solve problems or respond effectively to local issues. Indeed, the extent to which regional governments are perceived to interfere with local self-interest appears to be directly correlated with the degree of opposition to such entities.[23] Attempts to strengthen regional structures by giving them more authority or by changing the selection process of governing board members to make them more representative have not been successful. And there is little likelihood that stronger regional government structures will emerge in the foreseeable future.

On the other hand, there is growing support for organized entities that promote a return to a collective sense of civic mindedness. The extent to which the influential business leaders effectively promote this vision of the future will be the degree to which the general public believes that it has some chance of succeeding. Earlier indications in cities like Atlanta, Philadelphia, and Denver suggest that there may be a great deal of merit to this new form of regional problem solving.

But what seems more likely to occur is that a clearer distinction will be drawn between regional agencies that continue to function as governmental entities because their mission is to plan and implement regional infrastructure requiring massive capital investment (or because they are carrying out a federal mandate such as pollution control) and the emerging entities which function as loose affiliations. Local interest will reluctantly continue to support the more structured government entities because in the long run it is more cost effective. But successful as many of these agencies have been in influencing the infrastructure development process, they simply have not been capable of addressing issues of social equity, and thus the need to explore alter-

native structures to address these problems will become even stronger.

Regional entities which are emerging as partnerships between the business sector and non-profit institutions have the potential to address social equity concerns more directly. In no small part, this is because influential business people supporting these partnerships see that growing income and class inequalities within a region simply do not bode well for the future economic health of that region, let alone for promoting a more civil society.

Regional government is here to stay. As long as its primary function is to provide infrastructure capacity and implement federal or state regulatory mandates, it will receive tacit support from local municipalities and contribute little to the growing problem of regional inequalities. Regional organizations working both in concert with and independent of regional governments have a much higher probability of tackling the more politically volatile social equity issues facing every metropolitan area in the country. In the final analysis, however, dedicated leadership resolved to address these difficult social equity issues will be the factor which makes the difference.

Notes

1. Atkins, Patricia S. and Wilson-Gentry, Laura, 1992: "An Etiquette for the 1990s Regional Council" *National Civic Review*, Volume 81, Number 4, Fall-Winter, p. 466.
2. Wallis, Allan D., 1994: "Investing Regionalism: The First Two Waves" *National Civic Review: Realizing Human Potential*, Volume 83, Number 2, Spring-Summer, pp. 168–169.
3. Wallis, op. cit., p. 170.
4. Atkins and Wilson-Gentry, op. cit., p. 469.
5. Wallis, op. cit., p. 170.
6. ACIR, 1973–74: *Substate Regionalism and the Federal System*, Washington, D.C., U.S. Government Printing Office.
7. Atkins and Wilson-Gentry, op. cit., p. 469.

8. Ibid., p. 470.

9. McDowell, Bruce as cited in *Substate Regional Governance: Evolution and Manifestation Throughout the United States and Florida* (Tallahassee, Fla.: Florida Advisory Commission on Intergovernmental Relations, November 1991), p. 28.

10. Hartman, Richard, 1989: *A Report to the Membership*, Washington, D.C., National Association of Regional Councils, p. 1.

11. Ibid., p. 4.

12. Symonds, Richard N., Jr., 1992: Montana Discontinues Process," SPOC-NET, Vol. 7, No. 7, 19, February 1992, p. 1.

13. Atkins and Wilson-Gentry, op. cit., p. 468.

14. Dodge, William R., 1992: "Strategic Intercommunity Governance Networks" (Signets of Economic Competitiveness in the 1990s), *National Civic Review: Partnerships for Regional Cooperation*, Volume 81, Number 4, Fall-Winter, p. 412.

15. Wallis, Allan D., 1994: "The Third Wave: Current Trends in Regional Governance" *National Civic Review: Renewing America*, Volume 83, Number 3, Summer-Fall, p. 294.

16. Ibid., p. 303.

17. Rusk, David, 1995: *Cities Without Suburbs*, Second Edition, The Woodrow Wilson Center Press, Washington, D.C.

18. Lecture presented to the Graduate School of Architecture and Urban Planning, Spring 1995.

19. Peirce, Neal R. with Curtis W. Johnson and John Stuart Hall, 1993: *Citistates: How Urban America Can Prospect in a Competitive World*, Seven Locks Press, Washington, D.C.

20. Byrum, Oliver E., 1992: *Old Problem in New Times: Urban Strategies for the 1990s*, American Planning Associates, Chicago, Illinois.

21. Kirlin, John J., 1993: "Citistates and Regional Governance" *National Civic Review: Tales of Turnaround*, Volume 82, Number 4, Fall 1993.

22. Wallis, op. cit., 1994.

23. Baldassure, Mark, Joshua Hassol, William Hoffman, and Abby Kanarek, 1996: "Possible Planning Roles for Regional Government: A Survey of City Planning Directors in California" *Journal of the American Planning Association*, Volume 62, Number 1, Winter, pp. 179–183.

CHAPTER 34

GLOBAL COMPETITION AND URBAN REFORM

Theodore Hershberg

When historians render their judgments on the last quarter of the 20th century, they will conclude that its defining phenomenon was the emergence of a global economy. Driven by free trade, international capital markets, and extraordinary changes in communications and information technologies, this new economy will make the future very different from the past. In every field of endeavor, strategic thinkers are now asking how best to adapt to these changes, how to position their businesses, institutions, and organizations to take advantage of the new world marketplace. What should those of us interested in the future of America's cities learn from the remarkable transformations underway?

The first lesson of the global economy is that regions—not cities nor the suburban counties that surround them—will be the units of economic competition. As Neal Peirce, Kenichi Ohmae, and many others have argued, only regions have the necessary scale and diversity to compete in the global marketplace.[1] Only regions have an asset profile capable of projecting overall strength to compensate for the clearly less attractive profiles of individual counties or cities which lack either essential infrastructure or a sufficiently skilled pool of labor.

Regions, moreover, are the geographic units in which our goods and services are created. We hire from a regional labor force. We count on a regional transportation system to move the people and the materials involved in their production. We rely on a regional infrastructure to keep the bridges and roads intact and our sewers and pipelines functioning. We live in a regional environment where water and air do not recognize political boundaries.

If regions are the units of economic competition, *the second lesson of the global economy is that cities and their neighboring suburban counties must embrace strategies of regional cooperation.* To compete effectively, regions have to be cohesive. That is, they have to be capable of solving problems and seizing opportunities in a timely fashion. In a nation with precious few examples of regional government, this means that cities and suburbs have to find ways to work together for their mutual benefit.

Originally published as "Regional Cooperation: Strategies and Incentives for Global Competitiveness and Urban Reform," *National Civic Review*, Vol. 85, No. 2, Spring-Summer, 1996. Published by the National Civic League, Denver, Colorado. Reprinted with permission of the publisher.

The Global Economy Poses Three Regional Challenges

The good news in the global economy is that markets are enormously larger. There will be 6 billion people in the world in 2000 — more than 20 times the size of America's population. The bad news is that the competition will be fierce as our firms vie for profits and market share with their counterparts across the globe.

To succeed, regions must respond to three major challenges posed by the global economy. *First, regions must develop their human resources because human capital will be the source of comparative advantage in the future.* Between 1973 and 1992, while per capita GDP grew 25 percent (adjusted for inflation), only the top 20 percent of American male workers saw their real wages rise; the next 20 percent were stagnant, and the bottom 60 percent actually experienced a decline. Our standard of living did not fall at the same time largely because women entered the labor force in record numbers. But since 1989, even median household income has fallen despite the fact that Americans now work longer hours and a greater proportion now hold at least two jobs, more than in the last half century.

Inequality in the distribution of income and wealth, according to Lester Thurow, is also growing.[2] Among men working full time, the earnings gap between the top and bottom quintiles doubled in the last 25 years. Between 1979 and 1994, while the bottom three-fifths of American families lost ground in terms of real income, the second fifth gained 6 percent, the top fifth gained 25 percent, and the top 5 percent gained 44 percent. The share of wealth held today by the top 1 percent of the population now exceeds 40 percent, a proportion last observed in the late 1920s.

Why the sharply diverging trends in inequality? An informal poll of 18 prominent economists, conducted at the Federal Reserve Bank in New York at the end of 1994, concluded that 10 to 20 percent of the growing wage disparity was due to international trade; 10 percent came from declining union memberships and 9 percent from the erosion of the minimum wage. But almost half of the increases in income inequality resulted from technological changes that benefit the better educated.[3]

To counter these trends, regions should adopt rigorous, internationally benchmarked, academic standards and assessments for their students, expand greatly post-secondary training, make admission to their colleges and universities far more demanding, and increase the availability of advanced on-the-job training in the work place. Regions that respond to the human capital challenges brought by the global economy and rapid technological change will close the wage gap, ensure social stability, and improve the quality-of-life for all their inhabitants.

Second, regions must lower the cost of their goods and services to be competitive. The inefficiencies embedded in the configuration of local, state, county, and federal governments — duplicated personnel, facilities, and services, limited management incentives, and tax structures that distort the most efficient location for economic activities — lead to increased business costs. In a domestic economy, these higher costs did not matter very much because businesses passed them on to their customers in the form of higher prices, leaving their profit margins unaffected. Since all domestic producers did the same thing, no one derived competitive advantage.

But when the competition grows increasingly international — and, for whatever reasons, prices for foreign goods and services come in lower than our own — inefficiencies that spring from domestic practices undercut our competitiveness. In *World Class: Thriving Locally in the Global Economy*, Harvard Business School professor Rosabeth Moss Kantor illustrates the nature of global competition through the experience of a small American envelope manufacturer.[4] The company learns that the contract it has long held with a large local corporation has just been won by a Taiwanese competitor who provided a quality product at a lower price. After streamlining its internal operations, the local company reviews further options to stay competitive: It can reduce its profits; it can lower the wages of its workers; or it can look outside the firm to find ways to lower its costs.

When voters — workers and their families — understand that the choice they will increasingly face to maintain the competitiveness of American goods and services in a global economy is either to lower their wages or to find other ways of reducing costs, they will not surprisingly choose the latter. Government practices considered sacrosanct today will change far more rapidly than most people now appreciate because politicians will quickly grasp that Americans are more committed to their pocket books than to traditional governance structures.

Regions should be asking what size "service shed" is appropriate for individual services and, for that matter, whether government should produce the service or contract it out to the private sector. The issue is not structural — requiring the consolidation of governments into larger units, but functional — offering services at the most efficient geographic scale. Efforts to tackle this politically sensitive subject are underway in several regions, including promising starts catalyzed by SUNY Buffalo and the Rockefeller Institute of Government at SUNY Albany.[5]

Third, regions must use scarce investment capital more productively. When crime, drugs, homelessness, and other social problems spill over into adjacent suburban communities, the response of those who can afford it has been to move even farther away to more pristine areas at the peripheries of our regions. This process is embedded in the concentric rings of growth that emanate outward from our central cities.

Very troubling signs in the older, inner-ring suburbs suggest that the pace of out-migration and other indicators of deterioration — job loss, housing depreciation, drugs, crime and related social problems — are accelerating faster than in the central cities they surround. The reason is that these small communities lack the basic resources big cities rely on to slow down and mediate the process of decline. These inner-ring communities do not have large central business districts generating substantial tax revenues to underwrite essential services in the neighborhoods; they do not have large police forces to maintain safety and a sense of social order as the crime rate climbs; and they do not have the sizable public and not-for-profit social service agencies to address the needs of the poor and disadvantaged.

This out-migration from the cities and the inner-ring suburbs leads to new development in the exurbs, requiring new roads and highways, water mains and sewer lines, schools and libraries, homes and shopping centers, offices and sports complexes. When this happens, our scarce investment dollars are spent redundantly because we are essentially duplicating an infrastructure that already exists in older suburbs and central cities. Such growth also often represents a highly inefficient use of our land. In southeastern Pennsylvania between 1970 and 1995, for example, while population declined by 140,000, one-quarter of the region's prime farmland was lost to development.

This redundant spending imposes heavy opportunity costs because these dollars are not available for vital investments in productivity. While we build shopping centers, the Japanese are investing in research and development. To improve our competitive position in the global economy, America's regions would be far wiser to undertake more cost-effective development by adopting metropolitan growth rings, increasing residential and job densities in existing suburbs and cities, and investing the savings in research and development, plant and equipment and human capital. America should not behave in the 2000s as it did in the 1960s. The current practice of redundant spending is akin to eating our seed corn. The nation can ill afford public policy that leads to throw-away cities, throw-away suburbs, and throw-away people.

The Search for Solutions

Regions whose cities and suburbs succeed in finding ways to work together will fare better than those whose constituent governments choose to go-it-alone. Whatever the direction of causality, cities and suburbs are linked together through the integration of their regional economies. Whether they like it or not, or even whether they are aware of it or not, cities and suburbs are their region's primary stakeholders.

Unfortunately, one of the partners is not doing well. Most of America's cities are on greased skids, and what distinguishes one from the other is the angle of descent. Our political leaders act as if America will be a stronger nation and our regions will be more competitive in the future if we lose our cities and are left not simply with our current social problems, but ones far worse because they will have festered unattended. They behave much like the proverbial ostrich that sticks its head in the sand rather than contend with the dangers at hand. The presidential campaigns treat cities like tar babies — mention them and you're bound to get stuck in unpopular or costly solutions.

Yet there are credible responses to the urban question that involve neither significant outlays of cash nor failed policies. My colleagues at University of Pennsylvania's Wharton Real Estate Center are now engaged in an important study quantifying the costs to suburbanites of decline in the central cities they surround. Last year, for example, they calculated a conservative estimate for the value of taxable and exempt real estate in 10 of the nation's largest cities: $1.6 trillion.[6] A 10 percent decline in value would represent a loss of $160 billion — roughly what the savings and loan scandal cost Americans. Who are the big losers? Not city residents. Since the value of urban real estate is dominated by the large concentration of commercial office buildings in the downtowns, and these are owned by banks, insurance companies and pension funds, the losers turn out to be shareholders in these institutions, who not surprisingly live largely outside cities (along with 75 percent of the nation's population and a disproportionate share of our better-off citizens).

I look forward to the results of this research and the publication of more such examples of how urban decline affects the fortunes of suburban residents. These empirical findings are welcome weapons in the fight against the folly of disregarding the plight of our cities and their residents. But while these new data are necessary, they will not prove sufficient. To explain why the continued deterioration of our cities and the serious long-term consequences they pose for the nation are ignored, we have to look elsewhere.

Greater Philadelphia First, an organization of over 30 chief executive officers of the area's largest corporations, recently undertook an annual tracking survey to gauge public attitudes in a scientific sample of the region's population. In 1994 and 1995, roughly three-quarters "of suburban residents acknowledged a symbiosis between the city and the suburbs."[7] They appear to understand the economic consequences and the spillover of social problems into the adjacent inner-ring suburbs that inevitably follow the decline of the central city. These attitudes resemble those found by my graduate students in two dozen informal focus groups held in the last several years.

The reason suburbanites have not supported further efforts to aid urban centers, I suspect, is not the absence of empirical evidence documenting the negative effects on the suburbs, but widespread distrust and cynicism about what can be done to save our cities. There is an all-pervasive sense that taxpayers have been generous in the past. Just about everything has been tried with at best limited success, and there is no sense throwing good money after bad.

The work of a research team led by my Wharton School colleagues, Anita Summers and Joseph Gyourko, addresses these concerns. Their conclusion is that cities are beset by three major structural problems: the loss of jobs and population that undermined their tax base; a mismatch between the limited resources they possessed and the much larger set of social problems from which their residents suffered disproportionately; and the misuse of the available resources to address these problems.

Their *New Urban Strategy* argues that the federal government should accept responsibility for the costs of national problems — poverty and immigration — that are now borne disproportionately by cities. While there would be no net change in aggregate intergovernmental aid, they propose an "Urban Audit" that would first determine the extent of unfunded burdens that cities are bearing for the nation and then divide the pool of intergovernmental funds so that those bearing the largest burdens would receive the most aid.

The second component of the "Urban Audit" is intriguing and pregnant with potential for catalyzing urban reform: The federal government would adopt a rational incentive system that would define the road to "good government" and then reward cities which engage in reform and punish those which do not.[8]

Consider the experience of Philadel-

phia. In 1992, at the brink of bankruptcy, the city faced an accumulated deficit of $250 million. Working together, Mayor Ed Rendell, who is white, and City Council President John Street, who is African-American, produced a labor agreement that did not give away the store, consolidated health and related benefits that saved megabucks, and won back significant management prerogatives bargained away by previous administrations more interested in union support for the next election than in the day of fiscal reckoning another mayor would inevitably face. By 1996, the pursuit of reform policies produced an $80 million surplus. Under a rational incentive policy, cities like Philadelphia would receive more funding from the federal (and state) government, while cities which refused to make the tough political decisions would receive less.

Which cities would get rewarded and which cities would get punished would be determined not by politics, but by the empirically derived "Urban Audit" noted above. At this stage, the mechanism is incomplete and certain to be controversial. To be sure, the "devil is in the details," but the concept of a rational incentive system for the nation's cities is the right direction in which to move.

Cities *cannot* save themselves with their own resources and most *will not* save themselves given a deeply entrenched political culture which makes sustaining reform over the long term impossible. Cities lack sufficient funds to deal with the vast array of problems now concentrated within their borders, and scores of studies chronicling efforts over the last century prove that reform is at best temporary. As the energy of the reformers diminishes, the returning bureaucrats restore business as usual.

A rational incentive system — in crude terms, money for reform — could leverage and sustain good government. While there is no guarantee that suburban support will follow, there is also no doubt that suburban residents will refuse to provide further urban aid as long as the evening news remains filled with stories of mismanagement and corruption. Putting aside posturing and partisanship will not be easy for either urban or suburban politicians. The former, especially minorities, will fear a loss of power, and the latter will fear the strident opposition of suburban residents who dislike central cities, which in metropolitan Philadelphia is estimated in the 25 to 33 percent range.[9] But the large majority of urban and suburban residents understand the economic and social stakes of continued urban decline, and they can be mobilized by effective political leadership under a banner of rational incentives.

It is time for suburban Republicans to sit down with urban Democrats. Both sides would come to the table aware of shared interests. City politicians would recognize that the dollars they need depend upon political support from the suburbs. Suburban politicians would acknowledge their economic stake in the city, knowing that its decline will not destroy them as if by atomic blast, but realizing that they would suffer from the fallout.

What is the basis for a new quid pro quo? Under what circumstances are the suburbs prepared to help the cities? What behaviors are expected from cities to demonstrate that they are in fact sustaining reform? If the cities live up to their part of the bargain, what are the suburbs prepared to provide in return? We need concrete answers to these questions. Advocates of regional cooperation need to help specify the "Urban Audit" and define the "road to reform."

The other missing ingredient — effective political leadership — will be more likely to emerge if the signposts on the road to reform are spelled out in terms of coherent public policy. Ed Rendell could articulate this agenda as well as anyone in public life today if he put his mind to it. So could Indianapolis' Steven Goldsmith. Finding sub-

urban counterparts is always difficult. The sheer number of municipalities precludes productive collaboration among local governments and complicates even county-level partnerships. Republican governors could play these roles effectively.

To get the job done, of course, would require what most of us would associate with statesmanship. Politicians would have to want to solve the problems of the cities rather than position themselves for the next election. They would have to believe that partisanship is a luxury America can ill afford in the fiercely competitive global economy.

States have a pivotal role to play. The "devolution revolution" Richard Nathan has written about affords an opportunity to help cities as well as improve the competitiveness of regions in the global economy. States may soon receive large amounts of money in the form of block grants. Instead of disbursing these funds entirely to each county according to formulas hammered out in state capitols, governors and state legislatures could set aside a pot of dollars, perhaps 20 percent of the total. While each county would get its share of the 80 percent, the reserved portion of block grants funds would be available only to contiguous counties which come forward as regions with strategic plans demonstrating how resources could be better deployed on a regional, rather than a purely county basis. Duplicated facilities, personnel, and services abound within regions, and these regional proposals could identify new "service sheds" and rational allocations that would minimize costs and maximize service delivery. The plans submitted would have to contain real cost-benefit analysis so counties would not come together as regions simply to win the funds and then divvy them up among themselves.

The public policy that undergirded the Intermodal Surface Transportation Efficiency Act suggests how this might work. Funds were earmarked for highways and mass transit, but metropolitan planning organizations were given authority to spend an additional pot of "flex" dollars according to the unique circumstances of the region. "Regional allocation agencies," as Tony Downs refers to them, would similarly determine the best configuration of funds and delivery systems for health care, welfare, job training, education, environment, and the like.[10] These decision-making groups could be popularly elected as in Portland, Oregon, or appointed by the governor and the state legislature as in the Minneapolis-St. Paul area, or chosen by local governments.

In sum, success in the global economy requires cohesive and competitive regions. The future of the nation's cities is tied to the health of their regions, and the success of regions in the global economy depends in large part on the health of their central cities. Cities and the suburban counties that surround them should be working together to develop their human resources, lower the costs of their goods and services, and invest their scarce capital productively. A rational incentive system agreed to by city and suburban politicians and embedded in national and state policies can provide aid to cities and sustain them on the road to reform. The devolution of power from the federal to state governments and the wise allocation of new block grant funds can stimulate regional strategic planning and result in more cost effective service delivery and more cohesive and competitive regions. The growth of regional thinking over the last decade is succeeding in clarifying the policy directions in which the nation must move to save its cities and ensure the competitiveness of its regions in the global economy. The critical next phase depends upon recruiting a generation of political leadership capable of recognizing the trends, the real policy options, and the possibilities.

Notes

1. Neal R. Peirce with Curtis Johnson and John Stuart Hall, *Citistates: How Urban America Can Prosper in a Competitive World* (Washington, D.C.: Seven Locks Press, 1993); Kenichi Ohmae, *The End of the Nation State: The Rise of Regional Economies* (New York: Free Press, 1995); Theodore Hershberg, "The Case for Regional Cooperation," *The Regionalist* (September 1995).

2. Lester Thurow, "How Much Inequality Can a Democracy Take?" *The New York Times Magazine* (Nov. 19, 1995).

3. Jason DeParle, "Class Is No Longer a Four-Letter Word," *The New York Times Magazine* (March 17, 1996).

4. Rosabeth Moss Kantor, *World Class: Thriving Locally in the Global Economy* (New York: Simon and Schuster, 1995).

5. "Assessing Regionalism in Erie County," from *Governance in Erie County: A Foundation for Understanding and Action*, The Governance Project: State University of New York at Buffalo (January 1996); "Growing Together within the Capital Region," from *The Draft Report of the State Commission on the Capital Region* (February 1996).

6. Joseph Gyourko and Anita Summers, "Wharton Research Impact Conference Summary: A New Urban Strategy," *Real Estate Research Bulletin*, The Wharton School (Spring, 1995).

7. *The Attitudes and Opinions of Residents of the Greater Philadelphia Region*, conducted for Greater Philadelphia First by Response Analysis of Princeton, N.J., in 1994 and 1995.

8. Anita Summers, "A New Urban Strategy for America's Large Cities," Association for Public Policy and Management (Chicago, 1994).

9. This estimate is based on the proportion of suburban residents who would not "be willing to see a greater share of current state tax dollars directed to the region's urban problems" (see note 7 above); and a proprietary marketing survey done for a regional newspaper several years ago that concluded that "33 percent of those sampled had anti-Philadelphia attitudes."

10. Anthony Downs, *New Visions for Metropolitan America* (Washington, D.C. and Cambridge, Mass.: The Brookings Institution and the Lincoln Institute of Land Policy, 1994).

CHAPTER 35

REGIONAL EXCELLENCE IN THE 21ST CENTURY

William R. Dodge

A thousand years ago, in the late 900s, people literally feared the end of the world in some cataclysmic explosion.

Their fears caused them to consider reforms, especially of their spiritual behavior. Hoping that the end would coincide with the second coming, community leaders and citizens of the time, at least the Christian ones, dedicated themselves to a religious building campaign of colossal proportions. Their collaborative efforts resulted in constructing many of the monumental Romanesque cathedrals of Western Europe. Cluniac monk, Raoul Glaber, observed in 1003, "it was as if the whole earth, having cast off its age by shaking itself, were clothing itself everywhere in a white robe of churches."

Today, in the late 1900s, people fear the end of their local political worlds in some equally drastic change.

What used to be resolvable in their individual communities now defies resolution with neighbors across entire regions. What used to be clearly the responsibility of public, private, or nonprofit organizations now creates overlapping confusion. What used to be perceived as common — even American — values are increasingly contested by conflicted communities and interest groups.

Such fears have caused people to consider reforms, especially of their temporal behavior.

Not depending upon divine intervention for resolving their earthly challenges, community leaders and citizens are experimenting with new approaches to intercommunity and regional decision-making. These experiments have not yet reached colossal proportions, but they may preview a regional renaissance by the dawn of the 21st century.

Maybe, just maybe, our regions will be clothed with regional governance excellence in this change in millennia!

By regional governance, I do not mean metropolitan government, the one-big-government approach to regional challenges. Instead, I mean how we bring community leaders and citizens together to address challenges that cut across communities — from crime and drugs to economic competitiveness. This usually involves defining the challenge, assigning responsibility for addressing it to an existing or new regional mechanism, involving community leaders and citizens affected by it, designing a strategy for addressing it, negotiating responsibility and

Originally published as "Regional Excellence in the 21st Century," *National Civic Review*, Vol. 85, No. 2, Spring-Summer, 1996. Published by the National Civic League, Denver, Colorado. Reprinted with permission of the publisher.

implementing the strategy, and monitoring and evaluating success in addressing the challenge. By excellence, I mean doing this in a more timely, flexible, and effective manner with each new challenge, so as to take advantage of regional opportunities before they are lost and prevent regional threats from exploding into crisis.

Regional Governance Has Risen in Importance

Regions are organic systems organized in ways surprisingly similar to flowers, fish, mammals, and humans. They have evolved out of less complex — but not necessarily lower — life forms, especially in urban areas that started with small settlements that grew into cities that, in turn, expanded into regions containing suburbs and exurbs. As a result, regions have one or more vital organs — central business districts and suburban employment centers and shopping malls — tied together with the sinews of transportation, the arteries of commerce, and the protoplasm of community.

Healthy regions nurture us, their individual cells, by concentrating the resources and providing the connections to pursue a desired quality of life, locally and globally. In turn, they need our care and feeding, since, like other living beings, their health and happiness is determined by whoever or whatever shapes and controls their growth.

States and nations do not usually stir the same biological thoughts. As critical as they are to providing military security, setting uniform standards, redistributing wealth, and even supporting local and regional initiatives, they appear more to be human contrivances than living organisms.

It is not surprising, therefore, that the region has emerged again as it has repeatedly over recorded history. This time, it has become more important as the Cold War, which had required nations to develop competitive armies, cooled off, and the global common market, which now requires regions to develop competitive economies, heated up.

The era of the region is already being proclaimed worldwide. In Europe, the borders between nations are dissolving in the European community and a "Europe of Regions" is taking its place. In Asia, Hong Kong shows every sign of surviving its transfer from Great Britain to the Peoples Republic of China as a relatively independent region, one that now includes a considerable part of the Guangzhou province of China. I suspect that neither ideology nor nationalism will seriously restrict the behavior of this powerful living organism in the global ecosystem.

What might be surprising, however, is that this same Global Competitiveness, and four other major developments, or change drivers — Challenge Explosion, Citizen Withdrawal, Structure-Challenge Mismatch, and Rich-Poor Community Gap — have transformed regional governance from a nicety to a necessity.

Bottom Line: Community leaders and citizens need to focus priority attention on the growth development — the governance — of their own living organisms, their regions.

Pursuing Regional Governance Excellence Requires a Guiding Star

We have a long history of being easy "creationists" and reluctant "evolutionists" concerning the region.

On one hand, as easy "creationists," we have all too readily bought into the idea that a metropolitan government, in the form of a single monolithic structure that directs all decision making, would eventually be created, almost overnight, and guide regional development. It, I suspect, is doomed to be the eternal will-o'-the-wisp of regional governance.

No matter how creative we become, we cannot anticipate the range of challenges or nail down the geographic scope of the region long enough to have it governed by a single structure. Even those places that have annexed extensively, such as Columbus, Ohio; consolidated city and county government, such as Unigov in the Indianapolis region; or created two-tier governments, such as Metro Toronto, continue to be confronted with irrepressible sprawl leapfrogging across their borders into the great beyond.

Unless we are willing to pursue the highly unlikely option of making each region a state, and to then redraw state boundaries every decade to conform with the changing spheres of regional influence, we will need to build a "network" of regional decision making mechanisms — processes and structures — to address emerging challenges in each region.

On the other hand, as reluctant "evolutionists," we have resisted the evolution of regional decision-making mechanisms, condemning most of them to be ineffective "footballs without laces," giving all the appearances of addressing regional challenges but being genetically flawed in their powers, participants, practices, or perseverance. Or, even worse, we have flirted with the myth that the region was divisible — that the donut (the suburbs) is not connected to the hole (the central city). To borrow a metaphor from Peter Senge, author of *The Fifth Discipline*, dividing a region into parts has no greater chance of working than dividing any other living organism, such as an elephant, into parts; all one gets is a mess.

I believe that we now need to be strategic "pragmatists" and foster a regional renaissance. We need to pursue regional governance excellence in the closing years of the second millennium if we are to compete globally and thrive locally in the third. Achieving excellence, I further believe, requires launching initiatives to improve each

of five components of regional governance; that is, we need to make it prominent, strategic, equitable, empowering, and institutionalized.

Bottom line: The pursuit of regional governance excellence needs to be empowered by community leaders and citizens in each region and enjoy the involvement and support of state and national, governmental and non-governmental, organizations.

Achieving Regional Governance Excellence Will Strengthen, and Even Save, Our Federal System of Governance

Regional decision making complements local, state and national decision making by providing mechanisms for addressing cross-cutting challenges that cannot be sponsored by any one of those levels alone. It does not replace, but rather enriches and helps preserve our federal system of governance.

As regions continue to evolve, they will create a new political force in state capitals and Washington. At times, communities within regions will come together in a collective voice that has the clout to drive almost any agenda through the legislative process and shift funding streams to regional initiatives. Witness the success of regional lobbying efforts in many state capitals.

At times, these same communities will agree to differ and offer a divided voice but still probably make state capitals and Washington their battleground. In the Washington, D.C., region, for example, the political dividing line has shifted to the Beltway, with those inside who feel they are experiencing a declining quality of life — traffic congestion and resulting pollution, loss of contact with nature, increasing economic and racial segregation, and higher taxes to try to fix these issues — increasingly confronting those outside who still want to carve out a new place in the virgin hinterlands. Resolving regional challenges now consumes a considerable amount of the agendas of a city, two states and even the national government.

It might not be unreasonable to speculate that achieving regional governance excellence will someday result in strengthening the federal system. There is an excellent historical precedent for the impact of such challenges.

In 1785, representatives from the states of Virginia and Maryland met with George Washington at Mount Vernon to deal with the regional challenge of "jurisdiction and navigation" on the lower Potomac River. Finding that regional cooperation would not suffice and that part of the problem stemmed from the limitations of the Articles of Confederation that governed relations among the fairly autonomous states, the delegates decided to invite representatives from all of the states to a meeting in Annapolis the following year. The delegates at the Annapolis conference decided that the issues had such gravity that they decided to call a constitutional convention in Philadelphia the following year. The rest is history.

Will the challenge of jurisdiction and navigation on the growth streams sprawling out of our regions have a similar impact on national, state, and local government two centuries later? And this time, will it result in the ceding of critical authorities to regional governance mechanisms?

Bottom line: Resolving regional challenges could redefine our federal system of governance and breathe life into regional governance mechanisms.

Community Leaders and Citizens Need to Act Decisively Now to Achieve Regional Governance Excellence

ACHIEVING REGIONAL GOVERNANCE EXCELLENCE IS MORE AN ACT OF THE MIND THAN THE POCKETBOOK

The real fears of addressing challenges regionally have to do with confronting unfamiliar communities and peoples, especially those that are richer or poorer or of a different ethnicity, and unpopular challenges, especially future growth, since whoever shapes it controls regional decision making.

Not that this lack of interaction has made life better or governance cheaper for any of us. When central cities decline, when crime and drugs escalate, when impoverished school districts cannot graduate productive workers, when segregated populations cannot find jobs, or when suburban communities are paved over with highways and parking lots, when the only way to get anywhere is by personal auto, when we squander resources on inefficient services, when we mourn the loss of community — then we all suffer and pay.

ACHIEVING REGIONAL GOVERNANCE EXCELLENCE NEEDS TO BEGIN DECISIVELY, NOW

We have attracted the attention of community leaders and citizens and are experimenting with regional governance initiatives. That's positive, but it raises questions: Are we handling each new regional challenge better than the last one? Are we developing individual regional decision-making mechanisms that efficiently guide community leaders and citizens through equitable and empowering processes that handle the most pressing challenges?

We have also attracted the attention of economic interests that are already jockeying for influence in each of the regional economies that constitute the global common market. That's also positive, but it raises a second set of questions: Are we shaping regional growth and development so as to compete globally and thrive locally? If we are, are we also overcoming intercommunity disparities and building regional citizenship and a sense of regional community? And are we developing a "network" of regional decision-making mechanisms that interact seamlessly to provide regional governance excellence?

Finally, we are witnessing radical changes in the responsibilities and relationships of state and national governments. It's difficult to say whether this is positive or negative for regional governance, but it helps reinforce the need for community leaders and citizens to act decisively, now.

Community leaders and citizens in some regions are already beginning to launch their regional renaissances. They have started to consider the communities of the region in the singular, as *us*, and not just in the plural, as *you and me*. Community leaders and citizens in other regions may join them. I have no doubt that those who pursue this journey will live in the most desirable regions at the dawn of the 21st century.

CHAPTER 36

THE FUTRE OF REGIONALISM

Howard J. Grossman

The case for national substate regionalism is abundantly clear. The American landscape is already dotted with substate regional councils with a history of maturity, growth, passion, and excitement. It is also partially dotted with substate regional council difficulties that provide a most challenging approach to 21st century life in America. Substate regional councils have perhaps the most precise means with which to focus attention on key issues affecting the entire nation. If substate regionalism were carpeted across the nation, it would provide new and exciting opportunities to expand the delivery of citizen programs and to represent local concerns in a structured way — opportunities unlike any seen since the adoption of the Constitution in 1789. It would continue the progress begun in the late 1950s to reinvent government through the voluntary establishment of alliances, coalitions, partnerships, or networks.

The reinventing government craze filtering across the nation, led by David Osborne and Ted Gaebler with their fascinating and instructive book *Reinventing Government*, cuts across the wide swath of governmental practices throughout the nation. It continues to expand as a major invention of the latter days of the 20th century. In reality, however, the reinvention of governments has taken place much longer than since the 1990s began. It was in the latter 1950s that the practice of substate regionalism entered the history books and became a new chapter in the way problems and issues can be approached in these fading years of the 20th century. For all practical purposes, the invention of substate regionalism is the precedent for reinventing government.

There have been many examples of substate regionalism since its inception. Many practical successes, some failures, and continuing experiments impose both a theoretical construct and a pragmatic screen on the film of government pervading the delivery of services to residents of the United States.

During the height of Reaganomics, some regional councils went out of existence, while others took up the banner of entrepreneurialism and, though battered and bruised, survived the difficulties of that era. To the extent that financial support of substate regional councils diminished in the 1980s, substate regionalism reinvented itself through new and creative thinking regard-

Originally published as "The Case for National Substate Regionalism: Visioning the Future," *The Regionalist*, Vol. 1, No. 1, Winter, 1995. Published by the National Association of Regional Councils, Washington, D.C. Reprinted with permission of the publisher.

ing its mission, its financial base, and its work program. While divisiveness continues regarding substate regionalism's urban or rural needs or metropolitan versus non-metropolitan functions, it has progressed and made significant strides in the 1990s.

The main feature of substate regionalism is its ability to carry out activities which otherwise would not be accomplished by individual municipalities, counties, the private sector, or the not-for-profit sector alone. Although substate regionalism was built upon the platform of government, its innovation is characterized by networking, team-netting, and the constant building of affiliations and agility. If these words echo through the halls of the private sector, it's because they are deliberately crafted on principles and functions that the private sector authored and pioneered. These words also form the apex and strength of substate regionalism and lie well beyond the concepts and symbolisms of government only.

Natural Regionalism

Another way to interpret substate regionalism is through the concept of natural regionalism. Natural regionalism is the extension of two or more people, organizations, or governments, thinking about views and impacts both individually and collectively, as well as systematically, in order to afford the conditions which enable the sentiments of the minority to represent and take into account the interest of the minority.

Natural regionalism is a continuation of the principles outlined in the Magna Carta, the Greco-Roman laws of ancient times, and the various constitutional and legislative doctrines which have been established throughout history. The difference is that natural regionalism does not necessarily derive from constitutional or legislative law, but from the inherent rights of free assembly and public debate that have always been a cornerstone of democracy and among those freedoms granted by various leaders and groups throughout the centuries.

Natural regionalism proposes a higher order of life beyond the wisdom of the written words of legislative intent and constitutional theory. It suggests that the many levels of power and authority that override the conditions of human interaction derive not as much from political and legislative fiat, as from the inherent and expressed rights of communication and sharing, which are motivated by language, custom, and the oneness by which the population and the institutions of the world derived. While it may not make a great deal of difference in the actuality of regionalism, the ability to create a regional approach based on the laws of nature in addition to, or rather than, on the laws of humans becomes a principle, which may be more useful than any other.

Placing regionalism into a legislative format makes it all the more credible. Providing funding and support mechanisms so that regional councils can carry out their work becomes easier. A legislative format, however, does not make regionalism any more satisfying or important, and it is appropriate that both natural regionalism and human regionalism be powerful instruments — collectively — to enable regionalism to become an important contribution to society.

What Is Regionalism?

Substate regionalism must be viewed as a profession. Very often, however, it is portrayed as a governmental entity, part of the bureaucracy, just another layer of government, or a duplication of what already exists. It is none of these. It is new, different, innovative, opportunistic — it is a touchstone of people- and institution-focused functions that will achieve great results into and through the twenty-first century. It is more than planning, more than development, more than research, more than government, more than the private sector, and more than the not-for-profit sector. It is all of these, plus the ability to breathe new life into old structures and forms of activity which were designed for an agricultural society, honed by an industrial society, but incapable of dealing with an information society.

Substate regionalism is not thought of as a profession but should be. It is not recognized as a basic philosophy or concept but should be. It is not made of inherently designed and born regionalists but should be. It is not unified nationally through a carpeted nationwide structure but should be.

If substate regionalism had not been invented in the 1950s, it would have been invented today. In the American system of community life, substate regionalism is based upon volunteerism, utilizing federal and state grant support as incentive to local communities and the private sector to join together to reconcile community needs. These needs include infrastructure, resolution of major problems and issues affecting several jurisdictions, and planning and development. A planning process must be developed to enjoin and network the often competing and conflicting goals and responsibilities of many types of public, private, and not-for-profit organizations.

In the near and sometimes distant drumbeats of fiscal distress, downsizing, restructuring of industries, economic uncertainties, and classic internationalism, substate regionalism's role is far more important than ever before in its "thirtysomething" history.

Scope of Regionalism

The profession of substate regionalism is etched and carved in the bricks and mortar of public and private sector investments. It is the tones, shades, and variations structured on the palette of the early leaders of regionalism in the 1950s and 1960s. The profession is the over-arching dimension of single-mindedness which enables normally provincial thinkers to expand their insights toward regional needs and aspirations. It is an astonishing array of functions, services, technical assistance, and research capacities within a single organization, perhaps unparalleled within the circle of community or governmental institutions. It is the ability to be neutral, objective, a mediator, and, most importantly, a resourceful presenter of the strengths, weaknesses, opportunities, and threats facing the region.

The scope and breadth of substate regional councils is a commentary on the ingenuity of Americans to institute new ways of doing the business of government through a voluntary association of governments and private sector participants. There is no one way to plan, develop, and implement substate regionalism. There is a need to compile and disseminate information on the various ways that substate regional councils have been organized across the nation. The task of learning and disseminating was made easier by the establishment of the National Repository for Regionalism which collects materials, reports, documents, and papers on regionalism at The University of Georgia's Institute for Community and Area Development (ICAD).

The powerful surge of substate regionalism that occurred in the 1960s may be shifting in the 1990s and into the 21st century toward public/private sector partnerships, where the private sector becomes more embedded and deeply involved in substate regionalism. How this is accomplished and the exact structure and form it will take remains to be determined. Substate regionalism needs the strength of the private sector and requires the delicate balance of intergovernmentalism among and between all levels of government. Substate regionalism is a more influential institution when congressional and state legislative representation is possible and is a much more powerful force through an equal partnership of public, private, and non-profit sectors.

Substate regionalism should be a unique and creative institutional framework to supplement, not supplant. It should reinforce, not be a new government. It should be a potent source of positive production, not a bureaucratic body.

To achieve this dream requires a strategic vision of where the nation wants to go and how it wants to get there. It requires new thinking beyond the pale of conventional wisdom, which says what happened yesterday is what should happen tomorrow.

Municipalities are loaded with stress based upon the "F" word. Fiscal stability cannot be taken for granted, and local governments cannot withstand the pressures of service delivery in many regions without securing a new institutional framework. Substate regionalism means that certain programs that were traditionally provided at the local government level are now managed and administered at the substate regional level. The threats of take-over, job and prestige loss, "Big Brother," a loss of identity are all phantom images that do not do justice to the opportunities existing for substate regionalism. These opportunities include a 21st century concept of service delivery and program functions that has proven to be more effective and efficient than conventional means.

Nationalizing Substate Regionalism

In states where no specific legislation exists, regional councils have formed in a variety of ways including through executive order of the governor, interstate compact legislation, intergovernmental cooperation legislation, intergovernmental cooperation legislation, non-profit corporation legislation, regional planning commission legislation, and others. No one format fits the entire nation. In fact, arguments are made that in certain states there is no need for substate regionalism. Those states do not have enough counties, are too small, are too large and spread out, or have too many governmental agencies or bodies. Substate regionalism in relation to a national strategy can be rationalized only if an appropriate analysis of the entire governmental structure of the United States is accomplished.

Global Regionalism

A new dimension has been added to the justification for substate regionalism — the global connection. Global interdependence has become a prairie fire phrase, inhabiting the language of diplomats, economists, and politicians. But it is a valid phrase. As the nation, thus far unsuccessfully, bids for renewed leadership in a variety of categories where it ranked first historically, new approaches for success must be identified. Clearly, in terms of economic performance, the United States is no longer at the top and has fallen behind in a number of other categories such as health and education. Substate regionalism is not designed to solve these problems. The intensity of the problems, however, calls for significant and enlightened leadership to achieve economies of scale and more efficient means of production. These efforts are already being made by the private sector when it comes to the production of goods and services.

Regionalism: Its Many Forms

Regionalism takes many forms, tones, and creative energies. Substate regionalism is different in Pennsylvania and Alaska. Its focus and priorities are different in Maine and California. In Florida, its focus may be growth, while in New Mexico it may be lack of growth. Substate regionalism is characterized as a new experiment in states such as Alaska, with 13 relatively new regional development organizations. It remains on the youthful side of middle age in states such as Pennsylvania, where agencies have celebrated 25 and 30 anniversaries. Regionalism may be proposed as a major force through stringent legislation, as suggested in 1991-92 in California, or it may be loosely organized or nonexistent in states such as New Jersey.

The exciting adventure of substate regionalism is being tested in America's Last Frontier. From the Bering Sea to the Great Yukon, from the Kenai Peninsula and Southwest Alaska to the Pribilof Islands, and throughout the vastness of Alaska, substate regionalism is a new economic development stimulus for the benefit of all Alaskans. Problems in the state are compounded by the view of those in the Lower 48 that Alaska is the last symbol of a national environmental movement. The opportunities to create substate regionalism as the leading edge of economic activity in the state are enormous. With extremely limited resources, a limited number of professional staff, and new policy-making boards attempting to learn their awesome responsibilities, Alaska has created Alaska Regional Development Organizations (ARDOR). With a natural resource-based economy, small population, and extensive federal and state land holdings, Alaska offers a way of life unknown anywhere else in the nation. Therefore, its style of substate regionalism may well take an entirely different format in policy approaches and program initiatives.

On the other hand, some similarities to the substate regionalism found in the Lower 48 may exist. For example, the Anchorage Metropolitan Area faces revitalization, transportation, and housing issues, and many other issues that affect other medium-sized metro areas. In addition, Alaska has an astonishing amount of natural resources, environmental battles, water-related fishing economies, and budgetary battles that relate closely to the future of oil as an income-producing resource in the state. Imagine a state with 5.5 trillion tons of coal and little opportunity to develop this resource and market it to other countries. Imagine, however, the proximity of Alaska to the Commonwealth of Independent States and the opportunities for trade with nations who are slowly developing an evolutionary approach to democratization and privatization.

Alaska's situation is unparalleled in the experience of substate regionalism in America. It is, on the one hand, a challenge and an opportunity to showcase the benefits and assets of substate regionalism as never before seen in the United States.

This example is not meant to isolate Alaska from the other states. It is meant to describe briefly the excitement and vitality which, given a set of circumstances, can enhance how substate regionalism generates sound approaches to economic prosperity.

Irrespective of location, circumstances, growth, and economic deterioration, substate regionalism has a place in the spectrum of options available for determining the economic future of a region. Clearly, substate regionalism should and will be a model for overcoming many obstacles causing communities and regions to be uncompetitive from both an economic and quality-of-life view. In the next century, it will become even more important, in light of increasing reliance on cooperative partnerships, if the nation, its states, and constituent jurisdictions are to be as productive and quality driven as possible.

Clarifying the Role of Substate Regional Councils

Downsizing government and/or the service delivery system is obtainable only if appropriate substitutions are secured, such as those provided through substate regionalism. Too often, substate regional councils have been looked upon as paper shufflers and agencies that endanger grant opportunities. While there is a noticeable change in this regard, much more remains to be accomplished. One difficulty, while being an asset at the same time, is that substate regional councils differ as to philosophy and responsibility in various states and regions of the country. Some substate regional councils have focused on economic development. Other councils focus on transportation and land use. Still others are built upon uniform state legislation that spells out only what is required in that state. The argument is not so much for mandating uniformity, as it is for clarifying in the minds of others what substate regionalism constitutes and what role substate regional councils should play.

The difficulty of nomenclature provides a glimpse of the complexities of this subject. Known in some areas as regional councils, in others as regional planning commissions, in others as economic development districts, and in still others as councils of government, the difficulty in explaining what these institutions are has a powerful impact on their ability to become national treasures. Some have attempted to rationalize and clarify these institutions and their roles but no ready answer has been accomplished. One suggestion has been to call substate multicounty organizations "regional development organizations." Clarity could be enhanced substantially if the federal government were to establish an executive order, legislation, or both. This would identify substate regional councils as part of national policy and clearly delineate who they are, what their roles are, and how they interrelate with the public and private sectors.

Public/Private Sector Partnerships

Public/private sector partnerships were a hallmark of economic revitalization in much of the 1980s, and where the private sector actively participated in promoting economic revitalization while utilizing governmental funds as incentives, positive results accrued. Lessons can be learned from the massive changes occurring in Eastern Europe, the privatization occurring in several Latin American nations, and the increasing interest shown by other nations in the public/private sector model.

For example, the Appalachian Regional Development Model needs to be discussed, debated, evaluated, and utilized wherever appropriate in the United States. At the same time, the concept of regionalism needs to be stretched and stroked throughout the whole nation as a unique and structured process which can softly but effectively open new horizons as the nation gears for the 21st century. The ability to work *with* governments, and at the same time work *outside* the governmental arena and marry private sector programs with governmental incentives, is a beautifully timed, sensitive, and sensible arrangement offering the benefits of governmental services to all types of populations. At the same time, it brings in the expertise and involvement of the private sector that makes the investment decisions that directly affect the people and institutions of America.

No system of government currently in vogue provides all the answers to the problems and issues of the 1990s and the 21st century. The most powerful and potent argument for a structural change and the development of a national policy for regionalism is the very essence of American ingenuity and growth. Whereas the systems in which many Americans place great value were arguably satisfactory in the birth of the nation, that is not necessarily the case 220 years later as the United States hurls rapidly into a new millennium.

A national strategy for regionalism, on the other hand, neither means the death of local governments nor the institution of bureaucracy. Regionalism means capacity building. It means the potential for taking a national domestic policy and implementing it through a unified structured system with sufficient latitude on the part of states to adjust to the differences among those states. It means a more disciplined approach to the normally helter-skelter, irrational rivalry between and among urban, suburban, and rural interests.

Regionalism means a much more rational and responsible decision-making process involving those issues that clearly cross boundary lines and are incapable of reconciliation at a local or even county governmental level. Perhaps the most meaningful advantage of regionalism is its ability to bring to the table the major power brokers of the public and private sectors in a given region. While regionalism in its early days brought to the table only governmental leaders, its more advanced form allows both the public and private sectors, although to a large extent, most regional councils are still predominantly governmental agencies and are viewed in that context. If it is assumed that the private sector produces the goods and services that support the economy, the logic of a public/private sector form of regionalism becomes even more dominant.

Substate regionalism as a public/private sector partnership is a different institution than those established in the infancy of the discipline. It is not easy to convince local governmental officials that there should be equality between both sectors, and that from a structural viewpoint, the private sector should have equal voting rights to those of governmental officials. Furthermore, from a governmental viewpoint, involving higher levels of government in a voting capacity at the meeting table is not always an acceptable strategy. But these are issues detailed in scope, and with appropriate discussion, sensible solutions can be found. This is part of what may be called the prime directive strategy.

The Prime Directive

In the fictional representation of our global future as portrayed on the original *Star Trek* television series and on *Star Trek: The Next Generation* television show, there is only one prime directive. The directive involves helping citizens of heretofore unexplored worlds in the further reaches of space without interfering in the physical, economic, environmental, and social structure of the planets of the universe. In real life, there is no single prime directive. Instead, a multiplicity of forces interact with one another through a series of increasingly complex interrelationships between people and institutions, public and private sectors, and internal and external forces. These forces determine how this planet Earth, each nation, state, region, county, local government, neighborhood, and individual forms, expands, modifies, and contributes to the multiplicity of prime directives affecting the planning and regional decision-making process. This represents the principles embedded in substate regionalism.

All of us in this wonderful profession need to rethink and rededicate ourselves to leadership and capacity building and help create a vision which will take each citizen, official, and public or private sector institution toward a long-range strategic planning continuum, helping lead the people we serve to a global mindset. We need to examine how we can rediscover and re-energize substate regionalism as a professional approach to 21st century life. We must enable the people we serve to be highly motivated and fully involved in every facet of planning life, whether it be economic, physical, social, cultural, educational, or environmental, and truly make the year 2000 and the many years to follow the best in the history of humankind.

Throughout history, each time period has been projected as the most difficult, most complex, and most controversial, yet as each era goes by, we have every reason to believe that what follows may be even more difficult. The most recent era may be best characterized by the increasing reliance which every nation, including the United States, has on global interdependence and the role that economic development plays in bringing regions of the world much closer together. Despite the so-called end of the Cold War, the world has entered a new phase of nationalistic conflicts — the book of which has yet to be fully written.

Many substate regions and many parts of the world face serious new economic challenges. Total industrial restructuring of nations continues to be the great challenge of the 1990s, unlike any seen in the nation's history. The challenge for those moving into the working world and those seeking some form of higher education before doing so is to be aware of the need to emphasize productivity and quality, perhaps the two most important words in the economic setting of the 21st century. These prime directives will drive the economy of the nation through the next century, as competition for new economic growth continues to heat up.

A Covenant of Strength

There are many ways which regionalism can be a covenant of strength throughout the nation. Regionalism needs the union brought to the consensus table through the brotherhood and sisterhood of regional councils. There is no hard and fast rule for regionalism's success. There are covenants, however, that can cause regionalism to be a major force for the betterment of the people whom it is intended to serve. A covenant should be a sacred trust between parties, whether written or unwritten. A covenant from a regional council perspective is that which links volunteer board members, no matter where they live, to the duty and honor of upholding regional interests irrespective of the final decisions made by the regional council board. It is more an unwritten codicil than a constitutional or statutory principle built into the written documents that encompass the concept of substate regionalism.

Regional councils cannot perform their responsibilities without adhering to the basic tenets of substate regionalism. These tenets are more often found in the historical records and experiences of regionalism than in the strict rules and regulations that guide the many levels of government across the nation.

The Ark of the Covenant, through its Biblical and legendary interpretations, became a symbol of strength, unity, and religious fervor. Its mystical powers have been portrayed in books and movies. No such legend is ascribed to the covenant of regionalism, but substate regionalism needs the same fervor, trust, and recognition that the Ark of the Covenant has received over time.

Every so often, covenants need to be reinforced and a new look taken at how professions such as substate regionalism perform. Unlike the sacred schools of antiquity that form the rich texture and historical record of the past, there are no such instruments regarding the historical pathway of regionalism, although its practices and procedures have been written down and discussed in reports and massive tomes by organizations such as the Advisory Commission on Intergovernmental Relations.

Comparing or contrasting covenants of the past with the relatively short record of substate regionalism would be unfair. On the other hand, reexamining the origins of substate regionalism and recasting a new covenant of trust between those who participate in and benefit from the practices of substate regionalism is appropriate. With the next century ahead of us, the 21st century substate covenant would be an appropriate accomplishment and a contribution toward the goals and ideals that are likely to burst upon the American scene over the next several years. Such an action would create new interest and involvement of people who may not be familiar with substate regionalism and would reactivate and re-energize those born into the "thirtysomething" structure of regionalism.

Covenants cannot be broken automatically and should not contain a means by which parties can easily remove themselves from the original bonds of trust forming the covenant. This separates them from most agreements formed when governments or other sectors of the economy decide to work closely together. Those agreements often include language that enables parties to remove themselves from the agreement's original intent. Given the nature of today's society, this practice will likely continue into the foreseeable future.

On the other hand, in the case of the U.S. Constitution, which has been amended many times since its original enactment, the original bond of unity which enabled it to be written and approved has remained a stable and long-term commitment to the type, form, and structure of government that has guided this nation for over 200 years. Such an instrument of support may be the symbolic Olympic torch that carries substate regionalism to new heights in the 21st century.

Diversity

Regional councils have one characteristic not found in most other organizations—the characteristic of diversity. Most regional councils of any size include a wide range of disciplines and professions that, taken together, may be characterized as regional diversity. These professions represent a great many opportunities to affect in a holistic manner the great issues facing every substate region of the nation.

Beyond the professional talent that dictates the extent which regionalism can be successful, lies the diversity, or potential thereof, that characterizes the policy-making body of the regional council. Even where local elected officials make up the entire board of directors of a regional council, most elected officials are not full-time political leaders, but earn income through private sector positions. In those cases where a regional council's board of directors consists of a mixture of public and private sector personalities, diversity becomes even more useful in evaluating, developing, and carrying out plans and programs within the substate region.

This diversity may not have been utilized as effectively as it could be in shaping the future of a region. A sentiment exists that elected officials should be viewed only as such, that advisory board and committee members should be viewed only as representatives of their advisory organizations, and that private sector officials should be viewed only in the context of the particular position they hold. In fact, almost every regional council representative wears two, three, four, or more hats through participation on many non-profit boards and through other activities. It is difficult to realize how to tap into the many forms of regional diversity that exist. In fact, one full-time staff person would probably be required just to understand and maximize the diversity factor for the benefit of all concerned.

Few regional councils have achieved everything in the way of substate regionalism. While this is true of governments throughout the world as problems persist, especially in the financial relationships between demand for services and ability to provide such services, the search for perfection continues. Regional councils pursue new ways to do business and develop a corporate mentality that often does not exist in governmental circles. Substate regionalism also creates a shadow of strength and vitality not existing within many conventional governments. Diversity is part of the reason for this situation.

There is another side to regional diversity — the selection of issues to be placed on the regional council's agenda. What resources to deploy to handle different issues is always a perplexing decision facing regional councils. Only when regional councils have a limited agenda, wherein they receive funding from a minimal number of sources, does this problem dissipate. On the other hand, even larger and more urban regional councils have limited agendas, especially where they receive large amounts of funding for such issues as transportation or water quality. Their ability to accomplish comprehensive planning, economic development, and other functions fades in light of funding sources.

In more rural areas, there is a tendency to enhance regional agenda diversity since fewer agencies in the region compete with the role of the regional council. Therefore, regionalism and diversity are closely related to the numbers, type, and complexity of organizations that serve a given region and feel threatened by competition with a regional council.

The amazing strengths of regionalism are its ability to adapt from one function to another without losing stride and its ability to connect and network the region and appropriate parties to voice opinions and advice concerning regional issues. Regional diversity also implies the collection of views and attitudes from many different types of individuals and organizations in a given region, enabling these voices to be heard in the halls and boardrooms of regional councils. The regional role adequately and effectively brings together diverse thoughts and expressions and makes these expressions more than symbolic, meaningless utterances.

The diversity of regionalism should enable the profession to avoid being labelled as draconian. Openness, as opposed to elitism, is the hallmark of a respectable and truly professional form of regionalism diversity.

Thus, diversity comes in all forms, inhaling the fresh breath of inspirational regionalism and allowing a free and open process that does not exist in other circumstances and professions. Examining regionalism through the looking glass of diversity provides a new inciteful analysis of a profession on the cutting edge of 21st century life.

Our Lives, Our Fortunes, and Our Sacred Honor

"Our lives, our fortunes, and our sacred honor"— these words are found at the end of the Declaration of Independence. The powerful message they convey has not diminished in the 218 years since the founding fathers lent their signatures to a document which has developed a life and legend of its own. Since the founding of this nation, with its rich heritage and strength of values of people from many lands, the time-honored tradition of criticizing your own country has become a popular fashion statement. The tendency is to think that there are better ways to live, govern, and determine one's future, or that the "grass is greener on the other side." The right to criticize, however, is a cherished principle of the democratic system. The right to criticize without substantive facts and sensible comparisons is one which has become all too standardized across the United States.

The nation's heritage is not at stake — the nation's future is. This nation is strengthened by the obligations and actions that each generation brings to the table of life, flowing through the various governing structures created since 1776.

One of these structures, the substate regional council, has an obligation to inspire its communities, leaders, and public to be trustees of the founding father's principles that are emblazoned on our history. Regionalism is by no means the chosen and sole means for legacy transference. The profession can, however, touch a great many people and organizations and educate and explain the meaning that the Declaration's words signify to the nation builders of the present and the future. Since substate regional councils go beyond artificial boundary lines, they can bring the views of a wider range of participants to fact-finding tables, negotiating tables, consensus-building tables, and to many venues like those found during the pre–Constitution United States.

Some words are more important than others in any given document. Pledging of "lives, fortunes, and sacred honor" may have far more meaning than the issues pervading regional council discussions today, but the values of regional councils can be associated with the source of our revolutionary-based heritage.

Trust is a key word in the intent of the Declaration of Independence. It is also a word critical to the profession of substate regionalism. Regionalists are part of the system of institution building that is entrusted with the nation's future. Substate regionalists deal with the complex issues of employment, environmental sensitivity, housing, transportation, and the myriad issues and circumstances dictating the future. They cannot and should not be thought of as all things to all people and the solution to whatever ails the service area of the region. Regionalists can, however, contribute strongly to the nation's ability to meet the tenets of the Declaration of Independence in seeking to improve "our lives, our fortunes, and our sacred honor."

Substate regionalists reflect on the ideals of the nation and look backward into history, reflecting on how we arrived at this stage, and most importantly, projecting strategies, providing a vision, and helping implement the ideals of our heritage. Regionalists are wrapped in the enigma of rationalizing where we are, how we got here, where we are going, and who will be the winners and losers in the future. In the idealization of the future, substate regionalists seek equality and justice for all. Whether or not this is realistic or idealistic remains to be seen.

Translating the foundation of independent thought that the creators of this nation built in the Declaration of Independence into the complex world of today is difficult. Substate regional councils and regionalists across the United States can be major forces for duplicating what the signers of the Declaration achieved in the 18th century.

No sacred scrolls give the answers to the progress desired across the nation. Techniques and strategies can be used to help promote the best the nation has to offer. No thought was given 217 years ago, to the practice and profession of substate regionalism. What has been built into the process is a number of documents used to support and defend the innovations that occurred in the intervening years. The Declaration of Independence, the Constitution of the United States, the Emancipation Proclamation, the Atlantic Charter, the "I Have a Dream" speech of Dr. Martin Luther King, Jr., and even the Magna Carta of 1216 A.D. are a collection of words and wisdom of which we need to be reminded as the 1990s close and we head toward a new millennium.

The strength of substate regionalism is diversity — a collection of opinions and views, an exciting but sometimes overwhelming array of facts and information, and a mixture of plans that envelop our collective future. Substate regionalism continues to be an important way to implement that venerable document that begins: "When in the course of human events ... ."

The Next Century

The 21st century looms just over the horizon, bringing new thrills and possible new roles for substate regionalism to the national table. Because every state differs as to how it views substate regionalism, with legislative overview provided for the profession and funding available at different levels, there is both creative diversity and chaos. Even the word planning creates a dilemma because only the heartiest of souls believes that planning makes both immediate and long-term sense. Therefore, it may be that the substate regional council of the 21st century steers away from that word, away from other nomenclature that is not acceptable, and away from the language of those to whom the profession is less supportive.

Councils may move toward more uniform language, providing a more appropriate backdrop to the profession in the new century. What this language may be remains to be seen, but as more services are regionalized (as slow as that process may be) and as more stress is placed upon communities, areas, counties, and regions, the acceptability of substate regionalism should become more dramatic. Regional development, regional council, regional development organization, and generic terms of similar note are the ones to watch in the next century.

There may even be a move toward mergers of substate regional councils, thus creating larger geographic areas and boundaries in which regionalism becomes en-

sconced in the vocabulary of reinventing government.

Another trend may be the increasing involvement of the private sector in the work of substate regional councils. The private sector already holds a stake in substate regionalism both from the viewpoint of benefits derived and participation on the board of directors. This role does not come easy, but it should expand in the next century.

A major factor in the 21st century will be the delivery of services on the part of substate regional councils. The ability of substate regional councils to deliver a variety of governmental services such as, but not limited to, drug and alcohol programs, aging, the environment, and economic development has increased noticeably. As the thunderbolt of fiscal distress reaches across every part of the nation, new ways to deliver services will be sought. Substate regional councils are likely candidates for delivering these services to citizens within the jurisdictions served.

Another 21st century directive will be the expanded and diverse role of substate regional councils in many facets of regional life. This includes, but is not limited to, state-directed programs which focus on a substate regional council's role, policy development on controversial issues at the regional level, and technical assistance to both local governments and, most importantly, the private sector.

Perhaps the most generic and significant role of the regional council is the ability to act as a neutral disseminator of information, a neutral listener to positions taken by various sides, a mediator to bring options to the table for discussion, a convener to enable parties to meet and communicate, and a possible new role which few have considered — an adjudicator. Because so many disputes in America reach the level of legal action, the role of adjudicator may be one taken on by substate regional councils to provide a new structure to significantly relieve a crowded judicial system. These legal issues, that affect government, development, or other factors, are within the province of a substate regional council. The role of adjudicator might be controversial and take much insight, but it could be part of the new frontier of substate regionalism.

The most complex and aggravating obstacle to substate regionalism is the elimination of habits and philosophies which hearken back to our forefathers. Local governments are established as the centerpiece of the American governmental system. Their role differs from state to state, but the generality is that these local institutions are the strength and vitality of the American governmental system. It is difficult to erase or substantively change the institutional framework of more than 200 years. It is equally difficult to encourage local governmental officials to think of the region first and their jurisdiction second. Thus, if substate regionalism is to have an enlarged opportunity in the next century, the issue of facilitating appropriate changes in philosophy and attitude becomes important.

Another side to the 21st century view of substate regionalism exists. The ability to establish and implement a shared vision, a true partnership, and an electronic circuitry exists, where every part operates efficiently and with a spirit of teamwork unlike any seen in the past. While partners are considered the essence of substate regionalism, partnership has not always proven successful on controversial issues. This may explain why technical assistance on a one-to-one basis between the regional council staff and a specific local governmental organization has become a strong component of substate regionalism.

Substate regionalism in the next century should expand this type of partnering extensively to the private sector and, in some cases, to the not-for-profit sector. For example, one regional council is a designated affiliate library to the Foundation Center based in New York City. A strong element of affiliate library status is providing assistance to not-for-profit organizations in that region that seek technical support in finding foundation resources. This regional council may be the only regional development agency providing this type of service in the nation, and it is a service which could grow significantly in coming years.

Substate regionalism is a mutation of parts and pieces of local government that have stretched across the American governmental experience. It is a logical progression from an old-style format of government to a renewed and restructured basis for communitywide decision making. There are no magical solutions to the massive problems and obstacles facing local governments. From a 21st century perspective, the most ambitious and audacious program may be the considerable expansion of substate regionalism, causing public and private sector investments to be truly homogenized. The expansion of this concept should be one of the most challenging and inspirational highlights in the early days of the 21st century.

Singer John Denver wrote many songs expressing powerful feelings that reflect a calmness and attitude which might be termed counterculture. For example, in "I Want to Live," one of the most stirring and inspirational songs ever written, he includes the following refrains: "I want to grow," "I want to be," "I want to see," "I want to know," and "I want to share." These words may be the signature theme for substate regionalists of the 21st century and those who follow. They share a beautiful way to think about the present, prepare for the future, and become entangled in the opportunities and challenges that each of us face as we work through employment, recreation, and domestic life. It is the essence of why we are here on planet Earth, serving to find the most appropriate means for our future.

With the passage of time, regionalism has proven its worth even more, and its place on the cutting edge of institution-building represents a rare opportunity for the nation to turn a new page in its planning and development history. A national strategy for regionalism not only is an opportunity whose time has come, but also would help place the United States in a much more strategic competitive position internationally as the nation competes in a global battle for economic and quality-of-life survival through the 21st century.

CHAPTER 37

REGIONAL GOVERNMENT
RENAISSANCE

William R. Dodge

Community leaders and citizens in all regions are already laying the groundwork for a regional governance renaissance. The actions they are taking now will determine the degree of regional governance excellence each will achieve.

At the heart of this renaissance, we find community leaders and involved citizens dispelling old myths, adopting new truths, and pursuing regional governance excellence.

Old Regional Governance Myths

The old myths about regional governance that are being dispelled by the experiences of community leaders and citizens include:

- We can divide up crosscutting challenges and deal with them community by community.
- We can continue to afford endless flight to the hinterlands.
- We are too rich to have to worry about economic distress, too much of a melting pot to have to worry about ethnic and racial segregation.

- The answer to governing regions is structural; if desperate, we can always create an all-powerful metropolitan government.
- We can address regional governance challenges successfully with ad hoc approaches.
- Worst of all, regional governance is not that important — it is more of an intermittent nuisance than an ongoing necessity.

There is a myth, suggested 30 years ago, by Jane Jacobs in her classic work *The Death and Life of Great American Cities*, that community leaders and citizens were not ready to govern regions, that they should practice "metropolitan administration" first in our central cities:

Workable metropolitan administration has to be learned and used, first, within big cities, where no fixed political boundaries prevent its use. This is where we must experiment with methods for solving big common problems without, as a corollary, wreaking gratuitous mayhem on localities and on the processes of self-government ... If great cities can learn to administer, coordinate, and plan in terms of administrative districts at understandable scale, we may become

Originally published as "Regional Excellence: Governing Together to Compete Globally and Flourish Locally," *The Regionalist*, Vol. 2, No. 1, Spring, 1997. Published by the National Association of Regional Councils, Washington, D.C. Reprinted with permission of the publisher.

competent, as a society, to deal too with those crazy quilts of government and administration in the greater metropolitan areas. Today we are not competent to do so. (Jacobs, 427).

That old myth — that community leaders and citizens are not up to the task of regional governance excellence — has haunted us for decades and might be the most critical to dispel as our regions hurtle into the 21st century.

Emerging Regional Governance Truths

As this myth is being dispelled, community leaders and citizens are beginning to perceive some important truths about regional governance.

We are beginning to ask the right questions. We are at a stage in the evolution of regional governance at which we can begin to ask the right questions. We need to engage in a great deal more experimentation before we get the right answers.

One question, for example, is the one raised by George Latimer, the former mayor of St. Paul, Minn. at a National Civic League Conference: "How can we make government and economic forces support people where they live and derive values, how can we bring love of community back into the life of the region?" Another is one that I raised with the Annie E. Casey Foundation in the design of a new jobs initiative: "Is this to be another central city attempt to deal with a distressed community concern, with some regional involvement, or a new type of regional initiative to address a disparity challenge that cuts across poor and rich communities regionwide?"

We are beginning to develop a regional governance capability and capacity. Ongoing experimentation in regional problem solving and service delivery is strengthening community leaders' and citizens' capabilities to recognize workable and unworkable approaches. On bad days, this experimentation looks like the most confused polyglot of processes and mechanisms; on good days, one can begin to see a glimmer of governance in the 21st Century. The essence of this experimentation is presented in the following chapters of this book.

This experimentation is also developing a cadre of regional governance "pioneers," individuals and organizations who are willing to assist in designing strategies and supporting initiatives to address regional challenges. These include the "regional entrepreneurs," who take the lead in addressing regional challenges; the "regional wizards," who guide regional problem solving and manage regional service delivery; and the "regional champions," who provide financial, political, moral, and other support for improving regional governance.

We are beginning to explore some working guidelines and new models for improving regional governance. John Kirlin, a University of Southern California professor and dedicated regionalist, has suggested "10 emerging ideas that are likely to evolve, and perhaps be combined, into a framework for guiding creation of regional institutions."

- Responses must be developed within regions, not imposed from a state capital or Washington, D.C.
- Functional fragmentation must be overcome.
- Political accountability must be to the region.
- Regional and neighborhood governance both must be strengthened.
- Plans and ordinances are limited tools.
- Greater use should be made of decision rules and private market mechanisms in governance.
- The public and private sectors must be harnessed together.
- Equitable access and mobility must

be provided for those currently disadvantage.

- Vision is critical.
- Effective governance requires sustained effort. (Kirlin, 124)

Examples of new models for regional
governance include David Rusk's elastic
cities, Allan Wallis' cross-sectoral alliances or
my Strategic Intercommunity Governance
Network (SIGNET).

*We appear to be ready to modify ex-
isting traditions of local governance and
make new investments in rebuilding community, locally and regionally.* Stanford
University's John Gardner, former foundation and government official and the
founder of Common Cause and the Independent Sector, leads the Alliance for National Renewal movement, designed by the
National Civic League, to deal with the "social disintegration" of community. He
stresses that community is a regional concern: "It must not be thought, however, that
rebuilding of community is necessary only
in economically distressed areas. The sense
of community may be wholly absent in the
privileged family, in the affluent congrega-
tion, in the well-heeled suburb, clear consequences in terms of white-collar crime, substance abuse, child neglect and so on."
(Gardner, 1994, 377–9)

Gardner is concerned with turning
around the mood of the country and creating a "lend a hand attitude" that results in
communities that have wholeness incorporating diversity. He also has one of the potentially right questions: "How can the
American people be awakened to a sense of
purpose, a new vision and a new resolve?"
(Gardner, 1994, 377–9)

*We might even be conceding that re-
gional governance needs a legitimacy of its
own.* Regional stewardship is being seen as
an expression of our collective self-interest,
reflected in the comments of many experts.
"Today, national goals are being undercut
because the fragmented form of government

in metropolitan regions is inherently incapable of approving development patterns
which meet the needs of the entire region,"
according to Henry Richmond of the National Growth Management Leadership Project. (Richmond, 7) Community leaders and
citizens "must balance threatening excessive
centralization on one pole and ineffective
decentralization or narrow specialization on
the other," according to Allan Wallis, research director for the National Civic
League. (Wallis, 1994, 34) They need to
forge "strong bonds of community and social solidarity" that "link the residents of
metropolitan areas," according to Anthony
Downs. (Wallis, 1994, 44)

The challenge is to "reinvent regionalism"; to nurture, amplify and institutionalize efforts to improve regional governance.
(Wallis, 1994, 44) A new constitutional convention, such as was triggered by regional
issues in the 1780s, might not be needed,
but it might be timely to convene "regional
confabs," possibly modeled after a proposal
of a few years ago by the National Association of Counties to conduct a county governance congress for all levels of government.

*We might finally have the confidence
to pursue excellence in regional governance.* Alexis de Tocqueville confirmed
Americans' "can do" attitude on matters of
governance in 1831. While traveling by
steamboat down the Ohio River from Pittsburgh to Cincinnati, he wrote:

> There is one thing that America demon-
> strates invincibly of which I was hitherto
> doubtful. This is that the middle classes are
> capable of governing a state. I don't know if
> they would come off honorably from really
> difficult political situations, but they are ad-
> equate for the ordinary conduct of society,
> despite their petty passions, their incomplete
> education, their vulgar manners. Clearly they
> can supply practical intelligence, and that is
> sufficient. (de Tocqueville)

Perhaps community leaders and citizens finally believe they have the "practical

intelligence," the "covenant of strength," to pursue regional governance excellence, according to Howard Grossman of the Economic Development Council of northeastern Pennsylvania.

> Substate regionalism needs the same fervor, trust, and recognition that the Ark of the Covenant has received over time ... From a 21st Century perspective, the most ambitious and audacious program may be the considerable expansion of substate regionalism, causing public and private sector investments to be truly homogenized. (Grossman, 29)

Even earlier, in one of the first citystates, the citizens of ancient Athens took an oath that stated "I will transmit my city not diminished but greater and better than before." Today, many community leaders and citizens are developing the confidence to take a similar oath for their regions.

The final, emerging truth is that we need a regional renaissance to achieve regional governance excellence.

A Regional Renaissance

To transcend the current regional "merry-go-sorry" experience, I believe we need a regional renaissance, region by region, nationally. The original renaissance, between the middle ages and the industrial revolution, energized a revival of arts and literature, the beginnings of modern science, and the emergence of the nation-state. A regional renaissance, between now and the dawn of the third millennium, would energize community leaders and citizens in each region, inspire the best thinking of academic and other experts, and attract priority national and state as well as local resources.

Most important, a regional renaissance would raise our sights from treating regional governance as an ad hoc *expediency*, challenge-by-challenge, to pursuing regional governance *excellence*, holistically. Instead of

responding to each new challenge with still another decision-making mechanism, community leaders and citizens could create a network of mechanisms to address emerging challenges consistent with a vision for making their region work.

Achieving regional governance excellence, I further believe, requires pursuing initiatives to strengthen regional governance in five ways.

Collectively, efforts to improve regional governance need to make it:

- **Prominent — Visible and Important:** How can we make regional governance as important, and visible, as the challenges that it is addressing?
- **Strategic — Future Regional Governance Vision and Action Plan:** How can we develop a consensus future vision for regional governance excellence and collectively pursue strategies of priority initiatives for achieving it?
- **Equitable — Economically, Racially, and Fiscally:** How can we overcome economic disparities and ethnic segregation and the resulting widening gap between rich and poor communities and develop an "equal opportunity playing field" for all citizens and communities regionwide?
- **Empowering — Regional Citizenship and Community:** How can we develop our individual regional citizenship and create an overall sense of regional community that enables us to govern together regionwide?
- **Institutionalized — Regional Problem Solving and Service Delivery:** How can we foster experimentation that results in institutionalizing a regional decision-making capacity to address emerging challenges? How can we experiment with existing and probably many new regional problem-solving mechanisms, until

known and unforeseen crosscutting challenges are addressed in a timely manner? How can we redistribute responsibilities among existing and probably few new regional service delivery mechanisms, until strategies for addressing crosscutting issues are implemented flexibly?

These five components of regional governance excellence can be thought of as the five points of a regional governance star.

Finally, I suggest two hypotheses concerning launching a regional renaissance.

The first is that the five components need to be considered in approximately the order presented, reversing the all too frequently used process of jumping to institutionalizing some new regional governance mechanism and then picking up the pieces, or even finessing, making it prominent, strategic, equitable, and empowering.

- First, we need to raise the stature of regional governance — its visibility and importance — to attract the attention and resources of community leaders and citizens. We cannot achieve regional governance excellence if it has "second class" status.
- Second, we need to understand emerging regional challenges and our ability to address them and develop a future vision and strategies to guide our efforts to strengthen regional governance. Moreover, we need to assess our performance to determine whether regional decision making improves with each new challenge. Otherwise, we do not know whether our individual efforts contribute to, or detract from achieving regional governance excellence. We cannot ad hoc our way to regional governance excellence.
- Third, we need to address overcoming intercommunity disparities; otherwise the widening economic, racial, and fiscal gap between rich

and poor communities will be an Achilles heel undermining our collaborative initiatives to strengthen regional governance. We need to create an "equal opportunity playing field" for communities within a region.
- Fourth, we need to build regional citizenship and a sense of regional community; otherwise community leaders and citizens will not support, or breathe life into, initiatives to strengthen regional governance. We need the support of regional citizens to pursue priority initiatives for achieving regional governance excellence.
- Fifth and finally, we need to redirect existing problem-solving and service-delivery mechanisms, create new ones, and tie them together in a network that can address any regional challenge in a timely, flexible, effective manner. We need to institutionalize our capacity to achieve regional governance excellence.

In sum, we need to raise the *status*, design a *strategy*, balance the *scales* and find the *soul* of regional governance, before we tinker with its *structure*.

I am cautioned by John Gardner's advice that no matter how sound a strategy is for strengthening regional governance, implementation of priority initiatives will depend on taking advantage of the convergence of conditions beyond one's control. This sage prophet suggests in a letter:

> In a lifetime of watching a wide range of social problem solving, I've concluded that such problems rarely get solved by an orderly attack at the most logical point. I think one sees a lot of actions on a long ragged front with breakthroughs at often unsuspected spots. There are partial victories, and, with luck, enough to result in an overall victory. But it's untidy.

The second hypothesis is that any region that designs a consensus vision for the future of regional governance and aggressively pursues initiatives for addressing all five components can improve its regional governance performance and begin to achieve excellence by the turn of the millennium.

Many of the regional governance initiatives selected will probably build upon existing activities. Some of the initiatives will probably address two or more of the components simultaneously. All of the initiatives need proactively to pursue the unique future visions for regional governance excellence developed by community leaders and citizens in each region.

Initiatives for Pursuing Regional Governance Excellence

This volume presents regional governance initiative options to consider in a regional renaissance, one set for each component. Collectively, the three dozen initiatives, and hundreds of examples of their application, provide a "cafeteria of ideas" for community leaders and citizens to consider in strategies for achieving regional governance excellence. Each chapter presents:

- Background information on each component.

- Detailed explanations of initiative options, including a general description, specific examples of its application, accomplishments, strengths and shortcomings, future potential and contacts for additional information....

Although any of these types of regional governance initiatives can be considered for implementation as part of a SARGE (*s*trategy for *a*chieving *r*egional *g*overnance *e*xcellence), some will probably emerge as givens and others will offer debatable choices for achieving regional governance excellence.

More important, community leaders and citizens should select some regional governance initiatives that break new ground and offer the opportunity for preeminence in regional decision making, to become known as one of a handful of regions, nationally or even internationally, for pursuing particular types of experimentation in regional decision making. The regions that have established this reputation, such as the Minneapolis/St. Paul and Portland regions, are already reaping the returns in economic development and a high quality of life.

On the following exhibit is a regional excellence dozen, any combination of which, I believe, can make a region preeminent for its regional governance.

EXHIBIT 1
Regional Excellence Dozen: Regional Governance Initiatives to Make Regions Preeminent

Prominent

Create the critical mass of activities needed to capture the attention of community leaders and citizens and make regional governance important to them.

1. Sponsor an annual Regional Ex-

cellence Day (Prominent #5): Keep building community leader and citizen interest in regional governance with an annual celebration, including activities such as presenting regional governance awards for outstanding performance (Prominent #4), reporting on progress in implementing regional governance initiatives (Strategic #4), holding open houses at regional governance mechanisms, sponsoring dialogue on emerging regional challenges, and recruiting community leaders and citizens to work on regional projects.

Strategic

Maintain momentum in improving regional governance, systematically.

2. Institutionalize the Strategy for Achieving Regional Governance Excellence process (Strategic #2): Create an ongoing capacity to develop, implement, monitor, and update the SARGE, including securing the pledges of community leaders and citizens to pursue priority regional governance initiatives (Strategic #3), providing regular reports on the state of regional governance (Strategic #4), and creating regional governance fund/ foundation (Strategic #5).

Equitable

Educate community leaders and citizens on intercommunity disparities and reverse the widening service inequities, economic distress, and racial segregation among communities.

3. Offer regional interdependence dialogues for all community leaders and citizens regionwide (Equitable #1): Educate small groups of citizens from different communities across the region on the threats and opportunities of regional interdependence and recruit graduates as facilitators for the next round of small groups; recruit a coalition of academic, community, and religious groups to keep sponsoring new rounds of small groups until they are offered to all community leaders and citizens regionwide.

4. Combine regional tax sharing and service-delivery modifications to guarantee basic public services to citizens regionwide (Equitable #2): Generate adequate regional revenues, such as sharing some of the increased tax revenues resulting from new development, to guarantee basic public services in distressed communities; simultaneously, require service modifications, such as joint delivery by smaller distressed communities or between affluent and distressed communities, to assure effective use of the resources.

5. Combine intercommunity linkage projects, shared development of regional projects and urban growth boundaries to create economic opportunities for all communities regionwide (Equitable #3): Develop linkage projects between affluent and distressed communities, such as offering mobility to jobs in the former and redeveloping parcels in the latter; share benefits of regional employment centers and shopping malls across impacted communities; and establish urban growth boundaries to foster development, especially in distressed communities; overall, create an "equal opportunity playing field."

6. Offer affordable housing to create mixed income communities regionwide (Equitable #4): Require affordable housing in new housing developments, including subsidized units for the very poor, and convert public housing projects to mixed income projects, or tear them down.

Empowering

Develop regional citizenship, foster intercommunity relationships, and empower citizens in regional decision making.

7. Broaden regional leadership programs into regional citizenship programs (Empowering #1): Broaden the curriculum of regional leadership programs to include

followership and citizenship skills; open up participation to more community leaders and citizens; and channel graduates into assisting regional decision-making mechanisms and implementing SARGE regional governance initiatives.

8. Create ongoing "sister community" relationships between affluent and distressed communities regionwide (Empowering #4): Arrange sister community relationships between pairs of communities to exchange cultural and other groups, participate in regional interdependence small-group discussions, and pursue joint activities in each other's communities, with the support of corporate, academic, and other partners.

9. Establish citizen advisory boards or elect citizen representatives to regional governance mechanisms (Empowering #5): Either establish citizen advisory boards to review and comment on plans, budgets, and other actions of individual regional problem-solving and service-delivery mechanisms or directly elect citizen representatives to an empowered regional planning council (Problem-Solving #1), regional alliance (Problem-Solving #5), or regional planning and service district (Problem-Solving/Service-Delivery #3) that has authority to develop regional plans, set urban growth boundaries, and possibly deliver regional services.

Institutionalized

Provide the range of regional decision-making mechanisms needed to address regional challenges in a timely and effective manner.

10. Create at least one effective public, private, academic, and civic regional problem-solving mechanism (Problem-Solving #1–4): Each sector needs an effective regional mechanism to educate its members and develop positions on regional challenges as well as take the lead in addressing regional challenges, such as a regional planning council, regional chamber of commerce, or growth association, college or university regional affairs research institute, or public service program and regional civic organization; similar mechanisms could be created for labor, religious, and other sectors.

11. Institutionalize the capacity to launch regional alliances to address regional challenges (Problem-Solving #5): Build the capacity to turn to an existing regional problem-solving mechanism to sponsor a regional alliance representing all sectors of the region or create one or more ongoing regional alliances to address particular types of regional challenges as they emerge; expand the supply of regional "pioneers"— regional entrepreneurs to initiate regional alliances, regional wizards to guide their problem-solving processes, and regional champions to support the implementation of priority initiatives (Empowering #1).

12. Create a regional service-delivery coordinating group (Service-Delivery #5): Convene regional service-delivery mechanisms regularly to guide implementation of new regional services and develop cooperative arrangements for delivery of existing regional services; such a group could be free-standing, attached to a regional planning council or regional alliances, or be part of a regional planning and service district.

REGIONAL RESOURCE DIRECTORY

Major regional public agencies and nonprofit organizations included in the case studies in this volume.

Allegheny County
Office of the County Chief Executive
101 Courthouse
436 Grant St.
Pittsburgh, PA 15219
Telephone: (412) 350-6500
FAX: (412) 350-4360
Internet: *http://www.county.allegheny.pa.us*

Appalachian Regional Commission
Washington Office
1666 Connecticut Ave., N.W.
Suite 700
Washington, D.C. 20009-1068
Telephone: (202) 884-7799
FAX: (202) 884-7691
Internet: *http://www.arc.gov*

Atlanta Regional Commission
Comprehensive Planning Program
40 Courtland St., NE
Atlanta, GA 30303
Telephone: (404) 463-3250
FAX: (404) 463-3105
Internet: *http://www.atlantaregional.com*

Center for Greater Philadelphia
University of Pennsylvania
International House
3701 Chestnut St.
6th Floor East
Philadelphia, PA 19104-3199
Telephone: (215) 898-8713

FAX: (215) 898-9783
Internet: *http://www.cgp.upenn.edu*

City of Akron, Ohio
Economic Development Program
Office of the Mayor
166 South High St.
Municipal Building, Suite 200
Akron, OH 44308
Telephone: (330) 375-2133
FAX: (330) 375-2468
Internet: *http://www.ci.akron.oh.us*

City of Dayton, Ohio
Office of the City Manager
101 West Third St.
Dayton, OH 45402
Telephone: (937) 333-3333
FAX: (937) 333-4298
Internet: *http://www.ci.dayton.oh.us*

City of DeBary, Florida
Office of the City Manager
City Hall
137 South Highway 17-92
DeBary, FL 32713
Telephone: (407) 668-2040
FAX: (407) 668-4122
Internet: *http://www.debary.org*

City of Greensboro
Office of the City Manager
P.O. Box 3136

Greensboro, NC 27402-3136
Telephone: (336) 373-2002
FAX: (336) 373-2117
Internet: *http://www.ci.greensboro.nc.us*

City of High Point
Office of the City Manager
211 South Hamilton St.
High Point, NC 27261
Telephone: (336) 883-3293
FAX: (336) 883-3052
Internet: *http://www.high-point.net*

City of Springfield, Ohio
Economic Development Division
Office of the City Manager
City Hall
76 East High St.
Springfield, OH 45502
Telephone: (937) 324-7700
FAX: (937) 328-3497
Internet: *http://www.springfield.oh.us*

Contra Costa County
Growth Management Program
County Administration Building
651 Pine St.
11th Floor
Martinez, CA 94553
Telephone: (925) 335-1080
FAX: (925) 335-1913
Internet: *http://www.co.contra-costa.ca.us*

Denver Regional Council of Governments
Regional Growth and Development
4500 Cherry Creek Drive
South Suite 800
Denver, CO 80246
Telephone: (303) 455-1000
FAX: (303) 480-6790
Internet: *http://www.drcog.org*

Greater Baltimore Committee
Office of the Executive Director
111 South Calvert St.
Suite 1700
Baltimore, MD 21202
Telephone: (410) 727-2820
FAX: (410) 539-5705
Internet: *http://www.gbc.org*

Guilford County
Office of the County Manager
301 West Market St.
Greensboro, NC 27402
Telephone: (336) 641-3383
FAX: (336) 641-6833
Internet: *http://www.co.guilford.nc.us*

Metropolitan Council
Regional Administration
Mears Park Center
230 East 5th St.
St. Paul, MN 55101
Telephone: (651) 602-1000
FAX: (651) 602-1358
Internet: *http://www.metrocouncil.org*

Metropolitan Service District
Regional Planning Division
Metro Regional Center
600 NE Grand Ave.
Portland, OR 97232-2736
Telephone: (503) 797-1839
FAX: (503) 797-1911
Internet: *http://www.metro-region.org*

**Miami Valley Regional Planning
   Commission**
Office of the Executive Director
40 W. Fourth St.
Suite 400
Dayton, OH 45402-1827
Telephone: (937) 223-6323
FAX: (937) 223-9750
Internet: *http://www.mvrpc.org*

Montgomery County, Ohio
Office of the County Administrator
451 W. Third St.
Dayton, OH 45422-1375
Telephone: (937) 225-5802
FAX: (937) 496-7723
Internet: *http://www.co.montgomery.oh.us*

Port Authority of New York & New Jersey
Temporary Administrative Office
c/o Chief Financial Officer
241 Erie St.
Room 301
Jersey City, NJ 07310

Telephone: (201) 216-2564
FAX: (201) 216-2225
Internet: *http://www.panynj.gov*

Puget Sound Regional Council
Regional Transportation and Growth
  Management Planning
1011 Western Ave.
Suite 500
Seattle, WA 98104-1035
Telephone: (206) 464-7090
FAX: (206) 587-4825
Internet: *http://www.psrc.org*

San Diego Association of Governments
Regional Planning Program
401 "B" St.
Suite 800
San Diego, CA 92101
Telephone: (619) 595-5373
FAX: (619) 595-5305
Internet: *http://www.sandag.cog.ca.us*

Scientific & Cultural Facilities District
District Administrative Office
899 Logan St.
Suite 500
Denver, CO 80203
Telephone: (303) 860-0588
FAX: (303) 861-4315
Internet: *http://www.scfd.org*

State of Georgia
Coordinated Planning Program
Department of Community Affairs
60 Executive Park South, S.E.
Atlanta, GA 30329
Telephone: (404) 679-4940
FAX: (404) 651-5778
Internet: *http://www.dca.state.ga.us*

State of Georgia
Environmental Protection Division
Department of Natural Resources
205 Butler St., S.E.
Suite 1152 East Tower
Atlanta, GA 30334
Telephone: (404) 657-5947
FAX: (404) 651-5778
Internet: *http://www.ganet.org/dnr/environ*

State of Michigan
Tax Sharing Agreements
Library of Michigan
717 West Allegan St.
Lansing, MI 48909-7507
Telephone: (517) 373-3842
FAX: (517) 373-9620
Internet: *http://www.libofmich.lib.mi.us*

State of New Jersey
Department of Environmental Protection
401 East State St.
7th Floor, East Wing
Trenton, NJ 08625-0402
Telephone: (609) 292-2885
FAX: (609) 292-7695
Internet: *http://www.state.nj.us/dep*

State of Ohio
Joint Economic Development Districts
Department of Development
77 South High St.
Columbus, OH 43216-1001
Telephone: (614) 466-2480
FAX: (614) 644-5167
Internet: *http://www.odod.state.oh.us*

State of Virginia
Office of Community Revitalization
Department of Housing and Community
  Development
The Jackson Center
501 North Second St.
Richmond, VA 23219-1321
Telephone: (804) 371-7000
FAX: (804) 371-7090
Internet: *http://www.dhcd.state.va.us*

State of Washington
Office of Community Development
Growth Management Program
906 Columbia St., S.W.
Olympia, WA 98504-8350
Telephone: (360) 725-3000
FAX: (360) 753-2950
Internet: *http://www.ocd.wa.gov*

State of Wisconsin
Conservation Easement Program
Department of Transportation
P.O. Box 7910

Madison, WI 53707-7910
Telephone: (608) 266-3581
FAX: (608) 266-7186
Internet: *http://www.dot.state.wi.us*

Triangle J Council of Governments
Regional Planning Program
4222 Emperor Boulevard
Suite 200
Durham, NC 27703
Telephone: (919) 558-9320
FAX: (919) 549-9390
Internet: *http://www.tjcog.dst.nc.us*

U.S. Department of Transportation
(ISTEA & TEA 21 Program Information)

400 Seventh St., S.W.
Washington, D.C. 20590
Telephone: (202) 366-2332
FAX: (202) 366-9634
Internet: *http://www.dot.gov*

Volusia County
Office of the County Manager
Thomas C. Kelly Administration Center
123 W. Indiana Ave.
DeLand, FL 32720-4612
Telephone: (386) 736-5920
FAX: (386) 740-5245
Internet: *http://volusia.org*

NATIONAL RESOURCE DIRECTORY

Major national professional associations and research organizations serving local and regional governments.

Alliance for National Renewal
c/o National Civic League
1319 "F" St., N.W.
Suite 204
Washington, D.C. 20004
Telephone: (202) 783-2961
FAX: (202) 347-2161
Internet: *http://www.ncl.org/anr*

Alliance for Redesigning Government
c/o National Academy of Public
 Administration
1100 New York Ave., N.W.
Suite 1090 East
Washington, C.D. 20005
Telephone: (202) 347-3190
FAX: (202) 393-0993
Internet: *http://www.alliance.napawash.org*

Alliance for Regional Stewardship
785 Castro St.
Suite A
Mountain View, CA 94011
Telephone: (650) 623-3082
FAX: (650) 623-0900
Internet: *http://www.regionalstewardship.org*

American Planning Association
122 S. Michigan Ave.
Suite 1600
Chicago, IL 60603-6107
Telephone: (312) 431-9100
FAX: (312) 431-9985
Internet: *http://www.planning.org*

**American Society for Public
 Administration**
1120 "G" St., N.W.
Suite 700
Washington, D.C. 20005
Telephone: (202) 393-7878
FAX: (202) 638-4952
Internet: *http://www.aspanet.org*

Center for Neighborhood Technology
2125 W. North Ave.
Chicago, IL 60647
Telephone: (773) 278-4800
FAX: (773) 278-3840
Internet: *http://www.cnt.org*

**Center for Regional and Neighborhood
 Action**
1009 Grant St.
Suite 203
Denver, CO 80203
Telephone (303) 477-9985
FAX:(303) 477-9986
Internet: *http://www.crna.net*

**Council for Urban Economic
 Development**
1730 "K" St., N.W.
Suite 700
Washington, D.C. 20006
Telephone: (202) 223-4735
FAX: (202) 223-4745
Internet: *http://www.cued.org*

Government Finance Officers Association
180 North Michigan Ave.
Suite 800
Chicago, IL 60601
Telephone: (312) 977-9700
FAX: (312) 977-4806
Internet: *http://www.gfoa.org*

**International City/County Management
Association**
777 North Capitol St., N.E.
Suite 500
Washington, D.C. 20002
Telephone: (202) 289-4262
FAX: (202) 962-3500
Internet: *http://www.icma.org*

International Downtown Association
910—17th St., N.W.
Suite 210
Washington, D.C. 20006
Telephone: (202) 293-4505
FAX: (202) 293-4509
Internet: *http://www.ida-downtown.org*

**National Academy of Public
Administration**
1101 New York Ave.
Suite 1090 East
Washington, D.C. 20005
Telephone: (202) 347-3190
FAX: (202) 393-0993
Internet: *http://www.napawash.org*

National Association of Counties
440 First St., N.W.
Washington, D.C. 20001-2080
Telephone: (202) 393-6226
FAX: (202) 393-2630
Internet: *http://www.naco.org*

**National Association of Development
Organizations**
400 N. Capitol St., N.W.
Suite 390
Washington, D.C. 20001
Telephone: (202) 624-7860
FAX: (202) 624-8813
Internet: *http://www.nado.org*

National Association of Regional Councils
1700 "K" St.
Suite 1300
Washington, D.C. 20006
Telephone: (202) 457-0710
FAX: (202) 296-9352
Internet: *http://www.narc.org*

National Civic League
1445 Market St.
Suite 300
Denver, CO 80202-1728
Telephone: (303) 571-4343
FAX: (303) 571-4404
Internet: *http://www.ncl.org*

**National Community Development
Association**
522 — 21st St., N.W.
Suite 120
Washington, D.C. 20006
Telephone: (202) 293-7587
FAX: (202) 887-5546
Internet: *http://www.ncdaonline.org*

**National Congress for Community
Economic Development**
1030—15th St., N.W.
Suite 325
Washington, D.C. 20005
Telephone: (202) 289-9020
FAX: (202) 289-7051
Internet: *http://www.ncced.org*

**National Institute of Municipal Law
Officers**
1000 Connecticut Ave., N.W.
Suite 902
Washington, D.C. 20005
Telephone: (202) 466-5424
FAX: (202) 785-0152
Internet: *http://www.imla.org*

National League of Cities
1301 Pennsylvania Ave., N.W.
Washington, D.C. 20004-1763
Telephone: (202) 626-3000
FAX: (202) 626-3043
Internet: *http://www.nlc.org*

Partnership for Regional Livability
2125 W. North Ave.
Chicago, IL 60647
Telephone: (773) 278-4800, Ext. 135
FAX: (773) 278-3840
Internet: *http://www.pfrl.org*

Rails-to-Trails Conservancy
1100—17th St., N.W.
10th Floor
Washington, D.C. 20036
Telephone: (202) 331-9696
FAX: (202) 331-9680
Internet: *http://www.railstrails.org*

United States Conference of Mayors
1620 Eye St., N.W.
4th Floor
Washington, D.C. 20006

Telephone: (202) 293-7330
FAX: (202) 293-2352
Internet: *http://www.usmayors.org*

The Urban Institute
2100 "M" St., N.W.
Washington, DC. 20037
Telephone: (202) 833-7200
FAX: (202) 331-9747
Internet: *http://www.urban.org*

Urban Land Institute
1015 Thomas Jefferson St., N.W.
Suite 500 West
Washington, D.C. 20007-5201
Telephone: (202) 624-7000
FAX: (202) 624-7140
Internet: *http://www.uli.org*

BIBLIOGRAPHIC ESSAY

Bill Schechter

Historical Development of Regionalism and Metropolitan Governance

The best way to understand the current issues in regionalism and metropolitan governance is to review their roots and emergence over the last several decades. Allan Wallis' four-article compilation from the *National Civic Review: Inventing Regionalism* (1994) is a good place to start. The first essay, "Evolving structures and challenges of regional governance" organizes the changing geographic, economic, and social structures of American metropolitan areas into three phases: monocentric (central city dominance), polycentric (central city and suburbs competition) and networked ("complex complementarity and interdependency"). His next two essays relate those structures to three "distinct, but overlapping waves" of reform efforts.

In Wallis' first wave of efforts, governance in "monocentric regions," the focus is on structural solutions like city-county consolidations. For the early period, 1900–45, Paul Studenski's *The Government of the Metropolitan Areas in the U.S.* (1930)—published by the National Civic League—places the then-current developments into the context of Progressive era reforms. What is striking is how little the problems and issues have changed over the decades.

During what Wallis terms the second wave, corresponding to "polycentric" regions, the emphasis is on procedural reforms around improving program coordination and comprehensive planning, usually related to state and federal mandates. During what many observers consider the apogee period of federal influence, policy, and grant making, 1965–1979, the volume edited for Resources for the Future by Lowdon Wingo, *The Governance of Metropolitan Regions* (1972) provides a representative collection of essays.

The next period, 1980–89, is marked by the devolutionist tendencies of the "Reagan revolution" in its federalist incarnation. At the beginning of the decade, the National Academy of Public Administration prepared a *Metropolitan Governance Handbook* (1980) for HUD that was intended for the use of local government study commissions enjoying a minor vogue at the time. It was during this decade that many of the Federal programs that had required or encouraged regional decision making were eliminated or defunded.

According to Wallis, we are now in the third wave: "networked" regions with complex, complementary, and interdependent relationships calling for collaboration, governance, and the active involvement of the public, private, non-profit sectors. In the current period, 1990–96, the most influential work has been Robert Putnam, et al's *Making Democracy Work* (1993), even though it describes a decades-long

Originally published as "Metropolitan Governance: A Bibliographic Essay," *National Civic Review*, Vol. 85, No. 2, Spring/Summer, 1996. Published by the National Civic League, Denver, Co. Reprinted with permission of the publisher.

effort to regionalize governance in Italy. Offered as explanatory factors, Putnam's work has done much to popularize the terms "social capital" and "civic infrastructure."

Over the last three decades, the outstanding body of work has been the series of reports prepared for the U.S. Advisory Commission on Intergovernmental Relations (ACIR). Notable among these are *Metropolitan America: Challenge to Federalism* (1966), *Substate Regionalism and the Federal System* (1973), *The Organization of Local Public Economies* (1987), and *Metropolitan Organization: Comparisons of the Allegheny and St. Louis Case Studies* (1993). The later studies reflect the influence of the "public choice" school on these diagnoses and prescriptions of regional problems and possible governance solutions.

Forms of Metropolitan Government and Governance

Much of regionalism literature, both academic and popular, has focused on the forms and structures that have evolved or been consciously designed. David Walker's article entitled "Snow White and the 17 dwarfs..." (*National Civic Review*, 1987) provides a good overview of the permutations so far, arranged by their difficulty of implementation.

A much needed addition to the literature are collections of case studies that allow comparisons to be drawn and allow for the beginnings of systematic understanding. A good example is Rothblatt & Sancton (eds.) *Metropolitan Governance: American/Canadian Intergovernmental Perspectives* (1993), which has the added advantage of being comparative in a cross-national, as well as cross-regional sense. Both American regions (Boston, Chicago, Twin Cities, Houston, San Francisco) and Canadian regions (Montreal, Toronto, Edmonton, Vancouver) are covered.

Not all the literature on regionalism hides behind presume objectivity; much of it tends toward advocacy. The former mayor of Albuquerque, New Mexico, David Rusk develops the concept of "elastic cities" and holds an-

nexation of adjoining areas as the key in his *Cities Without Suburbs* (1993, 2nd Ed. 1996). His concerns with economic and racial segregation are bolstered by the 24 "lessons" from reform efforts so far that he offers.

In volume (#45) of the Urban Affairs Annual Review series entitled *Regional Politics: America in a Post-City Age* (1996), Hank Savitch and Vogel (eds.) offer a collection of essays on where these governance initiatives have been and where they are heading. A series of 10 case studies constitute the heart of this collection, arranged by three themes: "avoidance and conflict" (New York, Los Angeles, St. Louis); "mutual adjustment" (Washington, Louisville, Pittsburgh); and "metropolitan government" (Miami, Minneapolis-St. Paul, Jacksonville, Portland).

Growth Management & Infrastructure Development

But most people interested in regional governance issues see them as means, not ends. What they want are ways to design solutions to pressing problems of public policy, many of which don't respect the boundaries of existing local governments. Chief among these in recent attention have been issues relating to growth and physical infrastructure. John DeGrove's *Land, Growth, and Politics* (1984) is a good early introduction to the emerging problems and the varieties of nascent solutions to the management of growth.

As their title suggests, DiMento & Graymer (eds.), *Confronting Regional Challenges: Approaches to LULUs, Growth and Other Vexing Governance Problems* (1991) underscore the increasing importance attached to not only "governance," but the necessity for "regional" responses. Dealing with "locally undesirable land uses" (LULUs) have been difficult to deal with by other than regional strategies and the essays in this collection comment on successes (and failures) so far.

Anthony Downs' *New Visions for Metropolitan America* (1994) attempts to suggest solutions for the variety of growth-related problems now occurring in America's urban regions. Recommendations for transit-oriented development and other policy innovations ultimately depend on new forms of governance structures for their implementation. Downs targets fragmented land use powers as critical, maintains that the conventional vision of growth and urban development patterns are exacerbating tensions between cities and suburbs, and comments on the politics of choosing among alternative visions.

Economic Development and Regional Competitiveness

One key aspect of the recent fascination with "global competitiveness" has been the assertion that urban regions, not nations, are the crucial players in the new economic game. A good introduction to this line of thinking is the writings of Jane Jacob. Her *Cities and the Wealth of Nations: Principles of Economic Life* (1984) has been especially influential. She emphasizes the interdependency of cities and their regions and underscores the consequences of "faulty feedback" in the regional economies.

Applying this as a unifying theme and rationale, Neal Peirce and his colleagues collected a series of regional profiles they had worked on in *Citistates: How Urban America Can Prosper in a Competitive World* (1993). If urban regions are to be effective in this contest, then they must better organize for the task. After examining six cases (Phoenix, Seattle, Baltimore, Owensboro, Dallas, and St. Paul), they offer twelve "guideposts" for effective regional performance.

The best recent overview of the issues involved in this regional cooperation for global competitiveness is *North American Cities and the Global Economy* (1995) edited by Petr Karl Kresl and Gary Gappert. Here, 13 essays deal with the major issues faced by cities, the role of internationalization in urban revitalization, the importance of municipal networking and intergovernmental cooperation, bi-national case studies, and an extensive bibliography on cities and globalization.

HUD Secretary Henry Cisneros' essay on *Urban Entrepreneurialism and National Economic Growth* (1995) makes the case for a new emphasis on national urban policy. He emphasizes the need for identifying and building on the comparative advantages of the entire metropolitan area, making the region an "attractive place to do business," the importance of public/private coalitions in building the necessary institutional infrastructure, and the relative roles of national, state, and local government.

Social Equity and Regional Asset Sharing

From another point of view, for any region to be truly competitive, both suburbs and center cities must realize that they are *All in it Together* (1993) as Barnes & Ledubur's monograph for the National League of Cities advocates. In their sobering article "Ties that bind: central cities, suburbs, and the metropolitan region" (Economic Development Quarterly, 7:341–57, 1993), Hank Savitch, et al. make the case that despite patterns of segregation, regions are economically interdependent.

Not all the problems that urban regions face have to do with economics and infrastructure. The persistence of issues like access to affordable housing, tax base sharing, workforce development and job mobility remind us that there are race, income and distribution questions as well. In another essay, *Regionalism: the New Geography of Opportunity* (1995), HUD Secretary Henry Cisneros develops the policy implications of the distinction he makes between "things-regionalism" and "people-regionalism." Drawing on his experience as Mayor of San Antonio, he sketches the paradox of suburban growth with central city decline and points us toward civic life and civility as keys to forging the regional bonds that strengthen all its communities.

Advocates for the poor have often objected to many of the regional growth management initiatives, citing unacceptable trade-offs. Susskind & Podziba's *Affordable Housing*

Mediation (1990) outlines a regional approach to negotiated conflict resolution that they used in Connecticut.

Tax-base sharing as one way to reduce fiscal disparities and temper competition among jurisdictions has been used in some regions, notably the Twin Cities in Minnesota. Myron Orfield's *Metropolitics: A Regional Agenda for Community & Stability* (1996) describes their experience to date and offers advice on how to build the political coalitions necessary to implement this policy innovation.

Practical Guidance on Regional Capacity Building

Because citizens, interest groups, civil servants, and public officials have always looked for advice in helping solve their governance problems, a burgeoning literature has grown up to meet those needs. The Committee for Economic Development's *Reshaping Government in Metropolitan Areas* (1979) showed the way for that generation's concerns.

The final essay in the Wallis collection (1994) noted earlier, "Inventing regionalism, a two phase approach," advocates first using "consensus-based processes" to develop a vision for the region, and then, structuring "institutional capacity for sustained implementation of the vision." By emphasizing both legitimacy and capacity concerns, this approach reminds regional leaders and activists that governance requires a careful balancing of often conflicting values.

Much more recently, Bill Dodge's new *Regional Excellence*, (1996) for the National League of Cities promises a resource guide for those (in the words of its subtitle), interested in "governing together to compete globally and flourish locally." Dodge posits a five pointed lodestar for excellence in regional governance: initiatives must be prominent, strategic, equitable, empowering, and institutionalized. Emphasizing the importance of regional problem solving and service delivery networks, not metropolitan government, he provides dozens of examples of such governance mechanisms.

Associations, the Internet, and Other Resources

Books and articles aren't the only sources of information and guidance on regionalism and metropolitan governance topics. Civic organizations and professional associations provide crucial, practitioner-oriented resources. The National Civic League, its *National Civic Review* (now published four times a year) and its annual National Conference on Governance, have been especially useful. The National Association of Regional Councils publishes the monthly *Regional Reporter*, and recently established the Institute for the Regional Community, which in turn has begun a new quarterly journal, *The Regionalist*. The American Planning Association publishes the monthly magazine, *Planning*, and the quarterly *APA Journal*, which cover the regional beat.

Other good resources are such periodicals as *Governing, Journal of Urban Affairs, National Journal, Public Administration Review, Publius: The Journal of Federalism, Urban Affairs Quarterly* (now *Urban Affairs Review*), and *Urban Land*, which occasionally publish articles on regional and metropolitan governance topics.

The Internet is rapidly becoming not only an information resource on regional initiatives, but also a communications tool for scholars and practitioners. Besides the newsgroups and listserves that have been around for some time, the World Wide Web and its search engines are revolutionizing both research and publication. Good places to begin are such Web sites as the Alliance for National Renewal and the Alliance for Redesigning Government.

Editors Note

A national literature search revealed the following new publications in this field: *State of the Regions 2000: A Baseline for the Century of the Region* (NARC, 2001), *Multi-Region*

Economic Development Strategies Guide (NARC, 2001), and *How American Government Works: A Handbook of City, County, Regional, State, and Federal Operations* (McFarland, 2002).

This literature search was conducted from 1996, the date this annotated bibliography was published, forward to January 2002.

ABOUT THE CONTRIBUTORS

Affiliations are as of the time the articles were written.

American Planning Association, a nonprofit membership organization dedicated to building better communities through professional planning, Chicago, Ill.

William Beach, Senior Attorney, Miller, Canfield, Paddock & Stone, Detroit, Michigan.

Gail Cowie, Assistant Director for Programs, Institute of Community and Area Development, University of Georgia, Athens, Ga.

Susan R. Crow, Research Assistant, Institute of Community and Area Development, University of Georgia, Athens, Ga.

William R. Dodge, Executive Director, National Association of Regional Councils, Washington, D.C.

Robert T. Dunphy, Senior Director for Transportation, Urban Land Institute, Washington, D.C.

Lawrence D. Frank, Assistant Professor of City Planning, Georgia Institute of Technology, Atlanta, Ga.

Pamela Freese, Ph.D. Candidate in Urban Planning and Public Policy, University of Illinois at Chicago, Chicago, Ill.

Matt Greeson, Intergovernmental Coordinator, Office of the County Manager, Volusia County, Fla.

J. Eugene Grigsby III, Director, Advanced Public Service Institute, University of California, Los Angeles, Calif.

Howard J. Grossman, Executive Director, Economic Development Council of Northeastern Pennsylvania (now known as The Northeastern Pennsylvania Alliance), Pittston Township, Pa.

Jane Hansberry, Administrator (1990–1999), Denver Scientific and Cultural Facilities District, Denver, Colorado, and Ph.D. Candidate in Public Affairs and Public Administration, Graduate School of Public and International Affairs, University of Pittsburgh, Pittsburgh, Pa.

Terra Hargett, Assistant Editor, *American City & County*, Intertec Publishing Corporation, Atlanta, Ga.

Theodore Hershberg, Professor of Public Policy and History, and Director, Center for Greater Philadelphia, University of Pennsylvania, Philadelphia, Pa.

Benjamin G. Hitchings, Senior Planner, Triangle J. Council of Governments, Durham, N.C.

Tara L. Humphries, Public Affairs Specialist, North Carolina League of Municipalities, Raleigh, North Carolina.

Brian K. Jensen, Project Manager, Pennsylvania Economy League, Inc., Western Region, Pittsburgh, Pa.

Roger L. Kemp, Author, Editor, Futurist, and City Manager, Meriden, Conn.

Mary Ellen Mazey, Director, Office of University Partnerships, Department of Housing and Urban Development, Washington, D.C.

343

Bruce D. McDowell, Director of Government Policy Research, U.S. Advisory Commission on Intergovernmental Relations, Washington, D.C.

David Miller, Associate Dean and Professor, Graduate School of Public and International Affairs, University of Pittsburgh, Pittsburgh, Pa.

Jim Miara, Freelance Writer (on technology and development issues), Needham, Mass.

Marya Morris, Senior Research Associate and Assistant Editor, American Planning Association, Chicago, Ill.

Kim O'Connell, Freelance Writer (on environmental issues), Arlington, Va.

Brian W. Ohm, Assistant Professor, Department of Urban and Regional Planning, University of Wisconsin, Madison, Wis.

James B. Olliver, Jr., City Manager, Norfolk, Va.

Roger Richman, Professor of Urban Studies and Public Administration, Old Dominion University, Norfolk, Va.

Bill Schechter, Director, Washington Office, National Civic League, Washington, D.C.

Richard M. Sheehan, Accountant, Finance Department, Arapahoe County, Littleton, Colo.

R. Bruce Stephenson, Associate Professor, Environmental Studies Department, and Director, Growth Management Studies Program, Rollins College, Winter Park, Fla.

Richard Sybert, Director and Chairman, Governor's Interagency Council on Growth Management, Office of the Governor, State of California, Sacramento, Calif.

The Greater Baltimore Committee, a nonprofit organization dedicated to improving this inner-city community, Baltimore, Md.

Emanuel Tobier, Senior Fellow, Taub Urban Research Center, New York University, New York, N.Y.

James W. Turner, Managing Director, Pennsylvania Economy League, Inc., Western Division, Pittsburgh, Pa.

David B. Walker, Professor of Political Science, University of Connecticut, Storrs, Conn.

David Wallace, Founder, Wallace, Roberts & Todd, Philadelphia, Pa.

Allan D. Wallis, Director of Research, National Civic League, Denver, Colorado, and Assistant Professor of Public Policy, Graduate School of Public Affairs, University of Colorado, Denver, Colo.

Harry West, Director, Atlanta Regional Commission, Atlanta, Ga.

INDEX

www.ingramcontent.com/pod-product-compliance
Lightning Source LLC
Chambersburg PA
CBHW080548270326
41929CB00019B/3234